TRANSITIONAL JUSTICE AND CORPORATE ACCOUNTABILITY FROM BELOW

Bruno Tesch was tried, found guilty, and executed for his company's production and sale of the Zyklon B gas used in Nazi Germany's extermination camps. Tesch was not alone. More than 300 economic actors faced prosecution for crimes against humanity during the Holocaust. This book examines those trials and subsequent judicial and nonjudicial (truth commission) efforts up to the present to hold economic actors accountable for complicity in gross violations of human rights during armed conflict and authoritarian rule. It probes *what* these accountability efforts are, *why* they take place, and *when*, *where*, and *how* they unfold. It also explores obstacles blocking accountability efforts, particularly business veto power and weak international law. The book uses an original one-of-its-kind Corporate Accountability and Transitional Justice database to develop its argument. It claims that the truth and justice processes underway around the world constitute "accountability from below," a kind of Archimedes' Lever in which the right tools in weak hands can lift weighty international human rights.

Leigh A. Payne is Professor of Sociology and Latin America at the University of Oxford (St. Antony's College). She has won awards from the National Science Foundation, Economic and Social Research Council, the Arts & Humanities Research Council, British Academy, and others for her research on human rights, transitions from authoritarian rule and armed conflict, the armed right-wing, and business.

Gabriel Pereira is Associate Professor at the Faculty of Law and Social Sciences of the National University of Tucumán and researcher at the National Scientific and Technical Research Council, Argentina. He is also an affiliated researcher at the Latin American Centre of the University of Oxford.

Laura Bernal-Bermúdez is Assistant Professor at the Faculty of Law of Pontificia Universidad Javeriana in Bogotá, Colombia. She is also an affiliated researcher at the Latin American Centre of the University of Oxford.

T0371513

Transitional Justice and Corporate Accountability from Below

DEPLOYING ARCHIMEDES' LEVER

LEIGH A. PAYNE
University of Oxford

GABRIEL PEREIRA
National University of Tucumán

LAURA BERNAL-BERMÚDEZ
Pontificia Universidad Javeriana, Bogotá

CAMBRIDGE
UNIVERSITY PRESS

CAMBRIDGE
UNIVERSITY PRESS

University Printing House, Cambridge CB2 8BS, United Kingdom

One Liberty Plaza, 20th Floor, New York, NY 10006, USA

477 Williamstown Road, Port Melbourne, VIC 3207, Australia

314-321, 3rd Floor, Plot 3, Splendor Forum, Jasola District Centre, New Delhi - 110025, India

103 Penang Road, #05-06/07, Visioncrest Commercial, Singapore 238467

Cambridge University Press is part of the University of Cambridge.

It furthers the University's mission by disseminating knowledge in the pursuit of education, learning and research at the highest international levels of excellence.

www.cambridge.org
Information on this title: www.cambridge.org/9781108463508
DOI: 10.1017/9781108564564

First published 2020
First paperback edition 2022

A catalogue record for this publication is available from the British Library

Library of Congress Cataloging in Publication data
NAMES: Payne, Leigh A., 1956–, author. | Pereira, Gabriel, 1977–, author. | Bernal-Bermúdez, Laura, 1985–, author.
TITLE: Transitional justice and corporate accountability from below: deploying Archimedes' lever / Leigh A. Payne, University of Oxford, Gabriel Pereira, National University of Tucumán, Laura Bernal-Bermúdez, Pontificia Universidad Javeriana.
DESCRIPTION: New York, NY : Cambridge University Press, 2020. | Includes bibliographical references and index.
IDENTIFIERS: LCCN 2019020563 | ISBN 9781108474139 (hardback : alk. paper) | ISBN 9781108463508 (pbk. : alk. paper)
SUBJECTS: LCSH: Criminal liability of juristic persons. | Transitional justice. | Corporations–Corrupt practices. | Tort liability of corporations. | Human rights.
CLASSIFICATION: LCC K5069 .P39 2020 | DDC 346/.066–dc23
LC record available at https://lccn.loc.gov/2019020563

ISBN 978-1-108-47413-9 Hardback
ISBN 978-1-108-46350-8 Paperback

Contents

Figures

Tables

Images

Acknowledgments

This project was never conceived as a wholly academic enterprise. From its very origins it has been part of an "action-research" agenda. Our aim has been to produce knowledge that can advance victims' rights to truth, justice, reparations, and guarantees of nonrecurrence. We hope we have – even in some small way – delivered on that promise. We could not have even attempted to fulfill those objectives without support from so many people and institutions around the world.

The project could be said to have begun when Alexandra Guaguetá from the United Nations Working Group on Business and Human Rights discussed with us the possibility of our building a database to test the success of the Ruggie Principles. We became intrigued by the idea of constructing the database and started to work on that with Tricia Olsen from the University of Denver's Daniels School of Business. As we told Alex, our project would not test the Ruggie Principles, but it would attempt to create the first database and empirical study of corporate accountability. We are grateful to Alex for this spark of an idea that then ignited several projects, this book being one.

We undertook the coding of corporate accountability as part of the "Alternative Accountabilities" grant funded by the National Science Foundation-Arts and Humanities Research Council. On that project we collaborated with Kathryn Sikkink's team at the University of Minnesota. We thank Kathryn, Geoff Dancy, Verónica Michel, and Bridget Marchesi, in particular. Additional members of the research team included: Alec Albright, Brooke Coe, Emalie Coplan, Holly Dunn, Grace Fiddler, Katherine Franzel, Marie-Christine Ghreichi, Katrina Heimark, Daniel Johnson, Meagan Johnson, Maggie Loeffelholz, Moira Lynch, Cameron Mailhot, Florencia Montal, Zachary Payne-Meili, Farrah Tek, and Marcela Villarrazo. We also thank the Oxford team including Andrew Reiter (based at Mount Holyoke College),

Tricia Olsen (from the University of Denver-Daniels School of Business), Francesca Lessa, Emily Braid, Pierre Le Goff, and the three of us.

The project took on a dynamic of its own. We sought and received specific funding for the study of Corporate Accountability and Transitional Justice (CATJ). With the generous support from a range of agencies – British Academy; John Fell Fund – Oxford University Press; Economic and Social Research Council; Ford Foundation; and the Open Society Foundation – we began to build the CATJ database. That endeavor involved not only the three of us, but also Kathryn Babineau, Lina Malagón, and Julia Zulver. A part of that project involved studying the roots of transitional justice, corporate accountability following the Holocaust. The University of Minnesota's Human Rights Initiative and Grand Challenges grant provided support for Mary Beall and Ami Hutchinson to track down those cases. Others at Oxford also helped with the coding, specifically Ivo Bantel and Maike Sieben.

We received substantial institutional support from the University of Oxford, particularly from the Latin American Centre and the Sociology Department, for which we are ever grateful. One key administrator at Oxford stands out. Aileen Marshall-Brown, who manages the ESRC Impact Acceleration Account (IAA) and the social science division's HEIF Knowledge Exchange Fellowships program, provided invaluable feedback on our initial grant proposals.

We developed a close collaboration with partners around the world who formed part of the CATJ project. We have to especially thank Andhes, particularly Ana Laura Lobo Stegmayer, Josefina Doz Costa, and Cyntia Ovejero for administering the project and carrying out the coding of judicial files in the North of Argentina. CELS in Buenos Aires also participated in the early stages of the project up to the end. We thank Horacio Verbitsky, in particular, for his intellectual guidance in the project. Horacio, along with Gastón Chillier, and Diego Morales at CELS were involved in the project from the very beginning. In Dejusticia, we worked with a Colombian team who coded the Justice and Peace prosecution judgments, in particular Nelson Camilo Sánchez and Daniel Marín. César Rodríguez Garavito and Rodrigo Uprimny also participated in the design of the project from its early stages. Researchers at Dejusticia also played a key role in going through thousands of judgments. We particularly thank Lina Arroyave Velásquez, Sarah Dorman, Lindsi Allsop, and Paula Szy.

The action-research component of the project involved collaborations with other human rights organizations in Latin America. The group at Londres 38 in Chile engaged us in a number of energizing sessions around Chile's corporate accountability challenges. In particular, we thank Magdalena

Garcés. A core group of practitioner-researchers in Chile took a much broader approach to the economic accomplices of the dictatorship. We had an opportunity to work with them in Valparaiso in a book workshop organized by Juan Pablo Bohoslavsky, Karinna Fernández, and Sebastián Smart. Juan Pablo has been an enthusiastic supporter of our project from its very origins, involving us not only in the Chilean project, but also in projects on Argentina and Uruguay.

In Peru, Guatemala, and El Salvador we held stimulating workshops and discussions organized by APRODEH in Peru; Plataforma contra la Impunidad in Guatemala; and the Due Process of Law Foundation, the Instituto de Derechos Humanos de la Universidad Centroamericana (UCA), especially José María Tejeira, and the Comisión de Derechos Humanos de la Universidad de El Salvador in El Salvador. These workshops inspired working relationships that we look forward to continuing into the future.

We also participated in a working session in Cape Town, South Africa, organized by Louise Olivier and Borislav Petranov, of the Open Society Foundation, where we explored ways in which we could advance the impact of the project. Exciting ideas emerged from those sessions, some of which have made it into the book. In addition to Louise and Borislav, who have supported the project from the beginning, we also wish to thank Amanda Ghahremani, Daniel Marín, Emily Martínez, Michael Marchant, Angélica Neiszer, Nelson Camilo Sánchez, Karam Singh, Eleanor Thompson, Anneke Van Woudenberg, and Alan Wallis. The arrival of Pablo Camuña, Public Prosecutor of the Province of Tucumán, Argentina, and Pablo Gargiulo, an Andhes lawyer, simultaneously added levity and gravity. With Hennie van Vuuren we began to think about longer term collaborations around the issue of blood banking, one of the post-book projects we still hope to pursue, even if it will not mean a workshop in Llandudno.

Various units at the University of Oxford proved instrumental in advancing the project. With the Latin American Centre and St. Antony's College we ran a number of conferences over the years. Mansfield College and its Bonavero Institute, particularly Katherine O'Reagan and Annelen Micus, have supported our work in various ways. We reflect fondly on the memorable lunch in which Baroness Helena Kennedy, the Mansfield College Head of House, greeted each one of us. The group included Phil Bloomer; Juan Pablo Bohoslavsky; Gastón Chillier; José Durand; Matt Eisenbrandt; Katherine Gallagher; Marjorie Jobson; Judith König; Mauricio Lazala; Sheldon Leader; Lina Malagón, Roddy Brett, and baby Federico; Fernando Mendiola; Sabine Michalowski; Annelen Micus; Tricia Olsen; Fernando Luis Rodolfo Poviña; Francisco Quintana; Kiran Stallone; and Horacio Verbitsky.

The Argentine Embassy in London held events with us in 2014 and 2015. Ambassador Alicia Castro opened up her residence for two panel discussions, warm and generous empanada and Malbec receptions, and dinners. One of the most telling remarks about Ambassador Castro's role came from one of the participants, Fernando Mendiola, a Spanish scholar working on slave labor in the Franco-era working from the Public University of Navarre and a member of Memoriaren Bideak who participated in the 2014 event. He expressed his dismay at having an ambassador anywhere willing to take on these challenging themes.

In the final stages of the book, we held a workshop with those scholars and practitioners whose work we had relied on throughout the project. The North American Office of the University of Oxford opened up its offices to us. We have to particularly thank Alyson Goldman, Lisa Knudsen, and David Stiles for their help in making this a successful event. Some of the participants we had never met before; some were old friends and colleagues. Their incisive comments prompted us to make changes we really did not want to make, inspired us to make others, and motivated us to make one more round of revisions before submitting the manuscript to Cambridge University Press. They were tough, but constructive; exactly the kind of participants authors want at a book workshop. The book would have been out sooner except for the work they demanded; but it would have been a poorer version without their wisdom. We have thanked you before, but here we publicly thank you: Ruben Carranza, Douglass Cassel, Andrew Clapham, Pablo de Greiff, Michael Kelly, Daniel Marín, Verónica Michel, Tricia Olsen, Ron Slye, and Elizabeth Umlas. In particular, we have to thank Tricia Olsen for drawing the Archimedes' Lever for us with pencil and paper, and to Michael Kelly for encouraging us to make it a central theme of the book.

The book benefited from the care of our editor, John Berger. He tolerated our delays. He encouraged us to make it the best book it could be. We have so enjoyed working with him. Thank you to the anonymous reviewers. And also to the production team: Danielle Menz, Kevin Eagan, Ishwarya Mathavan, Anoop S. Kumar, and Joshua Penney. Several others outside the Press provided assistance in going over the text. We owe a debt of gratitude to Dorian Singh, who courageously took on the index for the project. We want to thank Stephen Meili and Julia Zulver in particular. All three would want us to take full responsibility for any remaining errors in the book that snuck past their careful scrutiny.

One of the most gratifying outcomes of the numerous encounters we have had over the years of this project is the emergence and endurance of a collaborative spirit. In 2014 we held a foundational event in Oxford. We invited human rights practitioners, legal practitioners, and academics to engage in a scoping exercise on corporate accountability initiatives, discuss challenges and opportunities to develop them, and explore potential collaborations and partnerships, many of which have been pursued further. Distinctive features of the action-research approach were praised by participants such as Gastón Chillier, executive director of CELS, who saw our initiative as crossing the deep north–south and academic-practitioner divides that often prevent equal partnerships and collaborations. Judge Poviña encouraged us to maintain at the forefront of the project the judicial actors working on the ground in isolated and often hostile environments, to consider how our study can bolster and encourage their human rights work.

The cover image for the book also represents partnership in the struggle for corporate accountability and transitional justice. We would like to thank La Garganta Poderosa for providing us with the photograph. Taken during the trial in Argentina of Ford Motor Company, it pictures the persistence of survivors, working in partnership with mobilized civil society groups and legal advocates, for *justicia y castigo* (justice and punishment) for crimes against humanity in which economic actors participated. The trial rendered justice and punishment, finding Ford Motor Company executives guilty and sentencing them to prison. The years represented in the image encompass the long struggle, from the beginning of the Argentine dictatorship with the 1976 coup to the year of the Ford Motor Company trial in 2018. Corporate complicity is represented by the iconic Ford Falcon automobile, the vehicle linked to the kidnapping of those who subsequently faced torture, illegal detention, death, and disappearance during the dictatorship. The years, the car's representation of companies' violations, and the call for justice, are emblazoned on the well-known *pañuelo blanco*, the white headscarf worn since the beginning of the dictatorship by Argentine mothers and grandmothers in search of their disappeared family members. The headscarf remains a powerful symbol of solidarity in Argentina, uniting civil society behind justice and "Never Again!" Here it extends that call to unity for corporate accountability for crimes against humanity.

The collaborative spirit that was essential to our research and impact also infused our working together. We recognized that we were demanding a lot of each other, but we also enjoyed each other tremendously. We communicated throughout with caring, understanding, laughter, and joy. None of us could have carried out this project alone. It was a true partnership.

That collaborative spirit was also found at home. Our partners picked up the slack for us when we travelled, spent weekends meeting deadlines that still seemed to slip into more weekends with deadlines. We have always given back, or tried to. Not every partner would have been as understanding. We cannot thank you enough, Stephen Meili, Fernanda Doz Costa, and Julian López Murcia. Our kids, even the older ones, continue to bring us joy in a troubling world. They remind us why we do this work. It is not only for us, or for them, but it is for a better world for their generation, future generations, and the generations of victims of corporate complicity. Never Again!

Introduction

Transitional Justice and Corporate Accountability

Bruno Tesch was tried, found guilty, and executed for his company's production and sale of the Zyklon B gas used in Nazi Germany's extermination camps. Tesch was not alone. More than 300 economic actors faced trial for crimes against humanity during the Holocaust. This book examines those cases and hundreds of other subsequent accountability efforts in trials and truth commissions around the world. These are examples of the uses of transitional justice for corporate complicity in gross violations of human rights during armed conflict and authoritarian rule. Until this study, such uses have been largely invisible.

Accountability for corporate complicity has been referred to as the "missing piece of the [transitional justice] puzzle, to pursue the full spectrum of justice" and remedy for authoritarian and civil conflict periods.[1] Corporate accountability also addresses a "victims' gap," a situation in which victims of corporate abuses have rights to truth, justice, reparations, and guarantees of non-recurrence under international human rights law, but they lack the effective mechanisms to fulfill those rights.[2]

---

[1] Juan Pablo Bohoslavsky and Veerle Opgenhaffen, "The Past and Present of Corporate Complicity: Financing the Argentinean Dictatorship," *Harvard Human Rights Journal* 23 (2010): 160.

[2] As Surya Deva says, "victims [of corporate human rights violations are] without any effective remedy." Surya Deva, "Multinationals, Human Rights and International Law: Time to Move beyond the 'State-Centric' Conception?," *Global Journal on Human Rights* 23, no. 2 (2015): 11. According to Pierre Kopp, that lack of remedy exposes "gaps in international law . . . by which member states, though obligated, remain unaccountable" for corporate complicity. Pierre Kopp, "Improving Sanctions through Legal Means," in *Profiting from Peace: Managing the Resource Dimensions of Civil War*, ed. Karen Ballentine and Heiko Nitzschke (Boulder, CO: Lynne Reinner Publishers, 2005), 390. See also: Anita Ramasastry, "Corporate Social Responsibility versus Business and Human Rights: Bridging the Gap between Responsibility

This book aims to find the corporate accountability piece of the puzzle to begin to narrow the victims' gap. It probes *what* these accountability efforts are, *who* they include, *why*, *when*, and *where* they take place, and *how* they unfold. It also explores obstacles that have blocked accountability efforts at the international and domestic level, in particular the absence of clear and binding international human rights instruments and economic actors' veto power.

WHAT IS CORPORATE ACCOUNTABILITY AND TRANSITIONAL JUSTICE

The trials for crimes against humanity after the Holocaust are considered to be the origin of transitional justice, defined as "the processes designed to address past human rights violations following periods of political turmoil, state repression, or armed conflict."[3] The International Military Tribunal at Nuremberg prosecuted and imprisoned those responsible for the Holocaust atrocities, including economic actors. The modern architecture of international human rights law emerged from those trials, aimed at punishing and preventing genocide and crimes against humanity, including torture, disappearance, and killing.[4] The response to the Holocaust led to what the United Nations (UN) asserts as states' obligations in transitional justice contexts embodied in a wide range of international human rights instruments today.[5] UN instruments

---

and Accountability," *Journal of Human Rights* 14, no. 2 (2015): 237–59; Nadia Bernaz, *Business and Human Rights History, Law and Policy – Bridging the Accountability Gap* (New York: Routledge, 2017).

[3] For definition, see Tricia D. Olsen, Leigh A. Payne, and Andrew G. Reiter, *Transitional Justice in Balance: Comparing Processes, Weighing Efficacy* (Washington, DC: USIP Press, 2010), 1. For the origin of transitional justice, see Ruti G. Teitel, *Transitional Justice* (New York: Oxford University Press, 2000); Ruti G. Teitel, "Transitional Justice Genealogy," *Harvard Human Rights Journal* 69 (2003).

[4] See for example, Michael P. Scharf, *Customary International Law in Times of Fundamental Change: Recognizing Grotian Moments* (Cambridge: Cambridge University Press, 2013); Michael P. Scharf, *Balkan Justice: The Story behind the First International War Crimes Trial since Nuremberg* (Durham, NC: Carolina Academic Press, 1997); Philippe Sands, ed., *From Nuremberg to The Hague: The Future of International Criminal Justice* (Cambridge: Cambridge University Press, 2003).

[5] See United Nations, "Guidance Note of the Secretary-General: United Nations Approach to Transitional Justice" (New York: United Nations, 2010), www.un.org/ruleoflaw/files/TJ_Guidance_Note_March_2010FINAL.pdf.

enshrine rights and duties to justice,[6] truth,[7] reparations,[8] and guarantees of nonrecurrence of violations (prevention).[9]

While the Holocaust trials played a formative and foundational role with regard to state perpetrators' atrocities, the same cannot be said for economic actors' complicity in those violations. The trials for the atrocities committed by Tesch and other economic actors have not had much of a legacy in contemporary transitional justice approaches.

We define corporate complicity as economic actors' assistance or participation in gross violations of human rights perpetrated by the state or state-like actors during authoritarian or civil conflict situations. Unpacking that definition, corporate complicity refers to economic actors' aiding and abetting the crimes against humanity carried out by state actors, paramilitaries, and rebel forces that control territory. Complicit economic actors may include state-owned, private, or mixed enterprises involved in authoritarian regime or civil conflict violence. Although conducting business with repressive authoritarian regimes or warring armies, and making profits from that business, might be considered immoral or unethical, our definition focuses instead on economic actors' direct or indirect participation in gross violations of human rights.

Among those gross violations of human rights are genocide, torture, kidnapping and forced disappearance, illegal detention, sexual assault, slave labor, and other crimes against humanity. A criticism of transitional justice is that it limits its approach to physical integrity abuses and sidesteps serious violations of economic, social, and cultural rights.[10] While we agree on the importance

---

[6] See Diane Orentlicher, "Report of Diane Orentlicher, Independent Expert to Update the Set of Principles to Combat Impunity – Updated Set of Principles for the Protection and Promotion of Human Rights through Action to Combat Impunity" (New York, NY: United Nations, 2005), Principle 19, https://documents-dds-ny.un.org/doc/UNDOC/GEN/G05/109/00/PDF/G0510900.pdf?OpenElement.

[7] Ibid.

[8] See United Nations General Assembly, "Basic Principles and Guidelines on the Right to a Remedy and Reparation for Victims of Gross Violations of International Human Rights Law and Serious Violations of International Humanitarian Law A/RES/60/147" (New York, NY: United Nations, 2005), https://documents-dds-ny.un.org/doc/UNDOC/GEN/N05/496/42/PDF/N0549642.pdf?OpenElement.

[9] See United Nations, "Guidance Note of the Secretary-General: United Nations Approach to Transitional Justice"; International Court of Justice, LaGrand (Germany v. United States of America) – Judgment (2001); Orentlicher, "Report of Diane Orentlicher, Independent Expert to Update the Set of Principles to Combat Impunity."

[10] Ruben Carranza, "Plunder and Pain: Should Transitional Justice Engage with Corruption and Economic Crimes?," *International Journal of Transitional Justice* 2 (2008): 310–30.

of those rights, we focus in this book on crimes against humanity that are unequivocally part of transitional justice processes. Our decision is not intended to support the claims that transitional justice *should* only address physical integrity rights, but rather to examine to what degree it *has* addressed the physical integrity violations that are clearly within its remit when they are carried out by economic actors.

Our definition includes four criteria for determining economic actors' complicity in those physical integrity rights.[11] Businesses may be engaged in direct complicity in criminal violence (e.g., joint criminal enterprise and conspiracy to violence). Violence may involve specific gross human rights violations with regard to labor (e.g., slave or forced labor). Financing repression, crimes against humanity, or war crimes are forms of indirect complicity in violence (e.g., bank loans to sanctioned regimes, or odious debt). Finally, corporate complicity results from enterprises or individuals engaged in illegal activity that knowingly procure or profit from, and thereby perpetuate, violence (e.g., trading in "conflict minerals"). When corporations engage in one or more of these four types of activities, they can be said to have committed gross violations of human rights and thereby may face accountability for complicity in past state violence. These four areas fall within transitional justice's remit.

We employ the shorthand "corporate complicity" and "corporate accountability," but we do not limit our study to corporations. Instead, we cast the broadest conceptual framework of "corporate" to include the array of economic actors engaged in gross violations of human rights during authoritarian or conflict situations. By "corporate," we mean the corporate structure of business as well as the definition of the term as "of, relating to, or formed into a unified body of individuals." Our use of corporate thus includes firms, but also individual economic actors who are part of a business enterprise or community. We include, for example, landholders who are not in a corporation but are part of a rural business sector. We also include business

---

[11] Tarek F. Maassarani, "Four Counts of Corporate Complicity: Alternative Forms of Accomplice Liability under the Alien Tort Claims Act," *New York University Journal of International Law and Politics* (2005): 39–65; Inés Tófalo, "Overt and Hidden Accomplices: Transnational Corporations' Range of Complicity in Human Rights Violations," in *Transnational Corporations and Human Rights*, ed. Olivier De Schutter (Portland, OR: Hart Publishing, 2006), 335–58; Jennifer A. Zerk, *Corporate Liability for Gross Human Rights Abuses: Towards a Fairer and More Effective System of Domestic Law Remedies* (Geneva: UN High Commissioner of Human Rights, 2014).

associations, or a unified group of individual economic actors and corporations in a single entity. Economic actors in our study include private, state-owned, or mixed enterprises. They comprise individuals who own or work for companies and other enterprises (such as a bank, farm, insurance company, or real estate concern) and commit violations as part of their role in the economic enterprise. We emphasize the economic activity of the individual or firm or association that links to the violent action. When economic actors participate directly or indirectly in the human rights violations carried out in armed conflicts or by authoritarian regimes, their actions constitute corporate complicity in those violations for which victims demand accountability. The use of the term "complicity," means that individual economic actors are not acting on their own. Instead, they form part of the violent structure in which human rights violations occur in authoritarian regimes and armed conflicts. They are directly or indirectly involved in the violations, not as individual citizens, but as economic actors.

We conceptualize corporate complicity in broad terms intentionally. Our operating assumption, shared by many, is that few transitional justice processes have included economic actors. To track accountability efforts, we therefore undertook the fullest possible range of economic actors who have faced transitional justice accountability mechanisms for gross violations of human rights. Our findings show who has been held accountable for what types of activities, where, when, and how.

Similarly, we adopt a broad accountability framework to include the full range of efforts. We do so to avoid seeing accountability only as guilty verdicts in criminal trials. Following Felstiner et al.,[12] we consider the act of claim-making by victims and their advocates as an effort to hold actors responsible, a kind of public truth-telling effort that attaches a cost – even if only reputational – to certain acts. Transitional justice includes institutional and informal truth-gathering processes among its mechanisms; we show that corporate accountability for past human rights violations is a hidden aspect of these processes. Guilty verdicts tend to be seen as the maximal form of accountability, yet transitional justice scholars have noted the impact of earlier, pre-judgment, efforts at judicial accountability as well as other forms of restorative

---

[12] William L.F. Felstiner, Richard L. Abel, and Austin Sarat, "The Emergence and Transformation of Disputes: Naming, Blaming, Claiming," *Law & Society Review* 15, no. 3/4 (1980): 631–54.

and reparative justice.[13] Consistent with other approaches to accountability, our study looks not only at outcomes or verdicts, but includes the full range of judicial actions as accountability efforts, from the formal initiation of legal processes to final judgments. This approach allows us to track the full extent to which transitional justice processes are being used to hold economic actors accountable for past human rights violations.

The specific set of accountability mechanisms is derived from transitional justice processes: domestic, foreign, and international human rights trials and truth commissions following periods of armed conflict or authoritarian rule. By domestic trials, we mean judicial actions investigated and/or decided by courts located in the same country in which the human rights violations took place. Foreign trials are the judicial actions investigated and/or decided by courts located in a country other than the one in which the human rights violations occurred. International trials are those judicial actions pursued in tribunals created by international organizations or alliances. The truth commission definition we use in this study is "a newly established, temporary body officially sanctioned by the state or an international governmental organization to investigate past human rights abuses."[14] We tracked these accountability efforts by constructing an original Corporate Accountability and Transitional Justice (CATJ) database.[15] Unlike other transitional justice databases, the CATJ is segmented into four discrete data sets of mechanisms.

The first set involves the "historical" data of trials for World War II human rights atrocities committed by economic actors in Nazi Germany and in Japan. When we first began researching the topic of corporate accountability at the Nuremberg and Tokyo Trials and their aftermath, we expected to find an existing and thorough study of all of the cases. Much to our surprise, it appears that no legal scholar or practitioner has systematically analyzed the full set of Nazi business trials or the economic actors held accountable in the Tokyo Trials. Some studies focus on specific companies, such as IG Farben or Krupp AG,[16] or specific courts, such as the Holocaust restitution and slave

---

[13] Geoff Dancy et al., "Behind Bars and Bargains: New Findings on Transitional Justice in Emerging Democracies," *International Studies Quarterly* 63, no. 1 (2019), 1–12.

[14] Olsen et al., *Transitional Justice in Balance: Comparing Processes, Weighing Efficacy*, 34.

[15] http://ahra.web.ox.ac.uk/.

[16] See, for example: Peter Hayes, *Industry and Ideology: IG Farben in the Nazi Era*, 2nd ed. (Cambridge: Cambridge University Press, 2001); Joseph Borkin, *The Crime and Punishment of IG Farben* (New York, NY: Free Press, 1978); William Manchester, *The Arms of Krupp, 1587–1968* (Boston, MA: Back Bay Books, 2003); Peter Mason, *Blood and Iron* (Victoria, Australia: Penguin Books, 1984).

labor cases in the United States.[17] Most studies mention only in passing the members of the business community charged or sentenced as part of the larger efforts at accountability for the mass atrocity. To fill that void, we collected all accessible data on all of the trials of Nazi businesses (and Japanese companies) and their outcomes. We are certain that more could be done to systematically analyze these cases of corporate complicity in the Holocaust (and in Japan). We looked for corporate accountability for the Holocaust and Japanese violations not only at the international tribunals, but also in foreign criminal and civil courts, and domestic civil and criminal courts. The data were gathered using online web searches as well as secondary research in academic publications. Our data set includes 349 economic actors in thirty-five judicial actions for their complicity in Nazi human rights atrocities and thirteen economic actors in ten judicial actions for Japanese abuses. From the Nazi cases, 43 percent (15) of the judicial actions ended with at least one conviction or adverse judgment, 37 percent (13) in settlements, 9 percent (3) in dismissals, and only 3 percent (1) ended in acquittal for all charges of individuals. For the remaining three cases we do not have information about outcomes. Of the ten Japanese cases (involving 13 economic actors), six ended in dismissals, one ended in a conviction that was later reversed by the Japanese Supreme Court, two ended in out-of-court settlements, and for one we were unable to determine the outcome.

The second set of accountability mechanisms data is official truth commissions. We established this data set by reading, searching, and coding every final truth commission report available. We looked for any mention of economic actors connected to physical integrity human rights violations carried out by authoritarian regimes or in armed conflicts. We tracked accountability for corporate complicity in twenty-three truth commissions in twenty countries around the world – half of the thirty-nine truth commissions with accessible final reports. These reports identified 329 economic actors by name for alleged abuses committed in armed conflict or authoritarian rule.

The third data set includes judicial accountability for corporate complicity in the violations occurring during the repressive regimes and armed conflicts of the 1960s to the present. We coded any judicial action that was initiated: a judicial investigation, a preliminary hearing, dismissal, settlement, a trial, an appeal, and final verdicts and sentencing. Using the Business and Human Rights Resource Centre (BHRRC) online archive, we first identified the economic actors mentioned for complicity in human rights violations in

---

[17] Michael J. Bazyler, *Holocaust Justice: The Battle for Restitution in America's Courts* (New York, NY: New York University Press, 2003).

armed conflict and authoritarian rule around the world. We faced great difficulty finding information on these judicial actions, and others not included in
the BHRRC archive. No single source compiled the information needed for
our analysis. Thus, our team of researchers searched for judicial action data
from a variety of national and international human rights organizations' press
releases and reports, reports from different government and UN bodies, scholarly articles and books, and articles from digital news agencies and newspapers.
In some cases, we had access to judicial archives. As a whole, we found
145 economic actors involved in 104 actions in 18 countries around the world.
Among the trials for violations that occurred in other countries, we found only
one international criminal, thirteen foreign criminal, and thirty-seven foreign
civil cases. At the domestic level, forty-two criminal and eight civil trials appear
in the database.[18] Of these 104 actions, only 17 have terminated in final convictions or adverse judgments, and 10 settled out of court. Although some were
dismissed (28) and some resulted in acquittals (5), others are awaiting appeal (7),
still others were withdrawn by the plaintiffs (2) or had an undetermined
outcome (1). The majority are pending investigation and final judgment (36).[19]

The fourth data set involves a unique process in Colombia. The highest
number of CATJ economic actors – 439 – appears in the Justice and Peace
judicial actions. The 2005 Justice and Peace Law (Law 975) enabled members
of the paramilitary group, United Self Defense Forces to demobilize and receive
a reduced sentence (five to eight years) in exchange for legal testimony (*versión
libre*) accounting for their acts and monetary compensation and restitution to
their victims. About 36,000 members of the paramilitary forces demobilized; ten
years later 195 have received judicial sentences.[20] We read the thirty-five rulings
issued by the Justice and Peace tribunals from 2011 to 2015.[21] These included a
section on the context in which the paramilitary unit under investigation

[18] We could not find the type of claim in two domestic cases.
[19] Two judicial actions ended with more than one outcome. The first one is the case brought
in US Courts against 52 companies, where 51 were acquitted and one reached a settlement.
The second one is a case in Chile where one of the defendants was convicted, and the second
was acquitted of all charges. We therefore have 104 judicial actions with 106 outcomes. Leigh
A. Payne and Gabriel Pereira, "Accountability for Corporate Complicity in Human Rights
Violations: Argentina's Transitional Justice Innovation," in *Outstanding Debts to Settle: The
Economic Accomplices of the Dictatorship in Argentina*, ed. Horacio Verbitsky and Juan Pablo
Bohoslavsky (Cambridge: Cambridge University Press, 2015).
[20] Contraloría General de la República, "Análisis sobre los resultados y costos de la Ley de Justicia
y Paz" (Bogotá, 2017).
[21] This work was done in collaboration with *Dejusticia*, as a result of the "Advancing Corporate
Accountability for Human Rights Violations during Past Dictatorships and Armed Conflicts
in Latin America" project, funded by Open Society Foundation – Human Rights Initiative.

operated, including claims they made regarding ties to politicians and economic actors. From that source, we coded information related to corporate involvement in paramilitaries' human rights abuses. Although these Justice and Peace proceedings are judicial actions, they are not judicial actions aimed at economic actors. Nonetheless, through these legal documents, companies named by paramilitaries have faced a form of judicial accountability. Moreover, Justice and Peace prosecutors have begun to investigate the alleged criminal activities of those economic actors as a result of paramilitary testimony. Any follow up trial of companies or business people initiated from the Justice and Peace process are included in the judicial action data set.

These four types of accountability mechanisms illustrate that transitional justice has included, and is including, corporate complicity in past human rights abuses. How to interpret this level of corporate accountability depends on perspective. Compared to an assumed level of complicity by economic actors in past human rights violations, the total number of judicial actions initiated, and the small number of outcomes, impunity seems to be a better description than accountability. We do not dispute that impunity prevails for corporate complicity in past human rights violations. Indeed, our findings show that despite significant efforts, corporate accountability faces formidable barriers. On the other hand, these data refute the notion that transitional justice has utterly failed to address corporate complicity in past violence.

In sum, *what* we examine is the phenomenon of corporate accountability and transitional justice from the Holocaust to the present. Despite increasing interest in business and human rights, this is the first systematic and global collection of data on the topic. It begins to track and analyze accountability efforts for economic actors engaged in indisputable physical integrity violations during authoritarian and conflict situations.

WHY HOLD ECONOMIC ACTORS ACCOUNTABLE

One reason *why* transitional justice should address corporate complicity in human rights violations during authoritarian regimes and armed conflict is the nature of past abuses. The CATJ database shows that businesses have been accused of widespread and systematic abuses over time and throughout the world. The alleged involvement of economic actors in human rights violations during armed conflict and authoritarian rule has not been peripheral, but rather is at the very core of, the logic behind, the violence. This was the argument made at Nuremberg in including businesses among those held to account for past atrocity.

It is also part of the argument about the rise of repressive bureaucratic authoritarian states of Latin America in the 1970s and 1980s, an approach

subsequently applied to other world regions.[22] Guillermo O'Donnell emphasized the alliance among the military, technocrats, and business that produced
those violent regimes. During the Cold War, and at a key developmental
phase in the most economically advanced countries of the Global South,
businesses and technocrats perceived authoritarian systems as the best way to
advance and protect "capitalist deepening" projects. Successive coups, and the
national security regimes they implanted, aimed at stemming the tide of
Communism and strengthening capitalism through wage repression and
violence against those labeled "subversives." Businesses actively collaborated
with those authoritarian regimes by creating blacklists of workers and union
leaders who subsequently faced kidnapping, illegal detention, torture, disappearance, and death, sometimes in companies' on-site detention centers.[23]
Not all members of the business community supported the coups and the
regimes. Some opposed them. Others withdrew their initial support owing to
state abuses, regimes' economic mismanagement, and the countries' loss of
prestige in international spheres that had a negative impact on business. Still
others were themselves the victims of state violence. Nonetheless, business
support provided an important degree of legitimacy, funding, and collaboration that sustained these regimes and their violence.

Economic actors are also key to the root causes of violence in armed
conflicts in Africa and Latin America. The human rights abuses related to
business partnerships with armed actors over "conflict minerals" (e.g., blood
diamonds) and illegal trade (e.g., arms and drugs) are well documented.[24]

[22] Nathan G. Quimbo, "The Philippines: Predatory Regime, Growing Authoritarian Features,"
Pacific Review 22, no. 3 (2009): 335–53; Hyung Baeng Im, "The Rise of Bureaucratic
Authoritarism in South Korea," *World Politics* 39, no. 2 (1987): 231–57; James Cotton,
"Understanding the State in South Korea: 'Bureaucratic-Authoritarian or State Autonomy
Theory?,'" *Comparative Political Studies* 24, no. 2 (1992): 512–31; Edmond J. Keller, "The State
in Contemporary Africa," in *Comparative Political Dynamics: Global Research Perspectives*, ed.
Dankwart A. Rustow and Kenneth Paul Erickson (New York, NY: Harper Collins, 1991); Eva
Bellin, "The Robustness of Authoritarianism in the Middle East: Exceptionalism in
Comparative Perspective," *Comparative Politics* 36, no. 2 (2004): 139–57.
[23] Leigh A. Payne, *Brazilian Industrialists and Democratic Change* (Baltimore, MD: Johns
Hopkins University Press, 1994); Horacio Verbitsky and Juan Pablo Bohoslavsky, eds., *Cuentas
pendientes: Los cómplices económicos de la dictadura* (Buenos Aires: Siglo Veintiuno Editores,
2013); Horacio Verbitsky and Juan Pablo Bohoslavsky, eds., *Outstanding Debts to Settle: The
Economic Accomplices of the Dictatorship in Argentina* (Cambridge: Cambridge University
Press, 2015).
[24] William Reno, "African Weak States and Commercial Alliances," *African Affairs* 96, no. 383
(1997): 165–86; Margo Kaplan, "Carats and Sticks: Pursuing War and Peace through the
Diamond Trade," *International Law and Politics*, no. 35 (2003): 559–617; Karen Ballentine and
Heiko Nitzschke, *Profiting from Peace: Managing the Resource Dimension of Civil War*, Project
of the International Peace Academy (Boulder, CO: Lynne Rienner, 2005); Tamo

These abuses also result from business involvement in state, paramilitary, or rebel "protection rackets"[25] to secure their legal or illegal business operations, or profit from the sale or trade in the tools of repression or war.[26] Banks also find lucrative investment opportunities in repressive or civil conflict systems, particularly when international aid is cut off to those regimes for humanitarian or human rights reasons.[27] The weak or nonexistent rule of law in conflict or authoritarian rule contexts, moreover, means that businesses commit abuses with impunity, lowering the cost of violation in highly lucrative sectors of the economy.[28]

Despite the prevalence and significance of corporate complicity in human rights violations in armed conflicts and authoritarian regimes, transitional justice scholars and practitioners have tended to ignore it, focusing instead on state actors. Such an approach fits the critique of the transitional justice field as liberal in orientation, rather than transformative. By adding corporate accountability to transitional justice, this study contributes to scholarship that grapples with the root causes of past violence.[29] For transitional justice to include corporate accountability, it would begin to reveal the economic and political power structures underlying authoritarian regimes and armed conflict violence. Analyzing corporate complicity thus begins to locate the root causes of violence as one of the missing puzzle pieces in transitional justice.

Acknowledging the role of economic actors as agents of violence links physical integrity rights and economic, social and cultural rights, a lacuna, or missing puzzle piece, in transitional justice approaches.[30] Corporate accountability for past human rights violations exposes the collaboration

---

Atabongawung, "Multi-Stakeholder Initiatives and the Evolution of the Business and Human Rights Discourse: Lessons from the Kimberley Process and Conflict Diamonds," in *The Business and Human Rights Landscape: Moving Forward, Looking Back*, ed. Jena Martin and Karen E. Bravo (Cambridge: Cambridge University Press, 2016), 75–105.

[25] William Stanley, *The Protection Racket State: Elite Politics, Military Extortion and Civil War in El Salvador* (Philadelphia, PA: Temple University Press, 1996).

[26] Deborah D. Avant, *The Market in Force: The Consequences of Privatizing Security* (Cambridge: Cambridge University Press, 2005); Neil Cooper, "State Collapse as Business: The Role of Conflict Trade and the Emerging Control Agenda," *Development and Change* 33, no. 5 (2002): 935–55.

[27] Juan Pablo Bohoslavsky, "El eslabón financiero en la justicia transicional uruguaya," *Revista Uruguaya de Ciencia Política* 2, no. 21 (2012): 153–79; Christopher Hutto and Anjela Jenkins, *Report on Corporate Complicity Litigation in the Americas: Leading Doctrines, Relevant Cases, and Analysis of Trends* (Austin, TX: University of Texas School of Law, 2010).

[28] Bazyler, *Holocaust Justice: The Battle for Restitution in America's Courts.*

[29] Paul Gready and Simon Robins, "From Transitional to Transformative Justice: A New Agenda for Practice," *International Journal of Transitional Justice* 8 (2014): 339–61.

[30] Dustin N. Sharp, *Justice and Economic Violence in Transition* (San Diego, CA: Springer, 2014).

between economic actors and political elites that violently consolidated and reproduced socioeconomic inequalities during authoritarian governments and armed conflicts.[31] It uncovers the role specific economic groups played not only in their moral and ideological support for authoritarian regimes and armed conflict, but in financing, instigating, committing, perpetuating, and knowingly profiting from, the violence."[32]

Non-state economic actors are not explicitly included or excluded from the focus of transitional justice. The International Center for Transitional Justice, for example, defines transitional justice as a response to "systematic or widespread violations of human rights ... [in] recognition for the victims and to promote possibilities for peace, reconciliation, and democracy."[33] The UN's definition is "the full range of processes and mechanisms associated with a society's attempt to come to terms with a legacy of large-scale past abuses, in order to ensure accountability, serve justice and achieve reconciliation."[34] Thus, if economic actors participated in the *systematic or widespread* human rights abuses of past authoritarian regimes and armed conflicts, corporate accountability advances transitional justice goals. The aim of transitional justice to come to terms with the legacy of abuses, to serve justice, and to recognize the rights of victims, suggests that economic actors as complicit in gross human rights abuses are, by the nature of their acts, a target of transitional justice processes.

And, indeed, they are. Our original CATJ database shows that transitional justice mechanisms have, in fact, investigated and held accountable economic actors complicit in the perpetration of grave human rights violations. They have done so in truth commissions and they have done so in human rights trials. These efforts do not constitute a witch hunt, as some members of the business community fear and claim, but rather recognize the direct and indirect role specific economic actors played in the abuses committed in authoritarian and armed conflict contexts.

Yet transitional justice scholars and practitioners are largely unaware of these accountability efforts. At a recent gathering of transitional justice and

---

[31] Josh Bowsher, "Law & Critique: Transitional Justice as 'Omnus et Singulatim,'" *Law Critique* 29 (2018): 83–106.

[32] Leigh A. Payne, Gabriel Pereira, and Laura Bernal-Bermúdez, "The Business of Transitional Justice," in *The Oxford Handbook of Transitional Justice*, ed. Jens Meierhenrich, Alexander Laban Hinton, and Lawrence Douglas (Oxford University Press, forthcoming).

[33] International Center for Transitional Justice, "What Is Transitional Justice?," www.ictj.org/about/transitional-justice.

[34] UN Secretary General, "United Nations Approach to Transitional Justice," 2010, www.un.org/ruleoflaw/files/TJ_Guidance_Note_March_2010FINAL.pdf.

business and human rights practitioners and scholars, not one of them knew the extent to which transitional justice mechanisms have included corporate accountability. Even those who have followed human rights trials around the world and read the same set of truth commission reports as we did were unaware of corporate accountability and transitional justice.[35] A goal of the project is to reveal the patterns of corporate accountability and transitional justice over time, to bring awareness to the relationship of corporate account-ability and transitional justice.

Visibility is an important part of our aims in the project, but so too is making transitional justice mechanisms more accessible and effective in addressing victims' rights. Although our study documents the use of transitional justice in corporate accountability, it also shows severe limitations on that process resulting in a "victims' gap." This project attempts to close that gap by revealing particular examples of accountability efforts that are accessible and adaptable to victims in a range of country contexts.

In sum, the *why* of corporate accountability is achieving the goals of transitional justice: addressing the rights of victims of widespread and system-atic abuse during armed conflict and authoritarian rule and building post-transition societies based on human rights and democratic principles.[36] With the truth about corporate complicity, and justice and reparations for those wrongs, victims' rights are fulfilled. Peace and human rights protections depend on the guarantee of non-repetition. Because the patterns of complicity are entrenched, a change in behavior on the part of businesses will likely only result from raising the legal, reputational, or financial costs to businesses of directly or indirectly participating in human rights violations. Advancing democracy, finally, hinges on respect for human rights, protection from violations, and access to justice and remedy when they occur, regardless of who perpetuates those abuses.[37]

---

[35] "The Business End of Human Rights: Book Workshop," University of Oxford North American Office, New York, September 12, 2018.

[36] Clara Sandoval, Leonardo Filippini, and Roberto Vidal, "Linking Transitional Justice and Corporate Accountability," in *Corporate Accountability in the Context of Transitional Justice*, ed. Sabine Michalowski (London: Routledge Press, 2013).

[37] John Ruggie, Special Representative of the Secretary General on the issue of human rights and transnational corporations and other business enterprises. John Gerard Ruggie, "Business and Human Rights: Further Steps toward the Operationalization of the 'Protect, Respect and Remedy' Framework," 2010, www2.ohchr.org/english/issues/trans_corporations/docs/A-HRC-14-27.pdf.

WHEN TO ADDRESS CORPORATE COMPLICITY

Transitional justice is often seen as a form of victors' justice or a witch hunt, at least by those perpetrators targeted by the accountability mechanisms. When applied to businesses the outcry over prejudicial treatment has been acute. This study confirms that not all economic actors are equally responsible for atrocities committed in all situations of authoritarian state or armed conflict abuses. It further verifies that doing business, and even profiting from business activity, during states of emergency, armed conflict, or authoritarian rule is not necessarily to be complicit in human rights violations. It also recognizes that some violations by businesses are unrelated to crimes against humanity committed by authoritarian states or during armed conflict, but rather constitute individual criminal acts for personal economic gain. Those types of violations can be addressed through the ordinary application of law. But when past state violence, or the extent of violence, would not have been possible without corporate sponsorship, when businesses provided the legitimacy for violence and the capacity to carry out that violence, and when businesses knowingly contributed to that violence directly or indirectly, they moved beyond "dirty" or immoral forms of business and into breaches of international human rights law as well as domestic laws. Corporate accountability for past human rights violations, therefore, must meet specific sets of criteria for transitional justice mechanisms to be applied.

Most global and local business communities already know these human rights standards. Norms of corporate conduct, underway and expanding via international voluntary agreements since the 1970s, embody human rights principles of respect, protect, and remedy. Firms and industry sectors have increasingly addressed companies' human rights behavior in their bylaws or voluntary associations. Soft law and voluntary principles on human rights conduct have been widely supported within the global business community. While companies and sectors may adapt these principles preemptively to avoid costly lawsuits or campaigns, corporate accountability and transitional justice aims to recognize the rights of victims after such violations occur. They show that businesses are not above the law. They aim to acknowledge and punish firms for past behavior, but also attempt to build democratic futures on a solid foundation of respect for human rights, equal protection under the law, and remedy when those rights are violated.

Much debate exists in the scholarly literature and in legal practice regarding whether and when a firm – rather than an individual as part of a firm – can and should be held accountable. Our study focuses on when any economic actor – an individual employee, a firm, or association of businesses – is complicit in past atrocities as part of business operations. Our study limits corporate accountability and transitional justice to situations when violations or alleged violations occur as part of an economic enterprise's practice or policy. Criminal codes in some countries, and civil codes in most countries, allow for corporate entities – as legal persons – to be held accountable for a range of behaviors.

In sum, *when* to apply transitional justice to advance corporate accountability depends on the set of events in which economic actors' behavior contributed to, financed, perpetuated, and prolonged, gross and systematic violations of human rights as part of an authoritarian regime system or armed conflict.

WHERE TO ADDRESS CORPORATE ACCOUNTABILITY

The phenomenon of corporate accountability and transitional justice has advanced in some form in every region of the world. Nevertheless, it remains "at the periphery of transitional justice work."[38] Although truth commissions have reported on corporate responsibility for human rights violations, these findings are not highly visible. Accountability in the form of criminal sentences or civil judgments are rare. Our aim in this book is to consider how to advance accountability to close the victims' gap in more post-transition contexts around the world.

Where transitional justice has gone the furthest in incorporating corporate complicity is in Latin America. There are more truth commissions in more countries in the region that name more companies involved in human rights violations than any other region of the world. There are more judicial actions and more accountability outcomes in Latin America than any other region of the world.[39] Latin America has taken the lead in transitional justice and corporate complicity.

It might be tempting to explain the region's protagonism as a result of the well-documented advances in the region in transitional justice in general. While it is perhaps not surprising that Argentina has moved the farthest in the world in advancing corporate accountability given its success in holding state agents of repression accountable,[40] Brazil has one of the weakest

[38] Dustin N. Sharp, "Interrogating the Peripheries: The Preoccupations of Fourth Generation Transitional Justice," *Harvard Human Rights Journal* 26 (2013): 782.

[39] Hutto and Jenkins, *Report on Corporate Complicity Litigation in the Americas: Leading Doctrines, Relevant Cases, and Analysis of Trends.*

[40] Bohoslavsky and Opgenhaffen, "The Past and Present of Corporate Complicity: Financing the Argentinean Dictatorship"; Verbitsky and Bohoslavsky, *Cuentas pendientes: Los cómplices*

accountability records for state perpetrators of repression and yet has advanced corporate accountability for complicity in the dictatorship's repression.[41] Colombia has barely begun its transitional justice process, but nonetheless has initiated efforts to incorporate corporate accountability into its transitional justice mechanisms. Our empirical analysis thus casts doubt on the assumption that existing transitional justice practice is a strong indicator of corporate accountability advancement. The explanation we develop for this regional phenomenon focuses on endogenous factors, ones that explain both transitional justice and corporate accountability efforts. That is, some of the same factors that explain overcoming impunity for state actors through transitional justice mechanisms in the region help explain advances in corporate accountability processes. We focus specifically on civil society demand and mobilization together with institutional innovators.

The *where* of corporate accountability and transitional justice, moreover, may be less of a regional phenomenon than a case of protagonism in a few countries in the region. Despite the apparent leading role those countries have taken, our data confirm that every part of the world has had some experience with these processes. We also show that the possibility of extending accountability efforts to additional countries is not out of reach for more countries in more regions given the *how* of corporate accountability and transitional justice.

HOW TO ADVANCE CORPORATE ACCOUNTABILITY

Some contend that transitional justice, as "a special kind of justice," is not necessary for corporate complicity when domestic tort law is available and sufficient. We do not concur that transitional justice is an exceptional form of justice.[42] The kinds of criminal trials that have held perpetrators accountable for past wrongs are standard in nearly all countries. Nonjudicial truth commissions do not differ substantively from presidential, parliamentary or congressional commissions of inquiry or special investigations. Reparations policies have been considered and sometimes adopted by political leaders to address past wrongs, such as the Civil Liberties Act that compensated for the Japanese internment camps in the United States. Rather than a special kind of

---

   económicos de la dictadura; Verbitsky and Bohoslavsky, *Outstanding Debts to Settle: The Economic Accomplices of the Dictatorship in Argentina.*
[41] Juan Pablo Bohoslavsky and Marcelo D. Torelly, "Financial Complicity: The Brazilian Dictatorship under the 'Macroscope,'" in *Justice and Economic Violence in Transition*, ed. Dustin N. Sharp (New York, NY: Springer, 2014).
[42] Teitel, *Transitional Justice.*

justice, the aim of transitional justice is to address extraordinary wrongs committed – the atrocities – and the need to take measures to prevent their reoccurrence. The notion of corporate accountability and transitional justice is less about inventing new forms of justice mechanisms than adapting existing institutional arrangements in countries to address unique contexts of violations, including tort law. But tort law alone is not enough. The full transitional justice toolkit includes the means to hold economic actors accountable for their role in the extraordinary criminal violence carried out with impunity during authoritarian rule and armed conflict.[43]

Transitional justice has been accused of focusing on the *how* of accountability through "top-down" sorts of accountability mechanisms, such as international courts. The burgeoning "business and human rights" literature considers "bottom-up" forms of accountability, in which powerful foreign courts in the Global North adjudicate transnational corporations for human rights violations that occur around the world. Our study bridges these two approaches and their distinct emphases on human rights accountability. We add to them a novel approach: "corporate accountability from below," or the efforts by domestic institutions in the Global South to hold economic actors accountable for complicity in human rights violations during dictatorships and armed conflict. Our database findings show the dynamic processes and outcomes of the "from below" level of accountability. Thus, the *how* in this study is "corporate accountability from below." These efforts resemble the truth commission and human rights trials in the Global South following authoritarian rule and armed conflict.

In a prior study on the effectiveness of domestic trials of state perpetrators to overcome impunity, we developed a "multidimensional approach." The study focused on the capacity to hold state actors accountable for their human rights violations during authoritarian regimes, particularly when those actors benefited from amnesty laws. The four factors we identified as necessary and sufficient for overcoming impunity – putting state actors on trial – are: strong civil society demand, strong domestic judicial leadership, strong international pressure; and weak veto players.[44] The process begins with victims and their supporters mobilizing to demand accountability. Without judicial leaders, however, civil society actors will lack the means to translate those demands

---

[43] Youseph Farah, "Toward a Multi-directional Approach to Corporate Accountability," in *Corporate Accountability in the Context of Transitional Justice*, ed. Sabine Michalowski (New York, NY: Routledge, 2013), 27–51.

[44] Francesca Lessa, Leigh A. Payne, and Gabriel Pereira, "Overcoming Barriers to Justice in the Age of Human Rights Accountability," *Human Rights Quarterly* 27 (2015): 728–54.

into action.[45] These judicial leaders rely on innovative strategies to overcome impunity. In that process, their efforts are bolstered by international pressure, mainly active agents promoting the global human rights accountability norm. The success of these processes will also depend on the power of veto players, the former perpetrators of human rights abuses and their allies.

In adapting the multidimensional framework to corporate accountability and transitional justice, we found that civil society demand remains critical to the process. Workers, unions, rural and indigenous communities, human rights groups, and victims of corporate complicity in human rights abuses, their families, and their advocates mobilize to demand accountability. Without that demand, corporate accountability processes would not begin. Yet to translate the demand into official action, civil society actors need more than "judicial leaders"; they need a broader set of institutional innovators. Truth commission staff, for example, do not constitute judicial leaders. Yet they are the institutional innovators who have converted the demand for corporate accountability (through victim testimony) into final reports. Human rights lawyers, prosecutors, and judges are the institutional innovators who advance corporate accountability cases through the judicial process, creatively blending domestic codes and statutes with international human rights standards. In the absence of clear, binding, and enforceable business human rights obligations in international law, international pressure rarely materializes in corporate accountability cases. This increases the importance of institutional innovators at the local level. They face a formidable veto player in the form of powerful global and domestic business communities.

The *how* of advancing corporate accountability therefore depends on overcoming weak international pressure and strong veto players' power. Our research finds that getting around the barrier of international pressure and business veto power has meant that these tools are more effective in corporate accountability from below. Where institutional innovators in the Global South respond to civil society demand for accountability, and develop the effective tools to advance those demands, they can sometimes overcome

---

[45] Our approach resembles that of Ezequiel González-Ocantos who explored *how* the interaction between civil society organizations and their human rights lawyers and judges operates and *when* such interaction produces positive accountability outcomes in transitional justice in the pursuit of justice for crimes against humanity. He showed that the mechanics of such interaction includes formal litigation as well as informal mechanisms through which litigants and human rights groups promote legal shifts and judges' legal skill development. Ezequiel González-Ocantos, *Shifting Legal Visions: Judicial Change and Human Rights Trials in Latin America* (Cambridge: Cambridge University Press, 2016).

impunity. To address the *how* of corporate accountability and transitional justice, we develop an Archimedes' Lever analogy.[46]

Archimedes asserted that with the right tool, weak actors can lift the world. The weak actors in our analysis are mobilized civil society groups and institutional innovators in the Global South. The right tool in our explanation is the combination of ordinary domestic laws with international human rights norms to advance corporate accountability. It is also the tool of working within truth commissions to be sure that they consider victims of corporate human rights abuses, thereby closing the victims' gap. The world that needs lifting is corporate accountability. How much force is applied by civil society actors on one side of the lever, and that applied by veto players on the other, is part of the equation for raising up corporate accountability. The other part of Archimedes' Lever is the important placement of the fulcrum. In our analogy, context is the fulcrum. Where it sits – a neutral position or one closer or further away from the weight of accountability – determines how much force will need to be applied by either side.

This book explores the challenges in overcoming corporate impunity, but also the potential of corporate accountability from below. We contend that under certain conditions, with powerful force applied by weak civil society actors and institutional innovators of the Global South, corporate accountability can rise.

CHAPTER OUTLINE

The book is organized around the "corporate accountability from below" argument. That theoretical framework is set out in Chapter 1, operationalizing and examining each of the component parts: context, international pressure, civil society mobilization, institutional innovators, and veto players. The subsequent chapters are the empirical applications of the approach organized in two parts. The first part – Chapters 2 and 3 – examines the barriers to corporate accountability: the absence of international pressure, the strength of the veto power, and unpropitious contexts that together block corporate accountability. The second part of the book – Chapters 4 and 5 – considers the mechanisms of the Archimedes' Lever that have allowed for weak actors in

---

[46] A special thanks to Rubens Carvalho for introducing us to the Archimedes' Lever concept. See Rubens Carvalho Gomes da Silva, "Values, Knowledge and Activism in the Brazilian Amazon: From the Boomerang to the Archimedean Lever," MSc diss. (Oxford: University of Oxford, 2010).

the Global South to advance corporate accountability in truth commissions and judicial action, the force applied by civil society mobilization and institutional innovators in propitious contexts. The empirical data in each chapter are derived from the CATJ database. The book's Conclusion explores the impact of "corporate accountability from below" on narrowing the victims' gap.

Corporate Accountability from Below

I should have accepted what they offered me as an exchange, because that is what they wanted: "to never see me again in Paine." But I thought that would be selling out ... [Landlord and transportation company owner] Don Francisco Luzoro was there. Even though he is a civilian, he seemed to be giving the orders [to the carabinero public security force]. Very strange. "You're late, Red (Colorín)," he said to me ... " You're going to have to tell us everything that you know ..." [After a severe beating,] I was yelling, telling them that I didn't know anything about anything, and that I didn't have any weapons ... And then another beating came. ... When night fell, they got out jugs of wine and they lit a fire for a barbecue. There were carabineros and civilians, most of them transportation company owners. There were some fifteen civilians and some eighteen carabineros. ... [Those detained were eventually lined up and shot] Pancho Luzoro yelled, "this one is dead!" and together with Daniel Carrasco he grabbed me by my feet and threw me in the water. ... What I want is justice. ... If it were all about money, I would have happily accepted the offer they made me way back then, and go up North and never speak about what happened, about the crimes they committed. But no way. No way I'm going to do this ... Dignity is more important. I am not a fucking sell-out.
— Testimony by Alejandro Bustos, Survivor of the Paine massacre[1]

In a remote region, south of Santiago, Chile there is a memorial to the event described by survivor Alejandro Bustos. The Paine Memorial remembers the seventy detained, disappeared, and executed in the weeks following the

---

[1] Martín Faunes Amigo, together with historian Eugenia Hortvitz and Oscar Montealegre, based on an interview with Alejandro Bustos in July 1992 and subsequently published as Martín Faunes Amigo, Eugenia Hortvitz, and Oscar Montealegre, "Paine: Testimonio de Alejandro Bustos 'el Colorín' sobreviviente de los fusilamientos realizados por civiles y militares," *Facebook*, 2015, www.facebook.com/notes/martin-faunes-amigo/paine-testimonio-de-alejandro-bustos-el-colorín-sobreviviente-de-los-fusilamient/10153474782834416/; Punto Final, "Camioneros en la represión," *Punto Final*, 2016, www.puntofinal.cl/850/camioneros850.php.

1973 coup that put General Augusto Pinochet in power. They had been the beneficiaries of the agrarian reform carried out by the two previous democratically elected presidents (Eduardo Frei Montalva and Salvador Allende). The 1,000 pine pillars arranged in a design that resembles the height and contour of the surrounding mountains also symbolize who remains standing: those who continue to struggle for justice. They are the family members of the Paine victims organized in an Association of Relatives of the Detained, Executed, and Disappeared who have worked for justice for the atrocity at Paine together with human rights lawyer Nelson Caucoto. On his visit to the Paine Memorial in 2017, Caucoto remarked, "[T]he women of this association are singular in their unwavering belief in justice; they have not taken revenge into their own hands. This peace, this hope, after so many years is owed to these women of the Paine Association." Paulina Maldonado, her grandfather, Carlos Chávez, one of the victims of the massacre, praised the lawyers for their genuine commitment "to move forward to seek justice for the seventy victims of Paine."[2]

Partial justice was received in what has been referred to as the first guilty verdict for a civilian for human rights violations during the Chilean dictatorship. Juan Francisco Luzoro Montenegro, mentioned in Bustos's testimony, a private landholder, transportation company owner, and director of the Business Association of Truckdrivers, was tried, found guilty, and sentenced to twenty years in prison by Chilean High Court Judge (San Miguel Appeals Court), Minister Marianela Cifuentes Alarcón.[3] At the trial, the only living survivor of the Paine massacre, Alejandro Bustos González, gave testimony, along with family members of the disappeared victims. The Paine families' lawyer Caucoto noted that the judge's ruling "begins to do justice for Paine, [a community] that has waited more than 40 years to resolve this very serious case."[4]

The trial was not the first – nor the last – effort at accountability for the Paine massacre. The first Chilean Truth Commission (Rettig) had previously referred to the collaboration of non-state actors in the repression at Paine. It referred to the region as "having suffered the highest per capita rate of

[2]   Paine Municipality, "Estudio de abogados de Nelson Caucoto visita el memorial Paine," *Paine Municipality*, 2017, www.paine.cl/estudio-de-abogados-de-nelson-caucoto-visita-el-memorial-paine/.

[3]   The Chilean state was ordered to pay the equivalent of US$3.4 million to Luzoro's victims as a form of restitution.

[4]   El Siglo, "Condenan a civil por violaciones de DDHH en 1973," *El Siglo*, 2017, www.elsiglo.cl/2017/11/17/condenan-a-civil-por-violaciones-de-ddhh-en-1973/. See also the case: http://expedientesdelarepresion.cl/wp-content/uploads/2018/03/sentencia-caso-Paine-episodio-Collipeumo.pdf.

disappearance of any Chilean settlement during the dictatorship."[5] The carabineros had also already been tried and found guilty for their involvement. Yet, the unprecedented Luzoro judgment is just the beginning, as Caucoto noted, of corporate accountability for the massacres. Luzoro admits that he did not act alone. While he has not named other non-state actors, the alleged responsibility of the Kast family has been mentioned by some, including by Bustos.[6] The Kasts, prominent in the region and nationally (owners of the Bavaria companies), distanced themselves from Luzoro and others under investigation, saying that they knew of them but had no relationship with them.

The Paine case is emblematic of the dynamics of the theoretical framework we set out in this chapter. It is a case of "corporate accountability from below," involving a truth commission and domestic judicial action linking past human rights violations with economic actors. It is part of the standard transitional justice process in Chile, yet invisible as such. The case hints at the dynamics of how these types of cases unfold. They occur at the local level – from below – in the absence of international agents or interest in these types of cases. They overcome potential business veto power where the economic actor is weak and the business community fragmented. They depend on the power of local mobilization and persistence accompanied by institutional innovators: their own legal counsel and the judge. That combination rendered some justice. But of the nine economic actors investigated – including Kast – only one has faced conviction for the murder and attempted murder of four of the seventy victims from the community. In other ongoing cases in Chile in which economic actors were involved, no one has been prosecuted. This suggests that economic actors retain a high degree of veto power over accountability outcomes. We argue that the absence of international pressure combined with this veto power is what has typically blocked corporate accountability. We also recognize context as a potential barrier. While Chile held two truth commissions for past human rights violations, it has only reluctantly adopted human rights trials and its amnesty law continues to retain legal standing. Thus, even during the presidency of Michelle Bachelet, Socialist Party member and victim of the dictatorship, transitional

---

[5] International Coalition of Sites of Conscience, "Memorial Paine," n.d., www
.sitesofconscience.org/en/membership/memorial-paine-corporacia-paine-un-lugar-para-la-
memoria-chile/.

[6] See also Javier Rebolledo Escobar, *A la sombra de los cuervos: Los cómplices civiles de la dictadura* (Santiago, Chile: Ceibo Ediciones, 2015).

justice has moved slowly, and even more slowly in the area of corporate accountability.

This chapter sets out the dynamics of the theoretical approach to "corporate accountability from below." In the first part, we focus on blocks to accountability. We contrast transitional justice accountability efforts with regard to state and rebel actors with corporate accountability efforts. In particular this section explores why the same international pressure that played such a crucial role in advancing accountability in other transitional justice processes has not emerged in corporate accountability efforts. We also look at veto players and examine how their power has remained so strong in corporate accountability processes compared to other transitional justice efforts.

Yet "corporate accountability from below" suggests that impunity for past corporate abuses – as the trial for the Paine massacre shows – can be overcome. In the second part of the chapter, we examine conceptually when and why local efforts succeed in doing so. In the process, we bridge transitional justice approaches with the business and human rights "bottom-up" approach. "Bottom-up" notions focus on domestic courts in the Global North in adjudicating contemporary corporate violations, thereby advancing global human rights. Our "from below" approach focuses on judicial and nonjudicial actors advancing corporate accountability in the Global South.

The concluding section draws together the two parts of the chapter to develop the Archimedes' Lever analogy for corporate accountability from below. It establishes the scope conditions and the key actors and factors at work. We contend in this section that corporate accountability from below is not merely an abstract analytical exercise. It is one grounded in, and in dialogue with, empirical, comparative, and historical analyses. It further aims to sharpen, refine, adapt, and make accessible to corporate accountability advocates, a set of tools to effectively advance corporate accountability. It is a framework for putting in the hands of weak actors the right tools to lift the weight of impunity and promote accountability for victims.

TRANSITIONAL JUSTICE AND CORPORATE ACCOUNTABILITY OBSTACLES

One of the criticisms of transitional justice is its "top-down" tendencies, or the undue influence of norms and practices in the Global North on the design and implementation of mechanisms. Such a process overlooks local understandings of past violence, human rights, and accountability. It imposes models of international human rights and justice on transitional countries in the Global South rather than responding to local demands and needs.[7]

Although we understand, we do not entirely accept that criticism of transitional justice. For us, transitional justice is many things, not "a thing" or "one size fits all." Although its history suggests a particular genealogy based on Northern norms, values, and practices, local actors of the Global South have participated in, and influenced the design of, transitional justice processes around the world. Many of the most dynamic aspects of transitional justice have emerged from actors on the ground developing alternative notions of justice. The contribution of traditional, or customary, justice is one example.[8] Nonetheless, many of these local practices have been bolstered by a global human rights accountability norm, and global agents supporting local-level processes.

International Pressure for Accountability

Our study of transitional justice in overcoming impunity for past human rights violations relies on international forces to pressure states as a key factor for success. International pressure is not the only component of our multidimensional approach; we find that impunity is more likely, however, where international pressure is weak or absent.[9]

We are not alone among transitional justice scholars who consider international pressure to be critical to advancing victims' rights in the aftermath of authoritarian state and armed conflict violence. For Ruti Teitel, the very origin of modern international human rights law and transitional justice processes emerged with international pressure for accountability following the Holocaust.[10] Mass extermination made clear that reliance on natural or customary law failed to protect against atrocity. Widespread agreement on universal human rights translated into post–World War II lawmaking with

---

7   Among a number of critiques, see Sally Engle Merry, "Transnational Human Rights and Local Activism: Mapping the Middle," *American Anthropologist* 108, no. 1 (2006): 38–51; Bowsher, "Law & Critique: Transitional Justice as 'Omnus et Singulatim.'"

8   Phil Clark, *Gacaca Courts, Post-Genocide Justice and Reconciliation in Rwanda: Justice without Lawyers* (Cambridge: Cambridge University Press, 2010); Mark A. Drumbl, *Atrocity, Punishment, and International Law* (Cambridge: Cambridge University Press, 2007); Joana Quinn, "Tradition?! Traditional Cultural Institutions on Customary Practices in Uganda," *Africa Spectrum* 49, no. 3 (2014): 29–54.

9   Lessa et al., "Overcoming Barriers to Justice in the Age of Human Rights Accountability."

10 Teitel, *Transitional Justice*; Teitel, "Transitional Justice Genealogy."

binding and enforceable human rights obligations on states and individuals in international conventions. Kathryn Sikkink considers international pressure one of the mighty streams that forms the "justice cascade," a torrent that impunity dams around the world could not block.[11] While these approaches do not necessarily endorse "top-down" notions of transitional justice, they nonetheless highlight international pressure as crucial to developing the global accountability norm that pressures states and contributes to overcoming impunity for past human rights violations.

By international pressure, we mean the active engagement of global agents in advancing the rights of victims in different spheres: in the international, regional, foreign, or in-country accountability arena; in policy-making, judicial, and nonjudicial bodies. Global agents may be based in international governmental institutions, such as the UN and its human rights agencies (e.g., Human Rights Council) and in regional bodies, such as the Inter-American Human Rights Commission and Court. They include those staff or independent experts in the UN system engaged in monitoring states' compliance to the UN Charter, international treaties, and human rights provisions. They have involved prosecutors and judges in domestic courts in foreign countries applying universal jurisdiction principles, such as the Spanish, French, and Mexican courts engaged in investigating human rights violations in Argentina. Global agents respond to demand from victims and civil society groups for truth, justice, reparations, and guarantees of non-recurrence. Local demands are heard and amplified by global agents who then pressure governments for change in the country where human rights violations occurred.[12]

Our study focuses on agents from international governmental organizations because of their powers of persuasion. There is no doubt that international nongovernmental organizations – e.g., Amnesty International, Human Rights Watch, International Crisis Group – have the power to name and shame and influence accountability outcomes. There is also little doubt that certain nongovernmental international institutions have accompanied, and designed, accountability processes, such as the norms "entrepreneurs" of the International Center for Transitional Justice.[13] Not to dismiss the power of nongovernmental organizations that have contributed so much to the global

[11] Kathryn Sikkink, *The Justice Cascade: How Human Rights Prosecutions Are Changing World Politics*, Norton Series in World Politics (New York, NY: W.W. Norton, 2013).

[12] Margaret E. Keck and Kathryn Sikkink, *Activists beyond Borders: Advocacy Networks in International Politics* (Ithaca, NY: Cornell University Press, 1998).

[13] Jelena Subotić, "The Transformation of International Transitional Justice Advocacy," *International Journal of Transitional Justice* 6, no. 1 (2012): 106–25.

accountability norm-making process, international governmental organizations have a different sort of pressure: the power to sanction. The pressure, therefore, is much more direct.

The effectiveness of these global accountability agents depends on access to effective tools. These tools at a minimum include widespread agreement on international human rights norms. To send an unequivocal message that states are bound by enforceable human rights agreements, these agents rely on global acceptance of a universal set of human rights norms considered to be inviolable, nonderogable, and embodied in international law. In particular, the Genocide Convention, the Torture Convention, and Crimes against Humanity legislation establish incontrovertible international human rights law prohibiting particular sets of crimes and requiring prosecution. The widespread international agreement behind these binding human rights obligations in international law provides an important tool to global agents promoting truth, justice, reparations, and guarantees of nonrecurrence. Global agents are able to translate victims' demands into the language of binding and enforceable human rights obligations in international law, and pressure states to comply with their duties to uphold the law.

Established global enforcement mechanisms reinforce global agents' promotion of victims' rights. These include international courts, international ad hoc tribunals, regional courts, and the application of universal jurisdiction in foreign courts. Where such courts exist, global agents can not only pressure states to fulfill their binding human rights obligations and advance victims' rights, they can independently pursue accountability to address those rights. Through pressure on states to act, or to advance accountability in foreign, regional, and international enforcement bodies, global agents endeavor to overcome patterns of impunity for human rights violations. International pressure for global accountability thus depends on key global agents with an effective set of tools, specifically the global human rights norm, binding obligations in international law, and enforcement mechanisms.

An illustration of international pressure for global accountability is the campaign against the amnesty laws that protected Latin American perpetrators of state violence from justice following the political transitions in the 1980s and 1990s. Responding to the demand for justice in the region, human rights groups took these claims to the Inter-American human rights system. The Inter-American Court on Human Rights adjudicated some of these cases, sanctioning transitional democratic states for failing to uphold their obligations under the American Declaration of the Rights and Duties of Man by granting amnesties for torture, disappearance, genocide, and crimes against humanity. The pathbreaking *Barrios Altos* v. *Peru* judgment issued by the

Court on March 14, 2001 extended the Court's decision beyond a single country to the region as a whole, increasing international pressure on countries to reduce impunity for state violence.[14]

The use by global agents of international human rights law and enforcement mechanisms effectively pressured states in the region to hold human rights trials, annulling, derogating, or otherwise weakening and circumventing amnesty laws. This process failed to occur in other parts of the world where regional bodies did not use codified international human rights law to pressure states.[15] Yet even in those areas, global agents – in the UN ad hoc International Criminal Tribunals for Yugoslavia and Rwanda, the International Criminal Court, and hybrid courts in Cambodia, for example – advanced human rights accountability.

The attempted trial in Spain of Chilean dictator General Augusto Pinochet provides an example. Responding to the universal jurisdiction claim that "some crimes are so heinous that a state is entitled or even obliged to undertake legal proceedings without regard to where the crime was committed or to the nationality of perpetrators and victims,"[16] in 1998 Spanish Judge Balthasar Garzón attempted to hold Pinochet accountable for violations by his regime in Chile. Garzón requested Pinochet's extradition from the United Kingdom, where he was convalescing after surgery. Although Garzón's request was rejected on humanitarian, and not legal, grounds, the use of universal jurisdiction lacked the widespread international support that might have rendered global agents' accountability efforts more successful.[17]

---

[14] Ezequiel González-Ocantos, "Communicative Entrepreneurs: The Case of the Inter-American Court on Human Rights' Dialogue with National Judges," *International Studies Quarterly*, 2018; Par Engstrom, "The Inter-American Human Rights System: Notable Achievements and Enduring Challenges," in *Contemporary Challenges for Understanding and Securing Human Rights in Practice*, ed. Corinne Lennox (London: School of Advanced Study, 2015); Santiago A. Cantón, "Leyes de amnistía," in *Víctimas sin mordaza: El impacto del sistema interamericano en la justicia transicional en latinoamérica: Los casos de Argentina, Guatemala, El Salvador y Perú*, ed. Due Process of Law Foundation and Comisión de Derechos Humanos del Distrito Federal (Washington, DC: Due Process of Law Foundation; Comisión de Derechos Humanos del Distrito Federal; United States Institute of Peace, 2007), 219–44, www.dplf.org/sites/default/files/1202485080.pdf.

[15] Ruti G. Teitel, "Transitional Justice and Judicial Activism – A Right to Accountability?," *Cornell International Law Journal* 48 (2015): 385–422.

[16] Madeleine Davis, "Universal Jurisdiction: National Courts and the Prosecution of Serious Crimes under International Law," *Human Rights Quarterly* 27, no. 2 (May 2005): 729–35.

[17] Judge Garzón pursued two tracks: (1) a universal jurisdiction track with regard to crimes against humanity committed in Chile for which signatories to the Universal Declaration and the international bill of rights had the right and responsibility to adjudicate and (2) the request for extradition of Pinochet to stand trial in Spain for the killing of Spanish citizens by his regime. Transitional justice scholars tend to focus on the universal jurisdiction initiative.

The initiative had a profound impact in Chile, nonetheless. Scholars contend that Judge Garzón did not instigate, but certainly accelerated, Chile's domestic courts' efforts to try General Pinochet for crimes against humanity.[18] International pressure on Chile came in the form of global agents using binding human rights obligations in international law, and enforcement efforts to advance victims' demand for justice for human rights violations. The event had an international impact beyond Chile's borders. The "Pinochet effect" is the concept that perpetrators of state violence risk detention and prosecution abroad if they travel, a recognition of a global human rights accountability norm, and potential enforcement mechanisms in foreign courts.

International pressure for accountability has challenged prevailing realist notions of state power. Realists typically view human rights law and accompanying institutions as too weak to promote change unless powerful nations promote such transformations to advance their own interests.[19] Yet powerful nations' interests do not appear to be behind the global accountability norm, and the regional (e.g., Inter-American Human Rights System) and international (e.g., UN International Criminal Tribunals, hybrid courts, and the International Criminal Court) mechanisms to promote it. Instead, global agents' human rights interests have successfully applied pressure on states previously resistant to accountability.[20]

The power and effectiveness of these global agents and their use of international pressure for accountability is illustrated by the backlash against them. Critics have argued that the overzealous adherence to international norms and enforcement mechanisms has eroded the flexibility necessary to navigate precarious political situations.[21] Amnesty laws protecting human rights violators became taboo, even when they provided states with leverage to advance

See Madeleine Davis, *The Pinochet Case: Origins, Progress and Implications* (London: Institute of Latin American Studies, 2003); Ellen L. Lutz and Caitlin Reiger, eds., *Prosecuting Heads of State* (Cambridge: Cambridge University Press, 2009); Naomi Roht-Arriaza, *The Pinochet Effect: Transnational Justice in the Age of Human Rights*, Pennsylvania Studies in Human Rights (Philadelphia, PA: University of Pennsylvania Press, 2005); Sikkink, *The Justice Cascade: How Human Rights Prosecutions Are Changing World Politics*.

[18]   David Pion-Berlin, "To Prosecute or to Pardon? Human Rights Decisions in the Latin American Southern Cone," *Human Rights Quarterly* 16, no. 1 (1994): 105.

[19]   Kenneth W. Abbott and Duncan Snidal, "Hard and Soft Law in International Governance," *International Organization* 54, no. 3 (2000): 421–56.

[20]   Francesca Lessa et al., "Overcoming Impunity: Pathways to Accountability in Latin America," *International Journal of Transitional Justice* 8 (2014): 75–98.

[21]   Mark Freeman, *Necessary Evils: Amnesties and the Search for Justice* (Cambridge: Cambridge University Press, 2009); Phil Clark, "Creeks of Justice: Debating Post-atrocity Accountability in Rwanda and Uganda," in *Amnesty in the Age of Human Rights Accountability: Comparative*

peace in complex situations emerging from civil conflict. Efforts to encourage paramilitary demobilization in Colombia, for example, were confounded when the Chief Prosecutor at the International Criminal Court made clear the institution's rejection of an amnesty in exchange for peace.[22] Rigid interpretations of international law emphasize states' duties to try perpetrators of gross violations regardless of the context in which the abuses occurred or the leverage an amnesty might provide to negotiate the end of conflict.[23] In legal terms, scholars suggest that the rigid implementation of the norm misinterprets law, by failing to recognize contexts in which amnesties are acceptable under international law.[24] They contend that there is more flexibility built into existing international law than the application of the global justice norm allows. What this debate over amnesty laws shows is effective international pressure for the global accountability norm: the use, or some would say "misuse," of international law by agents aimed at overcoming impunity and capable of overpowering potential veto players.

The existing set of tools is associated with agreement among the Allied forces following the Holocaust that certain atrocities required an international response. The accusations of "victors' justice" show the power of particular international forces – global agents – united to advance accountability for past atrocity. Efforts to hold perpetrators of post–World War II atrocities accountable also reflect initiatives and pressure from powerful global agents. The UN promoted ad hoc International Criminal Tribunals in Rwanda and Yugoslavia

---

and International Perspectives, ed. Francesca Lessa and Leigh A. Payne (Cambridge: Cambridge University Press, 2012).

[22] Office of the Prosecutor, *Situation in Colombia – Interim Report*, 2012, www.icc-cpi.int/NR/rdonlyres/3D3055BD-16E2-4C83-BA85-35BCFD2A7922/285102/OTPCOLOMBIAPublicInterimReportNovember2012.pdf; Mark Kersten, "The Great Escape? The Role of the International Criminal Court in the Colombian Peace Process," *Justice in Conflict*, October 13, 2016.

[23] UN peacemaking forces contend that the organization's outright rejection of amnesties means that they are barred from promoting them during a conflict, even if they provide the only means to convince warring parties to disarm and demobilize. Discussion of "Transitional Justice and Negotiating the End to Conflict," UN Mediation Support Unit, New York, February 13, 2015.

[24] The Geneva Convention Protocol II, for example, allows for an amnesty to negotiate the end of war. In addition, while the duty to prosecute grave violations identifies certain international crimes for which there cannot be impunity, there is no duty to prosecute every perpetrator of those crimes. See Max Pensky and Mark Freeman, "The Amnesty Controversy in International Law," in *Amnesty in the Age of Human Rights Accountability: Comparative and International Perspectives*, ed. Francesca Lessa and Leigh A. Payne (Cambridge: Cambridge University Press, 2012).

(ICTR and ICTY).[25] Hybrid international-domestic courts, such as the Extra-ordinary Chambers in the Courts of Cambodia (ECCC), resulted from a powerful political alliance within and outside the country.[26] The International Criminal Court, created with the Rome Statute of 1998, overcame the resist-ance by the United States to fill an enforcement gap. Global accountability agents, or transitional justice "entrepreneurs," also emerged in the UN to promote truth commissions, such as the ones in El Salvador, Guatemala, and Liberia. The UN eventually institutionalized its advocacy role by creating the UN Special Rapporteur on the promotion of truth, justice, reparation and guarantees of nonrecurrence. Even if victims throughout the world feel that justice has not reached them, there is no doubt that strong international pressure has attempted to advance global human rights accountability following authoritarian state and armed conflict violence.

This process has not evolved in corporate accountability and transitional justice. From time to time, and usually following atrocities, global agents have emerged. Their tools are not powerful. Widespread agreement on the clear, binding, and enforceable human rights obligations on business does not exist. The legal obligations that do exist are scattered among a range of different international human rights instruments. Thus, when economic actors violate human rights norms, they are only sometimes held accountable. Correspond-ing enforcement mechanisms are rarely used. As a result, little international pressure for corporate accountability exists on states or on economic actors.

In some international contexts, however, these global agents could, and have, advanced accountability. Conceptually, international pressure is distinct from international context. Disentangling global agents and their set of tools from the global context in which they operate is not simple, however. In our framework, we consider the global context to be a scope condition. There are more propitious global environments for international pressure and less propi-tious ones. The absence of geopolitical security concerns or threats to prevail-ing economic models creates a neutral international context, for example, in which global agents may effectively pressure or not, depending on the set of tools available to them. At other times, the international environment may be more favorable to international pressure. The aftermath of human rights

---

[25] See, for example, Victor Peskin, *International Justice in Rwanda and the Balkans: Virtual Trials and the Struggle for State Cooperation* (Cambridge: Cambridge University Press, 2008); Jelena Subotić, *Hijacked Justice: Dealing with the Past in the Balkans* (Ithaca, NY: Cornell University Press, 2009).

[26] See Alexander Laban Hinton, *Man or Monster? The Trial of a Khmer Rouge Torturer* (Durham, NC: Duke University Press, 2016). See also Drumbl, *Atrocity, Punishment, and International Law.*

atrocities on a global scale (such as the Holocaust) creates the context in which pressure from global agents is more effective, including the sharpening of their set of tools (widespread agreement on law and enforcement mechanisms). At other times, countervailing norms, such as global security (e.g., the Cold War era, War on Terror), may lead to a less propitious international context. In this context, and as we will show, even where global agents and their tools remain unchanged, they require additional force to advance corporate accountability.

In sum, the kind of "top-down" transitional justice – the effectiveness of global agents to advance accountability through the use of international law and enforcement mechanisms – has not had the same impact on corporate accountability and transitional justice. At certain moments, a set of agents with powerful legal and enforcement tools emerge, but they have not had a lasting effect. They lack widespread agreement around clear, consistent, binding, and enforceable international law and a corresponding set of international accountability mechanisms to address corporate human rights responsibilities. They lack the layers of international enforcement mechanisms – international, regional, foreign, and hybrid – that aid in pressuring states to adopt accountability mechanisms. Thus, where corporate accountability and transitional justice advances, it does so largely in the absence of international pressure, as a process "from below."

Accountability Veto Players

Another obstacle accountability efforts face, besides the absence of tools in the hands of global agents, is the power of veto players. George Tsbelis considers veto power to be the ability to stop a change from the status quo.[27] In transitional justice, veto players at the international and local level have the potential to block accountability, thereby stopping a change in the status quo of impunity. An extensive literature on the power of business to influence political outcomes would suggest that this veto power is likely to be effective.[28]

[27] George Tsebelis, *Veto Players: How Political Institutions Work* (Princeton, NJ: Princeton University Press, 2002).
[28] For a review of this literature see for example: C. Wright Mills, *The Power Elite* (New York, NY: Oxford University Press, 1959); Nicos Ar Poulantzas and Timothy O'Hagan, *Political Power and Social Classes* (London: Verso, 1978); Theda Skocpol and Margaret Somers, "The Uses of Comparative History in Macrosocial Inquiry," *Comparative Studies in Society and History* 22, no. 2 (1980): 174–97; Fred Block, "The Ruling Class Does Not Rule: Notes on the Marxist Theory of the State," in *The Political Economy: Reading in the Politics and Economics of American Public Policy*, ed. Thomas Ferguson and Joel Rogers (Armonk, NY: M.E. Sharpe,

Veto players have not been a central concept in the transitional justice literature, even though the roles of particular political, military, or combatant groups are recognized as obstacles, or potential obstacles, in the struggle for justice. Our discussion of amnesty laws enacted by exiting authoritarian regimes illustrates the efforts to block changes in the status quo of impunity by state forces. In peace processes, rebel forces also attempt to exchange arms for amnesty from prosecution, thereby attempting to gain leverage over the transition process. Overcoming veto players' power and leverage, thus, depends in part on global agents' pressure on states to adopt accountability measures. Global agents at specific international bodies, such as the Inter-American Court on Human Rights, the ad hoc International Criminal Tribunals for Rwanda and Yugoslavia, and the International Criminal Court, challenged the legal legitimacy of amnesty laws and the impunity they imposed. They thus pressured the newly emerging democratic states to hold such actors accountable, reducing the power of veto players. We also considered how certain scope conditions – international context – might strengthen or weaken the force of these global agents in their resolve to overcome the power of potential veto players.

Veto players' power is contingent. At times it is contingent on global forces or environments. It is also contingent on local sources of that power. Argentina is the example most often cited to show how potential veto players lost their ability to exert their power. The Argentine juntas negotiated amnesty laws as part of their exit strategy but lacked the power to enforce them. Discredited locally and internationally, as the result of the defeat in the Falkland Islands/ Malvinas War, their infamous human rights atrocities, and the country's economic collapse, the juntas and their allies failed to veto the changes to, and the eventual derogation of, the amnesty laws designed to protect them from human rights trials. Both international and domestic forces combined to hold state perpetrators accountable, overcoming the veto power of the former regime. The other extreme is Brazil, where the amnesty law has remained in force. No state perpetrators have faced human rights trials. In this context, regime forces retained legitimacy and power to veto human rights

1984); Charles Edward Lindblom, *Politics and Markets: The World's Political-Economic Systems*, Harper Colophon Books (New York, NY: Basic Books, 1977); Ralph Miliband, *The State in Capitalist Society* (London: Quartet Books, 1973); David Vogel, "Why Businessmen Distrust Their State: The Political Consciousness of American Corporation Executives," *British Journal of Political Science* 1, no. 8 (1978): 19–43; Claus Offe and Helmut Weisenthal, "Two Logics of Collective Action: Theoretical Notes on Social Class and Organizational Form," *Political Power and Social Theory* no. 1 (1980): 67–115; Payne, *Brazilian Industrialists and Democratic Change*, 1–15.

accountability processes. Domestic demand and the international pressure for prosecution are relatively weak compared to neighboring countries.

Chile represents a more variable form of veto power. The amnesty law remains in effect, but the country is divided over the legitimacy of the Pinochet regime. Polls show that the sector that once firmly backed Pinochet, his regime, and the amnesty for past human rights violations, has dwindled over time.[29] In this context, courts began to put perpetrators on trial – including Pinochet himself – with some degree of success. International pressure no doubt emboldened local accountability forces vis-à-vis veto players. Yet local factors also explain the reduced power of veto players. The once-powerful Pinochet supporters began to lose legitimacy. This resulted in part from increasing awareness that victims and the left were not inventing the abuses. Incontrovertible evidence linking the regime to atrocities convinced some former supporters to withhold their allegiance and accept accountability for past abuses. Information campaigns made it difficult for even some former regime supporters and bystanders to deny the evidence from two truth commissions and their reports, news stories, documentary films, monuments and museums, international rulings, and trial testimony. Some who had once denied as lies the accusations against the regime for its human rights violations began to see the truth and could no longer support the regime. This eroded the unity to fight against accountability. Pinochet's links to corruption, evident in the Riggs Bank scandal, provides an additional convincing argument for his loss of support, and the fragmentation of the accountability veto players. While some of his supporters may have felt that killing "subversives" was an acceptable cost for defeating Communism, illegally profiting from his position of power had no justification. Thus, the unity behind impunity began to erode. Reduced veto power made it possible to find ways to creatively circumvent the amnesty law and hold authoritarian state perpetrators accountable for human rights violations. The weakened power of veto players – whether emerging from national crisis, leadership crisis, loyalty crisis, or more powerful international or local accountability pressure – opens up the possibility of advancing accountability.

In corporate accountability and transitional justice, the business community has faced challenges to the status quo of impunity for human rights violations. Our database tracks truth commissions and international, foreign, and domestic trials that have attempted to advance accountability. It also looks at efforts to establish clear, binding, and enforceable corporate human rights

---

[29] Hugo Andrés Rojas Corral, "Indifference to Past Human Rights Violations in Chile: The Impact on Transitional Justice Success, 1990–2017," PhD diss. (University of Oxford, 2018).

obligations in international law. A powerful business veto power has emerged to halt those changes. Corporate veto power has succeeded in blocking the development of a global accountability norm, and corresponding enforcement mechanisms, for business human rights abuses during dictatorships and armed conflicts. Global veto players have thus impeded the use of pressure for corporate accountability.

The capacity of corporate veto players to block accountability stems in part from international contexts. We have discussed scope conditions – international context – in terms of the propitious or unpropitious conditions for global agents' international pressure on states. The same is true for veto players. In the face of the Holocaust, and international resolve to prosecute social sectors that produced it, veto players had little capacity to outweigh those forces. In the subsequent – Cold War – context, veto players recovered their power owing to their capacity to join the fight against Communism.

In neutral global contexts, business veto power emerges from within countries: their economic, social, and political connections with the ruling elite; state dependence on the private sector for income, employment, and resources; and active and direct lobbying and campaigning efforts. Businesses are, after all, critical to most economies. Much of the business and human rights literature focuses on the global might of companies compared to the states in which they operate. One such reference claims that "the largest multinationals now dwarf the economies of many countries and frequently mobilize greater political influence."[30] Another refers to the fact that "[n]early half of the world's largest economic entities are corporations, not countries. The revenues of Walmart recently exceeded the gross domestic product (GDP) of 174 UN member countries."[31] These references suggest that companies may not need collective action to leverage veto power over decisions made in the international and foreign, regional or domestic, arena since they have sufficient capacity individually to sway outcomes.

Hidden veto power may also result from perceived dependence on business for global or domestic economic stability and well-being. Businesses provide jobs, income, services, development, and products, for example. The fear of jeopardizing those contributions strengthens the veto power of businesses. Hypothetically, they have the option to pull out of countries that threaten to

---

[30] Simon Chesterman, "Oil and Water: Regulating the Behavior of Multinational Corporations through Law," *New York University Journal of International Law and Politics* no. 36 (2004): 307.

[31] Erika R. George, "The Enterprise of Empire: Evolving Understandings of Corporate Identity and Responsibility," in *The Business and Human Rights Landscape: Moving Forward, Looking Back*, ed. Jena Martin and Karen E. Bravo (Cambridge: Cambridge University Press, 2015), 25.

prosecute them. Such recognition of economic actors' function and leverage may lead, consciously or not, to an unwillingness to sanction abusive behavior.[32] Scholars have noted that firms in strategic sectors of the global or domestic economy enjoy fewer constraints on their behavior than firms in less critical sectors.[33] States may avoid hearing, investigating, or adjudicating corporate human rights violations if they anticipate repercussions of appearing hostile to business, such as a loss in foreign investment or business relocation to more permissive investment environments.[34] Even if international law established explicit human rights obligations on businesses, as some scholars claim that it does, states may prove less likely to sanction businesses for abusive behavior where those companies or sectors are integral to the national economy or national security.[35] This dependence on business for macroeconomic and political stability is likely heightened during processes of transition when states initiate post-conflict or post-authoritarian development efforts. In such contexts, states are more likely to face international pressure for reforms favorable to the private sector and global liberalism, rather than for corporate accountability.[36]

A similar source of power is the position of business people in the "power elite." Shared class, education, neighborhoods, and social networks mean that elite business people are part of the same communities as those judging their behavior. They sometimes hold (or held) government posts and thus have close professional and political connections as well. These connections shape perceptions, held broadly within society, that elites are not, and could not be, human rights violators. While there might be a willingness to see business-people involved in illegal trade as capable of committing atrocities, legitimate members of the business community tend to avoid that stigma.

[32] Uwem Ite, "Multinationals and Corporate Social Responsibility in Developing Countries: A Case Study of Nigeria," *Corporate Social Responsibility and Environmental Management* 1, no. 11 (2004): 1.

[33] Dorsati Madani, "A Review of the Role of Impact of Export Processing Zones," *Policy Research Working Papers* (Washington, DC: World Bank, Development Research Group, Trade, 1999); Michael Moran, "Misunderstanding of the Regulatory State?," *British Journal of Political Science* no. 32 (2002): 391–413.

[34] Christopher Dougherty, *Introduction to Econometrics*, 4th ed. (Oxford: Oxford University Press, 2011).

[35] Ite, "Multinationals and Corporate Social Responsibility in Developing Countries: A Case Study of Nigeria"; Madani, "A Review of the Role of Impact of Export Processing Zones"; Moran, "Misunderstanding of the Regulatory State?"

[36] Sabine Michalowski, ed., *Corporate Accountability in the Context of Transitional Justice* (Abingdon: Routledge, 2013).

These social, economic, and political ties between business and the rest of the power elite should not necessarily prevent accountability. We know that judges can decide cases based on legal arguments and evidence without undue social or political influence. Our empirical evidence seems to confirm this outcome. There are ways, therefore, to overcome what might be social or political biases in judicial decisions.[37]

The economic dependence and power elite sources of corporate veto power are intuitive and less empirically verifiable. They are also passive. There are active forms of veto power that they employ, however. Some of these forms of direct action depend on business financial resources, which, as we have shown, not all members of the business community equally possess. Thus, an international lobby depends largely on transnational corporations, but smaller enterprises can free ride to gain the benefit of blocking corporate accountability processes at the international level. Similarly, campaign contributions to influence presidential, judicial, or legislative office-holders to enhance veto power may depend on large companies' resources, but smaller companies benefit. Transnational or large domestic businesses have the capacity to use complex legal skills to fight against accountability efforts in courts, through challenges to jurisdiction, appeals processes, and counter suits. They can hire skilled lawyers in expensive firms, use legal strategies to dismiss, delay, or complicate trials, raising litigation costs for plaintiffs who can ill afford them, and reach confidential settlements before the case ends in judgment. In addition to legal resources, veto power can also involve media or public relations campaigns to counter the evidence in lawsuits. Economic actors have used unlawful practices of intimidation, threats, or violence aimed at lawyers, prosecutors, victims, or human rights defenders attempting to hold them accountable. They have engaged in lobbying efforts and campaign contributions domestically and internationally to influence the outcomes of policies and legislation. Divide and conquer strategies by businesses weaken the communities involved in cases against the companies, simultaneous strengthening economic actors' veto power. While all businesses have access to all of these strategies, some businesses are less likely to use them due to their cost or because of different priorities. Large companies more easily absorb the costs of veto efforts, or can pass them along to consumers, as the price of doing

---

[37] Joel B. Grossman, "Social Backgrounds and Judicial Decision-Making," *Harvard Law Review* 79, no. 8 (1966): 1551–64; Lisa Hilbink, *Judges beyond Politics in Democracy and Dictatorship: Lessons from Chile* (Cambridge: Cambridge University Press, 2007); Alexandra V. Huneeus, "Judging from Guilty Conscience: The Chilean Judiciary's Human Rights Turn," *Law and Social Inquiry* 35, no. 1 (2010): 99–135.

business. The willingness and capacity of members of the business community to incur these costs and to veto accountability outcomes is highly contingent on the characteristics of those companies. The community is fragmented geographically, by size and sector, and by political power and ideology. Thus, while veto power potentially exists, it is not always used or always effective.

Political and economic contexts can act as scope conditions influencing the effectiveness of the corporate veto over domestic accountability efforts. In more propitious local contexts, for example when presidents, judiciaries, or legislatures represent the business community, the corporate veto is more likely to be effective than in the opposite scenario. Similarly, during times of economic stress, greater reliance on business to help extricate the country from the crisis may enhance the veto power of companies over accountability efforts. In more politically neutral contexts, corporate veto power effectiveness depends more on its relative power vis-à-vis accountability agents.

In sum, corporate veto power capacity exists at the international and domestic levels. At the international level, powerful global accountability agents have only rarely overcome the corporate veto power to impose accountability. They have done so in historically contingent moments. At the domestic level, there is greater variation in the veto power of businesses. Their assumed power, as compared to the power of victims of corporate abuses, is tempered by ideological or political fragmentation, variation in resources, and perceptions of corporate wrongdoing within society. These potential weaknesses open up the possibility for local accountability agents to strengthen their power over veto players, even without international pressure. This is how corporate accountability from below is achieved.

CORPORATE ACCOUNTABILITY FROM BELOW

Despite accusations of being overly "top-down," the role of domestic actors – particularly, human rights organizations and victims' groups and their advocates – is emphasized in transitional justice studies. Domestic actors, for example, form one of the streams that converges with global agents in forming the justice cascade. In the notion of the "boomerang," domestic actors are critical to the demand for accountability, achieved after global agents amplify these demands and pressure states.[38] In our multidimensional approach, we also consider civil society demand to be the impetus behind accountability efforts. While transitional justice approaches recognize the importance of civil

---

[38] Sikkink, *The Justice Cascade: How Human Rights Prosecutions Are Changing World Politics*; Keck and Sikkink, *Activists beyond Borders: Advocacy Networks in International Politics*.

society mobilization behind accountability, civil society demand on its own is not sufficient to advance successful justice outcomes. International agents and local actors with accountability expertise complement the role of civil society demand in advancing accountability. As we have shown, international actors have not played a significant role in corporate accountability. Thus, our "corporate accountability from below" approach focuses on civil society mobilization and local institutional innovators as the key forces in overcoming corporate impunity.

An emphasis on corporate accountability through domestic processes is not novel in the business and human rights literature. "Bottom-up" strategies are identified as an effective way to bring about corporate accountability. As Kamminga and Zia-Zarifi state, "More concrete, and therefore more intriguing, examples come from the use of domestic courts to enforce international norms ... The advantage of enforcing international law in domestic courts is that they have relatively well-developed systems for addressing corporate entities and levying penalties against them. The disadvantage, of course, is that multinational corporations are set up precisely to avoid domestic jurisdiction over their activities."[39] The "bottom-up" approach in the business and human rights field is meant to address the constraints posed at the international level on corporate accountability. It locates accountability potential in courts in the Global North that might be more powerful than these multinational corporations, or at least in control of the legal tools to weaken their power. While our approach to "corporate accountability from below" also emphasizes the role of domestic accountability processes in transforming international human rights, it differs in important ways from "bottom-up" justice in the business and human rights literature; specifically in notions of accountability, the location of domestic courts, their aim, and their impact.

Our concept of "accountability from below" does not restrict forms of justice to trials only, in contrast to "bottom up" approaches. Truth commissions – absent from the business and human rights literature – are important nonjudicial forms of accountability included in the transitional justice toolkit. The business and human rights approach has not focused on past violations that occurred during dictatorships and armed conflicts, but ongoing human rights abuses, including those in democracies and rule of law systems. This may change, however. A recent truth commission initiative by the North

---

[39] Menno T. Kamminga and Saman Zia-Zarifi, "Liability of Multinational Corporations under International Law: An Introduction," in *Liability of Multinational Corporations under International Law* (The Hague: Kluwer Law International, 2000), 10.

Carolina Commission of Inquiry on Torture (NCCIT) addresses "The Rendition Project," the role of the private Aero Contractors, Ltd. company in conducting US government renditions.[40]

The "bottom-up"[41] focus on domestic legal efforts, moreover, emphasizes courts in advanced industrial countries – particularly in the United States, United Kingdom, Canada, the Netherlands, and Australia – considered to be integral to international lawmaking and public policy. The argument is that courts in powerful countries have the potential to shape international human rights through their judicial actions on business and human rights.[42] Janet Koven Levit describes "[b]ottom-up lawmaking [as] . . . a soft, unpredictably organic process that generates hard, legal results. Private parties, non-governmental organizations (NGOs), and/or mid-level technocrats coalesce around shared, on-the-ground experiences and perceived self-interests, 'codifying' norms that at once reflect and condition group practices. Over time, these informal rules become embedded, often unintentionally, in a more formal legal system and thereby become 'law.' Whereas top-down lawmaking, the type of lawmaking at the heart of the nationalist critique of international law, is a process of law internalized as practice, bottom-up lawmaking is a soft, unchoreographed pattern of practices externalized as law."[43] Recognizing that "the international lawmaking universe is disaggregating into multiple – sometimes overlapping – lawmaking communities," Levit expresses her desire to "celebrate this moment as one of possibility and promise" and "to invite new worlds."[44]

The Global South is not waiting for an invitation to this "new world" of "possibility and promise"; it has already constructed such a world. Underway in courts of the Global South are innovative practices that have begun to hold economic actors' responsible for international human rights violations.

[40] See Jayne Huckerby and Aya Fujimura-Fanselow, "The Truth about Rendition and Torture: An Inquiry in North Carolina," *Just Security*, December 14, 2017, www.justsecurity.org/49343/truth-rendition-torture-nongovernmental-inquiry-north-carolina/.

[41] Janet Koven Levit, "Bottom-Up International Lawmaking: Reflections on the New Haven School of International Law," *Yale Journal of International Law* 3, no. 32 (2007); Denise Wallace, *Human Rights and Business: A Policy-Oriented Perspective*, Studies in Intercultural Human Rights (Leiden, the Netherlands: BRILL, 2015).

[42] Sarah Joseph, *Corporations and Transnational Human Rights Litigation: Human Rights Law in Perspective* (Oxford: Hart, 2004); Christopher Avery, "Business and Human Rights in a Time of Change," in *Liability of Multinational Corporations under International Law*, ed. Menno T. Kamminga and Saman Zia-Zarifi (Cambridge: Cambridge University Press, 2000), 17–73.

[43] Levit, "Bottom-Up International Lawmaking: Reflections on the New Haven School of International Law," 395.

[44] Ibid.

These efforts are "multiple," but they only rarely "overlap" with efforts in the Global North. Thus, departing from the "bottom-up" approach, our "from below" approach focuses on domestic judicial and nonjudicial corporate accountability processes in the Global South. The two approaches locate the transformative effect of domestic forms of corporate human rights accountability in geographically distinct areas of the world.

Practitioners play a critical role in both approaches. Levit refers to these practitioners as "those on the ground, armed with intimate knowledge of their niche trade and/or interest areas, who constitute norms rooted in the nitty-gritty technicalities of their trade rather than the winds of geopolitics and diplomacy."[45] Her description resembles a transnational epistemic community with a set of technical (legal) skills based in the Global North oriented toward business and human rights.[46] Our "accountability from below" approach stresses the work of locally grounded truth commission staff and legal practitioners. While some developed their expertise in a long struggle for human rights advocacy both domestically and abroad, others have little to no experience in human rights, or international law, and instead fall into a category of "accidental" innovators. Not (yet) constituting an epistemic community, they have nonetheless, through standard lawyering techniques or through their work as staff in truth commissions, taken innovative steps.

The notion of "norms entrepreneurs"[47] fails to adequately describe the process and the actors involved. We contend that the set of individuals and groups are not all oriented toward promoting particular norms. Instead, in many cases, the innovation and the impact is a result of the quotidian work they do as lawyers, prosecutors, judges, and staff. They do not consciously or deliberately aim to transform or promote norms. Their work nonetheless has an impact.

How these processes potentially shape human rights outcomes are also somewhat distinct. As Levit states, "top-down lawmaking is a process of law instituted as practice, bottom-up lawmaking is a process whereby practices and behaviors gel as law."[48] She goes on to describe the process as finding "an alternative route to law that is inherently grounded and pluralist."[49]

---

[45] Ibid., 409.
[46] Peter M. Haas, "Epistemic Communities and International Policy Coordination," *International Organization* 46, no. 1 (1992): 1–35.
[47] Verónica Michel, *Prosecutorial Accountability and Victims' Rights in Latin America* (Cambridge: Cambridge University Press, 2018).
[48] Levit, "Bottom-Up International Lawmaking: Reflections on the New Haven School of International Law," 409.
[49] Ibid.

She suggests that such an approach "challenges us to imagine the promise of 'alternative futures' in international lawmaking."[50]

Our "accountability from below" approach leads potentially to an "alternative future," by promoting innovative practices in the Global South to overcome impunity for corporate complicity in human rights violations. Institutional innovators operationalize international human rights norms and law at the local level. They implement international human rights standards and economic actors' human rights responsibilities, through judicial and non-judicial action. When domestic courts hold economic actors accountable for crimes against humanity or forced labor, they challenge the contention that international human rights obligations do not apply to businesses. Domestic courts – through their practice and their interpretation of law – advance international human rights. When truth commissions address corporate complicity, they emphasize the dignity and the rights of victims of corporate complicity.

In addition, these local efforts play a role in human rights global practices. As these legal and nonjudicial practices spread and become visible, businesses become aware of the cost of ignoring their human rights obligations. Domestic courts and truth commissions erode the fortress of corporate impunity. These actions provide the weight of evidence that economic actors can – and sometimes will – be held accountable owing to their international human rights obligations. To instigate these types of innovative advances in corporate accountability, two sets of actors – civil society mobilizations and institutional innovators – use a set of tools accessible to them and to other actors in similar positions in the Global South.

Civil Society Mobilization

Although "civil society" is an overly broad and imprecise term, we use it as shorthand to refer to an overlapping set of actors primarily comprised of victims of abuse, their families, allies, and advocates. All are non-state, non-institutionalized, actors. Because of the very nature of corporate complicity, labor is key. Urban and rural workers, union and other labor leaders, mobilize as victims and activists against the role economic actors played in the repression and violence during authoritarian and conflict situations. These workers were targeted owing to their actual, or suspected, union, workplace, or political activity. Affected communities are also included, especially

---

[50] Ibid., 420.

working-class communities – urban or rural – associated with labor conflicts, and indigenous or African descendant communities that faced violent displacement or human rights violations resulting from environmental destruction. At times, members of the business community itself are targeted by other economic actors, either because they engaged in left-wing political activity or are accused of such activity, or for economic or political gain. Business victims rarely mobilize to demand justice. So-called subversives, or alleged or actual members of the armed left, have also been the victims of corporate complicity in acts of kidnapping, illegal detention, disappearance, torture, or killing. When they mobilize, they are less likely to identify as members of a targeted political group, but rather as individuals, union or labor leaders, community members, or other victims' group. The general population is also victimized, particularly by illegal trafficking enterprises and their security forces in armed conflicts.

Mobilization takes place through civil society organizations and networks, such as workers' organizations, victims' or relatives of victims' groups, solidarity groups, church or other religious organizations, community groups, human rights organizations, social movements, and activist networks. Support organizations and networks sometimes emerge before the end of authoritarian regimes and armed conflicts, but they also have emerged to advance accountability in the post-transition period. At times they work with transnational civil society organizations and even foreign or international governmental organizations and networks to amplify local demands.[51]

Despite what appears to be robust mobilization, civil society demand for corporate accountability is often stymied. Just as international law tends to focus on state perpetrators of human rights violations, victims may not see corporate complicity as separate from authoritarian state or armed conflict violence. The language and practice of human rights has focused on state, and not non-state, actors. Without clear understanding of the human rights obligations of business, those victims may lack awareness that they can denounce violations by non-state actors and make demands.

Nonetheless, they do. Our research suggests that certain civil society groups have been more active than others in denouncing corporate complicity. Labor movements, for example, have mobilized within truth commissions – where they represent a third of all victims of corporate complicity in our data base – and behind judicial action – where they represent about two-thirds of the victims in our database. Certain communities, particularly indigenous and

---

[51] Keck and Sikkink, *Activists beyond Borders: Advocacy Networks in International Politics.*

other ethnic groups, have also mobilized to demand truth, justice, reparations, and guarantees of nonrecurrence. Labor and community groups have mobilized in large part because they know their rights and have the organizational structure to act on them. These groups also have access to NGOs and legal representatives who promote domestic innovative institutional action to overcome the weakness of international pressure and the strong power of the business veto.

A limitation of civil society mobilization is its invisibility. Violations often occur in geographically isolated, culturally distant, or in politically and economically marginalized, populations. Relatively powerless in their societies, they may voice their demands, but they are not always heard given their lack of access to representatives or centers of power.

Thus, visible and audible civil society demands are critical to the process and increase the likelihood of instigating accountability. Demand would likely have such an effect where: individuals are organized in groups; those groups have a history or repertoire of rights-based collective action; where their mobilization – because of their historic role or the unconventional nature of their subsequent action – promotes media attention; or groups seek and receive alliances with agents able to translate their demands into accountability action. We further argue that where this kind of mobilization and alliance does not exist, we would not expect the demand for corporate accountability to emerge.

This kind of mobilization does not rely on societies with strong civil society organizations. Hypothetically, even weak groups could still mobilize to make demands for corporate accountability. This chapter started with the example of a poor rural community in Chile (Paine), severely repressed during the dictatorship, that engaged in mobilization efforts, linked to human rights organizations in the country, and demanded justice for past corporate complicity in the dictatorship's repressive violence. Yet, in other cases we find that such civil society groups have not emerged even though they have a strong mobilizational history. Despite a dense civil society network in Peru, with a history of mobilization for human rights, and an alliance between the authoritarian regime and business in the repression of workers, very little mobilization has occurred in relation to corporate accountability. Being seen or heard is much more likely where leadership, organizational structure, repertoires of collective action, media connections, and dense networks of alliances exist. It would seem that where there is pre-existing mobilization for transitional justice, we would expect those kinds of conditions. Yet, the mobilization we have encountered include those with long histories of transitional justice (Argentina, South Africa), those with very little (Colombia, Brazil), and those in-between (Liberia). For these reasons, neither transitional justice histories nor general civil society strength in the country are scope conditions for our study.

Visible and audible mobilizations are important because they can attract institutional innovators. Yet, at times, civil society actors themselves innovate, finding new ways to make demands public and visible, to influence accountability outcomes.

Institutional Innovators

In corporate accountability, civil society demand requires creative or innovative tactics to draw attention to economic actors' human rights violations, to bypass strong corporate veto power, to overcome the absence of international pressure, and to advance accountability efforts.

In judicial action, these "institutional innovators" comprise human rights lawyers whose institutional role is taking the cases to courts, prosecutors, and judges. They have the shared characteristic of taking on unpopular, even seemingly unwinnable, cases when they could avoid them. To transform these cases into winnable ones involves legal innovation. Otherwise ordinary domestic criminal codes, civil torts laws, labor law, or economic regulatory laws can be combined with international human rights law, incorporated into national statutes, to hold economic actors accountable. Institutional innovators thus think outside narrow legal strictures.

Judicial innovators do not emerge from a single background. While some may be steeped in a history of representing victims of human rights abuses and finding creative ways to circumvent amnesty laws aimed at blocking them from doing so, others may be skillful lawyers who use best practices to represent a client or defend a victim of an internationally recognized crime against humanity. The important distinction between institutional innovators and other legal actors is that innovators in corporate accountability cases cannot merely adapt already existing international human rights laws as legal actors did in traditional transitional justice processes. Corporate complicity cases do not fit narrow understanding of human rights abuses since they do not focus on state actors. The international human rights obligations on business remain unsettled. Thus, innovators must think creatively about appropriate legal strategies to advance corporate accountability cases.

At times, human rights lawyers working with victims of corporate complicity are part of those civil society organizations. Their legal work is within the organization, but they also prepare lawsuits to advance corporate accountability in courts. The innovative approach they take may result from dialogue within civil society organizations. They aim to provide the best legal argument and representation for their organizations.

Prosecutors, and not human rights lawyers, often argue the case. These institutional innovators in prosecutorial offices may rely on the legal arguments presented to them by civil society groups and their advocates. Sometimes institutional innovators exist within these offices, finding their own strategy to get around legal obstacles to advance accountability. One such legal action discussed further in the book involves the São Paulo state prosecutor's office in the Volkswagen case. The prosecutor initiated the innovative notion of a trial for declaratory judgment, rather than advancing a standard court case when doing so would have ended in dismissal given the legal standing of the country's amnesty law.

Judges respond to these arguments. Those with a narrow focus will tend to respond to domestic law only and ignore international human rights standards. For these reasons, it is critical for institutional innovators to base the argument on established domestic law that incorporates international human rights norms. Such a strategy makes it harder for judges to ignore the law. By accepting the argument that labor law violations sometimes constitute crimes against humanity, innovation can occur. Domestic law on its own would not work, given statutes of limitations on labor cases and other civil and criminal judicial actions. Since many countries around the world have ratified and incorporated international human rights law into their domestic legal systems, designating the violation as a crime against humanity, means that no statute of limitations applies. Combining such cases with ordinary domestic law allows institutional innovators to thereby advance accountability efforts. Even reluctant innovators might emerge in the judiciary by recognizing corporations' human rights duties. Similarly, hearing human rights violations in civil cases, rather than limiting them to criminal cases, represents an innovation. In the Vildoza case discussed in the book, the judge permitted what appeared to be a retroactive application of a money laundering law, by ruling that the defendant continued to profit from the ill-gotten gains and transfers. Because clear, binding, and enforceable human rights obligations on business do not exist at the international level, the accountability successes rely on these creative applications of domestic law.

These innovators have been referred to elsewhere as "justice operators."[52] That label implies a conscious decision to use the law and the judicial system to innovate, to advance accountability norms and processes. Some of the

---

[52] Maximiliano Mendienta Miranda, "Hydrocarbon Extraction in Guaraní Ñandeva Territory: What about the Rights of Indigenous Peoples?," in *Human Rights in Minefields: Extractive*

individuals and groups we analyze – human rights lawyers working with victims and activists, for example – do deliberately engage in these types of strategies. Prosecutors and judges are not necessarily part of a human rights network aiming to advance these processes. For these reasons, the innovative arguments might emerge from outside the institutions themselves, from the communities or their lawyers. If they are persuasive, they can render a judgment by individuals positioned to have an impact, but those individuals do not necessarily aim to have that impact.

Innovators in nonjudicial accountability institutions, such as truth commissions, may also be unaware of, and lack international encouragement to, investigate corporate complicity in human rights abuses. Neither are they likely to consciously or deliberately pursue innovative tactics. Corporate accountability does not require a commitment to innovation and transformation. Nor does it necessitate expanding the institution's mission or mandate, rule-breaking, or even rule-bending. In many ways, it is merely a byproduct of standard institutional practices.

For truth commission staff, corporate accountability is rarely part of the institutional mandate. Rigid adherence to the mandate, therefore, might exclude in the final report the testimony of victims of corporate human rights abuse. By interpreting the mandate as an objective to expose crimes against humanity and restore the dignity of victims, however, staff "innovate" by incorporating corporate abuse among the crimes against humanity for which victims demand justice. They find a way within the institutional framework to represent victims' truths. The innovation results from the work of sifting through testimony and sets of events to determine which will be included in the final report. Their motivation may be solely to fulfill their obligations in their professional position. They do not necessarily set out to deepen human rights norms in general, but rather to address the local needs of victims. It is in the process of their work or advocacy that they play an innovative role, not in the deliberate attempt to do so. By including corporate complicity, these staff play an innovative institutional role, even if they are unaware that they are doing so.

Truth commission staff illustrates that institutional innovators are not necessarily part of an epistemic community with a particular technical skill set. The fundamental skills involved are commitment to the goals of truth commissions and communication techniques. Communication skills link civil society demands to the broader truth commission objectives of victims' dignity, knowledge and acknowledgment, and building a human rights future.

Economies, Environmental Conflicts and Social Justice in the Global South, ed. César Rodríguez Garavito (Bogotá: Dejusticia, 2015).

Staff listen, record, and register victims' testimonies linking them to corporate complicity. Innovators salvage truths about past corporate complicity; they do not filter them out of the final report. Thus, even without a mandate to investigate corporate complicity, truths about economic actors' violations fit within the larger pattern of violations in authoritarian and conflict situations. How those truths arrive in truth commissions depend on civil mobilization and strategies of naming and shaming. In the absence of the connections of these civil society groups with commission staff, it is possible that these truths will not be told, that they would not be communicated in the final reports, and that they would not advance corporate accountability. Civil society groups can work with institutional innovators to assure that the truth about corporate complicity appears in the final report.

The "boomerang model" and the "justice cascade" reflect the role these local-level actors have played in attracting international attention. In that approach to transitional justice, the work of accountability depends on connections between local and international forces. In the "accountability from below" approach we adopt, local-level mobilization and innovation does not always, or even often, receive this kind of international attention or support. More international pressure, bolstering civil society demand and institutional innovation, would likely enhance local-level efforts. In the absence of international pressure, however, civil society groups and institutional innovators use local tools to advance accountability.

In sum, this book makes the controversial argument that the transformative process with regard to corporate accountability may already be occurring in the Global South. This is surprising, given the relatively weak power of local actors, and the legal and procedural difficulties victims and their advocates face in adjudicating corporate complicity cases in the Global South, as documented by many scholars.[53] The use of tools in the hands of civil society

---

[53] The legal barriers include: the difficulty of identifying the appropriate entity or entities against which to lodge a judicial action in relation to claims involving transnational companies; objections to such lawsuits based on doctrines of sovereign immunity, "act of State" and "political question"; the non-applicability of criminal law provisions to corporate entities in some jurisdictions; and, the existence of rules that place restrictions on the ability of individual victims, their representatives and other organizations (e.g., NGOs) to initiate and participate in legal proceedings. Zerk also includes practical obstacles blocking accountability in domestic courts, including but not limited to: scarce availability (or non-availability) of legal aid; "loser pays" rules; and lack of resources and specialized expertise within prosecution bodies. See Zerk, *Corporate Liability for Gross Human Rights Abuses: Towards a Fairer and More Effective System of Domestic Law Remedies*; Oxford Pro Bono Público, *Obstacles to Justice and Redress for Victims of Corporate Human Rights Abuse* (Oxford, 2008).

and the work of institutional innovators have helped overcome the barriers of powerful veto players and weak international pressure for accountability. When these processes advance, moreover, they provide adaptable models for corporate accountability around the world. In order to demonstrate how civil society demand together with institutional innovators have overcome the barriers of veto players and weak international pressure, we turn to the Archimedes' Lever analogy.

ARCHIMEDES' LEVER AND CORPORATE ACCOUNTABILITY

Archimedes developed a formula for explaining when the right tool in weak hands could lift the world. Our project adapts that formula to explain what types of tools in the hands of relatively weak actors of the Global South make it possible to elevate corporate accountability.

Three components are essential to Archimedes' Lever: the weight to be lifted; the force applied to lift the weight or to keep it down; and the placement of the fulcrum. By moving the fulcrum closer to the weight, Archimedes' showed, less force is necessary to lift even very heavy weights. Thus, the placement of the fulcrum allows for even weak actors to use the lever to lift great weights. In our analogy, the weight to be lifted is corporate accountability. Lifting it provides victims of corporate abuses with the rights to truth, justice, reparations, and guarantees of non-repetition. What is holding down the corporate accountability weight is the greater force applied by veto players compared to the force applied by civil society and institutional innovators. International pressure operates on either side of the lever or not at all. Global agents apply norms and laws that sometimes work for corporate accountability or against it. Global agents can, thus, tip the scale in one direction or other, but they are not always engaged in that process. The weight of corporate accountability, veto players' power, civil society mobilization, institutional innovators, and international pressure have been discussed previously in this chapter. The fulcrum merits more attention here.

The fulcrum is context – global or domestic – in which corporate accountability evolves. The fulcrum sits in three positions: neutral or in the middle; favorable to corporate accountability, or closer to the weight; or hostile to corporate accountability and further away from the weight. When the context is more conducive to corporate accountability, it is closer to the corporate accountability weight, reducing the amount of force necessary from civil society and institutional innovators to lift it. In contrast, when the context is less favorable, the fulcrum is farther away from the weight of corporate accountability, requiring much more force on the part of civil society actors

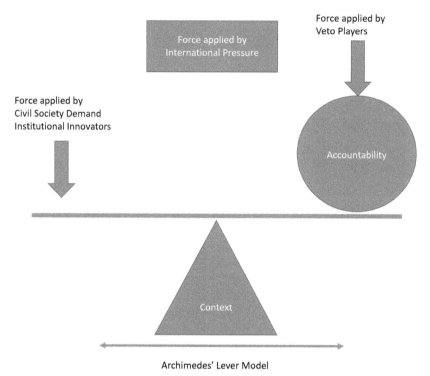

FIGURE 1.1 Archimedes' Lever Model
Source: The authors

and institutional innovators to lift it. When the fulcrum is in a neutral position, the force applied on either side of corporate accountability will determine the possibilities of lifting its weight (see Figure 1.1).

Context – the position of the fulcrum – is thus an important scope condition for corporate accountability. It is not determinative, however. Although in neutral contexts, the force applied by civil society actors will have to be strong enough to lift the weight of corporate accountability from under the force of veto players, it is still hypothetically possible for it to achieve the desired outcome. International pressure could add force to either side. Similarly, a favorable context does not guarantee the lifting up of corporate accountability. Such an outcome will still depend on some force on the side of civil society and institutional innovators to outweigh corporate veto power. Moreover, an unpropitious environment may make it nearly impossible for civil society actors and institutional innovators to lift the weight of accountability. Yet, with reduced power of veto players, and/or added force from international pressure on the civil society side, accountability outcomes may be achieved.

In sum, there are several moving parts in the model. We set out three contextual models related to particular global moments in history and the corresponding effect on domestic environments. These models illustrate how the Archimedes' Lever analogy works to promote corporate accountability, corporate impunity, and limited corporate accountability.

Corporate Accountability

In the corporate accountability model, the fulcrum is closer to the accountability weight. The international community reaches consensus that deterring future atrocities in which economic actors are involved requires accountability. Global agents emerge to add force to the side of accountability. Local-level demand and innovators may be weak, but as long as the fulcrum is closer to the accountability weight, sufficient force may lift the weight of accountability. Even if veto players are strong, their weight is overcome by civil society mobilization, institutional innovators, and international pressure.

This situation describes the years just following the Holocaust. At that time, international consensus existed around the atrocities and the need for preventing them in the future. International forces weighed heavily on the side of victims' demand for justice for Holocaust atrocities. Institutional innovators found ways to develop legal instruments – articulating universal norms and transforming them into law, the creation of the international military tribunal, and subsequent Allied forces' trials – that promoted – and achieved – the accountability outcome (see Figure 1.2).

The aftermath of military defeat in Germany and the US occupation created a context in which few barriers to accountability remained. Potential corporate veto players lacked sufficient strength in this context to stand up to international forces. Thus, the trials of companies for crimes against humanity moved forward. Accountability was the outcome, although it did not last.

Corporate Impunity

In the corporate impunity model, the global context is farther away from the weight of accountability. In addition, the corporate accountability weight is held down by the strong force of veto players and with added international pressure against accountability and in favor of impunity. In this scenario, it would take a force more powerful than the impunity forces to lift the weight of corporate accountability. Weak local civil society demand and institutional innovators may try to exert sufficient counter-force in this context, but they are unlikely to succeed.

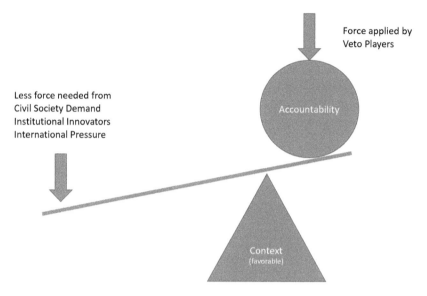

Corporate Accountability Model

FIGURE 1.2 Corporate Accountability Model
Source: The authors

This scenario is illustrated globally by the Cold War period. The international community considered private business and the capitalist economic model to be a bulwark against the threat of Communism.[54] In such a global context, veto players possessed substantial power, further reinforced by international pressure. Economic actors, imprisoned for the atrocities committed in the Holocaust, were released. To strengthen Germany and build the global capitalist infrastructure against Communism, German businesses – including those with owners or managers found guilty of Nazi-era atrocities – were restored intact.

The Cold War and the national security regimes it promoted around the world, targeting leftists engaged in social, economic, and political distribution projects, brought a legacy of human rights abuses. Multinational and some local businesses thrived in the military-capitalist alliances formed around the world. Before the fall of the Berlin Wall, the Cold War context thus made for unpropitious domestic contexts for corporate accountability. We find no judicial action cases during this era, no doubt resulting from the relative

---

[54] See Samuel Moyn, *Not Enough: Human Rights in an Unequal World* (Cambridge, MA: Harvard University Press, 2018).

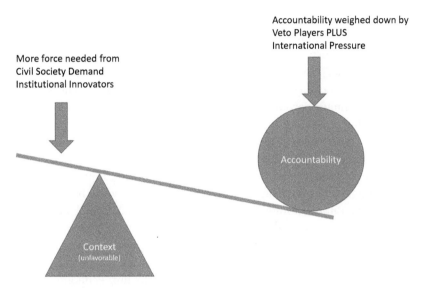

FIGURE 1.3 Corporate Impunity Model
Source: The authors

power of veto players in this context and the absence of international pressure for trials of economic actors. Economic actors did not have to apply much veto power in this context. Institutional innovators in truth commissions, however, responded to civil society demand and began to track corporate complicity in human rights violations even in this unpropitious climate. The weak use of veto power by economic actors allowed the forces on the side of accountability to lift up nonjudicial corporate accountability in truth commissions (see Figure 1.3).

Limited Corporate Accountability

A more neutral position emerges with the end of the Cold War. While there is generally strong support for transitional justice with the spread of a global human rights norm, the international community is neutral with regard to corporate accountability. In the wake of the oil crisis and global debt, neo-liberal solutions are promoted by international governmental organizations around the world. The aim, to strengthen economies through business development and free trade policies, coexisted with the aim to reestablish human rights and democratic regions in the wake of authoritarian rule and armed conflict. With regard to these competing interests, the context for corporate accountability, the fulcrum, is in a middle or neutral position. Veto players have power to continue to suppress corporate accountability. If they begin to lose that force (e.g., through fragmentation), greater opportunity exists for local civil society demand and institutional innovators to successfully apply – with the right tools – the force necessary to lift accountability. This scenario can render limited accountability outcomes, by reducing veto players' power or increasing civil society and institutional innovators' force.

This is the current international situation as we see it. International pressure for corporate accountability is weak. Force lies in the hands of relatively weak local civil society actors and the institutional innovators responding to their demand for accountability. Civil society has mobilized in some countries, through naming and shaming in formal institutions (truth commissions) and informal settings (campaigns and outings), to reveal atrocities carried out by economic actors and to point to the need for accountability and deterrence of future abuses. Victims and their families have also used their access to justice to link economic actors' behavior to international human rights violations embodied in domestic legislation. Such efforts have allowed for innovation in blending domestic and international human rights law and to overcome legal barriers, such as statutes of limitations. Without derogating amnesty laws that protect perpetrators of human rights violations, institutional innovators have found creative ways to circumvent them and to promote accountability by other means (e.g., truth commissions, truth trials, civil trials, and other ordinary domestic legal processes). In this way, they have innovated on standard transitional justice processes. They have also innovated in the field of business and human rights "bottom-up" practices by locating remedies in the Global South and finding ways to promote corporate accountability from below without relying on nonexistent global agents, binding international human rights obligations on business, and international enforcement mechanisms.

The international context is less unfavorable, more neutral, with regard to corporate accountability than it was during the Cold War. Yet domestic contexts during this period of time vary. We find, for example, that the spread of left-of-center governments in Latin America during the 2000s offered a neutral or more propitious environment for corporate accountability, followed in the last several years by unpropitious right-of-center governments. In some countries in Africa, like Liberia, we have seen that businesses and their political allies condemned in some transitional justice processes for their behavior during authoritarian rule and armed conflicts, have begun to reemerge and reassert their political and economic power, thereby strengthening the veto players' force over corporate accountability. Context, or the position of the fulcrum, moves over time.

The Paine case that opened this chapter provides an example. The local community of Paine organized into an Association that pressured for justice for the atrocities committed there. It did not benefit from international pressure to support its accountability endeavors. Nonetheless, the community's demands were amplified by local institutional innovators. Institutional innovators guaranteed that the country's first truth commission included the atrocities committed in Paine. By retaining the story of the Paine massacre, the truth commission staff recognized this atrocity in the country's official history of the authoritarian period. The community also worked with a human rights lawyer who was willing to frame their claims in legal language – domestic law and international human rights law – to advance the case through the courts. Holding even one businessman criminally accountable established an unprecedented outcome in the country. The outcome depended on the High Court judge assigned to the case, who accepted the human rights claims made against the economic actor. Victims' families, and the sole survivor of the atrocity, made sure to be heard, in the media and in the court. This case transpired in an environment in Chile in which human rights trials were occurring despite the legal standing of the amnesty law. In such an environment, it is perhaps not surprising that only one member of the business community accused of complicity in the massacre has been held accountable. The impunity of other, more powerful, economic actors involved in the atrocities, has rendered the outcome limited, rather than full, justice (see Figure 1.4).

Although we use the term "limited," we contend that justice is rarely ever total. The kinds of atrocities committed are not possible to remedy fully. The lives cannot be restored, the loss cannot be recovered, the harm cannot be undone.

CONCLUSION

In these limited outcomes, however, a great deal is achieved. At the local level, victims receive the recognition of wrongdoing: that someone harmed them. In a context of corporate impunity for past human rights violations, this acknowledgment begins to address victims' demands for truth, justice, reparations, and guarantees of nonrecurrence.

We make the bold claim, moreover, that such local-level actions contribute to global accountability in two ways. First, corporate accountability processes, even when they occur almost exclusively in the Global South, address the global rights of victims to truth, justice, reparations, and guarantees of

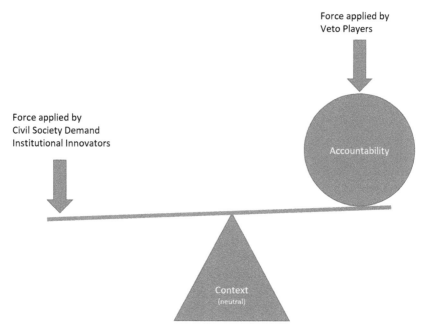

FIGURE 1.4 Limited Corporate Accountability Model
Source: The authors

nonrecurrence. Second, when corporate accountability occurs in the Global South, it not only contributes to state practice with regard to the human rights obligations of economic actors, it also fills an interpretive function. Truth commissions and courts play a role in interpreting international human rights norms as recognizing corporations' binding human rights obligations and states' duties to enforce those obligations. As these corporate accountability interpretive processes and practices in the Global South spread, they have the potential to affect change at the global level. They develop models that can be used in other countries. They bring justice – restorative and retributive – to victims, thereby narrowing the victims' gap. Thus, the Archimedes' Lever approach examines the way in which the right set of domestic accountability tools in the hands of relatively weak domestic actors, are being used to move the world to advance the rights of victims of corporate abuse.

The next sections of the book develop the Archimedes' Lever approach to corporate accountability from below historically, theoretically, empirically, and in practice today. The following two chapters focus more on impunity, the obstacles to corporate accountability. They do, however, explore moments in which these factors have led, or potentially could lead, to greater neutrality and even accountability. The remaining two empirical chapters consider the possibilities of accountability from below through mobilizations and innovations behind truth processes and domestic judicial action. In those chapters, we return to the theoretical framework to examine the contexts and factors that enhance or limit the use of sufficient force by local-level actors to overcome international pressure and veto barriers to advancing accountability. We also present the set of practical tools used by weak Global South actors with the potential to raise corporate accountability.

PART I

Obstacles to Corporate Accountability

2

International Pressure for Corporate Accountability

Si Frumkin wrote an essay that he called, "Why won't these SOBs give me my money? A survivor's testimony." He responds to his own question in the opening sentences of the essay: "Actually this is a rhetorical question. I know why they won't. Isn't it obvious? It is because they would rather keep it." He discusses not only his disillusionment with the company that had to be taken to court to compensate for its use of slave labor in Nazi Germany, but also his sense of betrayal by his own country, the United States: "my government prefers to uphold and defend the rights of giant German corporations rather than mine. The SOBs that anger me are many. The one I know best is the one whose slave I was, the one that worked my father to death, the one my government is protecting from me. It is called Philipp Holzmann A.G."[1]

Si Frumkin's indignation illustrates the victims' gap. Frumkin and so many other victims are the bearers of international rights to truth, justice, reparations, and guarantees of nonrecurrence in international human rights law. They have sought the fulfillment of those rights through international mechanisms, suspecting that the countries where the violations occurred would be less likely to address their demands. Their failure to receive the rights they deserve often leads to the sense of betrayal expressed in Frumkin's essay. This chapter examines the obstacles to corporate accountability at the international level: unsettled international law regarding the binding and enforceable human rights obligations of business entities, the absence of international enforcement mechanisms to hold economic actors accountable, and the related lack of international pressure on states to deliver to victims of corporate complicity their rights to truth, justice, remedy, and guarantees of non-repetition.

---

[1] Si Frumkin, "Why Won't These SOBs Give Me My Money? A Survivor's Testimony," in *Holocaust Restitution: Perspectives on the Litigation and Its Legacy*, ed. Michael J. Bazyler and Roger P. Alford (New York, NY: New York University Press, 2006), 92–100.

We do not claim that international pressure has always acted as a barrier. Looking back over the past seventy years, at key moments the international community has held economic actors accountable for grave violations of human rights. In the first part of the chapter, we track the historic cases of international judicial trials for companies' participation in crimes against humanity following World War II in Germany and Japan. Decades later, following the Rwandan genocide, international courts again held companies accountable. Foreign domestic courts also initiated investigations into international human rights abuses by economic actors in authoritarian and armed conflict situations beyond their national borders and by non-nationals. Regional bodies, such as the Inter-American Human Rights Commission and Court have also, at times, pressured states to address corporate complicity in past human rights violations.

These examples show that international pressure for corporate accountability occurs. The CATJ tracks those international and foreign judicial actions. Our findings show limited results in terms of judicial outcomes, leading to the disillusionment expressed by Si Frumkin, a sense that companies matter more to the international community than the victims of their abuse. This leads to a victims' gap, in which victims of economic actors' abuses cannot realize in practice their international rights to truth, justice reparations, and guarantees of nonrecurrence, that they possess on paper.[2] We contend that corporate accountability at the international level has occurred in rare and isolated moments, failing to build a legal legacy that could translate into international pressure on states and businesses to recognize human rights duties.

In contrast to transitional justice for state actors, a global human rights accountability norm and corresponding enforcement mechanisms for corporate actors have not emerged. While global institutional corporate accountability agents with the right set of tools pressure sporadically (i.e., when there is broad consensus around the norm following extreme atrocity that threatens

---

[2]   See the following discussions of the victims' gap: Justine Nolan, "The Corporate Responsibility to Respect Human Rights: Soft Law or Not Law?," in *Human Rights Obligations of Business: Beyond the Corporate Responsibility to Respect*, ed. David Bilchitz and Surya Deva (Cambridge: Cambridge University Press, 2013); Kopp, "Improving Sanctions through Legal Means"; George, "The Enterprise of Empire: Evolving Understandings of Corporate Identity and Responsibility,"19–50; Ramasastry, "Corporate Social Responsibility versus Business and Human Rights: Bridging the Gap between Responsibility and Accountability"; Bernaz, *Business and Human Rights History, Law and Policy – Bridging the Accountability Gap*.

global stability), economic actors more typically are seen as stabilizing agents. Thus, even these historic examples of corporate accountability face reversals when economic actors are perceived as necessary for national or global political objectives. International engagement is not based on underlying agreement around economic actors' clear and binding human rights obligations, but as a response to specific events. These events have not left a legacy in terms of developing norms and enforcement mechanisms for corporate complicity in past human rights abuses during authoritarian and conflict situations.

Why not? This chapter explores that question. First, to reveal discernible patterns, we look empirically at when and why international and foreign courts advanced corporate accountability and when they have not. Second, we discuss global power and context as key elements of international pressure, specifically international enforcement mechanisms, binding human rights obligations in international law, and international accountability agency. We conclude that inconsistent, weak, or absent international pressure has not blocked, but neither has it promoted, corporate accountability in the world. In addition, we conclude that corporate accountability is prevalent, particularly via domestic processes in the Global South.

INTERNATIONAL AND FOREIGN ENFORCEMENT

At certain historical moments, the international community has attempted to hold powerful economic actors accountable for their involvement in crimes against humanity during authoritarian and armed conflict situations. These moments are ephemeral, failing to develop into a widespread international agreement around the human rights obligations of economic actors and the duties of states and the international community to enforce those rights. Five sets of cases of international efforts at accountability are reviewed below: after the Holocaust; post–World War II for Japanese companies' crimes against humanity; following the Rwandan genocide; the application of the Alien Tort Statute in US courts; and other foreign courts' civil and criminal trials for corporate human rights atrocities around the world. Each period illustrates a limited form of accountability, suggesting what could be done with widespread international agreement. They also reveal an underlying obstacle to corporate human rights accountability. We contend that countervailing international pressures, around security and other concerns, block agreement, thereby leaving little legacy in terms of the binding and enforceable human rights obligations of business. This, in turn, removes an important international human rights tool that local actors could use to press for corporate accountability.

Accountability for Nazi Companies[3]

We must not forget that guilt is a personal matter; that men are to be judged not by theoretical, but by practical standards; that we are here to define a standard of conduct of responsibility, not only for Germans as the vanquished in the war, not only with regard to past and present events, but those which in the future can be reasonably and properly applied to men and officials of every state and nation, those of the victors as well as those of the vanquished. Any other approach would make a mockery of international law and would result in wrongs quite as serious and fatal as those which were sought to be remedied.[4]

Justice Robert Jackson, chief prosecutor for the Unites States in the International Military Tribunal, wrote these words. What sort of "future . . . applied to men and officials of every state and nation" that avoid becoming a "mockery of international law" did the Allied forces achieve following the Holocaust with respect to corporate human rights obligations and enforcement? We examine three moments of judicial accountability for corporate complicity in the Holocaust: the Nuremberg Trials, the industrialist trials, and the US civil restitution cases. We argue that comparing these attempts at corporate accountability reveals the factors that contribute to success: powerful global agents, potent legal tools, a propitious political climate, and the absence of formidable countervailing political pressures. Where those four factors have not prevailed, accountability outcomes decrease in likelihood. That is the case of Japan.

At first blush, the accomplishments at advancing corporate accountability seem great. Our research reveals 349 companies charged for crimes against humanity (excluding war crimes) in thirty-five judicial actions in three waves of accountability processes. These judicial actions have various outcomes depending on the charge and the role of the individuals involved. Forty-two

---

[3] Several researchers worked on the Nazi Business part of the database, most notably University of Minnesota Mondale School of Law students Mary Beall and Ami Hutchinson. Their research was supported by the Grand Challenges grant at the University of Minnesota during 2016–2017. In addition, University of Oxford researchers on the World War II cases of corporate human rights violations include Julia Zulver, Ivo Bantel, and Maike Sieben.

[4] United States v. Ernst von Weizaecker, *Trials of War Criminal before the Nuremberg Military Tribunals under Control Council Law No. 10, v. XIV ("Ministries Case")*, Judgment, 527 quoted in Michael Bazyler, *Holocaust, Genocide, and the Law: A Quest for Justice in a Post-Holocaust World* (Oxford: Oxford University Press, 2016), 107.

percent (15) of the judicial actions ended with at least one conviction or adverse judgment; 37 percent (13) in settlements;[5] 9 percent (3) in dismissals, and only 3 percent (1) ended in acquittal for all charges of all individuals.[6]

Why address corporate sponsors of Holocaust violence? The Nuremberg Trials anticipated holding economic actors accountable as "representative of important aspects of the dictatorship."[7] Along with Nazi regime leaders, three businessmen were charged at Nuremberg from November 20, 1945 to October 1, 1946: Walter Funk, Hjalmar Schacht and Julius Streicher.[8] Gustav Krupp von Bohlen und Halbach, from Krupp AG or Krupp Concern, would have been a fourth defendant. Although accused of war crimes, he was considered to be medically unfit to stand trial. Krupp thus avoided conviction and possible execution. Krupp's son (Alfried) was, however, subsequently tried for the company's complicity in war crimes and crimes against humanity, particularly the use of slave labor from Nazi concentration camps.[9]

From the Reichsbank, two bankers were tried: Walther Funk and Hjalmar Schacht. Richard Overy states that "[t]he unfortunate Schacht and his successor as economics minister, Walther Funk, were made to represent German capitalism."[10] Although Schacht was acquitted, Funk was found guilty on the count of crimes against humanity, as well as war crimes and wars of aggression. Funk had served as Hitler's personal economic advisor. In that role he had called together twenty-five leading industrialists in 1933 to provide financial and political support for Nazism.[11] As reported, "One tense moment in the trial occurred

---

[5] This number includes ten cases where there was a voluntary dismissal without prejudice by plaintiffs because this was a prerequisite to enter the compensation program organized by the German Foundation of "Remembrance, Responsibility, and the Future," which used funds from the German government and different industries to compensate victims.

[6] We did not have information regarding the outcome of three judicial actions, two in US Civil Courts and one in British Military Courts.

[7] Richard Overy, "The Nuremberg Trials: International Law in the Making," in *From Nuremberg to The Hague: The Future of International Criminal Justice*, ed. Philippe Sands (Cambridge: Cambridge University Press, 2003), 13.

[8] It might be possible to include Hans Fritzsche as a fifth economic actor held accountable at Nuremberg. It is not clear to us that he was an economic actor, but rather a state actor. He played a role in the state media enterprise controlled by the Goebbels' Ministry of Propaganda in promoting anti-Semitism. Fritzsche was acquitted.

[9] According to Overy, Jackson was adamant about putting Krupp on trial despite his age and debilitated condition. When he was unable to stand trial, Jackson attempted to have his son, Alfried, tried in his place but the other prosecutorial teams disagreed. Overy states that "the trial went ahead with no Prussian 'iron baron' in the courtroom." Overy, "The Nuremberg Trials: International Law in the Making," 13.

[10] Overy, "The Nuremberg Trials: International Law in the Making."

[11] Jewish Virtual Library, "Nuremberg Trial Defendants: Walter Funk," *Jewish Virtual Library*, www.jewishvirtuallibrary.org/nuremberg-trial-defendants-walter-funk.

when documentary evidence was presented by the prosecutor's staff that the Reichsbank received and held a large deposit from the SS. The deposit consisted of bags of jewelry and other valuables, including dental gold, taken from Jewish victims in Eastern Europe. Funk consistently denied knowledge of the contents of those bags and the prosecutors could never show conclusively that he did have such knowledge. Nor could they demonstrate conclusively that he was instrumental in planning military operations, or that he was directly involved in 'crimes against humanity.'"[12] He was nonetheless sentenced to life imprisonment but released in 1957 due to ill health and died in 1960.

Julius Streicher was found guilty at Nuremberg for crimes against humanity and hanged. Although he had held positions in the Nazi regime, his conviction was based on his inciting genocide in his newspaper *Der Stürmer*. His defense – that he only wrote and did not take action – was rejected by the Court. With only four defendants and three – controversial – convictions for Nazi business crimes against humanity, it is perhaps unsurprising that the historic Nuremberg Trials left little legal legacy in the area of corporate human rights obligations under international law.

The US prosecutorial team, under the command of Robert H. Jackson, dissatisfied with this limited level of accountability for Nazi businesses at the original Nuremberg trials, called on the Allied forces to carry out subsequent trials of alleged economic accomplices to the Holocaust atrocities. Jackson's motivation may have stemmed from his background as a New Deal Lawyer "who had cut his teeth on fighting America's powerful industrial corporations in the 1930s."[13] Churchill's deputy prime minister, Clement Attlee, also "argued forcefully that generals and business leaders should be dragged into the net," Overy quotes Attlee's view that "[o]fficers [presumably including those in companies] who behave like gangsters … should be shot."[14] Despite Overy's depiction of consensus among "Soviet lawyers, British socialists and Jackson's team of New Dealer lawyers [who] saw nothing unjust about including industrial magnates at Nuremberg," he nonetheless acknowledges opposition from "those who saw business activity as independent of politics and war-making."[15]

Powerful agents on the US prosecutorial team, and a lack of broad agreement among the Allied forces, drove the accountability process. We could not find a single trial for Nazi businesses in Soviet courts. The French military

---

[12] Ben S. Austin, "The Nuremberg Trials: Brief Overview of Defendants & Verdicts," Jewish Virtual Library, www.jewishvirtuallibrary.org/brief-overview-of-defendants-and-verdicts-at-nuremberg-trials.
[13] Overy, "The Nuremberg Trials: International Law in the Making," 6.
[14] Ibid., 10.
[15] Ibid., 10–11.

tribunal put one company on trial and sentenced its director, Hermann Röchling, to ten years' imprisonment and expropriated his assets. We found only nine economic actors tried by the British military tribunal, and very little information about their outcomes. We know that in the case of the Goering-works Factory in Brunswick, a British Military Court convicted Sigbert Ramsauer, a business person managing the factory in collusion with officials of the SS (Schutzstaffel, or the paramilitary wing of the Nazi Party) to life imprisonment. We also know that Bruno Tesch and an associate were sentenced to death by a British Military Court.

Our data set confirms what is widely acknowledged: the United States held the most extensive set of trials (41) from December 9, 1946 to April 13, 1949: the Flick Company (6 defendants); the IG Farben company (23 defendants); and the Krupp company (12 defendants). The trials ended with a significant level of convictions. Of the six defendants from Flick, three were found guilty and sentenced. Friedrich Flick faced the most severe – seven-year – sentence of the guilty parties.[16] The IG Farben trial convicted thirteen of twenty-three defendants with sentences ranging from 1.5 to 10 years (see Appendix C).[17]

The very powerful US judicial leaders behind these trials justified them based on interpretations of international law, domestic law in Germany, and the prospective need to stem future atrocities. Jackson is quoted as saying, "We propose to punish acts which have been regarded as criminal since the time of Cain and have been so written in every civilized code."[18] Judicial action was perceived as "conform[ing] to existing principles in international law but [also] to establish[ing] new rules of international conduct and agreed boundaries in the violation of human rights."[19] Overy concurs, challenging those who condemn the retrospective application of law. As he states, "[M]any of the acts covered by the Indictment were in fact known to be criminal at the time

---

[16] The acquitted include: Odilo Burkart, Konrad Kaletsch, and Herman Terberger. The other two convicted individuals were Otto Steinbrinck (five years) and Bernhard Weiss (two-and-a-half-year sentence). Flick was found guilty for war crimes and crimes against humanity through the use of slave labor, the deportation for labor of civilians of German-occupied territories, and the use of prisoners of war for war operations, war crimes, and crimes against humanity by participating in the plunder of public and private property, spoliation, and offenses against property which came under German occupation, and war crimes and crimes against humanity by participating in the murder, torture, and atrocities committed by the Nazi Party, and specifically the SS.

[17] Ten were acquitted and one defendant was removed from trial for health reasons. Michael J. Kelly, "Atrocities by Corporate Actors: A Historical Perspective," *Case Western Reserve Journal of International Law* 50 (2018): 49–89.

[18] Justice Jackson's Report to the President on Atrocities and War Crimes, June 7, 1945 cited in Bazyler, *Holocaust, Genocide, and the Law: A Quest for Justice in a Post-Holocaust World*, 84.

[19] Overy, "The Nuremberg Trials: International Law in the Making," 23.

they were committed, and would have been subject to criminal proceedings had the law not been perverted by dictatorship."[20] Linking business atrocities to other Nazi crimes, Jackson wrote to President Truman at the time, "A very large number of Germans ... remain unpunished. There are many industrialists ... whose guilt does not differ from those who have been convicted [at Nuremberg] except that their parts were at lower levels and have been less conspicuous."[21] Overy concludes that "[a]fter this grotesque historical experience, few could doubt, either then or now, that the international community required new legal instruments to cope with its possible recurrence,"[22] including the role of business in it.

This forceful and principled argument did not convince all Allied forces or even all the members of the US team. They did not share the interpretation of international customary law or the historical necessity of extending the trials to business leaders. This is evident in the lack of enthusiasm among the other Allied forces to hold "industrialist trials." Even within the United States, just a few years after the industrialist case convictions, John McCloy, the US High Commissioner for Occupied Germany, in 1951 granted clemency to "dozens of Nazi war criminals ... most notoriously the industrialist Alfried Krupp, who had been sentenced at Nuremberg to twelve years in prison for using concentration camp inmates as slave labor. Krupp, accompanied by most of his board of directors, walked out of the Landsberg prison in 1951 to a cheering crowd and a champagne breakfast – with his fortune and industrial empire intact."[23] McCloy's decision (discussed further in Chapter 3) could be characterized as "a consequence of a persistent reality in which power will always tend to triumph over justice."[24]

McCloy's decision reflects the view that the Nazi businesses did not deserve prosecution for alleged crimes against humanity and "that at most they were 'white collar criminals.'"[25] Michael Bazyler notes that "[c]onvicted insider traders today serve longer sentences than those served by Flick, Krupp, and the IG Farben executives."[26] He adds, "In 1957, *Time* magazine featured Krupp on its cover, lauding his contribution to restoring the economy of West

---

[20] Ibid., 22–23.
[21] See Bazyler, *Holocaust, Genocide, and the Law: A Quest for Justice in a Post-Holocaust World*, 91.
[22] Overy, "The Nuremberg Trials: International Law in the Making," 29.
[23] Joseph Finder, "Ultimate Insider, Ultimate Outsider," *The New York Times*, April 12, 1992, www .nytimes.com/1992/04/12/books/ultimate-insider-ultimate-outsider.html?pagewanted=all.
[24] Overy, "The Nuremberg Trials: International Law in the Making," 29.
[25] Bazyler, *Holocaust, Genocide, and the Law: A Quest for Justice in a Post-Holocaust World*, 108.
[26] Ibid.

Germany. His wartime deeds were barely mentioned. By that time, Krupp had become the richest man in Europe."[27] Bazyler views the industrial trials as "ancient history" by this time, "the forgotten stepchildren" of the Nuremberg Trials.

At the time of the clemency, McCloy's decision did provoke some outrage. Bazyler cites the reaction of chief prosecutor of the Einsatzgruppen trial, Benjamin Ferencz, in a letter in December 1951 to Telford Taylor, US Counsel for the Prosecution: "Noel, noel, what the hell?" Valerie Herbert wrote that as a result of the clemency, "[T]he Nuremberg trials' goals of justice and education were a failure."[28] Eleanor Roosevelt expressed her concern – "Why are we freeing so many Nazis?"[29] – reflecting the view that clemency in the face of grave crimes against humanity and war crimes was unacceptable. Taylor himself wrote an article with the title "The Nazis Go free" in which he stated that justice was the first casualty of the Cold War.[30]

McCloy's clemency decision shifted the momentum away from corporate accountability and toward corporate leniency. The moment for creating a corporate human rights accountability norm seemed to pass. The agent behind such a norm, Jackson with a background in fighting corporate economic abuses, with vast legal experience, and with strong backing, was replaced by an equally powerful and influential actor (McCloy) whose experience and support came from business. The two historical moments also could not have been more different. The immediate postwar period emphasized the deterrence of future genocides, including those in which businesses were involved. This contrasted with the beginning of the Cold War where powerful German businesses, once on the side of the enemy, were perceived as necessary to strengthening Europe and the West against the new Communist enemy.

Another moment returned, however, with the third wave of cases held in the United States in the 1990s. These were civil cases brought for restitution of property and reparations for slave labor in Nazi Germany. Out of a total of eighteen cases (after six were consolidated), most settled (13). The remaining five cases included three dismissals and two with unknown outcomes (see Appendix C). Businesses' financial settlements contributed to half of a reparations fund, with the German government covering the other half. Some researchers contend that by passing on half of the fund to the German

[27] Ibid., 102.
[28] Quoted in Bazyler, *Holocaust, Genocide, and the Law: A Quest for Justice in a Post-Holocaust World*, 105.
[29] Quoted in Kai Bird, *The Chairman: John J. McCloy and the Making of the American Establishment* (New York : Simon & Schuster, 1992), chap. 18.
[30] Bazyler, *Holocaust, Genocide, and the Law: A Quest for Justice in a Post-Holocaust World*, 105.

government, corporations failed to assume their responsibility for wrongdoing. The 3,000 firms that contributed paid "a nominal amount in proportion to their total assets" with most of the fund being offset by tax deductions, accepted as the cost of doing business, or passed along to consumers. Moreover, these 3,000 firms represent only a small fraction of the estimated 20,000 firms allegedly complicit in slave labor. The reparations paid to victims are estimated at $5,000 each, which is widely recognized as "too little too late."[31] Lawyers for the victims in these cases are criticized for profiting from atrocity or creating a legal enterprise to make money off slave labor cases.[32] The third wave did little to contribute to law-making, and some would also argue that it did very little to repair the harm to victims. Si Frumkin is one victim who would agree with that viewpoint.

Not all victims felt betrayed, however. Some were satisfied that businesses were held at least partially or symbolically accountable. An expert in these civil trials, Bazyler considers this third wave of (civil) trials as an alternative form of accountability. The restitution resulting from these trials, he argues, provided "recognition by the perpetrators of the wrongs committed against the victims and an issuance of an apology to those victims." He adds, "[T]he hidden role of German companies during the Nazi era came to light in the 1990s as these companies opened their archives to Holocaust historians to write reports on their wartime history ... The Holocaust restitution movement, therefore, yielded not only money; it also yielded new history and apology."[33]

What it did not yield was a corporate human rights accountability norm. The absence of the norm is evident in the debate over how to interpret the set of Nazi business trials in these three moments following the Holocaust. On one hand, William Schabas states that "there is nothing terribly innovative about an international instrument that would impose [human rights] duties upon economic actors,"[34] since those obligations exist in customary law. Yet others argue that economic actors – as such – were not held accountable following the Holocaust. Specific individuals, who happened to be owners and managers of businesses, were held accountable. In that sense, no innovation in the application of international law occurred. Gwynn Skinner

---

[31] Kara Ryf, "Burger-Fischer v. Degussa AG: U.S. Courts Allow Siemens and Degussa to Profit from Holocaust Slave Labor," *Case Western Reserve Journal of International Law* 33, no. 1 (2001): 178.

[32] See Bazyler, *Holocaust Justice: The Battle for Restitution in America's Courts*, chap. 8.

[33] Bazyler, *Holocaust, Genocide, and the Law: A Quest for Justice in a Post-Holocaust World*, 164.

[34] William Schabas, "War Economies, Economic Actors, and International Criminal Law," in *Profiting from Peace: Managing the Resource Dimensions of Civil War*, ed. Karen Ballentine and Heiko Nitzschke (Boulder, CO: Lynne Rienner Publishers, Inc., 2005).

questions that interpretation of the trials arguing that "corporations are bound by international law and thus liable for human rights violations."[35] While "[i]ndividuals were nominally on trial," the "company itself, acting through its employees, violated international law."[36] Skinner emphasizes that the court viewed the accused individuals as "acting within the scope of their employment or pursuant to their employment,"[37] and not as individual or independent citizens. Andrew Clapham, citing from the IG Farben case, further states that "[i]t can no longer be questioned that the criminal sanctions of international law are applicable to private individuals." Clapham's view concurs with Skinner's that the Tribunal "did in fact treat Farben as a legal entity (juristic person) capable of violating the laws of war."[38] He adds, "The US Military Tribunal in Nuremberg found that industrialists were members of an industrial organization which was connected with the commission of a war crime. Their *Farben* judgment can be read as implying that the Farben company itself had committed the relevant war crime, even though the Tribunal had no jurisdiction over Farben as such."[39] McCloy also, no doubt, saw those he released from prison as having been judged by their position as powerful members of the business community, rather than as individuals. He did not share Jackson's conviction about their individual or corporate responsibility for crimes against humanity.

As civil claims, the US restitution trials did not belabor the issue of individual guilt and focused on the responsibility of companies to compensate victims. Victims, particularly Jewish and non-Jewish slave laborers, found prestigious law firms and practitioners willing to take on their cases in US civil courts. Plaintiffs' lawyers became the global agents advancing corporate accountability. The ambiguous results in terms of accountability reflect yet another set of agents, tools, and political context. Accountability agents faced powerful companies' law firms. The post-Cold War climate constituted a neutral political context. The tools used blended domestic legal instruments with international human rights standards. The settlements reached hinged in

---

[35] Gwynne Skinner, "Nuremberg's Legacy Continues: The Nuremberg Trials' Influence on Human Rights Litigation in US Courts under the Alien Tort Statute," *Albany Law Review* 71, no. 1 (2008): 344.

[36] Ibid., 345.

[37] Ibid., 364.

[38] Andrew Clapham, "The Question of Jurisdiction under International Criminal Law over Legal Persons: Lessons from the Rome Conference on an International Criminal Court," in *Liability of Multinational Corporations under International Law* (The Hague: Kluwer Law International, 2000), 167.

[39] Ibid., 170–71.

large part on moving cases quickly before more victims of forced labor died without remedy for wrongs committed. These settlements also represented something of a compromise: victims received compensation, but companies' lawyers avoided precedent-setting legal outcomes that could hold future businesses accountable for atrocities such as these.

In sum, the future Robert Jackson envisioned in his statement has not transpired. What could not be sustained was the kind of moral and political leadership and commitment to corporate human rights accountability that Jackson embodied. Counterforces emerged in the figure of McCloy. Companies "lawyered up" and settled, avoiding legal judgment on their guilt or innocence. Propitious moments for understanding the importance of corporate accountability were followed by less propitious moments when countervailing security concerns trumped global accountability norms. Neutral moments then followed. Corporate accountability for Holocaust atrocities illustrates how international pressure exerted by global agents can play a powerful role on either the side of accountability or the side of impunity. It also shows the significance of context – the favorable, unfavorable, or neutral global context – in determining the amount of force that has to be applied by accountability actors to lift the weight of accountability. The efforts at corporate accountability following the Holocaust ended up facing such significant hurdles that they barely left a legacy. Indeed, the favorable international context, and the global agents who exerted pressure for accountability in the first two waves, did not even endure long enough to address corporate atrocities during World War II in Japan.

Trials for Corporate Complicity in Japan

The trials for corporate complicity in wartime atrocities in Japan are much more weakly represented in the scholarly literature and in subsequent case law than those in Germany. The International Tribunal for the Far East (IMTFE, or the Tokyo Trials) of 1946 tried twenty-eight military and political leaders for war crimes, but only one businessman. That businessman, Yoshisuke Aikawa of the Nissan Corporation, faced war crimes charges, not crimes against humanity, and he appears to have been released without standing trial.[40]

---

[40] Nearly 6,000 additional lower level individuals were held accountable in trials led by seven countries: Australia, China, France, the Netherlands, the Philippines, the United Kingdom, and the United States.

In our data set for corporate accountability in Japan, we found thirteen economic actors that faced trials in US and Japanese courts after Japan's military defeat and the 1951 peace agreement (see Appendix C).[41] Among the crimes included for prosecution were: prisoner abuse, rape, sexual slavery, torture, ill-treatment of workers, execution without trial, and inhumane medical experiments. The thirteen economic actors faced ten judicial actions in domestic Japanese courts (3) and in US courts (7). In Japan, three domestic trials were held involving Mitsui, Nishimatsu Construction Company, and Mitsubishi for alleged kidnapping and/or slave labor. Only Mitsui faced conviction by the Fukuoka District Court for slave labor, subsequently reversed on appeal to the Supreme Court of Japan.[42] The other two companies appear to have settled before conviction and were never charged in foreign courts. Mitsui faced additional charges – subsequently dismissed – in US District Courts (Northern California and Albuquerque) for alleged sexual slavery and kidnapping of "Comfort Women" and other counts of forced labor. It seems that all of the other cases brought against Japanese companies in US courts for sexual slavery, slavery, and kidnapping were dismissed.[43] In sum, nearly all of the cases that we found for businesses accused of crimes against humanity in Japan ended in dismissal or settlement. With only one conviction (later overturned), postwar Japan corporate complicity cases do not represent a clear indication of an international corporate accountability norm that extended from the Holocaust cases into atrocities committed elsewhere (see Appendix C).[44]

---

[41] These accountability efforts were carried out by the International Prosecution Section of the Supreme Commander for the Allied Powers (SCAP) rather than in the Tokyo Trials. The companies that faced trial included the Mitsui and Company, Mitsubishi Materials Corporation, Nippon Steel, Sumitomo Metal Corporation, Mitsubishi International Corporation, Ishikawajima Harima Heavy Industries, Nishimatsu Construction Co., Showa Denko K.K., Kawasaki Heavy Industries, Nissan Motor Company, Toyota Motor Company, Hitachi Ltd., NYK Line NA Inc./ Nippon Yusen Kabushiki Kaisha.

[42] The lower court had ordered the company in 2002 to pay compensation (165 million yen) to fifteen Chinese men. War.Wire, "Japanese High Court Overturns Order to Pay Chinese Forced Labourers," *War.Wire*, 2004, www.nytimes.com/1999/09/15/world/ex-pow-s-sue-5-big-japanese-companies-over-forced-labor.html.

[43] This includes Hitashi, Kawasaki, Mitsubishi, Nippon, Nissan, Showa Denko K.K., Toyota, and possibly Ishikawajima Harima Heavy Industries.

[44] Cases of slave restitution were brought and dismissed in the 1950s and again in the 2000s. See Anita Ramasastry, "Corporate Complicity: From Nuremberg to Rangoon, an Examination of Forced Labor Cases and Their Impact on the Liability of Corporations," *Berkeley Journal of International Law* 20, no. 1 (2002): 91–159; John Haberstroh, "In Re World War II Era Japanese Forced Labor Litigation and Obstacles to International Human Rights Claims in U.S. Courts," *Asian American Law Journal* 10, no. 2 (2003): 253–94.

Nonetheless, the efforts at accountability had something of an impact in Japan. The Japanese government acknowledged and apologized for the use of slave labor from South Korea, China, and over 900 US prisoners of war in factories during World War II. In addition, at least two companies – Mitsubishi Materials Corp and Nishimatsu Construction – reached an out-of-court settlement leading to an apology, compensation to Chinese slave laborers, and the construction of a memorial.[45] After a judge controversially applied the 1951 peace agreement between Japan and the United States to dismiss civil claims,[46] victims of slave labor sought, and sometimes received, an apology from companies. The political bargain behind the peace agreement put justice off the table, but symbolic forms of accountability occurred.

The outcome of the Japan cases, on the heels of the industrialist cases in Germany, confirms our framework. A judicial accountability agent, such as Jackson, did not emerge in Japan. The US courts acted more along the lines of McCloy, judging by political expediency rather than with a human rights deterrence framework. The application of the 1951 peace agreement to corporate accountability no doubt resulted from the perceived need for a stronger business and pro-Western country to stem the tide of Communism in Asia during the Korean War. Corporate impunity even for documented and acknowledged grave human rights violations by some of the most powerful companies in the world seemed preferable in that political context than accountability. Global agents in the form of a legal community emerged to defend victims' claims and they had legal tools and the precedent of the industrialist trials. Nonetheless, they could not overcome the power of veto players in that political environment of global insecurity. A victims' gap resulted.

US Army Tank Commander and Japanese prisoner of war (POW) Lester Tenney personifies that gap. He died at age 96 with an apology,[47] but no justice and no reparations for what he had experienced in Japan. This was not because he did not try. He worked tirelessly to bring attention to corporate

---

[45] Associated Press, "Japanese Firm Mitsubishi Used U.S. Prisoners of War as Slave Labor, Will Apologize 70 Years Later," *New York Daily News*, 2015, www.nydailynews.com/news/world/japanese-firm-u-s-prisoners-war-labor-article-1.2294061.

[46] Louis Sahagun, "Suit on WWII Slave Labor in Japan Voided," *Los Angeles Times*, 2000, http://articles.latimes.com/2000/sep/22/news/mn-25128.

[47] Prime Minister of Japan, Shinzo Abe, personally apologized to Tenney. Tenney also received an apology from Mitsubishi, although he had not been enslaved by that company. In 2015, Mitsubishi Materials issued a formal apology at the Los Angeles Simon Wisenthal Center. Hikaru Kimura issued the apology, bowing to James Murphy, a 94-year-old veteran who had been a slave in the mines, attending the event. Bazyler, *Holocaust, Genocide, and the Law: A Quest for Justice in a Post-Holocaust World*, 172–74.

wrongdoing in Japan during World War II. Tenney's story exemplifies the experience of many POWs. He claims that he was on the Bataan Death March, in which starving POWs were marched sixty to seventy miles, facing beating and other mistreatment along the way. Surviving the march, which many did not, he was forced into hard labor for three and a half years in a Mitsui-owned coal mine.[48] Tenney received more than many of his fellow POWs. Others died without an apology or even the acknowledgment of wrongdoing from firms that profited from their slave labor.[49]

It is surprising, even shocking, that US veterans, like Tenney, prisoners of war in a country that was roundly and militarily defeated, who were enslaved and mistreated by powerful companies in that country, who had lawyers in the United States fighting for them, still could not get justice in Japan or in their own country before they died. The Japanese case shows that the global agents with powerful tools developed in the industrialist trials lose force when the global context shifts. In that changed global context, business was seen as critical to global security rather than a threat to it. Corresponding to that change, powerful global agents applied pressure to resist corporate accountability.

Thus, by way of concluding this section, the historic cases from the Holocaust and Japan reveal the importance of global context. Global human rights agents, although they existed, could not apply sufficient pressure to outweigh the powerful veto from opposing global agents when the context shifted away from corporate accountability.

Rwandan Genocide

Following the World War II cases, we found only one international court – the UN ad hoc International Criminal Tribunal for Rwanda (ICTR) – that took on corporate complicity in past human rights violations.[50] The Media

---

[48] John Wilkens and Peter Rowe, "Lester Tenney, Army Tank Commander Who Survived Bataan Death March during World War II, Dies at 96," *Los Angeles Times*, 2017, www.latimes .com/local/obituaries/la-me-lester-tenney-20170227-story.html.

[49] According to Bazyler, the first lawsuit was brought by Ralph Levenberg, prisoner-of-war – against Nippon Sharyo Ltd. and its US subsidiary. This was dismissed in June 2000 by Judge Vaughn Walker for the San Francisco federal court and affirmed by the Ninth Circuit. The US Supreme Court refused to hear the case.

[50] Two other ICTR trials involve such loose connections to corporate accountability that we have not included them in our database: the Mugonero and Musema cases. In the Mugonero trial, Reverend Elizaphan Ntakirutimana and his son Dr. Gérard Ntakirutimana, were found guilty of aiding and abetting genocide. (See International Criminal Tribunal for Rwanda, "The Prosecutor v. Elizaphan and Gerard Ntakirutimana Cases No. ICTR-96-10 & ICTR-96-17-T," Trial Chamber I, 2003.) Rev. Ntakirutimana received a ten-year sentence. His son, with the

Case at the ICTR led to the conviction and imprisonment of three individuals for their participation in the genocide: Ferdinand Nahimana and Jean-Bosco Barayagwiza, both members of the Steering Committee that founded Radio Télévision Libre des Mille Collines (RTLM), and Hassan Ngeze, the owner, founder, and editor of the Kangura newsletter.[51] The ICTR referred to historical precedent, stating: "[T]he convictions were the first of their kind since the Allied Tribunal at Nuremberg in 1946 sentenced Nazi publisher Julius Streicher to death for his anti-Semitic publication *Der Stürmer.*"[52] The judges further highlighted the media's alleged atrocities, "which have not been addressed at the level of international criminal justice since Nuremberg," particularly "the power of the media to create and destroy fundamental human values ... Those who control the media are accountable for its consequences."[53]

The Media Case was appealed. In 2007, the Appeals Chamber acquitted the defendants on several counts: conspiracy, all genocide charges related to their involvement with RTLM and Kangura, and extermination as a crime

---

added charge of shooting two people to death, received a 25-year sentence. The Mugonero incident refers to an event on April 16, 1994 at the Mugonero Complex, a business project owned by the Seventh-Day Adventist Church, on April 16, 1994. The Ntakirutimanas were found guilty of leading and joining attackers, a group of Gendarmerie, in the massacre of hundreds of Tutsi who had sought refuge in the Complex. The link to corporate complicity is tenuous. Rev. Ntakirutimana, although the President of the West Rwanda Association of the Mungonero Compound, is identified in media reports not for his business role, but as the "first clergyman to be convicted of genocide by an international tribunal." (See Simon Marlise, "Rwandan Pastor and His Son Are Convicted of Genocide," *The New York Times*, 2003, www .nytimes.com/2003/02/20/world/rwandan-pastor-and-his-son-are-convicted-of-genocide.html.)

The other case involved Alfred Musema, the director of the state-owned Gisovu tea factory in the district of Kibuye. He was found guilty in 2000 of genocide, extermination, and rape as a crime against humanity. He was condemned to life imprisonment. The Appeals Chamber in 2001, acquitted Musema of the rape charge, but confirmed the other two judgments and the sentence. The charges against Musema stemmed from his involvement in several attacks against Tutsi who had fled to the hilly Bisesero region in the Kibuye district. He personally participated in, and authorized the use of company vehicles, uniforms, and personnel to carry out, massacres of Tutsi refugees who had fled to the region of Bisesero in the district of Kibuye. His personal role does not appear to be related to company policy or practice. (See Trial International, "Alfred Musema," *Trial International*, 2016, https://trialinternational.org/latest-post/alfred-musema/; International Crimes Database, "The Prosecutor v. Alfred Musema.")

[51] Sophia Kagan, "The 'Media Case' before the Rwanda Tribunal: The Nahimana et al. Appeal Judgement," *The Hague Justice Portal*, April 24, 2008.

[52] UN News, "UN Tribunal Convicts 3 Rwandan Media Executives for Their Role in 1994 Genocide," *UN News*, December 2003.

[53] Quoted in United States Holocaust Memorial Museum, "Incitement to Genocide in International Law," Holocaust Encyclopedia, n.d.

against humanity. The Chamber upheld the convictions for Nahimana and Ngeze, but acquitted Barayagwiza, on charges of direct and public incitement to commit genocide.[54] In the ruling, the Chamber clarified that merely owning or directing media outlets responsible for broadcasting or printing genocidal messages (the case of Barayagwiza in the Chamber's opinion) does not constitute the crime of genocide. The Chamber found sufficient evidence to uphold the conviction of Nahimana and Ngeze, specifically their direct involvement in the publications and broadcasts inciting genocide.[55]

With the appeal, the case moved from corporate accountability to certain economic actors' accountability for inciting genocide. For some, the failure to hold the businesses themselves accountable for their alleged role in the genocide, as opposed to specific individuals, limited the justice outcome.[56] The Chamber exonerated an individual who had directed a company whose policies and practices incited genocide (Barayagwiza-RTLM), and only held accountable those individuals who directly committed incitement at those companies through their own use of speech (Nahimana-RTLM and Ngeze-Kangura). By delinking the acts from the companies, the Appeals Chamber could be seen as merely applying international criminal law rather than advancing corporate accountability and transitional justice. The earlier innovative ICTR ruling, aimed at the role of companies, and those responsible for them, in inciting genocide, no longer prevailed.

The result of the Appeals Chamber ruling takes from the ICTR its potential role in promoting a global corporate accountability norm, legal innovation, or legal precedent. The ICTR cannot be viewed as a global agent deliberately

---

[54] Kagan, "The 'Media Case' before the Rwanda Tribunal: The Nahimana et al. Appeal Judgement."

[55] Bazyler, *Holocaust, Genocide, and the Law: A Quest for Justice in a Post-Holocaust World*, 246.

[56] One study states, "Although the case investigated the role of the media in the violence, only individuals were tried and the radio and newspapers involved were not prosecuted." Center for International Law and Policy, "Briefing Report: Transitional Justice and Corporate Accountability" (Boston, MA, 2016), 10. Another study made a similar claim: "In the case of Rwanda, Radio-Television Libre des Mille Collines (RTLMC) was launched by Hutu extremists to foster hate and galvanizing support for the forthcoming genocide. What is the responsibility of this station for its role? These questions remain difficult to answer and as a result the enterprises find themselves largely expunged." Sarah Federman, "Genocide Studies and Corporate Social Responsibility: The Contemporary Case of the French National Railways (SNCF)," *Genocide Studies and Prevention: An International* 2, no. 2 (2017): 16.

linking the acts of economic actors to the root causes, the perpetuation, or the intensity of the genocide. Instead, the judges, in the end, focused on individuals' acts, regardless of their role within companies or companies' policies and practices. The ICTR neither set out to be a global agent to deter future atrocities by identifying the role that economic actors played in the Rwandan genocide, nor did its rulings have that effect.

Nonetheless, some accountability was achieved. In the absence of settled international law, the Court still found ways to hold companies – through the direct action of individuals controlling those companies – accountable for genocidal acts. In the propitious environment in which the international community united to bring justice for a genocide it failed to prevent,[57] the ICTR addressed victims' needs. International efforts to stem genocidal acts addressed the behavior of broad sectors of society – including businesses – in fomenting that crisis. While "businesses" as such would not be held accountable, individuals inciting genocide – in businesses or not – would face accountability efforts. Such a ruling did not catalyze veto action in defense of businesspeople. Neither did global accountability agents emerge to apply a set of innovative tools to advance binding and enforceable obligations on business.

In sum, the ICTR delivered a limited form of justice to the victims of some businesses. It did not, however, transform the status quo of piecemeal international human rights obligations on business. It is unlikely that the ruling reverberated in the business community or would deter future violations elsewhere. Nonetheless, it did represent a way, within existing international human rights frameworks, to hold some individuals accountable who had perpetrated violations connected to their role as economic actors.

The Special Tribunal for Lebanon hints at ways in which international criminal courts could apply binding human rights obligations to economic actors if those duties existed in clear and settled international law. On July 15, 2016, Judge Nicola Lettieri entered a guilty verdict against two companies – New TV S.A.L. and Akhbar Beirut S.A.L. This was touted as the first time an international criminal tribunal prosecuted a company, rather

---

[57] Michael Barnett, *Eyewitness to a Genocide: The United Nations and Rwanda* (Ithaca, NY: Cornell University Press, 2002); Samantha Power, *A Problem from Hell: America and the Age of Genocide* (New York, NY: Basic Books, 2003); Roméo Dallaire, *Shake Hands with the Devil: The Failure of Humanity in Rwanda* (Random House Canada, 2003).

than an individual representing a company.[58] The tribunal interpreted "persons" broadly to include corporations.[59]

In general, however, the absence of binding human rights obligations on businesses has meant that international criminal tribunals have been unable to clearly enforce those duties. No clear international signal is sent that businesses have those duties and will be held accountable for failing to fulfill them.

"Bottom-Up" Foreign Trials

International human rights norms are not only applied in international courts, but also in foreign courts. By foreign courts, we mean those courts that adjudicate extraterritorial violations carried out by non-residents. Because the violations occurred in another country by actors in those countries, customary international law is applicable. Tracking corporate accountability in foreign trials in powerful courts of the Global North thus provides insights into the interpretations of customary international law regarding economic actors' enforceable human rights obligations.

Our database includes fifty corporate complicity cases in foreign courts. Nearly all of these cases (37 or 74 percent) involved civil rather than

---

[58] The companies published the names of confidential witnesses testifying before the Tribunal in violation of the court's order that such witnesses' identities be kept secret. Contempt proceedings were lodged against both corporations based on "willful interference with the administration of justice." Michael J. Kelly, *Prosecuting Corporations for Genocide* (New York, NY: Oxford University Press, 2016), 69; Ekaterina Kopylova, "Akhbar Beirut S.A.L. Guilty of Contempt, STL Found: One Small Verdict for a Tribunal, a Giant Leap for International Justice?," *Opinio Juris*, 2016, http://opiniojuris.org/2016/08/04/akhbar-beirut-s-a-l-guilty-of-contempt-stl-found-one-small-verdict-for-a-tribunal-a-giant-leap-for-international-justice/.

[59] As stated in the Statute, "The Special Tribunal shall have jurisdiction over persons responsible for the attack of February 14, 2005 resulting in the death of former Lebanese Prime Minister Rafik Hariri and in the death or injury of other persons. If the Tribunal finds that other attacks that occurred in Lebanon between October 1, 2004 and December 12, 2005, or any later date decided by the Parties and with the consent of the Security Council, are connected in accordance with the principles of criminal justice and are of a nature and gravity similar to the attack of February 14, 2005, it shall also have jurisdiction over persons responsible for such attacks. This connection includes but is not limited to a combination of the following elements: criminal intent (motive), the purpose behind the attacks, the nature of the victims targeted, the pattern of the attacks (*modus operandi*) and the perpetrators." Statute of the Special Tribunal for Lebanon, 2007. www.stl-tsl.org/sites/default/files/documents/legal-documents/statute/Statute_of_the_Special_Tribunal_for_Lebanon___English.pdf. See also Joseph Rikhof, "Analysis: The Special Tribunal for Lebanon: A Unique Institution," *Institut Philippe Kirsch*, 2018, www.kirschinstitute.ca/analysis-special-tribunal-lebanon-unique-institution/.

criminal (13 or 26 percent) litigation, owing to the concentration (32 or 64 percent) in US Courts applying the Alien Tort Statute (ATS). The ATS cases include allegations of companies complicit in abuses in authoritarian or armed conflict situations in Africa (7), North Africa and the Middle East (8), Asia (6), and Latin America (11). Five civil trials and thirteen criminal trials were initiated in the other foreign courts of the Global North (see Appendix E).[60]

Litigation in foreign criminal trials has produced little accountability. According to our database, there have only been four convictions in criminal courts. Six cases were dismissed. The remaining cases reached settlements (1) or are still ongoing (2).

The use of foreign civil courts to adjudicate human rights crimes is an innovation that transitional justice scholars and practitioners have largely ignored. It is a central mechanism for "bottom-up" business and human rights strategies of advancing corporate accountability through powerful courts in the Global North. Our findings, however, do not line up with the expectation "bottom-up" scholars have for positive accountability outcomes from foreign trials in the Global North. These trials have tended to maintain impunity, rather than promote justice. Twenty out of 37 – more than half of all cases brought in foreign civil courts in our database – were dismissed, for example. The ones that were not dismissed (17) involve: six pending cases, one acquittal, nine out-of-court settlements, and two withdrawals.[61] In sum, with no adverse judgments in civil courts and only four criminal convictions, the "bottom-up" approach has delivered a very thin form of corporate accountability.

Settlements could be viewed as a form of accountability, however. A company's decision to settle is viewed popularly as an admission of guilt. The settlement in the Ogoni case in Nigeria, for example, was evaluated in the following way: "The pay-out by Shell to the families of nine executed Nigerian activists who brought a lawsuit against the oil company in the United States has been rightly hailed as a victory for the relatives .... The settlement can be seen as a partial step toward holding companies such as Shell

---

[60] The other five foreign civil cases for corporate complicity were heard in Canada (Anvil Mining Ltd.), United States (Class Action) (Chevron), United Kingdom (BP Company), and France (BNP Paribas, Total). The thirteen criminal trials for corporate complicity in the database have been held in the United States (Chiquita Brands), France (Dalhoff, Larsen and Horneman – DLH, Lafarge, Qosmos and Total), Switzerland (Argor Heraeus, Cicolac-Nestlé), Germany (Danzer Group), Belgium (Abbas Macky and Aziz Nassour; Leonid Minin; Total), and the Netherlands (Guus Kouwenhoven and Frans Cornelis Adrianus van Anraat).

[61] The total number of outcomes is eighteen judicial actions, rather than seventeen, owing to two different outcomes — acquittal and settlement — in a single case.

accountable for the human rights impact of their operations."[62] The promise of financial remedy may provide a more immediate and necessary outcome for communities than jail sentences for a few employees.

What limits the role of settlements as accountability is the formal, and often public, disavowal of legal responsibility by companies. The settlement amounts also tend to be sealed, thereby eliminating the possibility of analyzing how much a company has paid out to resolve a case. Settlements also provide ways for companies to end disputes before the court reaches a judgment, reducing reputational costs and trumping efforts by victims to secure precedents that could play a role in subsequent cases. While settlements indicate that human rights allegations may be strong enough to force a company to provide some remedy to victims to avoid a ruling against them, they are the only form of accountability – and a weak one at that – that we have found in foreign civil courts.

These findings show that more cases have been heard in foreign courts than in international ones, concurring with the "bottom-up" approach that they are potentially a better pathway to shape international law regarding corporate accountability. On the other hand, the outcomes do not confirm that the strategy has worked. Further discussion of foreign courts and corporate accountability is thus warranted and provided in the next sections.

Alien Tort Statute and Corporate Accountability

In civil litigation for corporate complicity, the application of the ATS is significant both for the number of cases and its innovative use in the hands of global agents. ATS, established in the 1789 US First Judiciary Act, is a legal instrument providing federal district courts jurisdiction over "any civil action by an alien for a tort only, committed in violation of the law of nations or a treaty of the United States."[63] Designed to deal with piracy, in which no specific country held jurisdiction, ATS has been used by advocates to advance cases of crimes against humanity (law of nations), when perpetrated by foreign legal persons (including businesses), in another country, against foreign nationals. In 1997, US district courts ruled that ATS covered corporate liability

---

[62] Center for Economic and Social Rights, "Wiwa v. Shell Settlement Just One Small Step toward Ending Corporate Impunity," www.cesr.org/wiwa-v-shell-settlement-just-one-small-step-toward-ending-corporate-impunity. Center for Constitutional Rights, "Wiwa et al. v. Royal Dutch Petroleum et al.," www.ccrjustice.org/home/what-we-do/our-cases/wiwa-et-al-v-royal-dutch-petroleum-et-al.

[63] United States Congress, "28 U.S. Code Part IV Chapter 85 § 1350," n.d., www.law.cornell.edu/uscode/text/28/1350.

for human rights violations, opening up an avenue for corporate accountability for crimes against humanity in authoritarian and conflict situations.[64] Global advocates for victims began to use this innovative tool to advance corporate liability cases involving human rights violations in US civil courts.[65]

Despite this promise, and even before the US Supreme Court rulings in 2013 (*Kiobel*) and 2018 (*Jesner*) that constrained the use of ATS, corporate complicity cases had highly limited outcomes. We did not find even one judgment under the ATS against corporations for their complicity in authoritarian and armed conflict violence. Scholars' findings on the use of ATS in other corporate liability cases found the same results. All sixty cases analyzed by Michael J. Kelly ended without favorable judgments for the plaintiffs; cases were dismissed or companies settled before a final judgment and on the condition of no admission of wrongdoing.[66]

These results cannot be attributed to a lack of global agents or legal tools. Global agents successfully reached the settlement stage, suggesting that they produced powerful arguments that might have rendered an unfavorable judgment against the company. The case brought by the Lawyers' Committee for Human Rights used ATS to advance the international human rights violations claim against Shell Oil Company. The suit alleged that Shell had participated with Nigerian dictator Sani Abacha's army in the killing of Ken Saro-Wiwa and the Ogoni Nine owing to their protests of the company's destructive activities on protected cultural lands. In 2009, the Saro-Wiwa

---

[64] As one example, see U.S. District Court for the Central District of California, "Doe I v. Unocal, 963 F. Supp. 880 (CD.Cal.1997)."

[65] Richard L. Herz, "The Liberalizing Effects of Tort: How Corporate Liability under the Alien Tort Statute Advances Engagement," *Harvard Human Rights Journal* 21 (2008): 211; Chris Albin-Lackey, "Corruption, Human Rights and Activism: Useful Connections and Their Limits," in *Justice and Economic Violence in Transition*, ed. Dustin N. Sharp (New York, NY: Springer, 2013), 139–63; Michael J. Kelly, "Prosecuting Corporations for Genocide under International Law," *Harvard Law Policy Review* no. 6 (2012): 339–67; Wolfgang Kaleck and Miriam Saage-Maaß, "Corporate Accountability for Human Rights Violations Amounting to International Crimes: The Status Quo and Its Challenges," *Journal of International Criminal Justice* 8 (July 2010): 699–724; International Federation for Human Rights (FIDH), "Corporate Accountability for Human Rights Abuses: A Guide for Victims and NGOs on Recourse Mechanisms," *Globalisation and Human Rights Report*, May 11, 2016, www.fidh.org/IMG/pdf/corporate_accountability_guide_version_web.pdf.

[66] Kelly, "Prosecuting Corporations for Genocide under International Law." These findings are consistent with settlement trends in the United States. For example, de Gramont et al. point out that "Most analyses of US cases put the settlement rate in the range of seventy to ninety percent. Even when limited to contract/commercial cases, settlement rates in US litigation are typically estimated at well over sixty percent." Alexandre de Gramont, Michael D. Igyarto, and Tatiana Sainati, "Divergent Paths: Settlement in US Litigation and International Arbitration," *Fordham International Law Journal* 40, no. 953–72 (2017): 954.

litigation ended with a $11 million settlement approved by the US District Court for the Southern District of New York. Although the company did not accept liability, it expressed the hope that the settlement would contribute to reconciliation.[67]

The results also cannot be attributed to political environment alone. The conservative shift in the US Supreme Court that has been used to explain the *Kiobel* and *Jesner* decisions, does not shed light on the limited success rate – measured in settlements with no adverse judgments for businesses – prior to 2013. The lack of earlier judgments in favor of plaintiffs suggests that the political shift may not have as great an impact as it would seem. Nonetheless, institutional innovators and plaintiffs see the political shift and the recent rulings as significant obstacles to advancing corporate accountability in foreign courts.[68] The one significant area of ATS litigation that remains, however, appears to be US businesses involved in human rights violations outside the country, including corporate complicity in authoritarian and conflict situations.

Kiobel v. *Royal Dutch Petroleum* (2013)[69] involved a fairly narrow interpretation of ATS, specifically that there was not sufficient involvement of the US in the Shell company's violation for the Court to have jurisdiction. The Court decided that the US only had jurisdiction in cases "where the claims touch and concern the territory of the United States ... with sufficient force to displace the presumption against extraterritorial application."[70] Justice Breyer outlined the criteria for ATS application: (1) the tort occurs within the United States; (2) the company is headquartered in the United States; or (3) the company's conduct substantially and adversely affects an important US national interest. ATS did not apply, according to the Court, because Shell, as a Dutch company, had too little connection to the United States, its US headquarters had no connection to the acts perpetrated, and the victims were not US citizens. The decision ignored the universal jurisdiction concepts

---

[67] See Center for Constitutional Rights, "Wiwa et al. v. Royal Dutch Petroleum et al.," https://ccrjustice.org/home/what-we-do/our-cases/wiwa-et-al-v-royal-dutch-petroleum-et-al.

[68] Humberto Cantú Rivera, "The Kiobel Precedent and Its Effects on Universal Jurisdiction and the Business & Human Rights Agenda: A Continuation to 'a Human Rights Forum in Peril?,'" *Cuestiones Constitucionales: Revista Mexicana de Derecho Constituticional* 30 (2014): 209–22; Freshfields Bruckhaus Deringer, "Landmark Supreme Court Opinion Shuts Door to ATS Suits against Foreign Corporations," *Freshfields Bruckhaus Deringer*, April 2018.

[69] Kiobel v. Royal Dutch Petroleum Co., 133 S. Ct. 1659 (2013).

[70] Kiobel v. Royal Dutch Petroleum Co., No 10-1491, slip op., 5 (U.S. Sup.Ct. April 17, 2013) cited in Jernej Letnar Černič, "An Elephant in a Room of Porcelain: Establishing Corporate Responsibility for Human Rights," *Global Journal on Human Rights* 24, no. 1 (2015): 16.

behind ATS and how they had been previously applied in corporate and other human rights cases. As Bazyler states, "The *Kiobel* decision marks the death knell of most ATS litigation based on atrocities committed abroad" allowing only cases when "atrocities were committed by an American person or an American corporation abroad or when committed in the United States. The disparity with criminal law is startling. Under current federal criminal law, a genocidaire can be criminally prosecuted in the United States for atrocities committed abroad if found on American soil, but after *Kiobel*, cannot be civilly sued under the ATS for the same acts of genocide."[71] A legal scholar, questioning the *Kiobel* decision, remarks, "[W]hat is law in *Kiobel* isn't clear and what is clear in *Kiobel* isn't law."[72]

Jesner v. *Arab Bank, PLC* (2018) went further in eliminating the ATS pathway to corporate accountability and transitional justice. The Arab Bank was accused of holding accounts for terrorists, receiving funds in those accounts that would be used for terrorist activities, and providing funds from those accounts to suicide bombers. The Court upheld in April 2018 the decision by the Court of Appeals for the Second Circuit that "ATS does not allow lawsuits against corporations."[73] How such lawsuits might jeopardize foreign policy considerations were specifically referenced in the decision. In her dissenting opinion, Justice Sonia Sotomayor stated that the Court had exempted "corporations from responsibility under the ATS for conscience-shocking behavior." She added, "[T]he Court ensures that foreign corporations – entities capable of wrongdoing under our domestic law – remain immune from liability for human rights abuses, however egregious they may be."[74] The *Jesner* decision shows that political winds and whims can deepen the already negligible application of international norms and their enforcement by powerful domestic courts of the Global North.

The analysis of ATS cases for corporate complicity in past human rights violations reinforce the Archimedes' Lever analogy. During politically neutral moments – for example, before the *Kiobel* and *Jesner* rulings by the Supreme Court[75] – the placement of the fulcrum may lead to a balance of power

[71] Bazyler, *Holocaust, Genocide, and the Law: A Quest for Justice in a Post-Holocaust World*, 181.
[72] Ralph G. Steinhardt, "Kiobel and the Weakening of Precedent: A Long Walk for a Short Drink," *The American Journal of International Law* 107, no. 4 (2013): 841.
[73] Supreme Court of the United States, Jesner et al. v. Arab Bank, PLC, 2018.
[74] Ibid., 16–499 at 33.
[75] Analysts have highlighted the growing conservative profile of the US Supreme Court in the public domain. See Adam Liptak and Alicia Parlapiano, "Conservatives in Charge, the Supreme Court Moved Right," *The New York Times*, June 28, 2018, www.nytimes.com/interactive/2018/06/28/us/politics/supreme-court-2017-term-moved-right.html.

between the forces on the side of corporate accountability and those vetoing it. Unless one side can apply greater force, outcomes may not favor one side or the other. The high number of settlements, rather than judgments, illustrate this outcome. As the political context shifts away from corporate accountability – a context consistent with the recent Supreme Court rulings – the force on the side of victims will have to be much more powerful than the force on the side of veto players.

Foreign Courts beyond ATS

The political shift in the US Supreme Court does not necessarily represent a global shift, however. In the post-*Kiobel* and post-*Jesner* era, attention has turned to non-US foreign courts to advance corporate accountability. Our research did not locate a sufficient number of cases outside the United States to reveal a promising pattern of accountability outcomes from those courts.

Among the foreign civil cases, we found only four national courts that put five multinational companies on trial for corporate complicity in authoritarian and armed conflict human rights abuses.[76] One is pending. Of the remaining cases: one settled, two were dismissed, and one was withdrawn by the plaintiff because of financial difficulties. Table 2.1 summarizes the data on foreign civil (non-ATS) trials. As Table 2.1 shows, not one of these foreign

TABLE 2.1 *Accountability Outcomes: Foreign Civil Actions (Excluding ATCA)*

Name of Business	Country Where Abuse Took Place	Country of Court	Outcome
Total FinaElf	Myanmar	France	Settlement
Anvil Mining Ltd.	DRC	Canada	Dismissed
Chevron	Ecuador	United States	Dismissed
BNP Paribas	Rwanda	France	Pending
BP Company	Colombia	United Kingdom	Withdrawn

Source: Corporate Accountability and Transitional Justice database, 2016

---

[76] These include: Canada (Anvil Mining Ltd.), United Kingdom (BP Company), United States (Chevron), and France (BNP Paribas and TotalFinaElf). The case against BNP Paribas for its involvement in the Rwandan genocide is still pending before a French court. The Economist, "BNP Paribas Faces Accusations over the Rwandan Genocide," *The Economist*, 2017, www .economist.com/finance-and-economics/2017/07/08/bnp-paribas-faces-accusations-over-the-rwandan-genocide.

civil trials has (yet) rendered an adverse judgment against a company for past human rights violations.

Total is a multinational corporation incorporated in France accused of human rights abuses in Myanmar. Six Burmese villages filed a criminal complaint against company executives. A civil action for damages suffered by the victims followed the criminal complaint. Three years after the civil action was filed, the company and the claimants settled. The terms of the settlement were not disclosed to the public. Journalistic accounts reported that the company did not accept responsibility for wrongdoing, but paid EUR 10,000 for each claimant and contributed to a fund for social and economic programs in Myanmar.[77]

In the case of Anvil Mining Ltd., victims of murder, rape, arbitrary detention and looting brought a lawsuit against the company for its alleged logistical support to the Congolese military to commit those crimes. Anvil's incorporation in Canada meant that the claimants brought this case in the courts of the home state. Nonetheless, in 2012 the Quebec Court of Appeals dismissed the case on the grounds of insufficient connections to Canada. The Court held that evidence did not sufficiently link the abuses in the DRC to Anvil's Montreal headquarters.[78]

The Chevron-Texaco case in Ecuador involved severe environmental pollution in the region of Lago Agrio, allegedly caused by the company's operations between 1964 and 1992. The local communities of Lago Agrio have faced a long road through different courts. They first started in the United States, filing a class action in 1993. The claim was ultimately dismissed by the US District Court (Southern District of New York) in 2002 on the grounds of *forum non conveniens*, or the existence of a more appropriate court (in Ecuador) to hear the case.

Although four cases are insufficient to establish a trend, they do illustrate the obstacles victims face in taking claims to foreign courts. While universal jurisdiction offers an innovative pathway to hold companies accountable, it has not rendered positive results. Neither have the cases brought within the company's home jurisdiction, however.[79] We found only one such case in UK courts and it was withdrawn. Gilberto Torres, a Colombian trade unionist

---

[77] Benoît Frydman and Ludovic Hennebel, "Translating Unocal: The Liability of Transnational Corporations for Human Rights Violations," in *Business and Human Rights*, ed. Manoj Kumar Sinha (SAGE Law, 2013).

[78] See Canadian Centre for International Justice, "Anvil Mining (D.R. Congo/Canada)," Canadian Centre for International Justice, www.ccij.ca/cases/anvil-mining/.

[79] Business and Human Rights Resource Centre, "Briefing: Is the UK Living up to Its Human Rights Commitments?," *Business and Human Rights Resource Centre*, n.d.

TABLE 2.2 *Accountability Outcomes: Foreign Criminal Trials*

Name of Business	Country Where Abuse Took Place	Country of Court	Outcome
Abbas Macky and Aziz Nassour	Liberia	Belgium	Conviction
Frans Cornelis Adrianus van Anraat	Liberia	Netherlands	Conviction
Guus Kouwenhoven	Liberia	Netherlands	Conviction
Leonid Minin	Liberia	Belgium	Conviction
Chiquita Brands Inc.	Colombia	United States	Settlement
Dalhoff, Larsen and Horneman (DLH)	Liberia	France	Dismissal
Danzer Group	DRC	Germany	Dismissal
Argor Heraeus	DRC	Switzerland	Dismissal
Cicolac-Nestlé	Colombia	Switzerland	Dismissal
Lafarge	Syria	France	Pending
Qosmos	Syria	France	Pending
Total FinaElf	Myanmar	France	Dismissal
Total FinaElf	Myanmar	Belgium	Dismissal

Source: Corporate Accountability and Transitional Justice database, 2016

kidnapped and tortured by the AUC paramilitary groups in 2002, filed a lawsuit in the United Kingdom against BP, alleging that the company had paid the paramilitaries to kidnap him because of his activities as a union leader. In 2016 he discontinued the lawsuit due to legal, procedural, and financial challenges.[80]

The CATJ database includes a higher number of criminal cases (thirteen) for corporate complicity in six foreign courts for violations that occurred in six different countries (see Table 2.2). All of the cases involved armed conflict, rather than complicity with authoritarian regimes. This suggests that courts are less reluctant to hear corporate complicity cases when those violations threaten international security. The results, however, are not necessarily favorable to victims. Foreign criminal courts rendered guilty verdicts in only four of the thirteen cases. The rest ended in dismissal (6), settlement (1), or remain pending (2).

---

[80] See Business and Human Rights Resource Centre, "BP Lawsuits (Re Casanare, Colombia)," *Business and Human Rights Resource Centre*, n.d.

Three of the guilty verdicts involved atrocities committed in Liberia. Leonid Minin and Abbas Macky were accused of financing repression in Liberia by doing business with the government of Charles Taylor (buying blood diamonds and selling weapons). They were found guilty by Belgian courts of illegal diamond possession, but not for related war crimes or human rights violations. They were sentenced to two years in jail.[81] Guus Kouwenhoven was put on trial before Dutch courts. In 2017 he was convicted to 19 years in prison for being an accessory to war crimes and arms trafficking, for selling weapons to Liberia's then president Charles Taylor.[82] The willingness to put on trial the business associates of international pariah Charles Taylor may provide some explanation for the positive outcome for these cases. The verdicts and sentencing seem to reflect the courts' lack of attention to the allegations of serious human rights violations committed by these economic actors.

The fourth guilty verdict was rendered in the Dutch court case against a Dutch businessman operating in Iraq. Frans Cornelis Adrianus van Anraat was tried by the District Court of the Hague for conspiracy to commit genocide and conspiracy to commit war crimes by selling thiodiglycol, the chemical used in the production of mustard gas, to Saddam Hussein's regime for use in the Iran-Iraq war and against the Kurdish population. One scholar contends that "[e]ven though the charges were brought against an individual, it is arguable that they *de facto* addressed the corporate liability of van Anraat's one-man company."[83] In this case, the alleged perpetrator and his company were one and the same. He could not have committed the crime without the company, similarly the company could not have committed the crime without a directive from an individual. Van Anraat was thus held criminally liable for the atrocities he committed as part of his company. There is little doubt that van Anraat's association with internationally-reviled Saddam Hussein played a role in his conviction.

None of the other nine criminal cases brought before foreign criminal courts have ended in a guilty verdict. The US criminal investigation of Chiquita Brands for allegedly financing paramilitary and guerrilla groups in the course of the armed conflict in Colombia settled. The company admitted to financing the armed groups resulting in a fine (although victims

---

[81] Chernoh Alpha M. Bah, "Sierra Leone: Eight Lebanese Diamond Smugglers Jailed," *allAfrica*, December 13, 2004, https://allafrica.com/stories/200412140152.html.

[82] International Crimes Database, "The Public Prosecutor v. Guus Kouwenhoven," *International Crimes Database*, www.internationalcrimesdatabase.org/Case/2238.

[83] Černič, "An Elephant in a Room of Porcelain: Establishing Corporate Responsibility for Human Rights," 11.

did not receive reparations from the settlement).[84] Six cases were dismissed. The case against the gold refinery Argor Heraeus was dismissed by a Swiss prosecutor, because he did not find evidence to suggest that the company had any knowledge about the origins of the gold being refined. The claimants had argued that the firm refined three tons of gold ore pillaged from the DRC between 2004 and 2005.[85] A Swiss prosecutor dismissed the case against Nestlé also due to insufficient evidence to substantiate the case.[86] The company was accused of financing paramilitary groups in Colombia and ordering the murder of union members of SINALTRAINAL, the food company union. The French prosecutor dismissed the case against Dalhoff, Larsen, and Horneman, a timber company accused of purchasing timber from Liberia during the Charles Taylor regime, for lack of sufficient evidence. The case against the Danzer Group for allegedly aiding and abetting the Congolese military to perpetrate atrocities in the village of Bongulu in northern DRC in 2011 was dismissed in 2015 by the German prosecutor, also due to insufficient evidence to substantiate the legal claim.

A case brought to Belgian courts in 2002 against Total for complicity in violence in Myanmar was dismissed. A 1993 Universal Jurisdiction law allowed Belgian courts to hear cases related to international human rights violations, even if they occurred outside of Belgium by non-Belgian legal persons. The plaintiffs argued that the company financed the military dictatorship in Myanmar and was therefore responsible for the atrocities committed by the regime. In 2003 the universal jurisdiction law was modified to make it more difficult for noncitizens to use the law. In April 2005 the Constitutional Court decided that this change to the law was discriminatory. The following month the Cour de Cassation (court of highest appeal) decided that the plaintiffs had no standing to bring the lawsuit because they were not Belgian citizens (although one of them had recognized refugee status in Belgium). This is the first and only attempt so far to use universal jurisdiction in Belgium against corporations.[87]

---

[84] Business and Human Rights Resource Centre, "Chiquita Lawsuits (Re Colombia)," *Legal Accountability Report*, www.business-humanrights.org/en/chiquita-lawsuits-re-colombia.

[85] Business and Human Rights Resource Centre, "Total Lawsuit in Belgium (Re Myanmar)," *Business and Human Rights Resource Centre*, www.business-humanrights.org/en/total-lawsuit-in-belgium-re-myanmar.

[86] Business and Human Rights Resource Centre, "Nestlé Lawsuit in Switzerland (Re Colombia)," *Business and Human Rights Resource Centre*, www.business-humanrights.org/en/nestl%C3%A9-lawsuit-re-colombia.

[87] Business and Human Rights Resource Centre, "Total Lawsuit in Belgium (Re Myanmar)"; Frydman and Hennebel, "Translating Unocal: The Liability of Transnational Corporations for Human Rights Violations."

A French court also dismissed a criminal complaint filed against Total by victims of human rights violations in Myanmar. The Court of Versailles decided on legal and procedural grounds to accept the company's request to dismiss the case. The Court did not consider the crime of illegal confinement, which is an offense under French law.[88]

Two cases are pending in French courts, both involving French companies – Qosmos and Lafarge – operating in Syria. Qosmos was accused in 2012 of supplying surveillance equipment to the Bashar El-Assad government in Syria. Using one of the strategies described in Chapter 3, the company filed a defamation complaint against the human rights organizations that filed the claim. The claim is still pending.[89] The criminal case against Lafarge was filed in 2016 and the trial started in 2018. The firm is accused of possibly acting as an accomplice to crimes against humanity committed by the Islamic State in Syria.[90] The claimants allege that the firm financed the Islamic State (ISIS) in various ways (e.g., purchasing commodities for ISIS, paying fees and selling them cement). The future of these claims in France is uncertain.

The small number of outcomes in foreign civil and criminal courts is not a strong indicator of the "bottom-up" corporate justice notion. Yet, legal changes occurring in some foreign domestic courts indicate possibilities for "bottom-up" litigation in the future. Recent changes in the United Kingdom are promising regarding corporate accountability.[91] Legal initiatives in Switzerland and France have also made some headway in the global reach of their domestic courts in

[88] Frydman and Hennebel, "Translating Unocal: The Liability of Transnational Corporations for Human Rights Violations." See www.business-humanrights.org/en/total-oil-settles-french-lawsuit-over-forced-labourin-burma-will-set-up-%C2%A335-million-humanitarian-fund-campaigners-vow-to-keep-uppressure-for-divestment.

[89] Media Part, "Crimes against Humanity: The Ongoing Case against Qosmos at the Paris High Court," *Media Part*, October 28, 2018, https://blogs.mediapart.fr/jamesinparis/blog/281018/crimes-against-humanity-ongoing-case-against-qosmos-paris-high-court.

[90] The Guardian, "Lafarge Charged with Complicity in Syria Crimes against Humanity," *The Guardian*, June 28, 2018, www.theguardian.com/world/2018/jun/28/lafarge-charged-with-complicity-in-syria-crimes-against-humanity.

[91] In particular, the 2017 *Vedanta* case potentially limits the application of *forum non conveniens* and establishes the duty of care of parent companies to those affected by subsidiaries' behavior. See Gabrielle Holly, "Access to Remedy under the UNGPs: Vedanta and the Expansion of Parent Company Liability," *EJIL:Talk!*, October 2017. The potential may be checked, however, by legislation that raises the cost to victims and advocates to pursue such cases. See Leigh Day & Co., "Leigh Day Submission to the Joint Committee on Human Rights Inquiry on Business and Human Rights," 2016, www.leighday.co.uk/LeighDay/media/LeighDay/documents/Corporate accountability/2016_08_31-LEIGH-DAY-SUBMISSION-TO-THE-JCHR1.pdf.

addressing corporate human rights violations. Laws in these two countries seek to expand corporate liability to their subsidiaries and supply chains (Responsible Business Initiative in Switzerland and Duty of Vigilance Law in France). Legislative proposals to reform the law on corporate crime is also perceived as a way to lower the barriers to holding companies accountable.[92]

Some innovation also appears to be underway in the United States, in the wake of *Kiobel* and *Jesner*. One example is the use of the Dodd-Frank Act (Wall Street Reform and Consumer Protection Act of July 2010). Aimed at promoting financial stability for the United States by improving accountability and transparency in the financial system, the Securities and Exchange Commission (SEC) must report companies that use conflict minerals sourced from the DRC or adjoining countries. Because conflict minerals finance extreme levels of violence, including sexual and gender-based violence, the Dodd–Frank Act could be a "piece of US Government legislation – by means of SEC regulation – ... specifically targeted at human rights violations."[93] Efforts to weaken the Dodd–Frank Act may limit this potential.[94]

"Bottom-up" efforts represent potential tactics to overcome the victims' gap through international pressure. We have shown that certain global agents are willing and able to apply the necessary force to advance corporate accountability. They are up against opposing forces, however. The weight of forces against corporate accountability through foreign courts is reflected in this comment by Surya Deva: "[S]everal states are still not very keen to put in place a legally binding international instrument that imposes direct human

[92] Freshfields Bruckhaus Deringer, "UK Considers Reforms on Holding Companies Liable for Economic Crime," *Freshfields Bruckhaus Deringer*, 2017. Our search for reforms in German criminal liability law revealed no new law and criticism of existing ones: The Guardian, "Germany Approves Plans to Fine Social Media Firms up to €50m," *The Guardian*, June 2017; Andreas Lohner and Nicolai Behr, "Corporate Liability in Germany," *Global Compliance News Backer McKenzie*, n.d.; Andreas Rasche, "Corporate Criminal Liability in Germany – An Idea Whose Time Has Come," *The Business of Society*, November 2017.

[93] Mary E. Footer, "Human Rights Due Diligence and the Responsible Supply of Minerals from Conflict-Affected Areas: Towards a Normative Framework?," *Global Journal on Human Rights* 24, no. 1 (2015): 51–100.

[94] The Dodd–Frank Act has been under particularly vigorous attack during the Trump administration. The US Congress, for example, passed a new law that partially modifies it. According to the *The New York Times*, "The bill stops far short of unwinding the toughened regulatory regime put in place to prevent the nation's biggest banks from engaging in risky behavior, but it represents a substantial watering down of Obama-era rules governing a large swath of the banking system." Alan Rappeport and Emily Fitter, "Congress Approves First Big Dodd-Frank Rollback," *The New York Times*, May 22, 2018, www.nytimes.com/2018/05/22/business/congress-passes-dodd-frank-rollback-for-smaller-banks.html.

rights obligations on companies."[95] Thus, even where the political environment is neutral, in the absence of binding and enforceable corporate human rights obligations, the force is more strongly applied against, rather than for, accountability. We consider those obstacles in the next section.[96]

INTERNATIONAL FORCE AND
CORPORATE ACCOUNTABILITY

As we have shown in this chapter, the history of judicial action in corporate complicity cases demonstrates that at times businesses have been held accountable in powerful international and foreign courts. A few individuals at a few firms that committed atrocities during dramatic historical moments have faced legal punishment. Yet if businesses calculated the risk of being prosecuted for human rights violations in international and foreign courts, the evidence suggests that there is a low probability of such an outcome. In addition, states certainly cannot interpret these inconsistent sets of international or foreign trials as increasing pressure on them to hold corporate perpetrators of human rights violations accountable. Even in times of undisputed complicity within a political context of widespread condemnation (such as the Holocaust, Japanese slave labor, and the Rwandan genocide), economic actors – with a few exceptions – have evaded accountability.

The current situation of unsettled international human rights has meant that global agents have had to adapt innovative tools to advance corporate accountability. In the process, they have had to navigate around two legal obstacles: the lack of agreement over who is bound by human rights

---

[95] Deva, "Multinationals, Human Rights and International Law: Time to Move beyond the 'State-Centric' Conception?," 23.

[96] Regarding international enforcement mechanisms, a narrow window of opportunity opened at the International Criminal Court (ICC). The "French proposal" was not passed in the 1998 Rome Conference, which would have granted the ICC jurisdiction over legal persons, including businesses. By all accounts the barrier was time rather than political will. Former (and first) ICC chief prosecutor, Luis Moreno Ocampo, laments, "due to jurisdictional restrictions, my office was not able to bring a single case against an individual responsible for genocide through his [sic] financial or commercial contribution." Luis Moreno Ocampo, "Foreword," in *Prosecuting Corporations for Genocide*, ed. Michael J. Kelly (Oxford: Oxford University Press, 2016), xiii. Redrafting of the Rome Statute is in effect which might have provided the possibility to reconsider the proposal. Because the ICC can only bring individuals to trial, some innovation will be necessary to establish how to address the legal responsibility of individuals working for companies involved in human rights violations. Despite this promising avenue, we have not found any progress on this initiative.

obligations (corporations as legal persons) and the institutionalization of those obligations on business.

Business Human Rights Obligations

A statist perspective on international law posits that only states, and not businesses, have human rights obligations. In affirming that states are the focus of human rights accountability, businesses' own human rights duties remain unspecified.[97] The statist approach has been criticized as logically inconsistent with international human rights norms and practice. As Justine Nolan notes, "The traditional understanding of international human rights law is that it binds only states ... This focus on states as the bearers of human rights responsibilities has meant that some corporations ... have been able to operate largely in a legal vacuum, devoid of obligations at the international level."[98] Nicolás Carillo argues that "saying that human rights are only relevant in relation to states somehow goes against the intuitive understanding of their being *human* rights."[99] Surya Deva further challenges the claim: "[T]he argument that corporations do not have direct responsibility for human rights would be tantamount to saying that what individuals could do as employees of a corporation is much more permissible than what they would do as individuals. This is absurd."[100]

Critics of the statist view further contend that an obligation on states "does not imply that *only* [our emphasis] the state has such obligations."[101] David Weissbrodt cites from the Universal Declaration of Human Rights to show that "every individual and every organ of society ... shall strive ... to promote respect for these rights and freedoms ... to secure their universal and effective

---

[97] As one scholar states, there is "no basis in existing international law for the liability of corporations and, consequently, no rules of international law regarding the questions, which necessarily arise when a corporation is accused of wrongdoing." Declaration of Christopher Greenwood, "Presbyterian Church of Sudan v. Talisman Energy Inc, Republic of the Sudan Civil Action, 374 F. Supp. 2d 331 (S.D.N.Y, 2005), No.01 CV 9882 (AGS)," n.d.

[98] Nolan, "The Corporate Responsibility to Respect Human Rights: Soft Law or Not Law?," 146.

[99] Nicolás Carrillo, "Direct International Humanitarian Obligations of Non-State Entitites: Analysis of the Lex Lata and the Lex Ferenda," *Global Journal on Human Rights* 23, no. 2 (2015): 34.

[100] Deva, "Multinationals, Human Rights and International Law: Time to Move beyond the 'State-Centric' Conception?," 16.

[101] Jernej Letnar Černič, "Corporate Accountability for Human Rights: From a Top-Down to a Bottom-Up Approach," in *The Business and Human Rights Landscape: Moving Forward, Looking Back*, ed. Jena Martin and Karen E. Bravo (Cambridge: Cambridge University Press, 2016), 197.

recognition and observance."[102] He further cites from Article 30 of the Declaration: "Nothing in this Declaration may be interpreted as implying for any State, group or person any right to engage in any activity or perform any act aimed at the destruction of any of the rights and freedoms set forth herein."[103] Weissbrodt contends that the principle of universality and non-discrimination at the core of international human rights law means that the protection of an individual's rights cannot discriminate in terms of who commits those violations. Logically, if the perpetrator of the violation is more powerful than the state, as sometimes is the case with large transnational enterprises in weak states, then how could individuals seek remedy from the state?[104]

Douglass Cassel and Anita Ramasastry contend that the prevalent statist view has been weakened over time in the international legal arena.[105] Menno T. Kamminga and Saman Zia-Zarifi also hold that "[t]here is now a growing consensus that MNCs are bound by those few rules applicable to all international actors, plus a continuum of obligations that refer specifically to a corporation's activity and influence."[106]

The evidence from the CATJ shows that economic actors, and not only states, have been held accountable for violating human rights. Individual representatives of businesses were investigated, tried, and sentenced for their human rights violations in the Holocaust, the Rwandan genocide cases, and in foreign criminal trials. Yet, an interpretive battle has emerged: were

---

[102] David S. Weissbrodt, *The Beginning of a Sessional Working Group on Transnational Corporations within the UN Sub-Commission on Prevention of Discrimination and Protection of Minorities* (London: Kluwer Law International, 2000), 124.

[103] United Nations, *Universal Declaration of Human Rights* (New York, NY: United Nations, 1948).

[104] The anti-statist view is also famously held by these scholars in addition to the ones we cite: Nicola Jagers, "Transnational Corporations and Human Rights," in *To Baehr in Our Minds*, ed. Mielle K. Bultermann, Aart Hendriks, and Jacqueline Smith (Utrecht: Netherlands Institute of Human Rights, 1998); Peter T. Muchlinski, "Attempts to Extend the Accountability of Transnational Corporations: The Role of UNCTAD," in *Liability of Multinational Corporations under International Law*, ed. Menno T. Kamminga and Saman Zia-Zarifi (The Hague: Kluwer Law International, 2000); David S. Weissbrodt and Muria Kruger, "Human Rights Responsibilities of Businesses as Non-State Actors," in *Non-State Actors and Human Rights*, ed. Phillip Alston (Oxford: Oxford University Press, 2005), 315–49; Larissa van den Herik and Jernej Letnar Černič, "Regulating Corporations under International Law: From Human Rights to International Criminal Law and Back Again," *Journal of International Criminal Justice* 8, no. 3 (2010): 725–43.

[105] Douglass Cassel and Anita Ramasastry, "White Paper: Options for a Treaty on Business and Human Rights," *Journal of International and Comparative Law* 6, no. 1 (2016).

[106] Kamminga and Zia-Zarifi, "Liability of Multinational Corporations under International Law: An Introduction," 1.

businesses – as legal entities or persons – held accountable, or were individuals employed by businesses held accountable for their individual behavior?

One interpretation assumes that businesses are subject to enforceable international human rights obligations and the international community can use these past precedents to promote global accountability for economic actors' human rights violations. Legal scholar Gwynne Skinner, who argued that corporate accountability for human rights violations has been "legitimized and incorporated into the fabric of international law,"[107] contends that courts have held businesses, and not just individuals, accountable. This is important in shaping business behavior. Menno T. Kamminga and Saman Zia-Zarifi state, the "existing international legal system does place obligations on private [business] actors [. . .], and the shirking of these obligations can lead to liability."[108] Businesses ignore this obligation at their legal peril. But, as evidence from the CATJ show, the risk remains fairly low in international and foreign courts. A contending interpretation holds that only individuals, and not business entities, are subject to international human rights legal instruments. Jolyon Ford has promoted this view, arguing that "it cannot be said that international human rights law involves direct legal duties for businesses."[109] In which case, existing international law is unlikely to have a deterrent effect on business human rights violating behavior; individual employees, however, may have to calculate their degree of risk.

The distinction between putting employees on trial rather than companies can seem like procedural hairsplitting. In practice, it is not clear that individual, rather than corporate, liability poses a significant barrier to holding businesses accountable. Van der Wilt, for example, states that the position of power and knowledge required for a corporate agent to incur criminal responsibility for international crimes corresponds to that agent's internal position within the corporation that thus criminally implicates the corporate entity.[110] Andrew Clapham, agreeing that businesses have binding human rights

---

[107] Skinner, "Nuremberg's Legacy Continues: The Nuremberg Trials' Influence on Human Rights Litigation in US Courts under the Alien Tort Statute," 356–57.

[108] Kamminga and Zia-Zarifi, "Liability of Multinational Corporations under International Law: An Introduction," 1.

[109] Jolyon Ford, *Regulating Business for Peace: The United Nations, the Private Sector, and Post-Conflict Recovery* (Cambridge: Cambridge University Press, 2015), 37.

[110] Harmen van der Wilt, "Corporate Criminal Responsibility for International Crimes: Exploring the Possibilities," *Chinese Journal of International Law* 12, no. 1 (2013): 43–77. The author builds his arguments on the French proposal on corporate criminal liability, presented during the drafting process of the Rome Statute, as a preliminary normative framework. He tests his arguments analyzing case law of both domestic and international criminal courts in which individual business leaders faced trial on charges of complicity in international crimes.

obligations, nonetheless recognizes legal constraints in prosecuting companies rather than individuals representing those companies. He specifically mentions a corporation's requisite intent necessary to determine certain crimes, such as homicide. He adds, "[Y]ou can't put a corporation in jail."[111] Michael Kelly somewhat disagrees. He claims that international bodies can and do hold corporations accountable. He contends that international law in general, and the Genocide Convention in particular, are capable of forming both overall corporate intent and specific individual intent required to prosecute for genocide.[112] Interpreting the Holocaust, Rwandan genocide, and Kurdish genocide (van Anraat trial) as only holding individuals – and not companies – accountable constitutes legal fiction, rather than legal reality. The shift over time to use ATS to corporations engaged in international human rights violations further suggests that complicit businesses have, in fact, been considered legal persons in civil trials.

In sum, both theory and practice suggest that within the existing international legal and human rights framework, some instruments hold economic actors accountable for past abuses. In practical terms, even when individuals have been held accountable by international and foreign courts, they were not acting on their own. They were not individuals who alone kidnapped or murdered. They were the figureheads and representatives of economic entities complicit in the commission of international human rights violations by authoritarian regimes and in armed conflict. As such, and despite widespread disagreement over how to interpret human rights duties, judicial action has recognized the culpability of economic actors (individuals and the businesses in which they worked) for corporate complicity in human rights violations.

Institutionalizing Corporate Accountability

There have been efforts to make clear in international instruments the human rights obligations of economic actors. One international effort – the UN Draft Norms – endeavored to establish in a single instrument on business and human rights the obligations that exist in the "patchwork" of international law. This initiative was replaced, however, by the UN Guiding Principles, a voluntary instrument. Global agents operating in a fairly neutral

---

[111] Clapham, "The Question of Jurisdiction under International Criminal Law over Legal Persons: Lessons from the Rome Conference on an International Criminal Court," 139.

[112] Kelly, "Prosecuting Corporations for Genocide under International Law," 339.

international political environment provided legal and policy tools to advance these very different human rights instruments. The force applied by veto players was far greater than that applied on behalf of corporate accountability, thus thwarting the consolidation of the UN Draft Norms in favor of voluntary principles.

UN Draft Norms

The 2003 UN Sub-Commission on the Promotion and Protection of Human Rights drafted a document entitled "Norms on the Responsibilities of Transnational Corporations and Other Business Enterprises with Regard to Human Rights" ("UN Draft Norms").[113] The Preamble of the document states clearly "that even though States have the primary responsibility to promote, secure the fulfillment of, respect, ensure respect of and protect human rights, transnational corporations and other business enterprises, as organs of society, are also responsible for promoting and securing the human rights set forth in the Universal Declaration of Human Rights." It adds that "transnational corporations and other business enterprises, their officers and persons working for them are also obligated to respect generally recognized responsibilities and norms contained in UN treaties and other international instruments." The document lists those instruments and their embodiment of the human rights obligations of business, illustrating the "patchwork" nature of business human rights obligations in UN instruments (see Appendix A).

The UN Draft Norms make clear that "[t]ransnational corporations and other business enterprises shall not engage in nor benefit from war crimes, crimes against humanity, genocide, torture, forced disappearance, forced or compulsory labor, hostage-taking, extrajudicial, summary or arbitrary executions, other violations of humanitarian law and other international crimes against the human person as defined by international law, in particular human rights and humanitarian law." The UN Draft Norms further state that businesses and their employees "shall refrain from any activity which supports, solicits, or encourages States or any other entities to abuse human

---

[113] UN Sub-Commission on the Promotion and Protection of Human Rights, "Norms on the Responsibilities of Transnational Corporations and Other Business Enterprises with Regard to Human Rights" (United Nations, 2003). See also UN Sub-Commission on the Promotion and Protection of Human Rights, "Commentary on the Norms on the Responsibilities of Transnational Corporations and Other Business Enterprises with Regard to Human Rights, U.N. Doc. E/CN.4/Sub.2/2003/38/Rev.2" (New York, 2003); United Nations, "Other Multilateral Instruments and Guidelines for Corporate Behavior," http://hrlibrary.umn.edu/business/omig.html.

rights."[114] The head of the Subcommittee that devised the UN Draft Norms, Professor David Weissbrodt, contends that the exercise in which the Subcommittee was engaged did not invent business human rights obligations, but rather attempted to consolidate them in a single document. The Subcommittee interpreted the array of legal instruments as establishing clear obligations on business under international law and the possibility of enforcement. The members of the Subcommittee are not alone in adopting this perspective.[115] A vast literature has emerged that echoes this effort initiated by the UN Draft Norms to confirm the business human rights obligations already embodied in international law (see Appendix A). The Subcommittee reflected a view prevalent among international legal scholars and practitioners. Indeed, the initial resistance the Subcommittee encountered came from human rights organizations that felt the UN Draft Norms did not go far enough in developing binding and enforceable obligations. They were seen, instead, as a compromise, a cautious pathway to define norms from existing international instruments. As such, the UN Draft Norms passed in Committee.

Despite agreement in Committee, or maybe because of it, an organized sector of the business community mobilized against the UN Draft Norms. It saw them as a law-making effort, an attempt to transform nonbinding obligations in soft-law into binding and enforceable ones. This powerful business lobby proved capable of finding allies among the powerful members within the UN Commission on Human Rights (later UN Human Rights Council) and succeeded in defeating the UN Draft Norms.

The UNGPs Rollback

The defeat of the UN Draft Norms did not end the effort to establish international regulation of business human rights behavior. In 2005, UN Secretary General Kofi Annan appointed Professor John Ruggie as the Special Representative of the Security General on the Issue of Human Rights and Transnational Corporations and Other Business Enterprises (SRSG). In 2011, the Human Rights Council unanimously endorsed the UN Guiding

---

[114] UN Sub-Commission on the Promotion and Protection of Human Rights, "Norms on the Responsibilities of Transnational Corporations and Other Business Enterprises with Regard to Human Rights," sec. E.11.

[115] See, for example, International Commission of Jurists, "Proposals for Elements of a Legally Binding Instrument on Transnational Corporations and Other Business Enterprises" (Geneva, 2016), www.icj.org/wp-content/uploads/2016/10/Universal-OEWG-session-2-ICJ-submission-Advocacy-Analysis-brief-2016-ENG.pdf.

Principles on Business and Human Rights (UNGPs) drafted by SRSG Ruggie. The UNGPs were motivated by a desire to move a stalemate resulting from entrenched business opposition to the UN Draft Norms. Premised on the notion that persuasion and low-cost mechanisms are more likely to pave a secure pathway to improved corporate human rights behavior than judicial enforcement,[116] the UNGPs set out voluntary principles, or soft-law, on business and human rights.[117] As such, they have been viewed as having "the effect of rolling back the legal concretization of corporate human rights obligations."[118] Mary E. Footer argues that the UNGPs "do not go far enough ... [and] have not led to legal obligations that are binding on companies and other business entities."[119] She contends, "[T]he Guiding Principles provide no sanction whatsoever for companies that fail to fulfill their responsibility for tracking and reporting adverse human rights impacts in their business activities."[120]

While Ruggie boasts international "multi-stakeholder" backing of the UNGPs, his critics note the absence of support from the NGO, human rights, and international legal stakeholder communities. Other scholars caution against assuming a "multi-stakeholder initiative" could exist when corporations exert control over international negotiating environments. Business power over international fora can lead to a "race to the bottom that results in the adoption of norms that fail to do justice to local communities adversely affected by harmful business activities."[121] In particular, Denise Wallace contends that the International Commission of Jurists "expressed extreme dismay and regret" that Ruggie failed to consult jurists or provide explicit sets of

---

[116] John Balmer, Shaun Powell, and Stephen Greyser, "Explicating Ethical Corporate Marketing. Insights from the BP Deepwater Horizon Catastrophe: The Ethical Brand that Exploded and then Imploded," *Journal of Business Ethics* 102, no. 1 (2011): 1–14; William Laufer, "Social Accountability and Corporate Greenwashing," *Journal of Business Ethics* 43, no. 3 (2003): 253; Karin Buhman, "Navigating from 'Train Wreck' to Being 'Welcomed,'" in *Human Rights Obligations of Business: Beyond the Corporate Responsibility to Respect*, ed. David Bilchitz and Surya Deva (Cambridge: Cambridge University Press, 2013).

[117] John Gerard Ruggie, *Just Business: Multinational Corporations and Human Rights* (New York, NY: W.W. Norton & Company, 2013).

[118] Surya Deva, "Human Rights Lightly: A Critique of the Consensus Rhetoric and the Language Employed by the Guiding Principles," in *Human Rights Obligations of Business: Beyond the Corporate Responsibility to Respect*, ed. David Bilchitz and Surya Deva (Cambridge: Cambridge University Press, 2013), 80.

[119] Footer, "Human Rights Due Diligence and the Responsible Supply of Minerals from Conflict-Affected Areas: Towards a Normative Framework?," 52.

[120] Ibid., 59.

[121] Cedric Ryngaert, "Transnational Private Regulation and Human Rights: The Limitations of Stateless Law and the Re-entry of the State," *Global Journal on Human Rights* 2, no. 23 (2015): 108.

human rights obligations in existing international legal instruments.[122] NGO, human rights advocates, and legal scholars called on Ruggie to clarify in the UNGPs the existing international law on the human rights responsibilities of economic actors, sometimes explicitly questioning Ruggie's grasp of international law as set forth in the UNGPs.[123] Paul and Schönsteiner, for example, critique the UNGPs for producing "sometimes inaccurate representations of international law regarding certain aspects of states' obligation to protect; the lack of clarity on some aspects of the substantive dimension of the corporate responsibility to respect; and the absence of recommendations for effective enforcement mechanisms and of limits set for private reparations initiatives."[124]

Once adopted, the UNGPs prompted two practical questions. The first focused on the voluntary nature of the UNGPs, probing whether voluntary approaches are ever an effective means of shaping human rights behavior. The second explored whether the UNGPs explicitly or implicitly denied economic actors' binding human rights obligations.

The UNGPs have faced criticism for their voluntary nature, i.e., the lack of a credible threat of costly legal sanctions for abusive corporate behavior,[125] or even a system for monitoring business human rights behavior.[126] Surya Deva contends that the effectiveness of the UNGPs depends on states willing and able to exercise their "duty to protect" and companies willing to carry out their "responsibility to respect" human rights, "despite the absence of any legal bite flowing from the Guiding Principles."[127] Absent goodwill on the part of states or companies, Deva continues, the UNGPs leave "victims without any effective remedy in certain situations."[128] Denise Wallace shares with Amnesty

---

[122] Wallace, *Human Rights and Business: A Policy-Oriented Perspective*, 272–73.

[123] Bryan Horrigan, *Corporate Social Responsibility in the 21st Century: Debates, Models and Practices across Government, Law and Business* (Cheltenham: Edward Elgar, 2010).

[124] Genevieve Paul and Judith Schonsteiner, "Transitional Justice and the UN Guiding Principles on Business and Human Rights," in *Corporate Accountability in the Context of Transitional Justice*, ed. Sabine Michalowski (London: Routledge Press, 2013), 74.

[125] Clapham, "The Question of Jurisdiction under International Criminal Law over Legal Persons: Lessons from the Rome Conference on an International Criminal Court."

[126] Kaleck and Saage-Maaß further point out that none of the UN's existing human rights-related complaint procedures have the mandate to monitor corporate human rights behavior. Kaleck and Saage-Maaß, "Corporate Accountability for Human Rights Violations Amounting to International Crimes: The Status Quo and Its Challenges," 699–724.

[127] Deva, "Multinationals, Human Rights and International Law: Time to Move beyond the 'State-Centric' Conception?," 11.

[128] Ibid.

International and other NGOs the view of the UNGPs as a "smokescreen" behind which abusive practices continue, a "means to obfuscate the need for binding regulations and to forestall them indefinitely," and a failed project that "puts the language of human rights in the control of the wrong people."[129] The International Commission of Jurists also notes that the UNGPs "do not create a material or procedural basis for a cause of action by individuals for a violation of any of its contents. Nor can States that do not comply with the Guiding Principles be held accountable for that."[130]

More generally, many question the assumption that voluntary principles are effective in promoting best human rights practices by companies. Sir Geoffrey Chandler claims that "[h]istorically voluntarism has never worked."[131] It fails to raise the cost to corporations of committing human rights violations and, therefore, to deter future abuses.[132] It ignores businesses' rational calculations of costs and benefits associated with certain behaviors. Without altering the fundamental logic by which businesses adjust their behavior (i.e., increasing production costs or reducing profits), the UNGPs are unlikely to persuade businesses to comply with human rights norms.[133]

---

[129] Wallace, *Human Rights and Business: A Policy-Oriented Perspective*, 153–57.

[130] International Commission of Jurists, "Corporate Complicity & Legal Accountability" (Geneva, 2008), www.icj.org/wp-content/uploads/2012/06/Vol.1-Corporate-legal-accountability-thematic-report-2008.pdf.

[131] Geoffrey Chandler, "The Evolution of the Business and Human Rights Debate," in *Business and Human Rights: Dilemmas and Solutions*, ed. Rory Sullivan (Sheffield: Greenleaf Publishing, 2003).

[132] Weissbrodt and Kruger, "Human Rights Responsibilities of Businesses as Non-State Actors." See also deterrence theory claims regarding the need for perceived costly sanctions to deter future behavior: George Downs, David Rocke, and Peter Barsoom, "Is the Good News about Compliance Good News about Cooperation?," *International Organization* 50, no. 3 (1996): 379; Bruce Bueno Mesquita and Lawrence E. Cohen, "Self-Interest, Equity, and Crime Control: A Game-Theoretic Analysis of Criminal Decision Making," *Criminology* 33, no. 4 (1995): 483–518; Bill McCarthy, "New Economics of Sociological Criminology," *Annual Review of Sociology* 28 (2002): 417–42; Daniel S. Nagin, "Criminal Deterrence Research at the Outset of the Twenty-First Century," *Crime and Justice* 23 (1998): 1–42.

[133] Nicole Deitelhoff and Klaus Wolf, "Business in Zones of Conflict: An Emergent Corporate Security Responsibility?," in *The Business of Human Rights: An Evolving Agenda for Corporate Responsibility*, ed. Aurora Voliculescu and Helen Yanacopulos (London: Zed Books, 2011); Klaus Dieter Wolf, Nicole Deitelhoff, and Stefan Engert, "Corporate Security Responsibility," *Cooperation and Conflict* 42 (2007): 294–320; Michael E. Porter and Mark R. Kramer, "Strategy and Society: The Link between Competitive Advantage and Corporate Social Responsibility," *Harvard Business Review* 84, no. 12 (2006): 78.

Some of the treaty compliance literature concurs with this view.[134] Signing on to global initiatives is a low-cost activity that has the potential to provide cover for businesses to continue or even increase human rights abuses.[135] In contrast, as Clapham states, "[s]tressing potential criminal liability at the corporate and individual level is likely to generate greater attention than appeals to the importance of ethics in business. Corporations may not end up in jail but they are likely to be keen to stay out of the dock."[136] Similarly, attaching high economic costs to violations has been seen as a way to deter future abuses. In the landmark Filartiga case, for example, it was argued that "[b]ecause a violation of international law is an offense to all humanity, the trial court awarded the Filartiga family $10 million in punitive damages, stating that punitive damages must be awarded in an amount that will deter others from committing such outrageous crimes against humanity."[137]

Empirical studies testing the effectiveness of voluntary principles confirm their inadequacy in addressing corporate abuse. Kamminga and Zia-Zarifi state, "Our research indicated that voluntary codes of conduct are seldom useful in ameliorating the problems caused by MNCs."[138] Lim and Tsutsui's study refers to "organized hypocrisy," and not deep commitment to human rights obligations, among ninety-nine firms that signed on to the Global Compact that embodies the UNGPs' human rights responsibilities.[139] Two studies using Olsen and Payne's Corporate Human Rights Database[140] establish that voluntary principles are insufficient in remedying or redressing business human rights abuses. First, Kathryn Babineau's study of Peru found that Global Compact signatories were just as likely as businesses that did not

[134] Oona Hathaway, "Do Human Rights Treaties Make a Difference?," *The Yale Law Journal* 111, no. 8 (2002): 1935–2042.

[135] Ibid.; Alwyn Lim and Kiyoteru Tsutsui, "Globalization and Commitment in Corporate Social Responsibility: Cross-National Analyses of Institutional and Political-Economy Effects," *American Sociological Review* 77, no. 1 (February 1, 2012): 69–98; Wade M. Cole and Francisco O. Ramírez, "Conditional Decoupling: Assessing the Impact of National Human Rights Institutions, 1981 to 2004," *American Sociological Review* 78, no. 4 (June 18, 2013): 702–25.

[136] Clapham, "The Question of Jurisdiction under International Criminal Law over Legal Persons: Lessons from the Rome Conference on an International Criminal Court," 195.

[137] Ryf, "Burger-Fischer v. Degussa Ag: U.S. Courts Allow Siemens and Degussa to Profit from Holocaust Slave Labor," 176.

[138] Kamminga and Zia-Zarifi, "Liability of Multinational Corporations under International Law: An Introduction," 10.

[139] Lim and Tsutsui, "Globalization and Commitment in Corporate Social Responsibility: Cross-National Analyses of Institutional and Political-Economy Effects."

[140] Tricia D. Olsen and Leigh A. Payne, "Corporations and Human Rights Database," 2014.

sign on to be accused of human rights violations; they were, moreover, equally unlikely to remedy violations.[141] Government pressure, and not voluntary principles, proved more likely in this study to promote companies' positive human rights behavior. Second, Laura Bernal-Bermúdez also found few differences in human rights behavior among Colombian firms that signed on to voluntary principles compared to those that had not.[142] These empirical findings suggest that, at best, voluntary principles have done little to diffuse understanding of business obligations under international human rights law. Scholarship tends to confirm Kamminga and Zia-Zarifi's view of voluntary principles: they fail to achieve the goal of "protecting the rights of individuals hurt by the activity of multinationals … voluntary codes of conduct are seldom useful in ameliorating the problems caused by MNCs."[143]

The business community appears to view the effectiveness of the UNGPs in much the same way as critics. They supported them precisely because they removed the notion of binding obligations embodied in the UN Draft. Denise Wallace, for example, claims that the business lobbyists for the OECD seemed pleased that the UNGPs made no effort to "assign legal liability."[144] Citing the UNGPs, Shell Oil argued in a lawsuit that "companies do not have direct international law human rights obligations." Ruggie responded negatively to this view. In an amicus brief he referred to the company's misquote, misinterpretation, and misunderstanding of the UNGPs.[145] Ruggie stated that

[T]here [was] a problem with that inference. The quotation is taken from a section of my 2007 report that specifically surveyed UN human rights treaties. There I did say that 'the treaties do not address direct corporate legal responsibilities explicitly,' and 'it does not seem that the international human rights instruments discussed here currently impose direct legal responsibilities on corporations.' But the UN human rights treaties do not comprise the entire corpus of relevant international law; there are other bodies of treaty law, and the ATS specifically recognizes customary international law.[146]

[141] Kathryn Babineau, "Business as Usual? Corporations and the Challenge of Human Rights Remedy in Peru," MPhil diss. (University of Oxford, 2015).
[142] Laura Bernal-Bermúdez, "The Power of Business and the Power of People: Understanding Remedy and Corporate Accountability for Human Rights Violations. Colombia 1970–2014," PhD diss. (University of Oxford, 2017).
[143] Kamminga and Zia-Zarifi, "Liability of Multinational Corporations under International Law: An Introduction," 9.
[144] Wallace, *Human Rights and Business: A Policy-Oriented Perspective*, 267.
[145] Deva, "Multinationals, Human Rights and International Law: Time to Move beyond the 'State-Centric' Conception?," 7.
[146] John G. Ruggie, "Kiobel and Corporate Social Responsibility – An Issues Brief," 2012, 3.

Some scholars concur with Ruggie's intimation that the UNGPs are more binding than the business community assumes. The UNGPs, for example, establish that "[b]usiness enterprises should respect human rights. This means they should avoid infringing on the human rights of others and should address adverse human rights impacts with which they are involved."[147] The UNGPs, moreover, indicate expected behavior: "corporate entities have a responsibility to respect human rights," even though they reflect a lack of "external penalty or added profit to comply."[148]

Disagreement over business human rights obligations, even insofar as they are reflected in the UNGPs, has surfaced. Some scholars and practitioners claim that obligations exist, in soft-law and in international human rights norms, such as the UNGPs, even if they are not (yet) enforceable. Others argue that the obligations that exist are not (yet) binding and, therefore, not enforceable. In some cases, scholars themselves are blamed for ignoring existing corporate human rights obligations: "legal academia still seems reluctant to impose direct obligations on corporations."[149] Grear and Weston refer to academic obfuscation as "human rights betrayal ... deploying 'procedural' issues to exempt powerful corporate actors from accountability for human rights abuses ... [and] subversive of the quintessential claim that human rights are universal in character and [need] to be treated as such whenever and wherever they are threatened or denied."[150]

The debate over the UNGPs in legal academia and legal practice represents the way in which powerful global agents with effective tools can apply force on both sides of the corporate accountability weight. The near success of the UN Draft Norms prompted greater force on the side of veto players. In reaction to the adoption of the UNGPs, force is increasingly applied on the side of victims to raise corporate accountability. This force is illustrated in the new efforts underway to establish binding and enforceable human rights obligations on business.

---

[147] UN Human Rights Office of the High Commissioner, "Guiding Principles on Business and Human Rights: Implementing the United Nations 'Protect, Respect and Remedy' Framework" (New York and Geneva: United Nations, 2011), 13, www.ohchr.org/Documents/Publications/GuidingPrinciplesBusinessHR_EN.pdf.

[148] Jena Martin and Karen E. Bravo, "Introduction: More of the Same? Or Introduction of a New Paradigm?," in *The Business and Human Rights Landscape: Moving Forward, Looking Back*, ed. Jena Martin and Karen E. Bravo (Cambridge: Cambridge University Press, 2016), 5–6.

[149] Černič, "An Elephant in a Room of Porcelain: Establishing Corporate Responsibility for Human Rights," 19.

[150] Anna Grear and Burns H. Weston, "The Betrayal of Human Rights and the Urgency of Universal Corporate Accountability: Reflections on a Post-Kiobel Lawscape," *Human Rights Law Review* 15, no. 1 (2015): 21–44.

The Future of Binding Obligations

"For rights to have meaning, they must be enforceable," scholars of business and human rights have stated.[151] This has been seen as an evolutionary process that begins with an initial – soft-law – phase in which voluntary codes of conduct for businesses and states' human rights duties are verified followed by hard law that recognizes the gap between expectations and reality. Surya Deva states, "[T]his avenue has not proved to be very promising so far."[152] The current state of binding and enforceable corporate human rights obligations lacks consistency, clarity, and consensus.[153] No hard law has grown out of the UNGPs. The major international and regional treaties fail to explicitly address economic actors' binding and enforceable human rights obligations and states' duties with regard to corporate violations. We find only intermittently successful use of private litigation as an accountability measure. Another evolutionary approach might contend that the current state of corporate accountability – indeterminacy of law, contradictions, diagnostic struggles, and actor mismatch – represent the standard processes leading to settled law.[154] A third evolutionary approach might consider the UN Draft Norms and the UNGPs as evidence of emerging norm bandwagons,[155] or norm cascades, that will lead to crystallizing in international law those binding and enforceable human rights obligations. Rather than lamenting past struggles, or stasis, the dynamic processes underway may be establishing the foundation for binding and enforceable corporate human rights.

Our approach contends that such a process will require global agents with force to lift corporate accountability from under the weight of veto players. Two recent developments suggest that such processes and agency is on its way:

[151] Jonathan Drimmer and Lisa J. Laplante, "The Third Pillar," in *The Business and Human Rights Landscape: Moving Forward, Looking Back*, ed. Jena Martin and Karen E. Bravo (Cambridge: Cambridge University Press, 2015).

[152] Surya Deva, *Regulating Corporate Human Rights Violations: Humanizing Business* (London: Routledge, 2012).

[153] See Surya Deva's work that has called existing regulation inadequate. Deva, "Human Rights Lightly: A Critique of the Consensus Rhetoric and the Language Employed by the Guiding Principles"; Deva, *Regulating Corporate Human Rights Violations: Humanizing Business*.

[154] Terence C. Halliday and Bruce G. Carruthers, "The Recursivity of Law: Global Norm Making and National Lawmaking in the Globalization of Corporate Insolvency Regimes," *American Journal of Sociology* 112, no. 4 (2007): 1135–202; Sida Liu and Terence C. Halliday, "Recursivity in Legal Change: Lawyers and Reforms of China's Criminal Procedure Law," *Law and Social Inquiry* 34, no. 4 (2009): 911–50.

[155] Cass Robert Sunstein, "Social Norms and Social Roles," *Columbia Law Review* 96 (1996): 903–68.

the regional human rights systems in Latin America and Africa and the UN Human Rights Council.

Up to now, regional enforcement mechanisms have played an insignificant role with regard to corporate accountability. The Inter-American Commission and Court proved crucial in pressuring states to hold state perpetrators of past human rights abuse accountable, but it has rarely addressed corporate complicity in those violations. It is nonetheless regarded as having potential to do so. As we show in Appendix A, the Inter-American System has developed jurisprudence in relation to the interpretation of concepts often referred to in the context of corporate activities, such as the notion of "due diligence" and states' obligations to investigate corporate abuses.[156] One judicial action presented in Chapter 5, further illustrates the Inter-American System's potential. In 2002–2003, the Inter-American Human Rights Commission and Court pressured Colombia to prosecute palm oil companies working with paramilitary groups in the 1990s in the forced displacement of Afro-Colombian communities from their ancestral lands. This case suggests that where international pressure is applied, this may strengthen the side of corporate accountability. It is also significant in showing how regional courts could use innovative means to advance accountability. Rather than relying on unsettled international law on the binding and enforceable human rights obligations of business, the Inter-American System applied the American Convention of Human Rights.

Recent initiatives in the African Court on Human and Peoples' Rights to advance corporate accountability also look promising.[157] The 2014 "Malabo Protocol"[158] establishes jurisdiction over a broad range of crimes, including genocide, war crimes, and crimes against humanity, as well as mercenarism, corruption, money laundering, trafficking in persons, trafficking in drugs, trafficking in hazardous wastes, and illicit exploitation of natural resources, among others.[159] The Protocol establishes jurisdiction over natural persons and entities on established bases of consent, territory, nationality, passive

---

[156] International Federation for Human Rights (FIDH), "Corporate Accountability for Human Rights Abuses: A Guide for Victims and NGOs on Recourse Mechanisms," 164–65.

[157] The African Commission on Human and Peoples' Rights, for example, reviewed the Ogoni case in Nigeria and confirmed the responsibility of states to protect human rights from harm by foreign transnational corporations. International Federation for Human Rights (FIDH), "Corporate Accountability for Human Rights Abuses: A Guide for Victims and NGOs on Recourse Mechanisms," 144–46.

[158] This is formally titled the Amendments to the Protocol of the Statute of the African Court.

[159] Cassel and Ramasastry, "White Paper: Options for a Treaty on Business and Human Rights."

personality and protective principles.[160] As of November 2018, the Protocol had eleven of the required fifteen ratifications to enter into force.[161]

The Human Rights Council has become another potential global agent to advance corporate accountability. The Council initiated an international treaty process to regulate corporate human rights behavior. Ecuador and South Africa sponsored a treaty proposal resolution endorsed by Bolivia, Cuba, and Venezuela, and with support from twenty other countries. The proposal aims "to establish an open-ended intergovernmental working group with the mandate to elaborate an international legally binding instrument on Transnational Corporations and Other Business Enterprises with respect to human rights."[162] The Council further adopted by consensus the Norwegian member's proposed resolution for a binding instrument for the "effective implementation of the Guiding Principles," to "bridge governance gaps at the national, regional and international levels."[163]

A crucial step toward the treaty took place in July 2018, when the Intergovernmental Working Group (IGWG) released the first draft (called "Zero Draft") of the legally binding instrument and its optional protocol.[164] It is intended to "regulate business activities of a transnational character" (Article 3). It further establishes states' "duties to hold perpetrators criminally, civil and administratively liable for human rights violations in the context of transnational business activities through their domestic law [... and] to incorporate into their domestic law provisions for universal jurisdiction" (Article 10). Article 14 puts a committee of experts in charge of monitoring

---

[160] Matiangai Sirleaf, "The African Justice Cascade and the Malabo Protocol," *International Journal of Transitional Justice* 11, no. 1 (2017).

[161] See "Protocol on Amendments to the Protocol on the Statute of the African Court of Justice and Human Rights," https://au.int/sites/default/files/treaties/7804-sl-protocol_on_amendments_to_the_protocol_on_the_statute_of_the_african_court_of_justice_and_human_rights_5.pdf.

[162] United Nations Human Rights Council, "Elaboration of an International Legally Binding Instrument on Transnational Corporations and Other Business Enterprises with Respect to Human Rights A/HRC/26/L.22/Rev.1" (New York, NY: United Nations, 2014), https://documents-dds-ny.un.org/doc/UNDOC/LTD/G14/064/48/PDF/G1406448.pdf?OpenElement.

[163] United Nations Human Rights Council, "Human Rights and Transnational Corporations and Other Business Enterprises Res. 26/22, U.N. Doc. A/HRC/RES/26/22," 2014, https://documents-dds-ny.un.org/doc/UNDOC/LTD/G14/062/40/PDF/G1406240.pdf?OpenElement. Originally tabled on June 12, 2014, it was subsequently updated on June 17 and 23.

[164] Following the release of these documents, states began to negotiate the text of the treaty in the fourth session of the UN Working Group in Geneva in October 2018. The IGWG published a new draft business and human rights treaty on July 16, 2019. It was prepared by the Permanent Mission of Ecuador, on behalf of the IGWG, The draft is intended to serve as the basis for intergovernmental negotiations during the fifth session of the IGWG in October 2019. www.ohchr.org/EN/HRBodies/HRC/WGTransCorp/Pages/IGWGOnTNC.aspx.

and promoting the implementation of the treaty but no enforcement mechanisms were created. Instead, Article 5 states that "jurisdiction vests in the court of the State where such acts or omissions occurred or where the alleged perpetrator is domiciled."[165]

The draft and its protocol have been praised as positive steps toward the regulation of business behavior. Practitioners have raised concerns, nonetheless. Phil Bloomer, from the Business and Human Rights Resource Centre asserts that: "A contentious area of the Treaty's scope is its exclusive focus on 'business activities of a transnational character.'"[166] John Ruggie agrees and adds that the scope of the treaty is further limited to "for profit" economic activities, that would exclude some public or state-run companies.[167] Some practitioners raised objection to the "minimal discussion and provisions allocated within the Treaty on conflict-affected areas," asserting that the Treaty "fails to adequately address its relevance to, and implementation in, situations of armed conflict and occupation." Article 15(4) only references that "special attention shall be undertaken in the cases of business activities in conflict-affected areas." These critics contend that the Treaty fails to adopt the required language and specific legal framework pertinent to conflict-affected areas, such as international humanitarian law, which sets obligations and protections for state and non-state actors, including business enterprises, in situations of conflict.[168] Still others contend that the Treaty proposal does not incorporate the prior consultations that called for legal innovations that prescribe direct obligations for businesses that move beyond existing principles established in public international law.[169]

---

[165] "Legally Binding Instrument to Regulate, in International Human Rights Law, the Activities of Transnational Corporations and Other Business Enterprises – Zero Draft," 2018, www .business-humanrights.org/sites/default/files/documents/DraftLBI.pdf.

[166] Phil Bloomer and Maysa Zorob, "Another Step on the Road? What Does the 'Zero Draft' Treaty Mean for the Business and Human Rights Movement?," in *Compilation of Commentaries on the "Zero Draft"* (London: Business and Human Rights Resource Centre, 2018), 1–4.

[167] John Gerard Ruggie, "Comments on the 'Zero Draft' Treaty on Business and Human Rights," in *Compilation of Commentaries on the "Zero Draft"* (London: Business and Human Rights Resource Centre, 2018), 6–9.

[168] Shawan Jabarin and Maha Abdallah, Al-Haq, "The 'Zero Draft' Treaty: Is It Sufficient to Address Corporate Abuses in Conflict-Affected Areas?," in *Compilation of Commentaries on the "Zero Draft"* (London: Business and Human Rights Resource Centre, 2018), 4–6.

[169] Charlie Holt et al., "The Zero Draft Legally Binding Instrument on Business and Human Rights: Small Steps along the Irresistible Path to Corporate Accountability," in *Compilation of Commentaries on the "Zero Draft"* (London: Business and Human Rights Resource Centre, 2018), 9–11.

This process occurring at the international level has been closely followed and influenced by civil society. For example, a Treaty Alliance has emerged that unites large regional and international civil society networks advocating a binding and enforceable international instrument to address human rights abuses committed by transnational corporations and other business enterprises. The network operates in Geneva to influence UN decision makers. One of its members, the Economic Social and Cultural Rights Net, is comprised of over 230 organizations across more than 75 countries. It has worked to secure economic and social justice through human rights instruments. This network not only advances the development of a robust treaty,[170] but also attempts to exert international pressure "using the treaty process more broadly to encourage national, regional and international action to strengthen corporate accountability."[171] The Treaty Alliance creatively engages the UNGP as a useful mechanism to establish clear human rights obligations on businesses and to make progress toward enforcement mechanisms to solidify those obligations. The forty-seven states of the UN Human Rights Council (including the United States), acting by consensus, called upon "all business enterprises to meet their responsibility to respect human rights in accordance with the Guiding Principles."[172]

These new measures, despite criticisms of them, are promising. Having global agents with effective tools and a propitious political environment, these efforts may prove capable of applying the force necessary to lift the weight of corporate accountability. And yet, as the UN Draft Norms process indicated, veto players might emerge to block these initiatives from reaching the force of law. Our tracking of corporate accountability in the past leaves us skeptical, but nonetheless hopeful for the development of clear, binding, and enforceable international human rights obligations on business.

Limits of Applying International Human Rights Law

Until the changes promised in the discussion above are settled into clear, binding, and enforceable human rights obligations on business, those attempting to close the victims' gap are stymied in their efforts. A case study provides an illustration. Andhes, the Northeastern Argentine Association of

---

[170] There is a lively debate over the value and effectiveness of a treaty instrument for business and human rights. See: ESCR-Net, "About the Proposed Treaty," *ESCR-Net*, www.escr-net.org/corporateaccountability/hrbusinesstreaty/about-proposed-treaty; Business and Human Rights Resource Centre, "Reflections on the Zero Draft," *Business and Human Rights Resource Centre*, n.d.; CIDSE, "Value of a Future UN Treaty on Businesses and Human Rights Highlighted at EU Panel Debate," *CIDSE*, March 2017.
[171] ESCR-Net, "About the Proposed Treaty."
[172] Human Rights Council, "Resolution A/HRC/34/L.7" (New York, 2017).

Lawyers of Human Rights and Social Studies, has defended victims of human rights violations during the last Argentine dictatorship by consistently applying binding obligations in international law. It has also backed up its local-level defense of victims with support from the Inter-American Commission and Court of Human Rights. When it began to advance strategic litigation for corporate complicity in the dictatorship, its usual strategy of applying international human rights law seemed imprudent in the successful defense of victims.

Andhes' consultation with legal experts confirmed these doubts. Those experts viewed existing human rights obligations on business in international law as insufficiently clear, settled, binding, or enforceable to convince local judges on the merits of the cases. Andhes searched, without success, for criteria by which a company's behavior in an authoritarian regime could be legally connected to state atrocity and crimes against humanity. It sought clear standard-setting regarding the conditions under which business executives could be prosecuted for international human rights violations. It looked for clear precedents in historic cases. All to no avail.

The organization thus abandoned its traditional use of the international human rights framework to advance the rights of victims of corporate complicity. It opted instead to draw on broad international human rights law on crimes against humanity incorporated into Argentine legislation. It blended international human rights law with domestic legislation. These are the kinds of tools we see as advancing corporate accountability and closing the victims' gap. Even if the promising changes in Global North courts or at the regional or international level do not materialize in the short term, "corporate accountability from below" strategies can help overcome the barrier of unsettled international law in the area of corporate human rights obligations.

CONCLUSION

Andhes' experience reflects a central argument of this book. We contend that the international system, at present, weakens corporate accountability efforts. As one scholar concludes, "[T]he wide inconsistency in the rules which regulate corporate conduct creates a legal regime which goes against individual human rights and the human rights policy objectives of states, the international community, and individuals."[173] Although enforcement mechanisms exist, procedural hurdles, unclear and unsettled law, and the resources and capacity of economic actors to evade judgment, maintain the victims' gap. As

---

[173] Černič, "An Elephant in a Room of Porcelain: Establishing Corporate Responsibility for Human Rights," 30.

Erika R. George states, "The positivist position, to the extent that it supports the position that private commercial actors have no obligations under public international law, does little to address atrocities and to provide a remedy to those injured by private commercial actors."[174]

This has not always been the case. Archimedes' Lever helps illustrate the impact of shifts in the capacity to advance corporate accountability over time. In the past, when the international political environment moved closer to the weight of corporate accountability, less force was necessary to lift it. This is observed in the corporate trials following the Holocaust. During that period of time, global actors pressured for corporate accountability on behalf of victims and against veto players. The success can be measured in terms of guilty verdicts. The subsequent period is marked by an unfavorable global climate. During the Cold War, the fulcrum moved farther away from the corporate accountability weight, as business was seen as the bulwark against threats to the global economic and political order. Global agents acted alongside business veto players to weigh down corporate accountability.

Without a world-wide security crisis that has forged international consensus, the current global context since the 1990s seems to be one of neutrality. No single international threat trumps human rights concerns and vice versa. The positioning of the fulcrum to lift up corporate accountability is balanced. The weight of veto players against corporate accountability is great, however. Pressure on the other side – the use of effective tools in the hands of weak actors and the added strength of global agents – could begin to lift that weight. With the unsettled status of clear, binding, and enforceable international human rights obligations on business, such force does not yet exist. The accountability outcomes during this period can be measured in terms of one conviction in an international court (Rwanda), thirteen settlements of the Holocaust cases, and seven in the other foreign civil cases, and four convictions in foreign criminal trials.

These results do not suggest that either "top down" corporate accountability through international courts or "bottom-up" corporate accountability in foreign courts has gone very far in closing the victims' gap. Promising processes are underway at the international level to expand and strengthen international instruments to hold economic actors accountable for complicity in past human rights violations. At the moment, though, the gap persists.

---

[174] George, "The Enterprise of Empire: Evolving Understandings of Corporate Identity and Responsibility," 29.

In this international context, and as the Andhes example shows, "corporate accountability from below" may be the best, or even the only, option to address victims' rights. Local efforts are advancing the rights of victims by blending ordinary domestic legislation with international human rights standards, thereby achieving limited corporate accountability. We also see the emergence of dynamic actors from the Global South operating at the international level to establish binding and enforceable human rights obligations on business, which, if successful, will further add force to lift corporate accountability. The dynamic process underway is summarized in the comment that "much of international law that has been made and is being made today is actually bottom-up lawmaking."[175] Our study suggests that the changes underway are not, however, occurring in the "bottom-up" processes in the Global North courts, but rather in the Global South. We refer to this as "corporate accountability from below." The main obstacle to that form of accountability is the absence of international pressure to act as a counter weight to the powerful corporate veto, the subject of Chapter 3.

---

[175] Wallace, *Human Rights and Business: A Policy-Oriented Perspective*, 275–76, cited by Janet Koven Levit, "Bottom-Up Lawmaking: The Private Origins of Transnational Law," *Indiana Journal of Global Legal Studies* 15, no. 1 (2008): 49–73.

3

The Corporate Veto

In August 2016, the director of Legal Affairs of the Argentine Ledesma sugar mill sent a letter to Congresswoman Myriam Bregman. Bregman had spoken out in an official congressional meeting about the connection between Ledesma's owner, Carlos Pedro Blaquier, and alleged crimes against humanity that had occurred before and during Argentina's authoritarian regime (1976-1983). Her statements did not reveal any new information. As the well-known Argentine political figure Miguel Bonasso stated, "The acts carried out by Mr. Blaquier and his Ledesma sugar mill stopped being a secret many years ago thanks to the determination of Olga Aredez whose husband was kidnapped and taken away in a van with the Ledesma logo in one of the infamous 'blackouts' perpetrated by the dictatorship."[1] The letter to Bregman claims that the charges against Blaquier "were never proven." (In fact, the legal case against Blaquier and Ledesma is under appeal.) It goes on to accuse Bregman of publicly maligning Blaquier as a genocidaire and a beneficiary of social class privileges to secure impunity.

---

[1] Bonasso's statement refers to an event denominated the "Noche del Apagón," or blackout night, that occurred between July 20–23, 1976 in which the mill was allegedly involved. Nearly 400 people, many of them workers at the sugar mill, were taken to clandestine torture centers where they were tortured. Thirty-six of them were executed and disappeared. In 2005, nearly ten years before Bregman's statement in Congress, a well-publicized mobilization called for justice and punishment for the Noche del Apagón. Nearly five years before Bregman's statement, Blaquier faced charges from the Jujuy federal court for alleged involvement in twenty-six cases of illegal detention (Burgos case) and thirty-six disappearances during the Noche del Apagón. He had allegedly authorized the use of company vans for the kidnapping of those individuals and their subsequent transferal to clandestine torture centers. During the trial investigation, a 300-page document was found in the company archives, producing evidence of the company's illegal spying on individuals and groups who had participated in the 2005 mobilization for justice. Nonetheless, in March 2015, a year before Bregman's statement, Blaquier had been cleared of charges due to insufficient evidence by a second instance tribunal. This decision is being reviewed by the Supreme Court.

Bregman, and many others, interpreted the letter as an unlawful act of intimidation of an elected official.[2] Laura Figueroa, the lawyer in a number of genocide and crimes against humanity cases, referred to Blaquier's threats against Bregman as "a cowardly effort used by those with economic and political power against popular sectors ... particularly when they express anti-capitalist and democratic ideology."[3] Human rights lawyers, organizations, journalists, academics, politicians, and others expressed solidarity with the congresswoman and denounced the act of intimidation by the company. Bregman responded to the threat by stating "they are not going to silence us, we will continue fighting against impunity for all genocides."[4]

The Bregman-Blaquier incident illustrates the local power of certain businesses, the ample set of resources at their disposal, and their will and capacity to use those resources and that power to veto accountability efforts. At times, economic actors even resort to illegal tactics.

Transitional justice studies have paid insufficient attention to the role of veto players over accountability processes. The business and human rights literature, in contrast, places significant importance on how the economic resources businesses possess translates into power over accountability processes and outcomes. Our own data, containing a small number of successful judicial actions against businesses, seem to confirm this view.

This chapter aims to show with empirical evidence the veto power of business over corporate accountability. Following George Tsebelis's definition of veto power,[5] our study considers economic actors' ability to stop a change from the status quo. First, we examine the outcome of corporate accountability efforts as evidence of significant veto power. We explore who – what type of firm – has proved more successful in vetoing judicial accountability. We consider where – what type of court – that veto power over accountability occurs. We further analyze when – under what set of conditions – economic actors are most likely to successfully use their veto power over accountability. We then set out the strategies economic actors have deployed to maintain

---

[2] See: La Izquierda Diario, "Amplio repudio a la carta de Blaquier a Myriam Bregman," *La Izquierda Diario*, August 29, 2016, www.laizquierdadiario.com/Amplio-repudio-a-la-carta-de-Blaquier-a-Myriam-Bregman.

[3] Figueroa went on to describe Blaquier as "a powerful force" in the North of the country, where he "created a monopoly on sugar during the Onganía dictatorship" (1966–1970), by closing down competing companies in the region (ibid.).

[4] See: Telam, "Myriam Bregman calificó de 'intimidatorio' un escrito de abogados de Carlos Pedro Blaquier," *Telam*, 2016, http://memoria.telam.com.ar/noticia/bregman-llamo–intimidatorio–a-un-escrito-de-blaquier_n6625.

[5] Tsebelis, *Veto Players: How Political Institutions Work*.

impunity, specifically legal, nonjudicial, unlawful, and mobilizational. The third part of the chapter probes the possibility of weakening economic actors' veto power. This is consistent with our Archimedes' Lever approach. In neutral contexts, lifting the weight of corporate accountability depends on either civil society actors applying significantly more force than veto players, or reducing the force of veto powers. The conclusion to the chapter explores specific strategies that might contribute to reducing the power of veto players that weigh down corporate accountability.

VETO POWER AND ACCOUNTABILITY OUTCOMES

There is a natural assumption that owing to their economic power, businesses can block human rights accountability efforts. The pernicious effect of business's economic power on corporate human rights behavior – the capacity to escape justice for gross violations – has been described as "obvious and intolerable injustice … a mockery of a system that claimed to embody international law but did not cover the behaviour of actors whose role in international transactions – commercial, cultural, social – already rivaled that of States."[6] As yet, no study has systematically or empirically determined whether powerful firms have, indeed, avoided, or vetoed, accountability. We use the CATJ to do so. We look specifically at what types of firms seem to have escaped, or vetoed, justice, and which ones have not.

Veto in International and Foreign Judicial Cases

The post–World War II trials for corporate complicity challenge the notion that powerful companies have the power to veto accountability outcomes. Powerful companies were charged: Krupp, General Motors, BMW, Volkswagen, Ford, Bayer, Chase Manhattan Bank, DeutscheBank, Siemens, Nestlé, and Mitsubishi, among others. Their power at the time is evident in their key role in waging the war (military, chemical, healthcare facilities, and steel companies, for example) or for sustaining the regime (agriculture, manufacturing, and finance companies). Nonetheless, powerful industrialists went to prison. Others settled (see Appendix C). Thus, as we showed in the last chapter, in rare political moments, and with the efforts of powerful

---

[6] Kamminga and Zia-Zarifi, "Liability of Multinational Corporations under International Law: An Introduction," 2.

global agents with effective tools, members of the business community can be tried, found guilty, and sentenced severely for past atrocity. Getting around the veto power of businesses has resulted from propitious moments for corporate complicity and the application of force from determined global agents.

The outcomes of the other international and foreign trials tell a different story. The economic actors tried in the Rwandan genocide trials lacked the same global and financial power as in the historic cases. These might, thus, be seen as easier cases for corporate accountability. They, nonetheless, show that businesses do not enjoy total impunity for genocide or crimes against humanity. Although the guilty verdicts in foreign trials involved individual economic actors – not high-profile global companies – engaged in violence by internationally reviled regimes, they still represent sporadic instances of corporate accountability.

There is little evidence that corporate accountability in international and foreign trials has had a deterrent effect, however. Following deterrence theory,[7] if businesses perceive that there is a high and tangible cost attached to committing human rights violations (e.g., negative reputational, financial, or legal consequences), they will be less likely to commit them. Past accountability processes would then appear to predict subsequent business human rights behavior. If businesses avoided paying a high cost for the atrocities they committed in the past, they could react in one of two ways. They might perceive that they only narrowly avoided a high-cost outcome and thereby change behavior to avoid the risk of future convictions in a different political context with less lenient lawmakers. Alternatively, evading justice may lead businesses to calculate a low cost and low risk associated with corporate human rights violations, creating a permissive environment for committing such violations. If economic actors perceive that they have veto power over court judgments for human rights behavior, they will be less likely to change that behavior.

The CATJ cannot measure economic actors' perceptions of the risk of human rights violating behavior. It can examine whether past accountability efforts appear to have any effect on future behavior. It can do so by looking at judicial actions against the same firms in different violent contexts. Our findings are mixed. On the one hand, only a small number of the businesses in our data set (20) were accused of involvement in human rights violations in more than one situation of authoritarian rule or armed conflict. This does not

---

[7] Nagin, "Criminal Deterrence Research at the Outset of the Twenty-First Century," 1–42.

mean that only those companies were involved in human rights violations in other contexts, but they were not held accountable for them if they were. The set of cases is provided in Table 3.1.

Two characteristics of the pattern of corporate accountability seem to confirm deterrence theory. First, none of the German companies whose owners and employees faced prison terms for Holocaust atrocities are among the repeat offenders. This suggests that a high-cost sanction could curb business human rights abuses. Second, all of the companies involved in subsequent atrocities faced low-to-no sanctions for their earlier alleged complicity. Thirteen of the twenty companies were held accountable for Holocaust atrocities but settled in civil courts, a relatively low-cost sanction for large firms. The seven remaining companies faced accountability in truth commissions, or in pending cases without a sanction thus far, or the cases against them were dismissed or withdrawn. Low-level sanctions therefore appear to fail to deter future violations.

The Japanese firms could be seen as a challenge to the deterrence approach. All of the companies escaped justice historically and none of them appear to have been involved in subsequent atrocities. Thus, something beyond rational calculation of cost explains companies' involvement in human rights violations. In addition, while interesting, repeat incidents may not be the best way to assess business's perception of their ability to veto accountability outcomes. Economic actors may not have faced judgment themselves to know that there is a low likelihood of ever being held accountable. Our findings – the low level of verdicts and adverse judgments – reinforce that view. The cases are provided in Table 3.1.

Table 3.1 further suggests which types of companies are most often accused of complicity, or are more vulnerable to accusations. The sectors with the highest number of accusations of corporate complicity (three or four different contexts) are oil and gas corporations, that are arguably the strongest lobbying group worldwide. Vehicle manufacturing companies (Ford Motors, Daimler) also rank highest in the number of repeat accusations. This could suggest that such sectors have a "culture of operation" of no-tolerance for union or political activity. Or it may be that the global visibility of such firms might prompt accusations for strategic litigation purposes. The banking sector also figures prominently among the companies accused of multiple violations. This suggests that "blood banking" should be further explored to determine why banks continue to finance violence with impunity.

All of those accused in multiple violent situations are transnational corporations that operate directly or through subsidiaries in different

TABLE 3.1 *Repeat Accusations against Economic Actors*

Name of Company	Number of Cases	Countries of Abuse	Nationality	Sector
British Petroleum	3	Ecuador, South Africa, and Colombia	TNC	Oil and gas
Chevron-Texaco Corporation/Chevron-Texaco Global Energy/ Chevron-Texaco Overseas Petroleum Inc.	4	Ecuador, Nigeria, and South Africa	TNC	Oil and gas
Ford Motor Company	4	Holocaust, Argentina, Brazil, and South Africa	TNC	Manufacturing
Coca-Cola	3	Colombia, Guatemala, and South Africa	TNC	Beverages
Daimler Chrysler AG	3	Holocaust, South Africa and Argentina	TNC	Manufacturing
Elf Aquitaine	2	Nigeria and Brazil	TNC	Oil and gas
Exxon Mobil Corp.	2	Indonesia and South Africa	TNC	Oil and gas
General Electric	2	Brazil and South Africa	TNC	Energy
General Motors	3	Holocaust, Brazil, and South Africa	TNC	Manufacturing
Mercedes Benz	2	Argentina and Brazil	TNC	Manufacturing
Bayer AG	2	Holocaust and Guatemala	TNC	Manufacturing
BNP Paribas	3	Holocaust, Iraq, and Rwanda	TNC	Finance
Chase Manhattan Bank	2	Holocaust and South Africa	TNC	Finance

Name of Company	Number of Cases	Countries of Abuse	Nationality	Sector
Commerzbank	2	Holocaust and South Africa	TNC	Finance
Deutsche Bank	2	Holocaust and South Africa	TNC	Finance
Dresdner Bank	2	Holocaust and South Africa	TNC	Finance
Rheinmetall Group	2	Holocaust and South Africa	TNC	Military
Siemens	2	Holocaust and Brazil	TNC	Technology
Union Bank of Switzerland	2	Holocaust and South Africa	TNC	Finance
Volkswagen	2	Holocaust and Brazil	TNC	Manufacturing

Source: Corporate Accountability and Transitional Justice database, 2016

countries. This is not surprising. Because multinational companies operate around the world, they are more likely to be present in different violent contexts than domestic firms. The finding is significant in showing that multinational corporations are accused of involvement in more than one context. It further suggests that past accountability efforts do not seem to lead such companies to avoid human rights violations in subsequent armed conflict or authoritarian contexts. Volkswagen, for example, was accused of using thousands of forced laborers during the Holocaust; in Brazil it stands accused of providing the dictatorship with a list of unionized workers, facilitating their detention and torture. The company has evaded justice so far for both sets of events. Companies, or at least transnational ones, may intuitively grasp what our data reveal: they will face accountability efforts, but they will nearly always get away with alleged crimes against humanity.

Our data on foreign trials further indicate the veto power of powerful multinational companies. Of the thirty-seven economic actors that faced civil action, all were multinationals, 54 percent (twenty) of them operating in the extractive sector and 19 percent (seven) in the arms and military sector.[8] More than half of the cases brought against them were dismissed (twenty out of thirty-seven). Others settled (nine). None of the civil cases – all against multinational corporations – ended in adverse judgments. Of the thirteen economic actors involved in thirteen criminal actions (one action involved two business people and one company was involved in two actions), eight are multinationals and five are foreign nationals operating in the conflict. While all the foreign nationals were convicted,[9] none of the multinationals faced the same outcome. One multinational settled. Chiquita Brands, admitted to financing paramilitary and guerrilla groups in Colombia, but under duress. It agreed to pay a fine to the US government, none of which reached the victims. Two pending criminal cases involve large multinationals in construction and technology, operating in a context of war in Syria, and with capacity to prolong trial to delay judgment. The number of dismissals (six out of thirteen) might reflect the power of companies to persuade courts against the merits of the accusation. Four out of five companies[10] operate in the extractives sector, a sector that has great power in both domestic and global economies. The other company, Nestlé, is a Fortune 500 company with presence in over 189 countries around the world, and profits of a little over 10 billion dollars in 2017.[11] The criminal trials thus further suggest that multinational corporations have proved capable of "vetoing" negative judicial outcomes where national enterprises have failed.

Other scholars recognize the power of multinational corporations to evade justice outcomes in foreign courts. As one study contends, "More concrete, and therefore more intriguing, examples [of justice] come from the use of domestic courts to enforce international norms on MNCs. The advantage of enforcing international law in domestic courts is that they have relatively well-developed systems for addressing corporate entities and levying penalties

---

[8] The other 27 percent are distributed in companies operating in the agriculture (four), manufacturing (two), finance (one), retail (one), services (one), and unknown (one) sectors.

[9] All four cases involved illegal businesses (diamond and arms) trading with renowned enemies of Global North countries. Moreover, although the charges included human rights violations, only one of the individuals was convicted on those charges.

[10] Two judicial actions involve the same company: Total. And the two judicial actions ended with dismissals. Therefore, we have six dismissals involving five companies.

[11] Nestlé, "Annual Review 2017," 2018, www.nestle.com/asset-library/documents/library/documents/annual_reports/2017-annual-review-en.pdf; Fortune, "Fortune Global 500," *Fortune*, 2018, https://fortune.com/global500/search/.

against them. The disadvantage, of course, is that multinational corporations are set up precisely to avoid domestic jurisdiction over their activities."[12] Our data on multinational companies facing foreign domestic courts refine that observation. While multinational corporations have not always avoided domestic jurisdiction, they have escaped judgment, through dismissals and settlements. Settlements often involve specific conditions that decrease the reputational costs for businesses: the terms of the agreement are not disclosed to the public and they do not accept legal responsibility for the violations. Our findings on the outcome of corporate accountability efforts seem to confirm the particularly powerful veto power of multinational corporations in international and foreign courts.

Veto Power in Domestic Trials

In the next two chapters, we examine domestic accountability mechanisms in the Global South. That data also seem to confirm the power of multinational corporations over domestic courts. We found only two judgments against multinational companies in domestic courts of the Global South (Chevron-Ecuador and Ford-Argentina). This does not mean that multinational corporations were never charged. They are included in fifteen (28 percent) of the domestic judicial actions in our database, but domestic economic actors appear more frequently (thirty-eight, or 72 percent). Multinational firms have so far successfully avoided accountability efforts in domestic courts. Of the fifteen cases involving transnational corporations, there are ten (67 percent) pending (most of them for nearly a decade), one civil case where the company was found liable (Chevron-Texaco in Ecuador), one criminal case where company executives were convicted and is now under appeal (Ford in Argentina), and one dismissal (international banks in Argentina). Only three domestic economic actors succeeded in having their cases dismissed (executives of La Nueva Provincia, Ledesma and Fronterita in Argentina). In sum, mainly domestic economic actors have faced convictions and adverse judgments in our domestic judicial action data set. Transnational businesses have not blocked judicial action from initiating, but neither have they achieved acquittals or negative judgments. They still face a high

---

[12] Kamminga and Zia-Zarifi, "Liability of Multinational Corporations under International Law: An Introduction," 10.

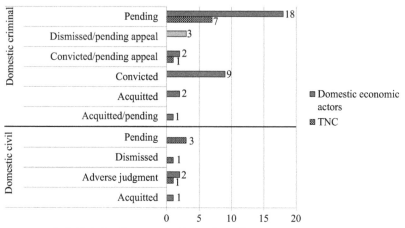

FIGURE 3.1 Judicial Action Outcomes by Nationality of Firm
Source: Corporate Accountability and Transitional Justice database, 2016

number of pending cases (ten).[13] If these follow the existing pattern, and veto power prevails, accountability is unlikely.

Veto Power in Truth Commissions

Our truth commission findings also have mixed results with regard to the power of multinational corporations to veto accountability. In truth commissions, as in judicial actions, domestic firms faced higher levels of accountability compared to multinational corporations. Most of the firms named in truth commissions were domestic (73 percent) rather than transnational (22 percent).[14] On the other hand, multinational corporations named in truth commissions were more likely to be the subject of subsequent post-truth commission legal action (69 percent, or eleven) than domestic companies or individuals (31 percent, or five). That legal action against multinationals, however, tended to occur

---

[13] An exceptional situation is the Justice and Peace data set. Nearly all of the pending cases (98 percent) involve only Colombian domestic companies and nationals.
[14] The nationality of the remaining 5 percent is unknown, suggesting they are domestic companies.

outside the country where the abuses were committed. The Chevron and Royal Dutch Shell in Nigeria cases, for example, appeared in the national truth commission report, but were brought to US civil courts through the ATS. In addition, the cases of five companies mentioned by the truth commission in South Africa were taken to court in the United States as part of an ATS claim originally involving over fifty companies.

The direct domestic and multinational veto power over truth commissions, as we show in Chapter 4, has proved less obvious until recently. We cannot attribute the lack of corporate accountability in half of the truth commission reports, for example, to veto power. Yet, there are hints in our study of indirect pressure. Tunisia's 2013 truth commission[15] aimed to investigate the full array of human rights violations (killing, rape and sexual violence, torture, enforced disappearance, and execution without fair trial) and economic crimes such as financial corruption and misuse of public funds during the Ben Ali regime (1987–2011).[16] What the truth commission did not do is link those economic crimes with physical integrity crimes. The Center for Strategic and International Studies considers the Ben Ali regime a poignant example of when "gross human rights violations are closely linked to widespread corruption."[17] Among the criticisms of the transitional justice process in Tunisia, including the truth commission, is the power of business elites who supported the Ben Ali regime over it. Former president of the International Center for Transitional Justice, David Tolbert, refers to the country's "reconciliation law" as having "nothing to do with reconciliation or truth, but has been characterized as a payoff to business elites."[18]

In the truth commission reports that did name companies, they most frequently named only one company. While truth commissions held large, medium, and small companies accountable by naming them, only a small number (three) included recommendations to follow up with judicial investigation of criminal activity or to compensate victims (Brazil, Ecuador, and Liberia). Thus, a high degree of impunity and invisibility prevails in the truth

[15] See Tunisia's Truth and Dignity Commission (TDC) established with the Transitional Justice Law of 2013.
[16] International Center for Transitional Justice, "Tunisia," *International Center for Transitional Justice Reports*, www.ictj.org/our-work/regions-and-countries/tunisia.
[17] Shannon Green, "On the Rocks: Tunisia's Transitional Justice Process," *Center for Strategic & International Studies: Commentary*, 2015, www.csis.org/analysis/rocks-tunisia's-transitional-justice-process.
[18] David Tolbert, "Hope Amidst Angst: The Tunisian Truth and Dignity Commission," 2018, www.linkedin.com/pulse/hope-amidst-angst-tunisian-truth-dignity-commission-david-tolbert.

commission reporting on corporate complicity, but a majority of the truth commission processes at least managed to publish names of allegedly complicit economic actors without facing the veto power of business. A kind of limited accountability thus occurred.

In sum, the CATJ findings indicate what types of companies are most likely to be held accountable by which sets of accountability mechanisms. We confirm that powerful multinational companies have avoided guilty verdicts and adverse civil judgments in courts of law, but they have not avoided judicial claims against them. In international and foreign courts, we found only accountability outcomes in the Holocaust trials, for which many of those imprisoned received clemency or settled out of court. We have only two judgments against multinationals in domestic court trials (Chevron-Ecuador and Ford-Argentina). Domestic firms have faced adverse judgments in domestic civil and criminal courts, however. Our findings suggest that a stronger international human rights framework for corporate accountability would increase international pressure for judicial action for violating companies, particularly multinational ones.[19] Without international pressure for corporate accountability, and with the evidence of economic actors' veto power over such processes, the victims' gap persists.

Domestic accountability mechanisms hold more promise in overcoming corporate veto power. Truth commissions have held national and transnational companies accountable in final reports, but without significant follow-up judicial action. Nearly all of the guilty verdicts in the CATJ were rendered by domestic courts against national economic actors. In general, domestic economic actors lack the same level of veto power as their multinational counterparts. One possible exception is the trial of Ford Motor Company in Argentina (see Chapter 5). These findings suggest that, corporate veto power does not apply to all economic actors or all forms of accountability. Moreover, it is not contingent solely on the size and power of companies, but also on their will and capacity to use anti-accountability tools and/or political linkages. We now turn to the sources of that potential veto power.

Veto Power through Political Linkages

Our findings partially challenge the notion that economic power alone explains corporate veto power over accountability efforts. Veto power may

[19] Sarah Joseph, "An Overview of the Human Rights Accountability of Multinational Enterprises," in *Liability of Multinational Corporations under International Law*, ed. Menno T. Kamminga and Saman Zia-Zarifi (The Hague: Kluwer Law International, 2000), 78.

depend as much on the intervening factor of social or political power. That is, economic power does not appear to directly guarantee veto power, but it might put businesses in a position to be able to veto accountability efforts through political linkages. Not all businesses have veto power, but those with connections to political or judicial authorities would likely have more power than others.

Emblematic cases of direct political linkages between those accused of corporate complicity and the government before, during, or after the dictatorship and armed conflict, indicate some of the difficulties victims and their representatives face in holding certain economic elites accountable. The examples we present in this chapter show that sometimes even those business elites with strong political linkages cannot always avoid accountability attempts. They do seem to avoid negative final judgments, however.

In Argentina, sixteen top executives from many of the country's leading companies held official positions in strategic areas of the authoritarian regime.[20] A paradigmatic example is José Alfredo Martínez de Hoz, who became Minister of Finance in the Argentine civil-military dictatorship. Martínez de Hoz came from the business sector. He ran Acindar, one of largest steel companies in the country and the region. During his term as the company's CEO, even before the 1976 coup, Acindar allegedly established a detention center that operated until the authoritarian regime created its own system of clandestine detention, torture, and extermination centers. It may have even served as a model for the subsequent clandestine detention centers emblematic of the Argentine dictatorship.

The election of a Socialist shop steward in 1975 at the Villa Constitución plant allegedly led Martínez de Hoz to use his family connections within the military regime to repress the company's workers. An estimated 300 workers were abducted, and most were killed. Martínez de Hoz was indicted in 1988 for human rights abuses. He spent seventy-seven days in jail before President Menem granted a pardon. When Menem's pardons were declared unconstitutional, the case against Martínez de Hoz was reinitiated. He was charged with the 1976 kidnapping and extortion of Federico and Miguel Gutheim, a local textile mill owner and his son. Martínez de Hoz was also prosecuted for the murder of his assistant at the Ministry, Juan Carlos Casariego. In both cases, Martínez de Hoz was accused of being part of an illegal

---

[20] Martín Schorri, "Industrial Economic Power as Promoter and Beneficiary of Argentina's Refounding Project (1976–1983)," in *Outstanding Debts to Settle: The Economic Accomplices of the Dictatorship in Argentina*, ed. Horacio Verbitsky and Juan Pablo Bohoslavsky (Cambridge: Cambridge University Press, 2015).

association leading to the human rights violations of the victims. In 2010, Martínez de Hoz was placed under house arrest (on humanitarian grounds owing to his advanced age of 85) where he died in 2013 while awaiting trial.

Similarly, in Chile, a case brought against one of the largest pulp and paper companies in Latin America, CMPC (Compañia Manufacturera de Papeles y Cartones, "La Papelera"), reveals the close connections between political elites and business. The paper mill is owned by one of the richest families in Chile, the Mattes. On the board of the company at the time of the 1973 coup in Chile was former president Jorge Alessandri (1958–1964). The company was targeted for expropriation and nationalization during the Allende government, leading to an anti-Allende campaign against the proposed action: "La Papelera No!" Members of the extreme right-wing Patria y Libertad (Nation and Freedom), fervent supporters of the coup, had links within the company and allegedly participated in the repression of workers and others on the political left in the aftermath of the coup. Nineteen people[21] from Laja and San Rosendo were disappeared after being picked up by the military police (carabineros) from their homes, neighborhoods, and workplaces in broad daylight. Eighteen were found in a common grave in 1978 in Yumbel, 38 kilometers from Laja and San Rosendo. The body of the nineteenth person was found in a building owned by Forestal Mininco, a company that was part of CMPC. The company and its employees were accused of complicity in the violence in a number of ways: providing the trucks connected to the disappearances, serving food and drink to the agents who disappeared people, providing the materials to cover-up the bodies left in a common grave, detaining some people in the company itself, and identifying workers to be disappeared.[22] The families of victims (Agrupación de Familiares de Detenidos Desaparecidos – AFEP) denounced the carabineros and the company employees to the Chilean Justice Department in 2010. The trial initiated in 2012, was subsequently shelved due to lack of proof, but has recommenced and is slowly moving forward. This is one of the pending domestic judicial actions in the CATJ.

These two cases in Argentina and Chile show that the political connections of certain businesses may make them targets for civil society campaigns that can lead to judicial action. These high-profile individuals and companies become, at times, the face of civil-military repression or paramilitary-business partnerships in armed conflicts. For this reason, they may attract more judicial

---

[21] Those detained included: fourteen CMPC employees from San Rosendo and two railroad workers from Laja, two students, and two teachers. One managed to escape.

[22] Rebolledo Escobar, *A la sombra de los cuervos: Los cómplices civiles de la dictadura.*

action than lesser known, less well-connected, companies. They may be in a powerful position to veto outcomes but seem unable to block the claims made against them. Where highly mobilized communities exist, and where institutional innovators assist them, sometimes the cases do move forward, even if very slowly and without a justice outcome.

Businesses do not require politicians in their companies to possess veto power. Sometimes an affinity exists with politicians without any direct economic benefit for the politician. The case of clemency granted to imprisoned Nazi businessmen in 1951 by the US High Commissioner during the US occupation of Germany, John J. McCloy, suggests a kind of political linkage that explains business veto power. McCloy could be said to be the iconic figure of these sorts of political-business connections. Referred to as "The Chairman" of the US elite "Establishment," he had worked as a lawyer in defense of corporations on Wall Street at a firm described as "counsel for the predatory rich,"[23] as a national-security manager in the powerful War Department during World War II, and as head of the World Bank, before becoming the High Commissioner. Following his three-year stint in Germany, McCloy went on to become director of Chase Manhattan Bank, the Ford Foundation, the Council on Foreign Relations, and the presidential Advisory Committee on Arms Control and Disarmament. He also served as legal counsel to all "Seven Sister" oil companies and as a member of the board of directors for a dozen corporations.[24]

McCloy did not see himself as ideological, but instead as someone who could make an "objective nonpolitical analysis of the issues."[25] He lacked "political ambitions ... His politics were less a matter of ideology than simple pragmatism. He had no constituency – except for his ties to Rockefeller family interests on Wall Street – and even in this case, for most of his career, he managed to make it seem that he was always able to rise above these private interests in order to discern the public interest."[26] As High Commissioner, he was, in the words of former German Chancellor Helmut Schmidt, the "architect of Germany's rehabilitation from an occupied country to an independent state."[27] Kai Bird's biography refers to "early postwar Germany, where

---

[23] Quote by John W. Davis about the law firm Cravath, Henderson and de Gersdorff, in Kai Bird, *The Chairman: John J. McCloy and the Making of the American Establishment* (New York, NY: Simon & Schuster, 1992), 63.

[24] Bird, *The Chairman: John J. McCloy and the Making of the American Establishment*, 18.

[25] Ibid., 307.

[26] Ibid., 19–20.

[27] Ibid., 16.

McCloy for three years wielded virtually dictatorial powers over the lives of millions of Germans."[28]

McCloy's biographer attributes the High Commissioner's attitude toward businesses to his connection to the US private sector and the geopolitics of the time. McCloy stopped the process of dismantling German companies linked to Nazism.[29] According to Bird, McCloy capitulated to Chancellor Konrad Adenauer's (1949–1963) insistence on maintaining in his Cabinet two powerful Nazi collaborator financiers, Hermann Abs and Robert Pferdmenges.[30] Bird is struck by McCloy's apparent bias: "[T]housands of schoolteachers and low-ranking civil servants who had been pressured to join the Nazi Party were penalized by the de-Nazification courts, while prominent industrialists who had given millions to the party – but never joined it – went untouched."[31] In general, though, Bird connects McCloy's leadership with greater worry "about the course of the Cold War than . . . about the fate of a few convicted Nazi war criminals" in the German business community.[32]

The backdrop of the North Koreans crossing the 38th parallel, the anticipated spread of Soviet communism in Europe, and the need for a strong Germany to fight international Communism, led to McCloy's "mass clemency," including the immediate release from Landsberg prison of Alfried Krupp and eight members of his board of directors. Although his action set off a storm of protest (see Chapter 2), McCloy claimed that he found "no personal guilt" in Krupp's actions. By returning the Krupp company property,

---

[28] Ibid. Bird's biography attempts to situate McCloy in the US legal profession at the time. On one end of the spectrum is Justice Louis D. Brandeis who he quotes as saying: "Instead of holding a position of independence, between the wealthy and the people, prepared to curb the excesses of either, able lawyers have to a large extent, allowed themselves to become adjuncts of great corporations and neglected the obligation to use their powers for the protection of the people." Ibid., 56, quoting from Lewis J. Paper, *Brandeis: An Intimate Biography of One of America's Truly Great Supreme Court Justices* (Secaucus, NJ: Citadel, 1983), 92–93. Bird locates McCloy's mentor at Harvard Law School, Felix Frankfurter, somewhere in the middle, a jurist who included among lawyers' professional responsibilities, "mediating between the powerful private and public interests" and "shaping a jurisprudence to meet the social and industrial needs of the time." Bird, *The Chairman: John J. McCloy and the Making of the American Establishment*, 56, quoting from Harlan B. Phillips, *Felix Frankfurter Reminisces: An Intimate Portrait as Recorded in Talks with Dr. Harlan B. Phillips* (New York, NY: Reynal, 1960), 81. Bird casts McCloy on the other end, stating "Like Frankfurter, he saw his role as an impartial mediator, objective, rational, and capable of discerning the greater public interest. Unlike Frankfurter, he saw no conflict between this and working for large corporate interests." Bird, *The Chairman: John J. McCloy and the Making of the American Establishment*, 56.
[29] Bird, *The Chairman: John J. McCloy and the Making of the American Establishment*, 326.
[30] Ibid., 329.
[31] Ibid., 330.
[32] Ibid., 336.

McCloy attempted to correct the previous confiscation that he characterized as "repugnant to American concepts of justice."[33] McCloy seemed to ignore the prosecution's evidence and findings, focusing instead on Krupp's unfair treatment. Krupp certainly was treated differently – as emblematic of industrialists involved in war crimes or crimes against humanity. He was not, however, selected for prosecution because of the size of the firm and its symbolic role in the Nazi war effort alone. Alfried Krupp and his father had made substantial contributions to the Nazi Party. Alfried had become a fervent Nazi and had requested on more than one occasion that slave labor from concentration camps work in the company. He was singled out not only because of his name, as McCloy suggested, but because of his association with the Nazis and the criminal acts he carried out through the company bearing his name.

The link between the clemency and the Korean and Cold Wars is obvious. Fritz Ter Meer, an IG Farben executive convicted and later freed by McCloy in August 1950, remarked that "[n]ow that they have Korea on their hands, the Americans are a lot more friendly."[34] The timing of the clemency and the need for a strong anti-Communist Europe was critical to McCloy's decision. Bird does not discount, however, that McCloy had "come under the influence of such prominent business leaders as Hermann Abs," one of the Krupp family's bankers. The expansion of the clemency to other elites (e.g., Nazi doctors and judges), leads Bird to claim that McCloy fundamentally doubted the guilt of "well-bred, highly educated, and sensible" people.[35] In Bird's writing, McCloy personifies the power elite: the political, social, and economic power to block or reverse corporate accountability.

Such power may explain why our database of cases includes mainly mid- and lower-level employees in small, national firms with less political and economic clout. High-level executives rarely (four out of fifteen cases) face convictions and adverse judgments in domestic, foreign and international courts. The case of the palm oil companies in Chocó, Colombia is rare in convicting two company owners (along with low-level employees and associated community members). Top executives of powerful companies, like Martínez de Hoz and Blaquier, tend to escape legal judgment on their guilt or innocence.

The previous two sections on corporate veto power through economic linkages and political linkages show that sometimes powerful companies and

---

[33] Ibid., 365.
[34] Ibid., 368.
[35] Ibid., 375.

powerful business leaders have faced accountability efforts in international, foreign, and domestic trials and in truth commissions. While economic actors have been unable to veto accountability processes, they are generally effective in avoiding accountability outcomes in the form of guilty verdicts, adverse judgments, or serving full sentences. A deeply entrenched legacy of impunity prevails. As a result, evidence from our database suggests that businesses would not interpret the results from judicial action and truth commissions as indicating a high cost to committing human rights violations. The probability of facing conviction is quite low even if businesses do nothing to actively avoid it. On the other hand, businesses may hope to avoid reputational costs resulting from claims of human rights violations and to avoid the risk of stigma or negative judicial outcomes. To achieve that end, businesses engage in specific veto strategies.

VETO STRATEGIES

Accountability outcomes for corporate complicity in human rights violations are low in number, but CATJ findings cannot entirely confirm an economic power explanation. Powerful domestic and multinational firms have faced trial. That few of these powerful individuals and firms have been convicted, or fulfilled their sentences, may attest as much to their use of effective veto strategies as to their economic or political power. In other words, economic and political power may enhance economic actors' success at deploying effective veto strategies. We discuss four sets of veto strategies: legal, divide-and-conquer, unlawful, and mobilizational.

Legal Strategies

Corporations' economic power allows them to hire high-priced, skilled lawyers, to defend them in complicated legal battles.[36] As a rule, businesses will have more economic resources to fight legal battles than victims. These economic resources enable them to hire experts with know-how to use the legal system to their advantage. The legal maneuvers used by businesses have led scholars to conclude that "[c]ourthouse doors are, for both legal and

---

[36] Michael Byers, "English Courts and Serious Human Rights Violations Abroad: A Preliminary Assessment," in *Liability of Multinational Corporations under International Law*, ed. Menno T. Kamminga and Saman Zia-Zarifi (The Hague: Kluwer Law International, 2000), 249.

practical reasons, generally closed to victims, particularly those who live in poverty."[37] The differential in resources thus further contributes to the victims' gap.

The legal strategies used by companies are not easily tracked due to the lack of accessible data. We managed to identify the legal strategy of companies in 323 cases, out of which 307 are trials for Holocaust atrocities. From the Holocaust civil restitution claims, 285 (89 percent) of the companies filed a motion to dismiss the case (with a low rate of success – only six cases have ended in dismissal). The other sixteen cases for which we have information, include Indonesia (Exxon Mobil), Ecuador (Chevron-Texaco), Argentina (Ford, La Veloz del Norte, Citibank and Bank of America, Techint S.A., La Nueva Provincia, Molinos Rio de la Plata, Mercedez Benz, Minera Aguilar, Loma Negra, Papel Prensa), Iraq (CACI Premier Technology Inc.), Colombia (Héctor Restrepo Santamaría, Drummond), and Brazil (Volkswagen). These include jurisdictional, evidentiary, national security, delay, counter-suits, and settlement strategies.

Forum non conveniens allows transnational corporations to argue that a different court, or forum, is preferred because of its particular characteristics, e.g., location of the company's headquarters or the location of the alleged violations and victims. This means that corporations can attempt, even if they sometimes fail, to move the judicial action from a court perceived to be less favorable to the company to one that is more likely to side with the company.

In Indonesia, Exxon Mobil, accused of murder, kidnapping, torture, and slave labor – by financing a military unit before and after the authoritarian period to guarantee security – argued that the case should not be heard by a US Court, but rather by an Indonesian court. The argument was that the allegations involved Indonesian plaintiffs injured by Indonesian soldiers on Indonesian soil. It is interpreted as a move to a more favorable court to escape justice. The decision on this request remains pending.

The controversial case of Texaco-Chevron in Ecuador provides another example. Texaco received favorable concessions from Ecuadorean authoritarian regimes (1964 and 1990) that allowed it to use operations that resulted in the alleged massive contamination of water and land, and the displacement of indigenous communities in the Lago Agrio region. The oil company employed one of the top and fiercest law firms on Wall Street to defend it against the claims brought by the community in US courts. Texaco

---

[37] Robert Thompson, Anita Ramasastry, and Mark Taylor, "Translating Unocal: The Expanding Web of Liability for Business Entities Implicated in International Crimes," *The George Washington International Law Review* 40, no. 4 (2009): 841–902.

successfully attempted to find a more favorable court based on the *forum non conveniens* doctrine. The move backfired, however, when the company's preferred Ecuadoran court entered a $9.5 billion judgment against the Chevron Corporation (merged with Texaco).[38] *Forum non conveniens* does not always lead to the sorts of judgments companies expect.[39]

Chevron has successfully moved the case to another jurisdiction, this time an international arbitration tribunal. The Permanent Court of Arbitration in The Hague ruled that Ecuador's 2011 Supreme Court decision should be annulled because it "was procured through fraud, bribery, and corruption and was based on claims that had been already settled and released by the Republic of Ecuador years earlier."[40] The Tribunal ruled that no part of the Ecuadorean ruling should be enforced by any state. Since the company's assets are all found outside Ecuador, the Hague decision voids the Ecuadorean ruling. The Arbitration Court ruling represents another example of how powerful companies can deploy legal strategies in different courts, even international tribunals, to avoid final judgment.

Economic resources also provide companies with the capacity to prolong the trial and delay judgment. The resources to sustain the trial over a long period of time tend not to be available to victims, their pro bono or NGO advocates, and state prosecutor's offices.[41] Costly delay tactics have included

---

[38] After receiving the prejudicial judgment, the company filed a racketeering lawsuit against the plaintiffs' lawyers and representatives in a US federal court. In 2014, the Court agreed with Chevron and barred Ecuadorian plaintiffs from collecting the $9.51 billion judgment because the "decision was obtained by corrupt means." An appeals court confirmed the decision in 2016. See BBC News, "Chevron Wins Ecuador Rainforest 'Oil Dumping' Case," *BBC News*, 2018, www.bbc.com/news/world-latin-america-45455984. See also Ted Folkman's posts, including Ted Folkman, "The Access to Justice Gap in Transnational Litigation," *Letters Blogatory*, 2011, https://lettersblogatory.com/2011/08/02/the-access-to-justice-gap-in-transnational-litigation/. There are controversies surrounding the legal tactics used by the company and by the plaintiff's lawyers. On one side of the issue, see Joe Nocera, "Chevron's Longtime Nemesis Hits the End of the Road," *Bloomberg Opinion*, 2018, www.bloomberg.com/view/articles/2018-07-12/chevron-nemesis-steven-donziger-pays-a-price-for-ecuador-lawsuit; Joe Nocera, "Behind the Chevron Case," *The New York Times*, 2014, www.nytimes.com/2014/09/23/opinion/joe-nocera-behind-the-chevron-case.html. The opposite view is posted in articles on the plaintiff lawyer's website: http://stevendonziger.com/.

[39] Christopher A. Whytock and Cassandra Burke Robertson, "Forum Non Conveniens and the Enforcement of Foreign Judgments," *Columbia Law Review* 111, no. 7 (2011).

[40] In September 2018, the Hague Permanent Court of Arbitration ruled in favor of the company, awarding the company hundreds of millions of dollars in costs. Karan Nagarkatti and Gary McWilliams, "International Tribunal Rules in Favor of Chevron in Ecuador Case," *Reuters*, September 2018.

[41] Daniel Blackburn, *Removing Barriers to Justice: How a Treaty on Business and Human Rights Could Improve Access to Remedy for Victims* (Amsterdam: Stichting Onderzoek Multinationale

hearings to dismiss the case or to clarify legal technicalities. Lengthy appeals processes further incur high costs and defer final judgment.[42] The high number of ongoing judicial actions in our database may reflect the use of delay tactics by businesses to avoid judgment.

In the Argentine cases, denial and insufficient evidence are the primary legal strategies. Companies argue for dismissal on the grounds that proof does not exist of the authorization of, or the provision of company's resources for, the crime.

National security was used as the legal strategy in the Iraq case. Former detainees in the Abu Ghraib prison brought a case against CACI Premier Technology Inc. claiming the use of torture. The lawyers for CACI applied the political question doctrine, alleging that the claim against the company was "nonjusticiable" because it would necessitate the court responding to political (national security), rather than legal, questions. The Eastern District of Virginia court dismissed the case on these grounds. On appeal, the Fourth Circuit court rejected this ruling and remanded the case to the District Court in 2016, stating, "It is beyond the power of even the President to declare [torture] lawful."[43] The case has faced a number of challenges and remains pending.

Investigation into Chiquita Brands' (Colombia) legal strategies illustrates the use of delay tactics by companies to avoid an unfavorable judicial decision. In 2007, the company admitted to making payments to the United Self-Defense Forces of Colombia (AUC), the largest paramilitary group in the country. This resulted in a criminal investigation that ended with a fine that did not reach the victims. A few months after this admission in July 2007, an ATS claim was filed in the US Federal Court in New Jersey. US Secretary of State Colin Powell had previously in 2001 designated the AUC a "foreign terrorist organization." Powell wrote, "This designation ... makes it illegal for persons in the United States or subject to U.S. jurisdiction to provide material support to the AUC; requires U.S. financial institutions to block assets held by the AUC; and enables us to deny visas to representatives of the group."[44] By Chiquita's own admission, it violated US law by funding and arming a known terrorist organization. The company was charged with

Ondernemingen (SOMO) and the Centre for Research on Multinational Corporations, August 2017), http://mhssn.igc.org/Removing-barriers-web.pdf.

[42] Zerk, *Corporate Liability for Gross Human Rights Abuses: Towards a Fairer and More Effective System of Domestic Law Remedies.*

[43] Center for Constitutional Rights, "Al Shimari v. CACI et al.," https://ccrjustice.org/home/what-we-do/our-cases/al-shimari-v-caci-et-al.

[44] Colin L. Powell, "Designation of the AUC as a Foreign Terrorist Organization" (Department of State Archive, 2001), https://2001-2009.state.gov/secretary/former/powell/remarks/2001/4852.htm.

complicity in extrajudicial killing, torture, crimes against humanity, and war crimes. Chiquita Brands has, at different stages of the judicial process, petitioned for dismissal and appealed negative decisions in lower courts. It was appealed all the way to the US Supreme Court where a hearing was denied. In this case, the plaintiffs had appealed the decision by the lower court to dismiss the case. The plaintiffs pursued litigation through the Cardona case in the Federal District Court in Florida. In early 2018, Chiquita reached an undisclosed out-of-court settlement with the families of victims. In August of that same year, the Colombian Prosecutor General's Office announced the decision to prosecute thirteen company executives for allegedly financing paramilitary groups.[45] The case in various forms has been ongoing for a decade in numerous fora within and outside the country, without a final judgment.

The Chevron case in Ecuador mentioned earlier is an example of Strategic Lawsuits against Public Participation (SLAPP suits). Companies have used these suits "to intimidate, harass, and silence activists who are working to expose corporate injustices and human rights violations. As intended, such lawsuits have a clear chilling effect on activism, silencing critical voices and stifling accountability."[46] Such suits can also be used by companies against communities of victims or their lawyers to sidetrack investigations into their human rights violations. In the Chevron case, the company brought a Racketeer Influenced and Corrupt Organizations Act (RICO) claim against the US lawyer Steven Donziger, the Ecuadorean lawyer Pablo Fajardo, and Luis Yanza, a local organizer for the 30,000 indigenous and nonindigenous Amazon rainforest villagers in Lago Agrio. RICO, a US federal law typically adopted in organized crime cases, was applied against Donziger over charges of fraud and extortion.[47] Amazon Watch referred to the RICO suit as "a complete miscarriage of justice," aimed at retaliation for the victory in the Ecuadorian court, an effort to deter

---

[45] See Business and Human Rights Resource Centre, "Chiquita Lawsuits (Re Colombia)."

[46] Otto Saki, "How Companies Are Using Lawsuits to Silence Environmental Activists – and How Philanthropy Can Help," Ford Foundation: Equals Change Blog, 2017, www .fordfoundation.org/ideas/equals-change-blog/posts/how-companies-are-using-law-suits-to-silence-environmental-activists-and-how-philanthropy-can-help/.

[47] For more information see, Daniel Fisher, "Appeals Court Upholds Sanctions against Donziger over $9.5 Billion Chevron Judgment," *Forbes*, August 2016, www.forbes.com/sites/danielfisher/2016/08/08/appeals-court-upholds-sanctions-against-donziger-over-chevron-litigation-in-ecuador/.

legal actions against companies, and to evade justice.[48] The company's commitment to use every legal tactic possible to avoid prosecution is summed up in the statement by a company official: "We're going to fight this until Hell freezes over – and then we'll fight it out on the ice."[49] Perhaps as part of that effort, the company has hired well-known human rights academic-practitioners to write *amicus curiae* briefs to support its claims.[50] One of those experts acknowledges receipt of payment from the company, but contends that he reached an independent decision regarding the plaintiffs' lawyers' unlawful acts. He further asserts that anyone carefully reviewing the record would come to the same conclusion of wrongdoing by Donziger.[51]

Donziger admits to "mistakes." But neither he nor the legal expert hired by the company believe that his legal missteps undermine the original case. Moreover, the law firm representing Chevron did not stop with a RICO claim against Donziger. Seventeen other organizations were also served. One of the members of that group has written about the legal wrangling in which he, and others, had to be involved. His own view is that Chevron's "bullying tactics" backfired, resulting in widespread and public criticism, including from Chevron's own investors. RICO and other SLAPP suit claims are nonetheless widely viewed as a way in which companies sidetrack and bog down the legal process, intimidate poorly resourced victims and their advocates, and thwart judgment on the merits of the case.

Although truth is usually a defense against slander cases in most countries, this is not true in all parts of the world. Thereby slander cases constitute another disruptive and costly delay tactic that businesses can use to prolong decisions. In Argentina, a top member of the national prosecutor's office revealed to us that a company's lawyers had threatened to file libel or slander cases against her, the team of lawyers in the Prosecutor's Office, and the human rights lawyers working on behalf of victims, as the result of opening an investigation against the company. The intimidation did not prevent the

[48] Steven Donziger, "Blog: Amazon Watch Response to Decision to Uphold Flawed Chevron Retaliatory Lawsuit," 2016, http://stevendonziger.com/2016/08/08/amazon-watch-response-decision-uphold-flawed-chevron-retaliatory-lawsuit/.

[49] Patrick Radden Keefe, "Reversal of Fortune," *The New Yorker*, 2012, www.newyorker.com/magazine/2012/01/09/reversal-of-fortune-patrick-radden-keefe.

[50] Corporate Social Responsibility (CSR) Newswire, "Notre Dame Law Professor under Scrutiny for Accepting Chevron Funds to Attack Ecuadorian Villagers," *CSR News*, 2015, www.csrwire.com/press_releases/38291-Notre-Dame-Law-Professor-Under-Scrutiny-for-Accepting-Chevron-Funds-to-Attack-Ecuadorian-Villagers.

[51] Personal communication with Douglass Cassel on September 12, 2018.

Prosecutor's Office from moving forward with the case, but it prevented us from making visible the specific company using this type of tactic. The prosecutor asked us not to name names that would lead to sidetracking the investigation in a likely slander suit.[52]

The Business and Human Rights Resource Centre (BHRRC) in London, a repository of claims against companies, has had to implement mechanisms to avoid costly slander suits. When it posts a claim against a company on its website, the company is given a chance to respond. BHRRC is also required to post the company's response if it is made. Only in this way can the NGO defend itself in slander suits. BHRRC staff calculate that 30 percent of its claims receive a response from the company. In the corporate complicity cases that we extracted from the BHRRC, we found company responses in five cases (out of twenty, or 25 percent).[53] All of the company responses denied the accusations except for Chiquita Brands. That company admitted having financed paramilitary groups but only under duress and with the expectation that the paramilitaries would protect employees from violence.[54]

Whether explicitly evoked or simply inferred, the threat of slander, calumny, or libel suits in Colombia has an impact on reporting claims against companies by victim or other groups. The Justice and Peace Unit of the General Prosecutor's Office of Colombia took testimony from paramilitary groups regarding their involvement in human rights violations. Although in their testimony members of paramilitary groups identified corporate complicity in those abuses, the Justice and Peace Tribunals, fearing a slander suit, limited their investigations into complicity to those companies for which it had corroborating evidence.[55] In other words, many more companies might have been subject to prosecution had the Court proved willing to consider

---

[52] We found evidence of similar types of slander suits brought against other entities exposing business violations of human rights. The London law firm Leigh Day was sued for libel by Trafigura after it represented 30,000 victims of the company's alleged dumped waste. Trafigura threatened other entities with legal action, such as the Norwegian State broadcaster NRK. The BBC also faced a libel suit from Trafigura for its 2009 story "Dirty Tricks and Toxic Waste in the Ivory Coast." See Blackburn, *Removing Barriers to Justice: How a Treaty on Business and Human Rights Could Improve Access to Remedy for Victims.*

[53] The cases with responses are from Ford and Ledesma in Argentina; Banacol and Chiquita Brands in Colombia; and Anvil Mining in the Democratic Republic of Congo.

[54] See Business and Human Rights Resource Centre, "Company Response Rates," *Business and Human Rights Resource Centre,* n.d., www.business-humanrights.org/en/company-response-rates.

[55] Bernal-Bermúdez, "The Power of Business and the Power of People: Understanding Remedy and Corporate Accountability for Human Rights Violations. Colombia 1970–2014," 80.

paramilitary testimony sufficient initial evidence to investigate company wrongdoing during the armed conflict. The Transitional Justice Unit of the Attorney General's Office, in response to a request for information, told us that by May 2017 paramilitary leaders had named 796 companies complicit in paramilitary violence, nearly twice as many cases that were included in the Special Prosecutor's rulings.[56] Magistrate Uldi Teresa Jiménez told us in an interview that courts have to be particularly careful about naming names in the rulings given the fear of libel suits by businesses.[57]

The complexity of corporate structures affords certain legal strategies that other defendants do not enjoy. Well-known difficulties faced in "piercing the corporate veil" derive from complex ownership and management arrangements, particularly with regard to multinational companies and their subsidiaries. Liability is less likely if the court accepts the argument that the parent company owes no legal duty of care to those affected by its subsidiary operations.[58] Lack of knowledge of the harm and the absence of evidence of direct orders have also been used to limit the responsibility of companies or top executives. For example, in the Urapalma case discussed in Chapter 5, the original guilty verdict charged mostly lower level employees. It appeared that these lower level employees – including Afro-Colombians who represented peasant organizations working with the company – were induced to take the fall for the top management. In July 2017, however, one of the top business people involved in this case, named by several of the people as one of the leading actors behind the strategy of dispossession and displacement of these communities, did face a sentence for his involvement.[59] Thus, these strategies to shield the company and top executives do not always work.

The capacity of companies to avoid accountability by claiming that they are not bound by international law, the use of *forum non conveniens*, the corporate veil, delay tactics, SLAPP suits, and other strategies, perpetuates the victims' gap. As Richard Meeran states, "The absence of either an international or domestic means of accountability would represent a total denial of access to justice for victims of multinational corporations' operations in developing countries."[60]

[56] Ibid., 84.
[57] Interview by Laura Bernal-Bermúdez to Magistrate Uldi Teresa Jiménez, May 25, 2017, Bogotá, Colombia.
[58] Richard Meeran, "Liability of Multinational Corporations: A Critical Stage in the UK," in *Liability of Multinational Corporations under International Law*, ed. Menno T. Kamminga and Saman Zia-Zarifi (The Hague: Kluwer Law International, 2000), 261.
[59] Bernal-Bermúdez, "The Power of Business and the Power of People: Understanding Remedy and Corporate Accountability for Human Rights Violations. Colombia 1970–2014."
[60] Meeran, "Liability of Multinational Corporations: A Critical Stage in the UK," 264.

Wealthy corporations can more easily afford the cost of prolonging the length of the trial processes than poorer victims of abuse. This strategy, while legal, constrains victims' access to justice.

Legal strategies also include settlements. We refer to settlements as a veto strategy because they allow businesses to avoid judgment and precedents that might tip the balance in favor of future claims by victims and heighten the cost of human rights violations to businesses. Economic actors tend to offer financial settlement when they anticipate losing a case. Moreover, businesses tend to reach the settlement on the condition of two terms: no acknowledgment of wrongdoing and the confidentiality of the reparation amount. All of the settlements in the CATJ are confidential except one. The *Wiwa* v. *Shell* case disclosed the amount ($15.5 million) of compensation to ten plaintiffs.[61] The company also agreed to establish the Kiisi Trust, explored further in this chapter.

Settlements, in other words, only sometimes contribute to accountability and remedy. At other times they reinforce veto power. They impede legal precedent that could strengthen future claims against companies. They prevent the interpretation of law to confirm businesses' binding human rights obligations. While it would appear to be counterproductive for the company's reputation to engage in a prolonged court case only to settle in the end, it can be a rational calculation. Winning a case is better for reputations than settling, but settling is better than losing. Thus, companies may draw out cases to see if they can win, or settle if they sense they will lose. By avoiding a final judgment, moreover, they win a longer game. They deter future claimants, precedent-setting judgments, and unfavorable law-making.[62] They provide a way for companies to escape legal judgment in the short term and retain veto power over future cases in the long run.

Nonjudicial Strategies: Divide-and-Conquer

In addition to the legal strategies companies use to avoid accountability, their economic power also affords them nonjudicial forms of leverage over community or victim groups that have been used to attempt to block claims against them. Two examples from the CATJ – the Urapalma case in Colombia and

---

[61] Ingrid Wuerth, "Wiwa v. Shell: The $15.5 Million Settlement," *American Society of International Law*, September 9, 2009, www.asil.org/insights/volume/13/issue/14/wiwa-v-shell-155-million-settlement.

[62] See a study on US civil claims for insights, Catherine Albiston, "The Rule of Law and the Litigation Process: The Paradox of Losing by Winning," *Law & Society Review* no. 33 (1999): 869–910.

the Volkswagen case in Brazil – reveal divide-and-conquer strategies used by companies but that failed to stop judicial action.

The Urapalma S.A. case involved several Colombian palm oil companies' displacement of an Afro-Colombian community. To undermine the judicial claim of illegal and violent land expropriation, the companies sought business partnerships with certain members of the community.[63] To a certain degree this strategy worked. The community divided over how to best resolve the land occupation by the companies. Those who had accepted the partnerships with the companies opposed the adversarial legal process. Arguing that the community would benefit from the business opportunities offered by the companies, they advocated informal negotiations to resolve the dispute. The company further exploited divisions by allying with certain organization leaders who claimed to be the community's legal representatives. Against the company were community members allied with the church and NGOs. They persisted in their pursuit of judicial action and won. Their success is no doubt a result of the institutional support they received. It is probable that other poor, marginalized, less well-organized, and unsupported communities might not survive division and would accept company incentives to drop the case. Such communities would calculate that their likelihood of winning in court is low against well-resourced companies with social, political, and other connections.

Similarly, in the Volkswagen case in Brazil, union leaders worried that the company would attempt to avoid legal judgment by making private reparations to the named plaintiffs, thereby dividing and conquering solidarity behind the union movement's broader goal. Brazil's reparations law had already granted indemnity to individual victims. Moreover, the country's prevailing amnesty law prevented the pursuit of a legal judgment against the company. Thus, the union movement attempted to use legal action against the company to achieve other objectives: collective reparations, acknowledgment of wrongdoing, and exposing the widespread and systematic nature of corporate complicity in past human rights violations. Volkswagen was the first case, but the union movement aimed to prepare legal actions against more companies. The aims were thus greater than the single judicial action against Volkswagen. The movement hoped to reveal the alliance of companies

---

[63] The companies reached out to leaders of the community, urging them to create local business associations that would work together with the companies to apply for state funding and to benefit from the exploitation of their lands. Other members of the community started working as employees of the companies. See Bernal-Bermúdez, "The Power of Business and the Power of People: Understanding Remedy and Corporate Accountability for Human Rights Violations. Colombia 1970–2014."

before, and sustained throughout, the dictatorship to roll back workers' rights and representation that had been won in decades of labor movement struggles. A "cheap settlement" to a few plaintiffs, would not achieve those goals. The union leaders developed solidarity strategies to build support for the broader objectives. They succeeded in having the prosecutor's office reject the company's initial offer to settle by erecting a commemorative plaque. With the case ongoing, it is too early to know if the union movement will overcome a potentially divisive company indemnity strategy and achieve its truth, memory, and acknowledgment goals.

As stated previously with regard to settlements, private pay-offs are appealing to companies to offset the reputational and legal costs of judgment. Yet divide-and-conquer efforts are not always effective. In the Urapalma and Volkswagen cases, communities proved resilient in resisting the temptation to reach out-of-court agreements. In both of these cases, the communities worked with unions and NGOs to avoid such an outcome. Strong civil society movements can thus undermine divide-and-conquer strategies even when they are used by powerful companies with substantial economic resources and eager to protect their reputation. In some cases, as Urapalma shows, communities will hold out for a judicial sentence even when the odds of winning are quite low.

Unlawful, Intimidation, and Coercion Strategies

Bribery, violent threats, intimidation of witnesses, and outright violence are among the set of unlawful mechanisms used by businesses to block accountability efforts. We began this chapter with a well-publicized case of intimidation by a powerful company in Argentina against a member of Congress. Because they are often illegal, these tactics are difficult to track and document.

When communities have experienced these tactics in the past, or when they suspect that companies will engage in them, they will tend not to pursue claims for justice. Human rights lawyers building cases against companies in Argentina explained to us that many victims and witnesses of corporate violations fear personal reprisals against themselves or their relatives still working for those companies, and thus want to, but feel they cannot, participate in legal processes. These reprisals are often difficult to prove because companies find ways to disguise them as sanctions or dismissals for common workplace disputes unconnected to the claims of past human rights violations.

We also came across unlawful threats and intimidation by companies against legal practitioners engaged in investigations of corporate complicity in past human rights violations. Those individuals have asked us not to reveal details of these tactics in our publications. They also do not report them to authorities. Their reasons are that these kinds of tactics can become the main focus of the case, drawing attention toward an ongoing legal matter and away from past human rights abuses. The threats, moreover, are very difficult to connect to the business accused of a past human rights violation. They are rarely directly or obviously carried out by the company itself, but rather through a surrogate. Much effort would have to be spent proving intimidation and threats in the present, thereby derailing the focus on the past actions by the company.

Nonetheless, some of these cases have been registered. Front Line Defenders, the BHRRC, Amnesty International, the Inter-American Commission on Human Rights, and other governmental and nongovernmental organizations have begun to do so.[64] Front Line Defenders, for example, has documented the death threats and other forms of violent intimidation against members of the Comisión Intereclesial de Justicia y Paz (CIJP) as a result of their involvement in the palm oil (Urapalma) case. Five members of this Catholic Church-supported NGO have faced violent threats, including Danilo Rueda, one of the most active advocates for the Afro-Colombian and indigenous communities facing the palm oil companies, and Father Alberto Franco, the executive secretary of CIJP. These acts included a break-in at CIJP, the theft of computers and documents, an assassination attempt, and written and phoned death threats.[65]

Some of these efforts at intimidation are subtler and indirect, signaling a threat without constituting illegal behavior. In our own work, we have faced two such attempts. In the first, we were warned against pursuing our work on corporate complicity in human rights violations by a reviewer for an application for research funding. Presumably a scholar, this anonymous reviewer suggested that, given the power of business, we would destroy our careers if we pursued our line of research on corporate complicity in human rights

[64] On the efforts to protect indigenous human rights defenders from mega-projects, see Nancy Tapias Torrado and the Inter-American Commission on Human Rights, "Criminalization of Human Rights Defenders" (Washington, DC, 2015), www.oas.org/en/iachr/reports/pdfs/criminalization2016.pdf; Amnesty International, "Defending Human Rights in the Americas: Necessary, Legitimate and Dangerous" (Amnesty International: London, 2014).

[65] See Frontline Defenders, "Threats and Harassment against Members of the Comisión Intereclesial de Justicia y Paz," 2013, www.justiciaypazcolombia.com/threats-and-harassment-against-members-of-the-comision-intereclesial-de-justicia-y-paz/; Frontline Defenders, "Shots Fired at Vehicle of Human Rights Defender Father Alberto Franco," 2013, www.frontlinedefenders.org/en/case/case-history-father-alberto-franco; Frontline Defenders, "Break-in at Home of Human Rights Defender Mr Danilo Rueda and Theft of Items Containing Sensitive Information," 2011, www.frontlinedefenders.org/en/case/case-history-danilo-rueda.

violations. We did not receive the grant. But more importantly, we were given a warning to stop investigating companies. Second, after presenting a public report on our research findings on Colombia, several articles in the press written by groups associated with businesses accused the study of undermining the private sector. In one, our report was identified with "guerrilla" tactics to "change the political model" in the country on the "the corpse of the business sector."[66] Because Colombians have been murdered for assumed associations with the revolutionary left-wing agenda, we and our other colleagues in Colombia interpreted the statements as intimidation. Taking this subtle act of intimidation to court for slander would have proved lengthy, costly, and ultimately unlikely to succeed.

Mobilization Strategies: The Business Lobby and Campaigns

The use of intimidation and illegal tactics may reflect a sense of weakening business veto power and thus the need to take action. Mobilizing against international and domestic policies or laws that challenge impunity may also reflect a sense of weakness and the need to reassert power when it is threatened. In particular, funding and sponsoring campaigns that guarantee impunity are likely to occur when the business community senses that its control over outcomes is beginning to slip away.

At the international level, David Weissbrodt suggests, for example, that the reason why the UN Code of Conduct was never adopted and the OECD Code of Conduct failed to focus on human rights "may have been the result of opposition by transnational corporations to such specific binding standards."[67] One additional forceful and nearly successful effort to develop binding efforts was defeated in the final stage by a powerful international business lobby with allies within influential states. This is the case of the UN Draft Norms, discussed in Chapter 2.

According to Weissbrodt and his associates, and documented in other studies, the UN Draft Norms were narrowly defeated only after an

---

[66] The text stated, "What we cannot forget is that in exactly this way, the guerrilla had a totalitarian political project that implied the seizing of power. Dejusticia and the connected organizations have a project to 'change the model' that implies stepping on the corpse of the business sector. And destroying it starts with discrediting it." Mauricio Botero Caicedo, "Entre la ignorancia y la mala fe," *Las2Orillas,* 2018, www.las2orillas.co/entre-la-ignorancia-y-la-mala-fe/.

[67] Weissbrodt, *The Beginning of a Sessional Working Group on Transnational Corporations within the UN Sub-Commission on Prevention of Discrimination and Protection of Minorities,* 127.

international business lobby mobilized. Weissbrodt describes a constructive dialogue with the US mission in the months leading up to the vote. The response changed when the International Chamber of Commerce contacted the White House, alarmed by the "problematic" UN Draft Norms. The US representative on the Sub-Commission, who had not previously raised any concerns, confronted Weissbrodt, asking, "What is this all about?" Brochures also appeared at the Commission on the day of the vote, prepared by the International Chamber of Commerce (ICC), the International Organization of Employers (IOE), and the International Confederation of Free Trade Unions (ICFTU), who opposed the passing of the UN Draft Norms.

In the joint statement prepared by the ICC and the IOE on the UN Draft Norms, they referred to themselves as "the most representative global business organizations." Among their various arguments, the organizations highlighted that business did not have human rights obligations under international law. The UN Draft Norms, they stated, "are predicated on the belief that human rights can best be advanced by circumventing national political and legal frameworks and establishing international legal obligations for multinational companies that do not exist at the national level and do not apply to domestic companies."[68] Because of the effective lobbying by these forces, several votes assumed to be favorable to the UN Draft Norms turned negative, defeating them.[69] Weissbrodt notes that the lobby's effectiveness reflected business power and influence over the representatives to the Council, particularly in the US and the UK missions.

Jena Martin and Karen E. Bravo describe the defeat of the UN Draft Norms as "a combination of full-throated objection and silent rejection."[70] Denise Wallace suggests that through the defeat "these business groups lobbed a cautionary threat to the HRC that it would be business as usual – obstruction, avoidance, and political pressure – if the Council veered from the dictates of

---

[68] International Chamber of Commerce and International Organization of Employers, "Joint Views of the IOE and ICC on the Draft Norms on the Responsibilities of Transnational Corporations and Other Business Enterprises with Regard to Human Rights. U.N. ESCOR, 55," in *International Human Rights: Law, Policy, and Process*, ed. David S. Weissbrodt, Joan Fitzpatrick, and Frank Newman (Cincinnati, OH: Anderson Pub. Co., 2001).

[69] The UN Guiding Principles (or "Ruggie Principles") replaced the UN Draft Norms. Ruggie himself has noted that binding agreements around human rights were unacceptable to the business community and therefore only nonbinding agreements would pass the Council. See Ruggie, *Just Business: Multinational Corporations and Human Rights*.

[70] Martin and Bravo, "Introduction: More of the Same? Or Introduction of a New Paradigm?," 3. See also Giovanni Mantilla, "Emerging International Human Rights Norms for Transnational Corporations," *Global Governance* 15, no. 2 (2009): 279–98.

business ... These business lobbyists are unequivocal in their promise to intentionally obstruct any attempts to enact binding regulations."[71]

John Ruggie, who drafted the UN Guiding Principles (UNGPs) that replaced the UN Draft Norms after the defeat, does not refer to the business lobby. Instead, he calls the UNGPs the solution to a "stalemate,"[72] boasting support from multi-stakeholder groups.[73] Such a depiction ignores the absence of human rights groups in the endorsement of the UNGPs.[74] These groups attempted in vain to lobby Ruggie, specifically to avoid "the lowest common denominator" approach to business and human rights, to recognize businesses' human rights obligations, states' duties to enforce them, and apply "legal jurisprudence and doctrine concerning the direct applicability of international law to private actors."[75] The process and the outcome of the UNGPs' adoption is a story of business's organizational power and influence.

Weissbrodt rejects the notion that the UN Draft Norms are dead, arguing instead that "they keep coming back ... people still use them."[76] The way in which they have been revived in the Human Rights Council could be seen as a form of "corporate accountability from below." An "international legally binding instrument on transnational corporations and other business enterprises with respect to human rights" in the Human Rights Council was sponsored by Ecuador and South Africa,[77] co-sponsored by Bolivia, Cuba,

[71] Wallace, *Human Rights and Business: A Policy-Oriented Perspective*, 267.
[72] John Gerard Ruggie, "Interim Report of the Special Representative of the Secretary-General on the Issue of Human Rights and Transnational Corporations and Other Business Enterprises U.N. Doc.E/CN.4/2006/97," in *International Human Rights: Law, Policy, and Process*, ed. David S. Weissbrodt, Joan Fitzpatrick, and Frank Newman (Cincinnati, OH: Anderson Pub. Co., 2001).
[73] Ruggie, *Just Business: Multinational Corporations and Human Rights*, xxi.
[74] Scholars echoed concerns over the absence of key NGOs. Denise Wallace argues that "individuals and indigenous peoples, the victims of corporate human rights abuse ... [were] ... noticeably missing" in the group of stakeholders involved in the discussion of the UNGPs. Wallace, *Human Rights and Business: A Policy-Oriented Perspective*, 267.
[75] Amnesty International, "Letter from Joint NGO's to John Ruggie, Special Representative to the U.N. Secretary-General on Business and Human Rights, Joint NGO Position on the Interim Report from the Special Representative of the U.N. Secretary General on Business and Human Rights," in *International Human Rights: Law, Policy, and Process*, ed. David S. Weissbrodt, Joan Fitzpatrick, and Frank Newman (Cincinnati, OH: Anderson Pub. Co., 2001).
[76] Interview with Barbara Frey and David S. Weissbrodt by Leigh A. Payne and Mary Beall, Human Rights Center, Mondale School of Law, University of Minnesota, April 20, 2017.
[77] See United Nations Human Rights Council, "Elaboration of an International Legally Binding Instrument on Transnational Corporations and Other Business Enterprises with Respect to Human Rights A/HRC/26/L.22/Rev.1."

and Venezuela, and subsequently by Algeria, El Salvador, Nicaragua, and Senegal. The twenty votes in favor of the Resolution came from Latin America, Africa, Asia, or Eurasian representatives.[78] The abstaining votes were also from the Global South.[79] In contrast, all of the fourteen countries that opposed the measure, with the exception of Korea and Japan, were European or North American.[80] Should this initiative pass, and surpass the potential veto power of business, it will confirm the argument regarding "corporate accountability from below."

Business mobilization in foreign courts can also act as a veto strategy. The ideological shift in the US Supreme Court that led to the *Kiobel* and *Jesner* decisions weakening corporate accountability for foreign firms in US courts, did not happen by accident. Corporations are known for their campaign contributions that help elect presidents and legislators in the United States who are favorable to business. Those presidents then nominate, and the Senate confirms, Supreme Court judges. A careful study confirms the findings that the current US Supreme Court is more favorable to business than at any time since World War II.[81] Studies further suggest that the pro-business bent of the US Supreme Court, as well as the lower courts from which those justices are typically drawn, has resulted from increased business electoral campaign contributions that have circumvented disclosure rules and constraints on funding limits.[82] These contributions also enable well-connected members of the business community to make suggestions to, or lobby, executives about possible judicial candidates for consideration, further reinforcing veto power and the status quo of corporate impunity.

Colombia provides another example of business lobbies and campaigns to sustain the status quo of impunity. There is evidence that economic actors financed the No campaign against the approval of the peace agreement via a referendum in 2016. A journalistic investigation from Verdadabierta.com

---

[78] Algeria, Benin, Burkina Faso, China, Congo, Côte d'Ivoire, Cuba, Ethiopia, India, Indonesia, Kazakhstan, Kenya, Morocco, Namibia, Pakistan, Philippines, Russian Federation, South Africa, Venezuela (Bolivarian Republic of), and Vietnam.

[79] Argentina, Botswana, Brazil, Chile, Costa Rica, Gabon, Kuwait, Maldives, Mexico, Peru, Saudi Arabia, Sierra Leone, and United Arab Emirates.

[80] Austria, Czech Republic, Estonia, France, Germany, Ireland, Italy, Japan, Montenegro, Republic of Korea, Romania, the former Yugoslav Republic of Macedonia, the United Kingdom of Great Britain and Northern Ireland, and the United States of America.

[81] Lee Epstein, William M. Landes, and Richard A. Posner, "How Business Fares in the Supreme Court," *Minnesota Law Review* 97 (2013): 1431.

[82] Billy Corriher, "Big Business Taking over State Supreme Courts," *Center for American Progress*, 2012, www.americanprogress.org/issues/courts/reports/2012/08/13/11974/big-business-taking-over-state-supreme-courts/.

revealed, for example, that three firms and a businessman that financed the campaign had been named by a paramilitary leader as financial supporters of the Bloque Bananero (Banana Growers Bloc) of the AUC paramilitary groups.[83] Two members of that Bloc have been accused of forced displacement and forced evictions in the Urabá Region. When on October 2, 2016 the No vote won, the Government was forced to renegotiate the agreement and to satisfy some of the requests from those leading the No campaign, including the business sector.

One of the business community's main concerns is the design of the transitional justice process. In particular, it feared the Special Jurisdiction for Peace (JEP) would lead to a witch hunt where members of illegal armed groups would falsely and indiscriminately accuse firms and businesspeople of human rights abuses. After the defeat of the government's referendum on peace, former President Álvaro Uribe, a businessman, asked for the new agreement to exclude the possibility of the JEP prosecuting third parties to the armed conflict, especially businesspeople. Although the government did not succumb to this pressure to exclude business groups, it clarified that the new peace agreement would only include those members of the business community who had played active and decisive roles in the armed conflict. This agreement was approved by Congress in December 2016.

On April 4, 2017, Congress issued Legislative Act No. 01 of 2017 regulating the JEP. The Constitutional Court reviewed the Legislative Act. In November 2017, it decided that the JEP was not the appropriate court for business accountability cases, referring them instead to ordinary jurisdiction where impunity has been the rule.[84] A researcher from the prosecutor's office, who asked to remain anonymous, explained that strong veto power of business is undermining corporate accountability efforts through ordinary jurisdiction. In his view, this is the work of top officials within the prosecutor's office allied to the business community and the Duque government (endorsed by Colombian business). As a result of these efforts, the reports and investigations revealing the role of some economic actors in the conflict are quietly being shelved.[85]

In sum, the following set of strategies were used by businesses to avoid accountability: legal, nonjudicial divide-and-conquer, unlawful and

---

[83] Verdadabierta.com, "Los cuestionamientos a bananeros detrás del No," *Verdadabierta.com*, 2016, https://verdadabierta.com/los-cuestionamientos-a-los-bananeros-detras-del-no/.

[84] See Sentencia C-674 de 2017 of the Colombian Constitutional Court, available at www .elespectador.com/sites/default/files/pdf-file/c-674_de_2017.pdf.

[85] Interview with public official of the Prosecutor's Office in Colombia by Laura Bernal-Bermúdez on August 28, 2018. The official asked to remain anonymous.

intimidation, and lobbying. We have suggested that in addition to these direct strategies, businesses' most successful veto power is invisible: the social, political, and economic influence over how a judge interprets evidence or how member companies on international bodies evaluate businesses as potential abusers. Although we show that the business community and individual businesses have substantial power, we have further argued that they do not always use that power, and when they do, they do not always win. Thus, one way to effectively apply force to lift corporate accountability is by reducing corporate veto power.

REDUCING VETO POWER

What we refer to as business veto strategies over corporate accountability, other scholars have called the "logics of limiting responsibility." They add that these logics are "subversive of the quintessential claim that human rights are universal in character and to be treated as such whenever and wherever they are threatened or denied."[86] While the logics may persist, the veto strategies used by business may not be as powerful as they once were. Some scholars in the business and human rights field have made this claim and attempt to explain it. Douglass Cassel mentions the fear of public criticism as a motivator behind shifts that may enhance corporate human rights.[87] Barbara Frey also refers to corporations' willingness to consider the human rights implications of their activities as a shift in attitudes.[88] These shifts no doubt exist within the business community, but we have not found that they are sufficient to remove business opposition to binding and enforceable human rights obligations. To assess the possibility of reducing business veto power, we look at some of the indicators of shifts: from corporate social responsibility to business and human rights; firm-level investigations into past violations; voluntary victims' reparations funds; and companies as human rights defenders.

---

[86] Grear and Weston, "The Betrayal of Human Rights and the Urgency of Universal Corporate Accountability: Reflections on a Post-Kiobel Lawscape," 23.

[87] Douglass Cassel cited in David S. Weissbrodt, "The Beginning of a Sessional Working Group on Transnational Corporations within the UN Sub-Commission on Prevention of Discrimination and Protection of Minorities," in *Liability of Multinational Corporations under International Law* (The Hague: Kluwer Law International, 2000), 119–38.

[88] Barbara A. Frey, "The Legal and Ethical Responsibilities of Transnational Corporations in the Protection of International Human Rights," *Minnesota Journal of Global Trade* 6, no. 153 (1997): 188.

From Corporate Social Responsibility to Business and Human Rights

Companies' adoption of corporate social responsibility (CSR) initiatives since the 1970s has been interpreted as a shift in the attitudes of economic actors regarding human rights.[89] These initiatives intensified in the 1980s and 1990s, following industry disasters, such as Bhopal and Chernobyl. Efforts to control negligent and abusive firms, and to salvage industries' reputation through business-led initiatives, resulted. At the very least, these initiatives marked a rhetorical commitment in the business community to adhere to international human rights standards and standards of ethical behavior.[90] Further emphasizing this normative commitment, Cassel and Ramasastry refer to a reputable survey in which senior corporate executives overwhelmingly acknowledged firms' responsibility to protect human rights.[91] Because recognition of norms is the first step toward the development of a norms cascade,[92] this would appear to be a positive shift.

This shift from earlier views is often noted in reference to the statement attributed to Milton Friedman that "there is only one social responsibility of business – to use its resources to engage in activities designed to increase its profits."[93] That oft-repeated refrain leaves out the second part of Friedman's statement: "So long as it stays within the rules of the game, which is to say, engages in open and free competition without deception or more." Unless one were to cynically argue that Friedman was unaware of rules regarding

---

[89] Tagi Sagafi-nejad and John H. Dunning, *The UN and Transnational Corporations: From Code of Conduct to Global Compact* (Bloomington, IN: Indiana University Press, 2008).

[90] Alex Wawryk, "Regulating Transnational Corporations through Corporate Codes of Conduct," in *Transnational Corporations and Human Rights*, ed. Jedrzej George Frynas and Scott Pegg (Palgrave Macmillan, 2003); Virginia Haufler, "Disclosure as Governance: The Extractive Industries Transparency Initiative and Resource Management in the Developing World," *Global Environmental Politics* 10, no. 3 (2010): 53–73; Laura Bernal-Bermúdez and Tricia D. Olsen, "Business, Human Rights and Sustainable Development," in *The SAGE Handbook of International Corporate and Public Affairs*, ed. Phil Harris and Craig S. Fleisher (London: SAGE Publications, 2017).

[91] Cassel and Ramasastry, "White Paper: Options for a Treaty on Business and Human Rights."

[92] See Martha Finnemore and Kathryn Sikkink, "International Norm Dynamics and Political Change," ed. Martha Finnemore, *International Organization* 52, no. 4 (1998): 887; Thomas Risse and Stephen Ropp, "Introduction and Overview," in *The Persistent Power of Human Rights*, ed. Thomas Risse, Stephen Ropp, and Kathryn Sikkink (Cambridge: Cambridge University Press, 2013); Sunstein, "Social Norms and Social Roles."

[93] Milton Friedman, *Capitalism and Freedom* (Chicago, IL: University of Chicago Press, 1963); Milton Friedman, "The Social Responsibility of Business Is to Increase Its Profits," *The New York Times Magazine*, September 13, 1970, www.colorado.edu/studentgroups/libertarians/issues/friedman-soc-resp-business.html. See also discussion in Wallace, *Human Rights and Business: A Policy-Oriented Perspective*, 90.

business respect for human rights, it is clear that even this statement, made nearly five decades ago, viewed human rights abuses as antithetical to the ethics of profit-making and corporations' social responsibility. Nonetheless, Friedman's statement does not go as far as more recent refrains circulating in business communities that "human rights are good for business."[94] The idea that good human rights practices could enhance profit-making is addressed in Chris Avery's coverage of the point of view from business on this topic. He quotes Marjorie Kelly, editor of *Business Ethics* magazine, who states, "We're going through a mind-change. Most of us still carry around the subliminal idea that ruthless behavior beats the competition and good behavior is money out of pocket. But the data shows that the traditional idea is wrong. Social responsibility makes sense in purely capitalistic terms."[95]

Some scholars have noted the irony in the absence of support for international regulation of business behavior. Kamminga and Zia-Zarifi, for example, state, "In contrast to their great enthusiasm for binding international rules that protect and facilitate their activity, MNCs have argued vociferously against any sort of international rules that would hold them accountable for any damages they cause." These authors add that "[i]t is now fashionable, and strongly encouraged by MNCs themselves, to discuss the responsibilities of corporations in terms of social accountability, good governance, responsible citizenship, or other such formulations, in lieu of international legal obligations."[96]

Avery warns against this attitude among businesses. Traditional CSR, he contends, exposes companies to risk in ways that a business and human rights (BHR) approach does not. The BHR framework overcomes the top-down, selectively applied, profit-oriented, and company-centered CSR approach. He highlights the work of the Business Leaders Initiative on Human Rights (BLIHR) attempting to "mainstream human rights within their operations" to make human rights central to "the social dimensions of business responsibility

---

[94] Among other works, see Margaret Jungk, "Why Businesses Say Human Rights Is Their Most Urgent Sustainability Priority," *Business and Social Responsibility*, October 13, 2016, https://www.bsr.org/en/our-insights/blog-view/why-businesses-say-human-rights-most-urgent-sustainability-priority; Grace Segran, "Mary Robinson: Human Rights Are Good for Business," *Insead: Knowledge*, July 26, 2008, https://knowledge.insead.edu/ethics/mary-robinson-human-rights-are-good-for-business-2093.

[95] Quote from Bennett Daviss, "Profits from Principle: Five Forces Redefining Business," *The Futurist*, 1999, 30. Cited by Avery, "Business and Human Rights in a Time of Change."

[96] Kamminga and Zia-Zarifi, "Liability of Multinational Corporations under International Law: An Introduction," 9.

and issues of corporate governance."[97] Although the number of companies that joined the BLIHR have increased since Avery wrote that article, it remains small, from eleven to fourteen.[98] In looking at the BLIHR firms, most of them are not well-known or even clearly businesses (rather than foundations). Among the businesses, four are in our database as having faced some form of accountability for human rights obligations. Coca-Cola has faced litigation in the United States for its alleged role in atrocities during Apartheid in South Africa and in Guatemala. Paramilitary leaders in Colombia also mentioned the company as allegedly financing the conflict. General Electric was also involved in the ATS Apartheid trial in the United States and was also mentioned in the Brazilian truth commission report for alleged complicity with the dictatorship. Hewlett-Packard was also included in the ATS Apartheid trial. Novartis was included as a defendant in the ATS Apartheid trial and in one of the Holocaust class actions before US courts. Follow-up research could determine if past costs of litigation or reputational costs engender these firms' push for business and human rights.

There is evidence, in other words, of change within the business community. It is slow in coming and it does not yet enjoy widespread support within countries or among major companies in the world. It is unlikely that businesses will voluntarily reduce their veto power without pressure from states or the international community, or serious threats to impunity for human rights violations.

Economic Actors' Truth-Gathering Efforts

Individual efforts within companies or business associations also provide evidence of their willingness to accept the notion of corporate human rights responsibility. By investigating and documenting past violations, certain economic actors acknowledge wrongdoing and seemingly condemn such behavior in the future. This is not a new strategy by companies. Several firms acknowledged their complicity in Nazi regime atrocities and hired historians to investigate their role. In some cases, these historians went beyond in-firm projects to make public the company's past. The Deutsche Bahn's historian, for example, put together a "Special Trains to Death" exhibition in the central station that claimed "without the Reichsbahn [its predecessor] the industrial

---

[97] Christopher Avery, "The Difference between CSR and Human Rights," *Corporate Citizenship Briefing*, August/September 2006, issue 89, www.business-humanrights.org/sites/default/files/reports-and-materials/Avery-difference-between-CSR-and-human-rights-Aug-Sep-2006.pdf.

[98] ABB, AREVA, Barclays, Coca-Cola, Ericsson, General Electric, Gap, HP, National Grid, Newmont, Novartis Foundation for Sustainable Development, Novo Nordisk, StatoilHydro, Zain.

murder of millions of people would not have been possible."[99] Notably, this recognition of the company's involvement in past atrocity occurred when the threat of judicial action was no longer present.[100]

Volkswagen was another of the companies that hired a historian to investigate its past in Nazi Germany. When investigations began against Volkswagen for its involvement in the repression of workers during the Brazilian dictatorship, the German company sent its historian to explore the allegations. In November 2016, Volkswagen sent Professor Christopher Kopper from Bielefeld University to conduct a study about the charges raised by the union movement of the company's collaboration with the dictatorship and complicity in human rights violations.[101] Kopper's investigations revealed "regular cooperation between the Brazilian factory security service and the police,"[102] hinting at corporate complicity in the repression of the company's workers during the dictatorship. Kopper derived this information from the repressive police (DOPS) archives that documented conversations overheard in the employee locker room, information that only the company could have compiled. The historian also found the "blacklists" of so-called subversive employees that the company had helped produce and circulate among firms located in the industrial belt surrounding São Paulo. Kopper's investigations cast doubt on the company's claim that the German headquarters was unaware of the Brazilian subsidiary's action. As reported by the *Folha de São Paulo* newspaper: "Kopper stated that it is feasible the VW headquarters was not entirely aware of the Brazil plant's activities throughout most of the dictatorship. But that changed in 1979 when a group of Brazilian workers went to Wolfsburg for a conference and confronted then-CEO Toni

---

[99] Suzanne Kill, cited in Kate Connolly, "German Railways Admits Complicity in Holocaust," *The Guardian*, January 23, 2008, www.theguardian.com/world/2008/jan/23/secondworldwar.germany.

[100] The 1973 trial of Albert Ganzenmüller, secretary of transport and deputy director of the Reichsbahn, for the firm's involvement in the deportations to death camps, ended after he had a heart attack on the first day. Ganzenmüller lived twenty-three years after the trial ended without threat of further prosecution.

[101] The company had previously sent an historian to Brazil who met with workers and the prosecutor's office and appeared to find sufficient evidence of the company's culpability. Shortly after returning to Germany, however, the historian resigned his position, and was replaced. While the timing suggests that he was forced to resign due to his probes and promises in Brazil, the most common interpretation is that it was a coincidence, that his relationship with the company's management was already strained because of a separate incident.

[102] Deutsche Welle (DW), "VW Worked Hand in Hand with Brazil's Military Dictatorship," *Deutsche Welle*, July 24, 2017, www.dw.com/en/vw-worked-hand-in-hand-with-brazils-military-dictatorship/a-39814070.

Schmücker about the arrests."[103] According to a German news source, in 1979 former President Luis Inácio Lula da Silva, when he was a trade union leader, informed Chancellor Helmut Schmidt of the company's involvement in the dictatorship's repression[104] Kopper reportedly admitted to the newspaper that the company should apologize for its involvement.

In Argentina, we found two such truth exercises carried out by economic actors. In the first, the National Stock Exchange (CNV) began looking into corporate complicity in human rights violations. The CNV hired three academics to investigate and reveal to the public the role different member businesses had played in the repressive apparatus during the dictatorship.[105] In this way, it acted as a kind of business association within the state investigating business human rights abuses. In the second, the new owners of an Argentine firm turned over its archive to the national prosecutor's office, presumably to avoid any connection between the current firm and past owners' alleged complicity in human rights abuses.

These examples suggest that at times companies and economic actors' associations might collaborate with investigations and participate in truth-gathering exercises to understand business's role in past violations. The few cases we have found of such exercises suggest that this is a rare occurrence, however. In some cases – such as the Volkswagen case and the Argentine firm that turned over its files – the motivation has less to do with a new view toward human rights, full disclosure, or remedying past harm, than with the desire to avoid corporate liability. That is, by investigating economic actors' own history of human rights violations, the current managers and directors will be less likely to be held judicially accountable for decisions taken by their predecessors.

Nonetheless, the acknowledgment of wrongdoing through these firm-level or association-level truth-gathering efforts may have two effects in terms of the veto power of business. First, they show that businesses themselves, as well as the corporate communities in which they operate, can no longer deny

---

[103] Jean-Philip Struck, "Historian Reveals Ties between Brazilian Volkswagen Affiliate and the Military Dictatorship," *Folha de São Paulo*, April 8, 2017, www1.folha.uol.com.br/internacional/en/brazil/2017/08/1907170-historian-reveals-ties-between-brazilian-volkswagen-affiliate-and-the-military-dictatorship.shtml.

[104] Deutsche Welle (DW), "VW Worked Hand in Hand with Brazil's Military Dictatorship."

[105] See Alejandra Dandan and Hannah Franzki, "Entre analisis histórico y responsabilidad jurídica: El caso Ledesma," in *Cuentas pendientes: Los cómplices económicos de la dictadura,* ed. Horacio Verbitsky and Juan Pablo Bohoslavsky (Buenos Aires: Siglo Veintiuno Editores, 2013); Maria Celeste Perosino, Bruno Nápoli, and Walter Bosisio, *Economía, política y sistema financiero: La última dictadura cívico-militar en la CNV* (Buenos Aires: Comisión Nacional de Valores, 2013).

complicity in past violence. Second, this exposure to the truth from the business sector may motivate some companies unblemished by such past wrongdoing to take a stand against such behavior. With businesses willing to distance themselves from such activity, the community begins to fragment and lose some of its power to veto accountability efforts. This is more likely when civil society mobilization brings to light corporate complicity in the violence.

Contributions to Remedy Victims

Businesses have, at times, paid into compensation funds, though their motives in doing so may be far from pure. For example, the German Foundation for Remembrance, Responsibility, and the Future (EVZ) was established as a result of class action lawsuits filed in US courts in 1998 and pressure from US groups and the US government.[106] The Foundation received $5 billion contributed equally by the government and industry to compensate surviving forced laborers during World War II. It is not clear how many or which industries made contributions,[107] or based on what motivations. Because the donations did not materialize until after forced laborers initiated lawsuits against companies, they are viewed by some as efforts to avoid litigation. While contributions, such as the Volkswagen donation, recognize "moral responsibility," they explicitly deny "legal responsibility."[108] Ryf claims that "German industries have paid only nominal amounts to slave labor victims, and most victims have not received any compensation."[109] The Foundation is considered to be a way for firms to whitewash their complicity in Nazi era crimes rather than any serious effort at accountability or remedy.

---

[106] "Nazi-Era Claims against German Companies," *American Journal of International Law* 94, no. 4 (2000): 682.

[107] The American Jewish Committee found 255 corporations that had employed forced labor and only 17 that contributed to the compensation fund. Norman Kempster, "Agreement Reached on Nazi Slave Reparations," *Los Angeles Times*, December 15, 1999, http://articles .latimes.com/1999/dec/15/news/mn-44055. Another study mentions 6300 corporate donations to the compensation fund. Toby Helm, "Germany to Compensate Nazi Slave-Labourers," *The Telegraph*, May 31, 2001, www.telegraph.co.uk/news/worldnews/europe/germany/1332474/ Germany-to-compensate-Nazi-slave-labourers.html. In addition, individual companies such as Volkswagen and three major Swiss banks set up independent foundations to pay out compensation. Edmund L. Andrews, "Volkswagen to Create $12 Million Fund for Nazi-Era Laborers," *The New York Times*, September 11, 1998, www.nytimes.com/1998/09/11/world/ volkswagen-to-create-12-million-fund-for-nazi-era-laborers.html.

[108] Andrews, "Volkswagen to Create $12 Million Fund for Nazi-Era Laborers."

[109] Ryf, "Burger-Fischer v. Degussa Ag: U.S. Courts Allow Siemens and Degussa to Profit from Holocaust Slave Labor," 155–78. Cited to Burger-Fisher, 65 F. Supp.2d at 271; Ferencz, supra note 3 at 209–11.

The process in South Africa is also shrouded in doubt regarding companies' motivations. Certain economic actors attended the Special Hearings held by the South African Truth and Reconciliation Commission; they were not required to do so. Those who appeared recognized, at the very least, that they had been the beneficiaries of a violent and illegitimate regime. Some of the members of the business community recognized their debt to South African society for their passive complicity with the Apartheid regime, specifically their failure to help end it. These businesspeople contributed to the voluntary reparations fund. The contributions were quite small relative to the numbers of victims and the vast wealth some of the companies derived from Apartheid's exploitative labor and natural resources systems.

The Kiisi Trust was established in 2009, using funds from the settlement of the US ATS Saro-Wiwa case against Shell. The case accused Shell of complicity in the Nigerian military's arbitrary detention, torture, and execution of the Ogoni people who protested the company's cultural and environmental destruction of their community and land. Trust Africa states that "[t]he settlement is recognized as a victory for human rights and environmental justice in Nigeria and as a pivotal step towards holding corporations accountable for complicity in human rights violations, wherever they may be committed." Rather than individual reparations, the fund supports "education, health, community development, educational endowments, skills development, occupational development, women's programmes, small enterprise support, and adult literacy."[110] The Kiisi Trust had potential to overcome the weaknesses of past reparations funds and to create a model replicable in other judicial settlements. In 2014, five years after it had been established, *Africa Confidential* lamented the fact that the Trust still had not distributed any funds. In April 2018 the Fund was still seeking applicants for posts. But by August 2018, the Fund announced its scholarship program, with deadlines for applications in December 2018.

No systematic study exists of corporate reparations funds. Few such funds exist, and those that do lack information. While they are touted as a positive way to recognize the debt companies owe to victims, they do not hold businesses legally accountable for directly and indirectly contributing to human rights violations. They are thus often viewed cynically by victims and human rights groups as either "blood money" to avoid prosecution or shallow compensation for guilt.

---

[110] Trust Africa, "The Kiisi Trust Benefit the Ogoni People," *Trust Africa*, n.d., www.trustafrica .org/en/programme/philanthropy-advisory-services/kiisi-trust-fund.

On the other hand, if they are popularly viewed as a form of accountability for past complicity, they do play a role in reducing business veto power. They show that businesses have not always had full impunity for violations and at moments they have paid the price for past activity. The problem with this strategy to reduce business veto power is monitoring or enforcing those payments and their equitable distribution to victims and their communities, particularly when they are voluntary.

The Fragmented Business Community

When an executive in BP's political risk analysis division announced to one of the authors of this book that "human rights is good for business," he was not referring to the legacy of human rights violations in authoritarian regimes and armed conflict. During those times, complicity seems to have been better for business. South African businesses that participated in the TRC honestly attested to how they profited from their complicity in the Apartheid structures. Economic actors benefited from authoritarian regimes and armed conflict through: wage repression, violent control of unions and left-wing workers, suppression of strikes and other labor actions, clearing land for rural development, stimulus packages to heighten private investment, and impunity for illegal trade and profit. In those situations, what was good for business was a pro-business repressive apparatus or armed protection.

Different truth-gathering exercises have also shown how businesses used the repressive apparatus during authoritarian regimes to undermine other businesses. One highly controversial case involves the Papel Prensa company in Argentina. Owned by David Graiver, the company provided newsprint for the major newspapers in the country. Graiver, who died in a mysterious airplane accident in Mexico in 1976, was the assumed banker for the Montonero guerrilla group. After his death, the Argentine military repressive apparatus allegedly picked up Graiver's wife and brother. Under coercion, possibly including torture, the Graiver family turned over the newsprint company to the military. A state company was formed that was subsequently sold to the top three print media companies in the country at the time (Clarín, La Nación, and La Razón), providing them with a monopoly on the print media industry.

The details of use of the repressive apparatus in the case are murky. Some contend that Graiver faked his death. Graiver's wife and brother have changed their testimonies over time, further confusing the story. The simple story advanced by the Cristina Fernández de Kirchner government cast the Graiver family as victims of the civil (business)-military violence due to their support for the left-wing movements for social change; this version of the Papel Prensa case does not entirely hold up to scrutiny.[111] Nonetheless, evidence does confirm that business people denounced others as leftists to the security apparatus to gain economic advantage, specifically acquiring those firms when the owners were detained by the military for suspected subversion.[112]

The Brazilian National Truth Commission report reveals the ostracism within the business community of those who did not embrace the coup and the regime it implanted. According to the report, two powerful businessmen in Brazil – Emilio de Morães and José Mindlin – did not succumb to the pressure from their colleagues. Their example shows that businesses did not have to be complicit; they could have acted morally, legally, and responsibly to avoid participating in the violence. While it may be true that these two enterprises had become so powerful that their owners could avoid reprisals for taking an independent course, it is also true that other powerful companies did not follow that same path. If more firms had proved unwilling to collaborate in the repression, the regimes would have lost an important base of financial support and legitimacy and collapsed sooner rather than later. Tens of thousands of lives likely would have been saved.

Although some companies did not endorse authoritarian regimes, we found no evidence of economic actors who took action to defend human rights during these periods of repression and conflict. We have looked for, but have not found, modern-day "Schindlers," or economic actors who aimed to stop violence and protect victims or potential victims of atrocity. Contemporary Schindlers might recognize that they and their companies benefited – even if only indirectly – from a system that violated human rights and assume their responsibility by paying generously into an effectively designed reparations fund to support the community of victims in the new – post-dictatorship, post-conflict – society. They might engage pro-actively in efforts to remedy victims

---

[111] Before Graiver mysteriously died, he was under investigation for embezzlement by Manhattan District Attorney Robert Morgenthau due to the 1976 American Bank & Trust failure. Morgenthau eventually dropped the case, but he assumed that Graiver faked his death to escape conviction. Graiver was also accused by the Montoneros for stealing the funds they had invested with him; another reason he is suspected of faking his death to avoid retaliation.

[112] The study conducted for the Argentine National Stock Exchange (CNV) and its role during the dictatorship, reveals that some members of the business community had denounced their competitors as "subversives" and they were subsequently detained by the repressive apparatus. Once detained, their shares or their companies were sold to those who denounced them. Some of the detained businessmen were never seen alive again; others survived torture and lived to tell the story.

through jobs, community development, or other strategies.[113] They might participate more widely in initiatives like the BLIHR.

In Colombia, some efforts are underway to directly engage companies in the peace process. Rather than appealing to their guilt over the past, these initiatives establish business opportunities to invest in Colombia's future. The "Sabores de la Reconciliación"[114] efforts undertaken by the Bogotá Chamber of Commerce is one example. The Chamber has organized events in which victims and perpetrators prepare a meal using local ingredients to serve to members of the business community, academics, and civil society organizations. The event allows for an informal encounter – social engagement – of victims, perpetrators, and the business community. It also provides an opportunity for businesses to invest in the community through companies that can develop ingredients or foods commercially, hire local cooks, or contribute to post-conflict development in other ways. This initiative produced several videos, one of them discussing the opportunities for business people to help in peace-building efforts.[115]

In addition, one of the results from the peace process includes policies that seek to incentivize investment by companies in areas of the country that have been highly affected by the armed conflict (ZOMAC in Spanish). In theory, the communities will benefit because private investment will likely improve infrastructure, access to public services and secure new jobs and opportunities for local communities. In turn, the companies benefit from tax reductions and special conditions to operate.[116] By April 2018, 407 businesses had already entered the ZOMAC areas.[117] The entrepreneurial nature of these types of

[113] A study of B-corps (Benefit Corporations, or socially responsible businesses) contends that these firms have done remarkably little for human rights. Joanne Bauer and Elizabeth Umlas, "Do Benefit Corporations Respect Human Rights?," *Stanford Social Innovation Review*, 2017. The attention to the founder of Chobani yogurt, Hamdi Ulukaya, and his hiring of refugees in the United States has suggested that every once and a while, Schindlers do appear. See Christine Lagorio-Chafkin, "This Billion-Dollar Founder Says Hiring Refugees Is Not a Political Act," *Inc.*, 2018, www.inc.com/magazine/201806/christine-lagorio/chobani-yogurt-hamdi-ulukaya-hiring-refugees.html.
[114] See Cámara de Comercio de Bogotá et al., "Los sabores de la reconciliación," n.d., www.ccb .org.co/Transformar-Bogota/Paz/Acciones-por-la-Paz/Los-sabores-de-la-reconciliacion.
[115] See Canal Capital, *Los sabores de la reconciliación: Beneficios y oportunidades para la paz* (Colombia, 2017), www.youtube.com/watch?v=jGeayQzKnUE&index=6&list= PLg308Sxb8FcFWSS6DIr_RrbFphNoGjGbx.
[116] El Tiempo, "Por invertir en antiguas zonas de conflicto se pagarán menos impuestos," *El Tiempo*, 2017, www.eltiempo.com/politica/proceso-de-paz/plan-de-inversion-para-las-zonas-mas-afectadas-por-el-conflicto-zomac-139498.
[117] Revista Dinero, "Las ZOMAC ya tienen 407 nuevas empresas," *Revista Dinero*, 2018, www .dinero.com/pais/articulo/407-empresas-se-han-creado-en-las-zomac/258141.

efforts seems to calculate that businesses will participate in peace-building when they see it in their economic interest to do so. Such efforts are intended to reduce the likelihood of future human rights violations and corporate complicity in them.

Additional direct action is targeted at Colombian companies that benefited from the fifty years of conflict and became Colombian-based multinationals. The Colombian Agency for Reintegration (Agencia Colombiana para la Reintegración) began a process a decade ago in which companies trained and employed victims and perpetrators from the conflict. Companies including Sodexo, El Éxito, Cemex, and Bancolombia are part of this initiative called "Reintegración desde la Empleabilidad" (Reintegration through Employment). The Agency acts as an intermediary between the companies and the workers who have demobilized, either as paramilitaries or left-wing combatants.[118]

While finding a novel way to engage business actively in the peace process, these Colombian examples have not revealed potential Schindlers. Individuals within the business community calling on other members of the economic sector to take risks for the well-being of victims have not emerged. Neither have members of the business community advanced accountability for businesses' human rights wrongs. They focus on shifting the calculation from making profits during conflict to profit-making during peacetime.

In other words, existing projects to engage businesses have not separated out those economic elites who reject the notion of business human rights violations in armed conflict or authoritarian regimes from those who acknowledge it, condemn it, and aim to do something about it. Such a division could fragment the business community in such a way as to reduce its veto power over corporate accountability.

Without such a process from within the business community, fragmentation has tended to come from outside. In particular, when states begin to hold businesses accountable, they can fragment the community's resolve to work together to defeat corporate accountability. Some companies begin to distance themselves from those held accountable. In Chapter 5, we show an example of this process in the Colombian case of the Fondo Ganadero de Córdoba.

In sum, inducements, reputational concerns, and fear of judicial action seem to have played a role in generating only a rhetorical shift in the business community, without creating human rights leadership for, or a sea change in,

---

[118] Radio Santafe, "Sodexo, reconocida por la ACR gracias a sus esfuerzos en empleabilidad," *Radio Santafe*, December 14, 2016, www.radiosantafe.com/2016/12/14/sodexo-reconocida-por-la-acr-gracias-a-sus-esfuerzos-en-empleabilidad/.

business human rights attitudes or behavior. A persistent denial of wrongdoing and avoidance of accountability and remedy coexist with rhetorical commitments.

We could not find meaningful initiatives within the business community – beyond those which benefit corporate self-interests – to break the veto power over corporate accountability. From this investigation, we conclude that most of the effort at shrinking that veto power will need to come from below. Civil society mobilization and institutional innovators will have to sufficiently raise the cost of committing atrocities such that businesses will recognize their economic and self-interest in avoiding such behavior. This fragmentation could lead to a distancing within the business community from those economic actors who do not respect and defend human rights. It would thus reduce the veto power over corporate accountability initiatives.

CONCLUSION

This chapter reveals the corporate veto power over accountability for human rights violations. It shows the power of certain companies, alone or in concert, to avoid legal judgment for their involvement in past human rights atrocities. National and multinational firms have faced trials in every kind of court. Only two courts since the World War II cases have rendered guilty verdicts against multinational companies for corporate complicity in human rights abuses during dictatorships and armed conflict (Chevron-Ecuador and Ford-Argentina). This demonstrates the extraordinary veto power of certain companies over judicial accountability. Business veto power has also shaped and constrained international human rights law by blocking binding and enforceable corporate human rights obligations. This has had the added effect of limiting international pressure on states to do so.

This chapter has examined the social and political linkages that have bolstered veto power. It also looked at the set of judicial, nonjudicial, illegal, and mobilizational tactics that sustain veto power. Our study finds little evidence to support the view of a positive shift in business attitudes towards human rights (e.g., CSR and BHR). The business community as a whole seems no more willing to accept binding and enforceable human rights obligations, and state's duties to enforce them, than in the past. Like the states in which they operate, they may give lip service to human rights protections, but will rarely take action to actively promote and defend them unless it is in their self-interest.

Returning to the Archimedes' Lever model, we find that business veto power remains intact, weighing down corporate accountability. In neutral or unfavorable political contexts, and in the absence of international pressure, efforts from below require exceptional force to lift up corporate accountability from under this weight.

The chapter reveals certain strategies that could be undertaken from below to lessen corporate veto power, the weight holding down corporate accountability. Fragmenting the business community's resolve to thwart accountability efforts is a central strategy. An example of such a strategy involves raising public knowledge of corporate complicity in human rights violations and intimidation and threats against victims and their human rights advocates. Some companies, recognizing the reputational costs of association with past abuses, may begin to denounce them, albeit tepidly. This could include rhetorical statements, donations to victims' support funds, or opening up employment opportunities to survivors. Such efforts weaken the resolve to fight accountability efforts. They acknowledge within the business community a no-tolerance for human rights violating behavior. The visibility of truth commission findings and successful judicial action against companies heightens this awareness and promotes understanding of the need for regulation. In terms of law-making, the mobilization behind the treaty that has emerged from, and is supported by, the Global South, may have the capacity to reduce the veto power of business vis-à-vis those on the side of civil society. Thus, more force from below depends on mobilizing behind visibility campaigns, truth commissions, judicial action, and law-making.

The findings in this chapter also suggest that certain political moments may be more propitious than others. The visibility campaign is most likely to work in neutral or favorable political contexts by influencing public opinion through media attention to past corporate complicity in violations, ongoing struggles for justice, and efforts by businesses to thwart those processes.

As an example, in our collaboration with Dejusticia, we prepared a report on corporate accountability and transitional justice published and launched in a public setting in Bogotá. When business groups attacked the report, they did so ideologically and not by refuting the evidence. On the other hand, some individual members of the business community recognized the quality of the research and invited us to meet with them to further discuss the findings and to try to reach a shared view on what can be done in the future. They even suggested that we have a joint session with the truth commission. This could be seen as a clever technique to overpower our academic project. Or it could be seen as an effective and sincere strategy by some members of the community to make clear that they do not endorse corporate complicity in the past conflict and their hope to prevent such acts in the future. Some economic actors seem to be distancing themselves from those who allied with paramilitary forces to carry out violence against workers and communities. In doing so, they weaken corporate veto power. They might only do so with the threat of possible reputational, legal, and financial costs. Those potential costs result from efforts from below.

In the next two chapters, we analyze those efforts. We show how local actors have advanced corporate accountability in truth commissions and domestic judicial action in the Global South. We look at the political context, the positioning of Archimedes' fulcrum, as well as the relative force applied on either side of the corporate impunity weights.

PART II

Accountability from Below

4

Truth-Telling from Below

The disappeared ... were all kidnapped from their homes on 27 July 1976, they were almost all Ledesma company workers. In the middle of a general black-out, uniformed troops broke into their houses, detaining more than 200 people. They were all taken to the Guerrero clandestine detention center where they faced brutal torture ... more than 70 people remain disappeared to this day.
— Humberto Campos, survivor, testimony to the Argentine
CONADEP truth commission[1]

Our weapons, ammunition, uniforms, vehicles, radios and other equipment were all developed and provided by industry. Our finances and banking were done by bankers who even gave us covert credit cards for covert operations.
— Craig Williamson, Apartheid "spy and planner of assassinations," testimony
to the South African TRC[2]

These excerpts from two iconic truth commissions tell a story about "corporate accountability from below." They show that the very first truth commission in the world – in Argentina – held businesses accountable for complicity in the infamous junta's repressive apparatus. They also show that one of the most celebrated truth commissions in the world – in South Africa – identified companies allegedly complicit in Apartheid's violence. They are not alone in holding economic actors accountable for human rights violations in non-judicial mechanisms; more than half of all truth commissions' final reports have done so.

---

[1] Comisión Nacional sobre la Desaparición de Personas, *Nunca Más*, 1983.
[2] The quote is from a memorandum submitted to the Commission at the Armed Forces hearing in Cape Town on October 9, 1997 and reproduced in the South African Truth and Reconciliation Report, Volume IV, p. 24. Williamson's "title" is provided by Shaun de Waal, "Apartheid Killings and Awkward Questions," *Mail & Guardian*, March 23, 2018.

Until we completed our study, few knew this story. The aim of this chapter is to expose the truths about corporate complicity hidden in those final reports. To achieve that goal, the chapter begins with an overview of truth commissions' efforts to unveil corporate complicity in past authoritarian state and armed conflict violence. We explore the location of those truth-telling exercises and their impact. The chapter examines the types of violations revealed and their connection to the root causes of violence. We use the Brazilian and Liberian examples of how reports identify the role of economic actors in the root causes of authoritarian state and armed conflict violence. We then analyze, using the Archimedes' Lever analogy, how efforts at truth-telling about corporate complicity in violence emerged. We emphasize the role of civil society mobilization, including campaigns and outings to enhance the visibility of corporate complicity in past authoritarian and armed conflict situations. We also highlight the role truth commission staff play in the process of including victims' testimony to corporate complicity in the final reports. In the conclusion, we identify strategies to promote corporate accountability in truth commissions.

COMPARING TRUTH COMMISSIONS
AND CORPORATE ACCOUNTABILITY

Argentina's 1983 CONADEP,[3] National Commission on Disappeared Persons, produced the first truth commission report in the world. Its *Nunca Más* (Never Again) report names eleven companies allegedly complicit in the authoritarian regime's kidnapping, arbitrary detention, disappearances, and torture. The newest truth commission in Colombia,[4] inaugurated in November 2018, has begun to explore the role economic actors (as "terceros civiles," or third-party civil actors) allegedly played during a half-century of armed conflict. From Argentina to Colombia, in twenty-three truth commissions in twenty countries, over a thirty-six-year period, these experiences reveal that there is nothing new, and nothing unusual, about truth commissions and corporate accountability.

---

[3] Comisión Nacional sobre la Desaparición de Personas, *Nunca Más*. Other studies have noted earlier truth commissions that either lacked legitimacy or completion: Pakistan (1971), Uganda (1974), and Bolivia (1982).
[4] Comisión para el Esclarecimiento de la Verdad, la Convivencia y la No Repetición (Truth, Coexistence and Non-repetition Commission).

Overview of Corporate Accountability and Truth Commissions

Twenty-three of the thirty-nine truth commissions with final reports,[5] or 59 percent, not only mention corporate complicity in human rights violations during past authoritarian regimes or armed conflict, they name names of economic actors allegedly involved in those abuses. Because some countries had more than one truth commission report, an even higher proportion of transitional countries – twenty out of thirty, or 67 percent – recognize corporate complicity in past human rights violations. A total of 329 companies were named in these reports in Africa, Asia, and Latin America. Although no truth commissions with corporate accountability appeared in Europe or the Middle East and North Africa (MENA), we still assert that truth-telling about corporate complicity in past human rights violations is neither a unique nor isolated phenomenon.

When we began this study, we did not expect to find more than a handful of commission reports acknowledging corporate complicity, and certainly did not expect that they would reveal names. We are not alone in finding our results surprising. Most truth commission and transitional justice scholars are unaware of this phenomenon. Even country experts where corporate complicity is included in the reports, and those who, like us, read through all the reports, are unaware of the extent of corporate accountability in truth commissions.[6] In the next sections, we set out the key characteristics of corporate accountability in truth commissions: their geographic distribution, their impact, the types of complicity included in them, and their discussion of corporate complicity as a root cause of violence.

Geographic Distribution of Corporate Accountability and Truth Commissions

The timeline presented in Figure 4.1 shows an increasing number of truth commissions that name economic actors allegedly complicit in past human rights violations. From 1990 to 2012, every year or two a final truth commission report includes economic actors' abuses. A gap of six years exists between the 2012 Brazilian and the 2018 Colombian truth commission. During that period, the Egyptian and Tunisian commissions did not examine corporate

---

[5] There are more than thirty-nine truth commissions in the world. Not all truth commissions prepared final reports, however. In addition, some of the final reports that were prepared were not accessible to us.

[6] Discussion at "The Business End of Human Rights: Book Workshop," University of Oxford North American Office, New York, September 12, 2018.

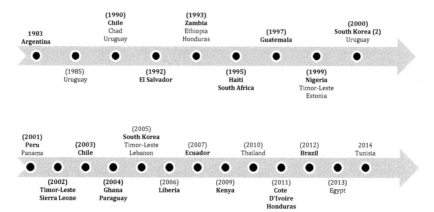

FIGURE 4.1 Truth Commissions and Corporate Complicity
Note: Truth commission countries in bold name economic actors allegedly involved in human rights violations.
Source: Corporate Accountability and Transitional Justice Database, 2016

complicity in human rights violations, but did address economic crimes in which businesses were involved.[7]

The timeline hints at the global spread of truth commissions naming economic actors allegedly complicit in human rights violations. They are not, however, distributed evenly across world regions (Figure 4.2). Most are concentrated in Latin America: ten countries (50 percent) and eleven truth commissions (48 percent). Most of the companies named in truth commission reports are also found in Latin America (232, or 71 percent). Africa follows close behind in terms of the number of truth commissions (eight, or 35 percent) and number of countries (eight, or 40 percent). The region has a far lower number of companies referenced, however (ninety-three, or 28 percent). Asia trails the other two regions with only four truth commissions (17 percent) in two countries (10 percent) and listing only four (1 percent) of the named companies.

These patterns could cast doubt on corporate accountability as a global phenomenon. It could be seen, instead, as Latin American protagonism, a further development in its leadership role in transitional justice. It makes logical sense that where transitional justice has gone the farthest and the deepest, in Latin America, that corporate accountability would accompany

---

[7] Our focus on gross violations of human rights excluded those truth commissions that only investigated corporate complicity in economic crimes, i.e., Chad, Egypt, Thailand, and Tunisia. Some of those included in our dataset investigated both human rights violations and economic crimes by businesses.

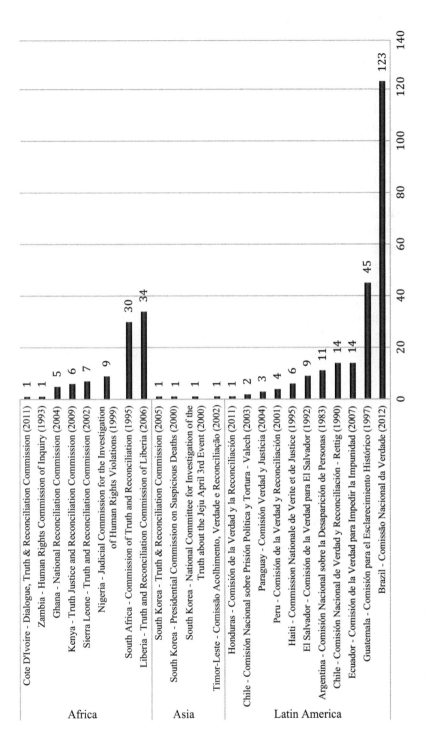

FIGURE 4.2 Distribution of Cases by Region
Source: Corporate Accountability and Transitional Justice database, 2016

it.[8] The example of Argentina, with the first truth commission, its numerous trials for crimes against humanity, and its image as a "human rights protagonist,"[9] appears to confirm this logic.

Our study recognizes the leading role Latin America has played in corporate accountability. Yet evidence does not support the claim that the region's history of transitional justice explains that concentration. Argentina's truth commission reported on corporate complicity in a very early stage of transitional justice, before it began human rights trials. Brazil's truth commission named more companies than any other country's reports, and yet it is one of the weakest adopters of the region's transitional justice models. It has not prosecuted a single perpetrator of human rights violations in its past dictatorship.[10] Its amnesty law remains firmly intact. Its truth commission was adopted with great ambivalence by state authorities, nearly fifty years after the coup that installed the authoritarian regime.[11]

The distribution of companies named in truth commission reports further defies a regional explanation. While Latin America as a whole ranks above the rest of the world in terms of the concentration of companies identified (71 percent), those numbers are driven mainly by two countries: Brazil with

---

[8] Bohoslavsky and Torelly, "Financial Complicity: The Brazilian Dictatorship under the 'Macroscope.'"

[9] Kathryn Sikkink, "From Pariah State to Global Protagonist: Argentina and the Struggle for International Human Rights," *Latin American Politics and Society* 50, no. 1 (2008): 1–29.

[10] Other sorts of transitional justice mechanisms have been used in Brazil, however. Abrão and Torelly list the sets of reparations policies and innovations on amnesty processes, contending that the absence of trials is not the same as the absence of transitional justice. Paulo Abrão and Marcelo D. Torelly, "Resistance to Change: Brazil's Persistent Amnesty and Its Alternatives for Truth and Justice," in *Amnesty in the Age of Human Rights Accountability: Comparative and International Perspectives*, ed. Francesca Lessa and Leigh A. Payne (Cambridge: Cambridge University Press, 2012). Paulo Abrão and Marcelo D. Torelly, "O programa de reparações como eixo estruturante da justiça de transição no Brasil," in *Justiça de transição – Manual para a América Latina*, ed. Félix Reátegui (Brasília/Nova Iorque: Ministério da Justiça/ICTJ, 2011), 473–516.

[11] The link between the strength of transitional justice processes and corporate accountability does not hold outside the region either. South Africa could be seen as confirming the relationship given that it was one of the truth commission that named the highest number of companies (fourth place) and its truth commission is globally recognized as a model to emulate, despite its numerous critics. South Africa, however, has not pursued other transitional justice mechanisms with equal vigor. It had a (widely criticized) reparations program. The perpetrators who failed to apply for, or who were denied, amnesty in exchange for truth about their past atrocities, have generally avoided justice. Antje de Bois-Pedain, "Accountability through Conditional Amnesty: The Case of South Africa," in *Amnesty in the Age of Human Rights Accountability: Comparative and International Perspectives*, ed. Francesca Lessa and Leigh A. Payne (Cambridge: Cambridge University Press, 2012), 238–62.

123 (37 percent) and Guatemala with 45 (14 percent). Together, those two countries' truth commissions represent half of the economic actors named in all truth commissions' reports. They are in first and second place in terms of the numbers of companies named. When the third and fourth place truth commissions (Liberia with thirty-four, or 10 percent, and South Africa with thirty, or 9 percent) are added, four countries' reports name 71 percent of all companies identified. Those four countries are split between two world regions: Latin America and Africa.[12]

Further casting doubt on Latin America's protagonism is the fact that the region is also highly represented among the set of countries whose truth commissions fail to address corporate complicity. As Table 4.1 shows, six truth commission final reports in three countries of the Americas do not mention corporate complicity.[13] Three countries' truth commissions in the MENA also fail to address corporate complicity in grave violations of human rights.[14] Africa has three country reports that do not mention corporate complicity, Asia has two, and Europe has one such report.

In sum, while there is a higher concentration in Latin America of truth commissions that name economic actors complicit in human rights violations, the phenomenon is not exclusive to the region. In our explanation of corporate accountability and truth commissions, we consider those factors leading to regional concentration. Before doing so, we examine the impact of corporate complicity truth-gathering exercises.

Impact of Corporate Accountability and Truth Commissions

One of the greatest limitations on the impact of corporate accountability in truth commissions is the lack of visibility. Although many commission reports cover corporate complicity, in many countries, and with many names of economic actors, this phenomenon remains largely unknown.

---

[12] At the average of fifteen companies named per commission, only the four countries mentioned meet and exceed that average, and only two other countries' truth commissions come close: Chile and Ecuador each name fourteen companies. At the median of six, Latin America and Africa are more balanced. Latin America has six reports and Africa has five.

[13] The final report in Honduras does, however, talk about the media and freedom of expression issues, as well as economic crimes.

[14] The Tunisian Truth and Dignity Commission set out to "examine the relationship among repression, resource extraction in the south and land use in the north, to large-scale unemployment and marginalization." See Ruben Carranza, "Transitional Justice, Corporate Responsibility and Learning from the Global South," April 28, 2015, http://jamesgstewart.com/transitional-justice-corporate-responsibility-and-learning-from-the-global-south/. We could not find evidence of those findings, however.

TABLE 4.1 *Truth Commissions without Corporate Complicity*

Country	Region	Name of the commission	Year
Chad	Africa	Commission of Inquiry into the Crimes and Misappropriations Committed by Ex-President Habré	1990
Egypt	MENA	Fact Finding Commission	2013
Estonia	Europe	International Commission for the Investigation of Crimes against Humanity	1999
Ethiopia	Africa	The Special Prosecution Process in Ethiopia by the Office of the Special Prosecutor	1993
Honduras	Latin America	National Commissioner for the Protection of Human Rights (Comisionado Nacional de Protección de los Derechos Humanos, CONADEH)	1993
Lebanon	MENA	International Independent Investigation Commission Established Pursuant to Security Council Resolution 1595 (2005)	2005
Pakistan	Asia	The War Inquiry Commission (Hamoodur Rahman Commission)	1972
Panama	Latin America	Panama Truth Commission (Comisión de la Verdad de Panamá)	2001
Thailand	Asia	Truth and Reconciliation Commission of Thailand	2010
Timor Leste	Asia	The Commission on Truth and Friendship of Timor Leste (CTF)	2005
Timor Leste	Asia	International Commission of Inquiry on East Timor	1999
Tunisia	MENA	Truth and Dignity Commission	2014
Uruguay	Latin America	Parliamentary Investigative Commission on the Situation of Disappeared Persons and Its Causes	1985
Uruguay	Latin America	Investigative Commission Requested by Senator Juan Carlos Blanco Regarding His Conduct in the Ministry of External Relations in the Case of Elena Quinteros	1990
Uruguay	Latin America	Peace Commission (Comisión para la Paz)	2000
Uruguay	Latin America	Investigative Commission on the Kidnapping and Assassination of Former National Representatives Zelmar Michelini and Héctor Gutiérrez-Ruiz	1985

Source: The authors

In part, this results from the superficial quality of the investigations, the shallow depth of information, and the hidden findings. There is rarely a separate section of the report devoted to corporate involvement in past violence. Few commissions conducted thorough investigations or in-depth case studies. Instead, the truth about corporate complicity tends to emerge organically from scattered evidentiary fragments, lists of events, appendices, or testimony with little follow-up research. One has to be looking for corporate accountability in truth commissions to find it.[15] Thus, while as a whole the findings on truth commissions and corporate accountability are impressive, few individual reports are particularly elucidating.

This kind of investigation may be the result of truth commission mandates. Despite the volume of reports covering corporate complicity, only four truth commissions had official mandates to investigate economic actors' human rights violations: Chad, Timor-Leste, Kenya, and Liberia. Even those mandates are underwhelming in their scope. Chad's 1990 commission's mandate to investigate past violence linked economic and human rights crimes: "all violations of human rights, illicit narcotics trafficking and embezzlement of state funds."[16] Yet, we did not find any specific references in Chad's report to corporate complicity for human rights violations. Timor-Leste's 2006 commission mentioned "corporations and other individuals" among a list of those involved in "massive violations." The Commission vowed that "[a]ny account of 'the truth' relating to a conflict will be incomplete if it does not include the actions of all of these parties."[17] Despite this mandate, only one company was named – PT Freeport Indonesia – for financing the violence carried out by Indonesia's occupying military forces. Kenya's 2009 commission's mandate included investigation into politically motivated violence and its link to land displacement and major economic crimes.[18] As we discuss later in the chapter, it faced constraints in doing so, but still mentioned six specific cases. The International Center for Transitional Justice refers to the Liberia's 2008 truth

[15] The 1990 National Truth and Reconciliation Commission in Chile ("Rettig Commission"), provides an example. Volume I mentions incidents in which victims were held in on-site detention centers at companies, disappeared, or shot. Yet the information on the role of companies is scant, as the following entry shows: "On 3 October 1973, Hugo Manuel Rojas Cortes, 38 years old, worker at the Luchetti company died. The victim was detained at the Luchetti company after a raid on the 13 September 1973. He was then taken to the National Stadium [where he died]. Comisión Nacional de Verdad y Reconciliacion, *Informe de la Comisión Nacional de Verdad y Reconciliación*, Volume I, 1991, 171, www.derechoshumanos.net/lesahumanidad/informes/informe-rettig.htm. www.ddhh.gov.cl/ddhh_rettig.html.
[16] Commission d'Enquête du Ministère Chadien de la Justice sur les Crimes du Régime de Hissène Habré, *Report* (Chad, 1992).
[17] Truth and Reconciliation in Timor-Leste Commission for Reception, *Chega!*, 1999, www.cavr-timorleste.org/en/chegaReport.htm.
[18] Truth, Justice and Reconciliation Commission of Kenya, *Report of the Truth, Justice and Reconciliation Commission*, 2013. And also United States Institute of Peace, Truth Commission: Kenya, n.d. Reports and other relevant resources available here: www.tjrckenya.org/index.php.

commission mandate as "innovative" in its approach to "understanding the dynamics of the Liberian conflict,"[19] specifically the link between economic crimes, exploitation of natural resources, and human rights abuses.[20] Liberia has the third highest number of companies named.

Some commissions lacked an explicit mandate, yet economic actors' human rights violations fell within their scope of operations. The 2002 commission for Sierra Leone identified "perpetrators [of human rights violations as] ... both natural persons and corporate bodies, such as transnational companies or corporations."[21] Other commissions referred to "all human rights violations," without explicitly excluding non-state business perpetrators of those abuses. Mandates, therefore, did not overly constrain commissions' inclusion of corporate complicity in final reports. A majority of reports in three regions – Africa, Asia, and Latin America – reveal the truth about corporate complicity with, but mainly without, a mandate to do so. Mandate does not completely explain the lack of visibility. It may explain, however, why much of the information on corporate complicity is buried in the report since these sets of investigations were rarely emphasized as a priority by commissions or their mandate.

The highly limited impact may also result from the scant recommendations by commissions regarding corporate complicity in human rights violations. The number of reports with specific recommendations is low (twelve of twenty-three). Most of the recommendations, moreover, seem unlikely to deter future complicity in human rights violations. An example is voluntary reparations from businesses.[22] South Africa's voluntary

---

[19] Paul James-Allen, Aaron Weah, and Lizzie Goodfriend, "Beyond the Truth and Reconciliation Commission: Transitional Justice Options in Liberia," 2010, https://ictj.org/sites/default/files/ICTJ-Liberia-Beyond-TRC-2010-English.pdf, 3 and 6.

[20] Liberia's Truth and Reconciliation Commission mandate is stated as follows: "An economic crime is any prohibited activity committed for the purpose of generating economic gains or that in fact generates economic gain. It applies to any state or non-state actor with a link to the conflict in Liberia, including but not limited to public and private individuals, corporations, and other business entities whose economic activities contributed to gross human rights and/or humanitarian law violations in Liberia or that otherwise perpetuated armed conflict in Liberia, as well as those who benefited economically from armed conflict in Liberia." Truth and Reconciliation Commission of Liberia, *Final Report*, Volume I, 2008, 69, http://trcofliberia.org/reports/final-report.

[21] Sierra Leone Truth and Reconciliation Commission, *Witness to Truth: Report of the Sierra Leone Truth and Reconciliation Commission*, Volume I, 2004, 35–36.

[22] Two examples of voluntary reparations are Timor-Leste's CAVR and the South African TRC. More information exists on the TRC. The South African TRC hoped to adopt through voluntary contributions from businesses: a wealth tax; a one-off corporate and private income tax; a single donation of 1 percent for each company on the Johannesburg stock exchange; a "business reconciliation fund"; and donations to SASRIA (South African Special Risks Association) to provide insurance against material loss arising from political conflict. Truth and

reparations recommendation has faced criticism. Christopher Colvin contends that in its design, "[T]he culpability of domestic business has ... not been seriously considered. Business either ignores the question or makes absurd offers to 'manage' the disbursement of reparations funds."[23] The Truth and Reconciliation Commission (TRC) report itself refers to the voluntary private sector donations to the Business Trust as "a paltry amount when one considers the massive amount needed to repair the inequities and damage caused to entire communities." It added, "In these disappointing circumstances, it seems essential to restate the proposals made by the Commission for ways in which business could generate funds for this broader project of reparation and restitution."[24] The Commission noted that businesses in South Africa at the very least had "a moral obligation to assist in the reconstruction and development of post-apartheid South Africa through active reparative measures ... business, possibly through the Business Trust, needs to commit itself to a far more focused programme of reparation."[25]

Recommendations aimed at regulating business human rights behavior also appeared in some final reports. The 2004 Paraguayan commission, for example, called for "norms for transnational and other business enterprises, recognizing their obligation to promote, guarantee the enjoyment of, respect for, and protection of human rights, as well as the rights and interest of indigenous communities, and other groups facing vulnerability and risk." It further recommended greater ministerial oversight of "contracts and working conditions of indigenous peoples working in ranching, forestry, agriculture and other businesses."[26] We could not find an evaluation of the implementation of these recommendations.

Reconciliation Commission of South Africa, *Truth and Reconciliation Commission of South Africa Report*, Volume VI, section 2, chapter 5, 1998, 143, 319. See also Christopher J. Colvin, "Overview of the Reparations Program in South Africa," in *The Handbook of Reparations*, ed. Pablo De Greiff (Oxford: Oxford University Press, 2006), 199.

[23] Colvin, "Overview of the Reparations Program in South Africa," 205.
[24] The commission noted that the Business Trust received approximately 800 million rand, or around US$100 million. The trust is not directly connected to corporate complicity in the Apartheid era or companies' moral obligation to contribute to the new South Africa or to compensate victims in light of past corporate abuse. Truth and Reconciliation Commission of South Africa, *Truth and Reconciliation Commission of South Africa Report*, Volume VI, section 2, chapter 5.
[25] Truth and Reconciliation Commission of South Africa.
[26] Comisión Verdad y Justicia de Paraguay, *Informe final*, Volume I, 112–13.

Only three commissions – Brazil, Liberia,[27] and Ecuador[28] – recommended judicial investigations into possible criminal or crimes against humanity activity by businesses. The follow-up on these recommendations for judicial investigations has been weak. Only two economic actors in Brazil (Fiat and Volkswagen) are facing trials. In Liberia, two of the economic actors named in the report have faced trial, but in foreign, rather than Liberian courts. None of the economic actors named in the Ecuadorean commission have faced trial.

Indeed, few economic actors named in any truth commission reports have faced judicial action. Eighteen of the 329 economic actors named in truth commission reports are facing trial in domestic courts (Argentina [3], Brazil [1], and Peru [1]) and foreign courts (for alleged violations in Timor-Leste [1], Guatemala [1], Liberia [3], Nigeria [3], and South Africa [5]).[29] This low level of follow-up judicial investigation further suggests that truth commissions have had highly limited impact. Moreover, truth commission information on the few named economic actors facing trial are only rarely used in these judicial actions. Thus, truth commissions have played no significant role in advancing the legal accountability of economic actors in past violence.

In sum, while corporate complicity is revealed through a large number of truth commissions around the world, this information has not commanded any attention even within the countries where the commissions conducted their work. As a result, the surprising level of corporate accountability in truth commissions has had little impact. It has not exposed economic actors' complicity in human rights violations and thus contributed to victims' rights to truth, justice, reparations, and guarantees of non-repetition. One task for our project is to reveal the truths about corporate complicity hidden in these reports, so as to advance victims' rights.

[27] "The Extraordinary Criminal Tribunal for Liberia named individuals, corporations and institutions recommended for prosecution or, in some cases, for further investigation." United States Institute of Peace, Truth Commission: Liberia, 2006, www.usip.org/publications/2006/02/truth-commission-liberia; Truth and Reconciliation Commission of Liberia, *Final Report*, Volume II, 2009, http://trcofliberia.org/resources/reports/final/volume-two_layout-1.pdf; Truth and Reconciliation Commission of Liberia, *Mandate*, 2006, http://trcofliberia.org/about/trc-mandate; Truth and Reconciliation Commission of Liberia, *Official Website*, n.d., http://trcofliberia.org. Truth and Reconciliation Commission of Liberia, *Final Report*, Volume II, 370–71.

[28] In Ecuador, the 2007 Truth Commission to Impede Impunity, focused on economic crimes: "a list of 26 individuals were recommended for prosecution," an additional "19 corporations, institutions and state actors," and a "further investigation of 54 individuals and corporate entities for their actions." The Commission further "charge[d] the Ombuds office and the Ministry of Justice and Human Rights to implement human rights codes of conduct, recognizing international obligations, for transnational enterprises and other commercial businesses, that work with populations affected by their projects." Comisión de la Verdad de Ecuador, *Informe de la comisión de la verdad de Ecuador*, Volume II, 372, 374–75, 454l.

[29] One company – Royal Dutch Shell – has faced foreign civil judicial action for alleged violations in Nigeria and South Africa.

Types of Corporate Complicity

The breadth of coverage in the set of truth commission reports is extensive. The time period usually begins during the Cold War, but several include origins of corporate abuses in colonial and independence periods.[30] The reports include a full range of economic sectors allegedly complicit in past violence (in order of frequency): agriculture, manufacturing, natural resources extraction, and finance. The type of company varies, including multinational, state, and large, medium, and small private domestic enterprises.

Truth commission reports concentrate on four (sometimes overlapping) sets of victims of corporate complicity: members of political opposition groups (32 percent); rural and urban labor (28 percent); local community groups (21 percent); and the general population (19 percent). The Latin American reports concentrate on victims in the political opposition (97 percent) and in labor (80 percent), whereas the African commissions capture mainly the "general population" (90 percent) and local communities (52 percent). The Asian truth commissions include all categories (except general population) at a very low (2–3 percent) level.

In some truth commissions only one type of victim of corporate complicity is mentioned. Nigeria's Oputa commission focused on local (indigenous) communities, protesting alleged exploitation on plantations or environmental destruction of communal lands. El Salvador's truth commission report mentions political opposition as the focus of privately funded death squad activity. The Zambia report includes only one category of victims of corporate complicity: labor in copper mines.

Argentina's CONADEP report mentions only workers, victims of the repression unleashed by a business-military alliance behind the neoliberal economic restructuring.[31] Powerful testimony by Adolfo Omar Sánchez in the report

---

[30] The Guatemalan, Kenyan, and Liberian commissions look further back in time. The Guatemalan report discusses racism from the colonial period to the present. The colonial legacy is identified as an explanation for the violent power of economic actors over the powerlessness of the victimized indigenous community. The armed conflict exacerbated those historical roots of violence. In the Kenyan report, colonialism's unequal distribution of land continued into the post-independence era. In the recent violence, inequality and legal and illegal land grabs often resulted in massacres of local communities. (See especially Volume 2A.) Liberian slave labor at the Firestone Rubber and Tire Co. plantation dates back to the 1920s when the ruling Whig Party forced indigenous peoples to work for the company (Volume II, p.15).

[31] Indeed, CONADEP's *Nunca Más* (Never Again) report identified workers as the largest single category of victims (30.2 percent) of human rights abuse overall during the civil-military dictatorship. Comisión Nacional sobre la Desaparición de Personas, *Nunca Más*.

recounts an emblematic event at the Ford Motor factory in General Pacheco, Buenos Aires province. Sánchez claims that he was tortured at a detention center at the Ford plant following a union meeting with the manager of labor relations. The manager told the union representatives that the company would no longer recognize worker delegates and he joked with them as they left, "Say hello to my friend Camps when you see him," referring to the notorious police torturer in the province. Sánchez recounts that those who detained him sought additional union leaders, and asked him specifically about Juan Carlos Amoroso. They told Sánchez that "they were going to kill us both and all the Peronists, and throw us into the river." This testimony, among others, revealed the truth about the kidnapping, torture, and on-site detention of twenty-four Ford employees.[32]

The coverage in the reports is extensive. Although some reports include only vague references to general participation in repression or violence, others track direct and indirect involvement in specific violations. In order of frequency mentioned, we found the following sets of corporate complicity in human rights violations included in final reports: financing abuses, illegal detention, kidnapping, torture, extrajudicial killing and forced disappearances, property and environmental wrongs, sexual and gendered violations, slave labor, and indifference or passivity.

Financing

Financing violence is the most frequent category of corporate complicity mentioned in the reports. The commissions that included the most entries of companies allegedly financing violence are Brazil, Liberia, and South Africa, although each reflected a different kind of financing activity. Brazil's commission focused on companies that allegedly financed the coup and the repressive apparatus subsequently established by the authoritarian regime. In Liberia, the commission focused on financing through corruption linked to illegal natural resource extraction that fueled the conflict. As examples of truth commissions and corporate complicity as root causes of violence, a discussion of both reports follows later in the chapter.

The 1995 South African Truth and Reconciliation Commission documented several types of financing activities that allegedly fueled violence: general economic support by business, banking, and odious debt. In terms of general economic support the report states, "[b]usiness was central to the economy that sustained the South African state during the apartheid years." The growth of the private sector in mining, agriculture, the security apparatus, and the military industrial complex occurred in a "racially structured context" of land, labor, and

---

[32] Comisión Nacional sobre la Desaparición de Personas.

repressive policies favorable to business. The report highlights, in particular, "white agriculture with privileged access to land and firms connected to the security apparatus." The report identifies certain sectors, such as mining, as instrumental to the design and implementation of Apartheid policies.[33]

Banks were also critical. Following on the quote from Craig Williamson at the beginning of the chapter, the South African Truth and Reconciliation Commission stated: "the use that was made of covert credit cards cannot be ignored. The particular banker involved may not have had direct knowledge of why specific cards were being used. However, there was no obvious attempt on the part of the banking industry to investigate or stop the use being made of their facilities in an environment that was rife with gross human rights violations." The report describes Swiss banks (Credit Suisse and UBS) as allegedly "important partners of Pretoria during apartheid" from its institution-alization in 1948 through the marketing of South African gold and funding infrastructure in homelands during the Apartheid era.[34] A quote from the report illustrates the alleged link between banks and the Apartheid state: "After the Sharpeville massacre in 1960, the chairman of the largest Swiss bank, UBS, was asked: 'Is apartheid necessary or desirable?' His response was: 'Not really necessary, but definitely desirable.'"

"Odious debt" is another financing activity raised in the TRC final report. The Commission describes the Apartheid state's need for financing after UN sanctions were imposed.[35] As the report states, "Swiss banks came to the rescue." The Swiss Parliament understood the strong support in the country for the economic sanctions, but nonetheless allowed the financing of the Apartheid regime. As one parliamentarian reportedly stated, "Let's be honest. Our businessmen just want to do business in South Africa at any price. And this policy is not a sound policy for our country internationally. One of these days it's going to come back and haunt us.'"[36]

---

[33] Truth and Reconciliation Commission of South Africa, *Truth and Reconciliation Commission of South Africa Report*, Volume V, 1998, 251.

[34] Truth and Reconciliation Commission of South Africa, *Truth and Reconciliation Commission of South Africa Report*, Volume IV, 1998, 144.

[35] The report describes the history in this way: Following the 1976 Soweto uprising, the United Nations condemned Apartheid as a crime against humanity, expelled South Africa, and countries around the world adopted economic sanctions. The gold boom that had once supported the Apartheid state was followed by a bust, forcing the regime to search for loans coinciding with shrinking opportunities owing to the sanctions. Truth and Reconciliation Commission of South Africa, *Truth and Reconciliation Commission of South Africa Report*, Volume VI, section 2, chapter 5.

[36] Truth and Reconciliation Commission of South Africa.

Other types of financing of human rights violations – through private security forces, public security forces, and death squads – are also covered in the reports. Sierra Leone's commission alleges that the "the South African private security firm, Executive Outcomes (EO) was efficient in combating the RUF (Revolutionary United Front) during the conflict ... a large number of civilians were killed when Executive Outcomes helicopter gunships attacked RUF jungle bases between 1995 and 1996."[37] The Peruvian commission report notes alleged private sector financing of violence through "irregular" security forces. As the report states: "violence was not unknown in trade union-business relations, not even in its most extreme form (assassinations). What was never investigated at the time was the use of irregular groups, information systems, and intimidation. These are areas of anti-democratic activity by employers that need investigation. It is not a secret that many of the acts of intimidation were carried out by private security organs."[38]

Chega!, the Timor-Leste report, focuses on private company financing for the Indonesian military. An example is the PT Freeport case. The report mentions the company's abuses in relation to the protection it sought from the military.[39]

In El Salvador's report, all references to corporate complicity involve funding death squads.[40] As the report states, "Because of the clandestine nature of their operations, it is not easy to establish all the links existing between private businessmen and the death squads. However, the Commission on the Truth has absolutely no doubt that a close relationship existed, or that the possibility that businessmen or members of moneyed families might

[37] Sierra Leone Truth and Reconciliation Commission, *Witness to Truth: Report of the Sierra Leone Truth and Reconciliation Commission*, Volume II, 2004, 403–4.
[38] Truth and Reconciliation Commission of South Africa, *Truth and Reconciliation Commission of South Africa Report*, Volume V.
[39] General references, without names of companies, are also made to Australian, British, and Canadian firms that financially supported the occupation and its violence.
[40] The Guatemalan and Peruvian final reports also provide examples of corporate complicity in funding death squads. Guatemala's *Memoria del Silencio* report documents cases of businesspeople funding death squads. One entry refers to the conviction for murder in 1976 in which the defendant confessed to being a member of a death squad funded by Guatemalan businessman Elías Zimeri Nassar. In another, the report identifies a landlord, Carlos Thompson, who created a death squad in La Palma (Río Hondo, Zacapa). Comisión para el Esclarecimiento Histórico, *Guatemala, memoria del silencio*, 1999, 148. Fn 191 quoting from *Amnesty International Briefing*, 1976; See also p. 1097. In the Peruvian commission report, businessman Jorge Fung Pineda is alleged to have used his close personal connections within the military to call on the Colina Group, a notorious death squad, to violently repress workers. Comisión de la Verdad y Reconciliación del Perú, *Informe final*, Volume VII, 2003, 563, 576.

feel the need and might be able to act with impunity in financing murderous paramilitary groups, as they did in the past, poses a threat to the future of Salvadorian society."[41] In particular, the truth commission identified the strong financial and political support allegedly received from business to a notorious death squad leader:

> Former Major D'Aubuisson drew considerable support from wealthy civilians who feared that their interests would be affected by the reform program announced by the Government Junta. They were convinced that the country faced a serious threat of Marxist insurrection, which they had to overcome. The Commission on the Truth obtained testimony from many sources that some of the richest landowners and businessmen inside and outside the country offered their estates, homes, vehicles and bodyguards to help the death squads. They also provided the funds used to organize and maintain the squads, especially those directed by former Major D'Aubuisson.[42]

Illegal detention

Illegal detention is the second most frequently mentioned type of violation in the reports. The truth commissions discovered the use of clandestine detention centers on-site at company plants. While Latin American reports contain frequent references to this form of complicity,[43] South Korea's commission investigation into the April 3rd massacres at Jeju also hints at the role some companies played in holding prisoners who were subsequently killed and their bodies hidden. The report alleges that "the Absolute [sic] Alcohol (Oriental Development Company) warehouse in Jeju-eup ... [and in] Seogwipo, the potato factory above Jeongbang Falls and the warehouse near Cheonjiyeon Falls were used as camps."[44]

---

[41] Comisión de la Verdad para El Salvador *De la locura a la esperanza: La guerra de 12 años en El Salvador*, 1993, 129.

[42] Ibid., 127. The report mentions that D'Aubuisson had allegedly taken credit privately for the planning of Monsignor Romero's assassination (ibid., 27). The report identified certain individuals as allegedly funding death squads without referring to them as members of the business community; we discovered their business links by cross-checking their names against other lists of private funders for the death squads.

[43] In addition to Argentina, see Brazil, Chile, and Guatemala.

[44] The incident took place in 1948–1949. National Committee for Investigation of the Truth about the Jeju April 3 Incident, *The Jeju 4.3 Incident Investigation Report*, n.d., www .jeju43peace.or.kr/report_eng.pdf; Hun Joon Kim, "Seeking Truth after Fifty Years: The National Committee for Investigation of the Truth about the Jeju 4.3 Events," *International Journal of Transitional Justice* 3 (2009): 406–23, 559.

Kidnapping and torture

Kidnapping and torture in which economic actors were involved came primarily from Latin American reports.[45] The Peruvian commission highlighted a number of incidents of kidnapping on remote landed estates. In one such case on July 25–26, 1987, two local priests and four others were kidnapped and held on the Sota farm of the Umachiri rural business, some of them for up to twelve hours, presumably by a paramilitary group.[46] Corporate complicity in torture was covered in reports from Africa (Ghana and Liberia) and Asia (South Korea). Regarding Ghana, the most extensive reporting on alleged torture took place at the Vacuum Salt Company Limited in Songhor Lagoon near Ada. In 1982, residents of the region challenged the Company's monopoly on salt production and sales. The Company allegedly retaliated against them, calling in soldiers and the police. The report refers to the "ill treatment that in some cases amounted to torture" that fifteen citizens faced. This included being forced to eat salt and drink salty water, stare at the sun for long periods of time, and crawl on stones. They also reported slapping, kicking, and beatings sometimes with a rifle butt. Some testified to illegal detention up to three weeks, during which time they faced torture. One example is Aku Sebie of Hwakpo, who was seven months pregnant and miscarried while she was in custody.[47]

Extrajudicial killing and disappearances

In corporate complicity in extrajudicial killing and disappearances, Latin America is once again disproportionately represented.[48] The Peruvian commission refers to the killing of a union leader that the workers directly attribute to the mining company Centromín, but notes the lack of definitive proof.[49] Demetrio Martínez was allegedly assassinated after a worker safety demand was rejected by the company.[50] His cousin, also an employee, testified at the Commission that the company had an extermination unit that had killed other union leaders like Demetrio.[51] The Ecuadorian truth

---

[45] See Argentina, Brazil, and Guatemala, as well as Peru for economic actors involved in kidnapping. For torture, see Argentina, Brazil, Chile, and Guatemala.

[46] Comisión de la Verdad y Reconciliación del Perú, *Informe final*, Volume III, 2003, 394.

[47] National Reconciliation Commission of Ghana, *National Reconciliation Commission Final Report*, 2004, 36, 55.

[48] See Argentina, Brazil, Ecuador, and Guatemala, in addition to Peru.

[49] The report states that the Maoist Shining Path terrorist group might have been involved as a way to intensify the crisis.

[50] Martínez had allegedly tried to persuade the mining company to provide extra funds and medical benefits to compensate for the health effects of the chemicals used by workers in the mining operations.

[51] Comisión de la Verdad y Reconciliación del Perú, *Informe final*, Volume V, 2003, 202, 218.

commission report identifies the mining company La Tigrera as implicated in killing and disappearances in El Oro province.[52] Testimonies from the community to the Commission reported two extrajudicial killings, twelve illegal detentions, twenty-one wounded, and forty-seven tortured.[53] According to leaders and survivors, various disappearances also occurred.[54] The Haitian truth commission reported on an operation against political opponents in the state-owned enterprise, Telecó, in October 1991, that allegedly ended in the firing of forty to fifty employees and a forced disappearance.[55]

Africa is the only other region that documents extrajudicial killing.[56] Many of these killings are linked to illegal trafficking in conflict minerals and arms. As the Sierra Leone commission describes: "Simply put, diamonds were both an indirect cause of the war in Sierra Leone and a fueling factor."[57]

Property and environmental violence

Property and environmental violence are covered in commissions in Latin America and Africa. The only kinds of corporate complicity in the Kenyan report are property and land claims. The report states that distinguishing the business class from the political ruling class is nearly impossible due to their very close connections and the use of land for political favors before elections. Still, the National Land Commission noted "a very close linkage between land injustices and ethnic violence in Kenya . . . land related injustices are prominent factors that precipitate violence between and within ethnic tribes in Kenya."[58]

---

[52] The report refers to national security forces during the dictatorship of León Febres Cordero (1984–1988) who ousted community members from El Oro province. The land invasions backed by military and civilian forces took place on four occasions in 1987. The report describes "an enormous level of violence that affected the entire community," including "indiscriminate shooting at the local population." La Tigrera mining company is identified as having been involved in transporting some of the dead bodies from these land displacements in their trucks, hidden under banana leaves. Those individuals remain among the disappeared. Comisión de la Verdad de Ecuador, *Informe de la Comisión de la Verdad de Ecuador*, Volume II, 2010, 55 and 44, http://repositorio.dpe.gob.ec/handle/39000/1312.

[53] *Informe de la Comisión de la Verdad de Ecuador*, Volume I, 2010, 340.

[54] Comisión de la Verdad de Ecuador, *Informe de la Comisión de la Verdad de Ecuador*, Volume II.

[55] Rodrigue Jacques, a renowned member of the Lavalas Party of ousted President Jean-Bertrand Aristide was identified as disappeared. Commission Nationale de Vérité et de Justice, *République d'Haïti: Rapport de La Commission Nationale de Vérité et de Justice*, 1996, 188–89.

[56] Cote D'Ivoire, Ghana, Liberia, Nigeria, Sierra Leone, and South Africa all mention this type of corporate complicity.

[57] Sierra Leone Truth and Reconciliation Commission, *Witness to Truth: Report of the Sierra Leone Truth and Reconciliation Commission*, Volume II.

[58] The Commission lists the injustices that spark conflict as: illegal alienation and acquisition of individual and community land by public and private entities, illegal alienation of public

Environmental destruction is linked to human rights violations in the final
reports of truth commissions in Brazil, Ecuador, Guatemala, Nigeria, and
South Africa. The Oputa commission in Nigeria focused on corporate complicity in the oil-producing areas of the country.[59] The most well-documented
case occurred in Ogoniland in the Niger Delta. The Ogoni people had
protested the impact of Shell on their socio-economic and cultural well-
being for over thirty years after oil was discovered in the 1960s. Such protests
were violently repressed with allegations of company involvement. As the
Oputa Commission stated: "The violence, which is usually affected by the
police or the military, may be at the instance of the state or the oil multinational corporations. The latter often prefer inviting the security agencies
whenever their operations are threatened by the local people, rather than
engaging them in genuine dialogue. Oil multinational corporations often use
divide and rule tactics among the communities especially with regard to
giving token compensation that they sometimes give to their host community.
In the process, the oil multinational corporations play communities, groups
and even youth elements or organizations against each other in order to
promote their interest. The result is usually violent conflicts amongst communities and groups."[60] Testimony at the Oputa Commission revealed the
violence related to environmental devastation of Ogoniland, specifically "the
arrest, detention, torture and killing of the Ogonis" by public security forces.
The witness "informed the Commission about the alleged complicity of Shell
Petroleum Company in importing arms and ammunitions into the country for
the purpose of suppressing agitation by the Ogonis about the environmental
degradation of their land by Shell Petroleum Company."[61]

land and trust lands, preferential treatment of members of specific ethnic groups in
settlement schemes at the expense of the most deserving landless, forced resettlement of
members of a community outside of their homelands, forced evictions and the phenomenon
of land grabbing, especially by government officials. Truth, Justice and Reconciliation
Commission of Kenya, *Report of the Truth, Justice and Reconciliation Commission*, Volume
IV, 2013, 52.
[59] In one incident in 1998, a leak in a pipeline operated by Shell Petroleum Development
Company in the Jesse community (Niger Delta) caught fire, killing 1,000 people and injuring
1,500.
[60] Human Rights Violations Investigation Commission (Oputa Panel), *Human Rights Violations
Investigation Commission*, Volume III, 2005, 43.
[61] Ibid. Similar issues emerged in the Truth, Justice and Reconciliation Commission of Kenya.
Recommendations by the Commission corresponded to the findings: "the oil MNCs must be
made to operate according to internationally acceptable minimum standards as they do in the
developed or their home countries. Companies that do not observe this rule should be
appropriately sanctioned." Truth, Justice and Reconciliation Commission of Kenya.

Sexual and gendered violence

Sexual and gendered violence as a form of corporate complicity in human rights violations only appears in a few truth commission reports. Guatemala and Sierra Leone provide examples. The sexual violence reported in the Guatemalan Truth Commission mainly affected indigenous women on private landholdings. One case involves what appears to be an alliance between the military and the landholder of the Finca San Francisco.[62] In a mission to eliminate guerrillas from the region, the military reportedly accused the Mayan descendant (Chuj speaking) workers on the Finca of guerrilla collaboration. The military allegedly forced the workers to hand over their possessions, such as food, money, and radios. The report continued, alleging that the military then raped the women and burned them alive. Men were killed. Children were forcibly removed from a church by their feet and swung against wooden poles. The village was burned after the military feasted on the stolen food. An estimated 350 people were killed in this single event.

The Sierra Leone report considers how generalized conflict associated with illegal trade victimized women. The killing of men often left women as heads of households without access to land or credit. As the report states, "Many war widows complain of being forced out of farmlands that belonged to their husbands."[63] Because of laws restricting women's land ownership or access to credit, high concentrations of women among displaced peoples resulted.[64]

Forced or slave labor

A few countries (Guatemala, Liberia, and Sierra Leone) listed forced, or slave labor, as part of corporate complicity. The Guatemala report refers to La Perla farm in which at least two women were allegedly held against their will and obligated to work. Juana Hermosa was reportedly detained with her four children, tortured, and made to work from 1985 to 1991. Micaela Paz Sánchez was purportedly detained for a year and forced to work on the coffee harvest without pay. Rural villagers in Sierra Leone made testimony to the truth commission about the RUF system of slave labor they experienced. They were forced to produce coffee and cocoa and to carry the heavy bags to Liberia

---

[62] Retired Coronel Víctor Manuel Bolaños had stopped visiting the land in 1981 after the manager of a neighboring farm was killed by the guerrillas. On July 17, 1982, the military arrived at the Finca to forcibly force out guerrillas from the zone.

[63] Sierra Leone Truth and Reconciliation Commission, *Witness to Truth: Report of the Sierra Leone Truth and Reconciliation Commission*, Volume IIIB, 2004, 115–16.

[64] Ibid., 115–16, 144.

for trading for arms, which they then returned to Sierra Leone. Throughout the process they faced beatings, killings, and illegal detention.[65]

Indifference and passivity
We found two references to indifference and passivity in the business community as complicity in the violence. The Paraguayan commission stated, "during the 1954–1989 dictatorship, the personal and institutional attitude of private businesses and their associations, particularly Feprinco and the Unión Industrial Paraguaya, maintained a dismissive and indifferent attitude in the face of human rights violations and in some cases they supported the government. For these reasons, the business sector holds a passive political responsibility [for those violations]."[66] The Peruvian commission also referred to economic actors' indifference to the high level of political violence during the conflict. Instead of seeking solutions to the violence, they found ways to insulate themselves, and limit their engagement in society to activities that increased their profits, such as promoting favorable economic and labor policies.[67]

This diverse set of violations shows the array of corporate complicity in gross violations of human rights covered in truth commissions around the world. They demonstrate that in many instances economic actors were more than peripheral to the violence. The allegations made in reports link the violence directly to particular economic actors' abusive behavior. Indeed, because of its centrality to past human rights violations, economic actors' complicity is examined in some truth commission reports as a root causes of the violence, as revealed in the next section.

Root Causes of Violence

Scholars and practitioners have associated economic actors with the origin and logic, intensity, extension, and endurance of human rights violations in authoritarian regimes and armed conflicts. In the "authoritarian state model" of violence, a tight alliance formed between those in political power and those

---

[65] Sierra Leone Truth and Reconciliation Commission, *Witness to Truth: Report of the Sierra Leone Truth and Reconciliation Commission*, Volume IIIA, 2004, 481–82, www .sierraleonetrc.org/index.php/view-the-final-report/download-table-of-contents/volume-one/ item/witness-to-the-truth-volume-one-chapters-1-5?category_id=11.

[66] On the page before, the report recognizes the "political and moral" responsibility that businesses, along with other sectors hold for the grave violations of human rights. Comisión Verdad y Justicia de Paraguay, *Informe final*, Volume I.

[67] Comisión de la Verdad y Reconciliación del Perú, *Informe final*, Volume I, 2003, 341–42.

in economic power to implant a new neoliberal economic model to expand trade, income, and profits. Seen as being built on the backs of labor, the model cut wages, social spending, and worker protections, rolling back decades of labor victories in struggles for justice. To suppress labor activism aimed at defending rights and protesting anti-worker policies, repressive laws and violence attempted to crush labor mobilization. In the "armed conflict mode," the root causes of violence emerge from, on one hand, systemic inequality and the use of violence by rebel forces to reverse that pattern, and, on the other hand, economic actors engaged in violent illegal activity and violent security schemes to protect their businesses and profit.

Although the first – authoritarian – mode is generally associated with Latin America, these comments from the South African truth commission suggests a similar pattern: "To the extent that business played a central role in helping to design and implement apartheid policies, it must be held accountable. This applies particularly to the mining industry . . . Direct involvement with the state in the formulation of oppressive policies or practices that resulted in low labor costs (or otherwise boosted profits) can be described as first-order involvement. This is clearly of a different moral order to simply benefiting from such policies. Businesses that were involved in this way must be held responsible and accountable for the suffering that resulted."[68] Similarly, the armed conflict mode tends to be associated with Africa, but the Colombian conflict exhibits some of the same dynamic, that the President of the truth commission, Francisco de Roux, attributes to the country's history of poverty and impunity.[69]

In the next section, we provide an in-depth look at corporate complicity as a root cause of authoritarian state repression, through the 2012 Brazilian National Truth Commission (CNV). After examining the Brazilian report, we turn to an in-depth look at corporate complicity as a root cause of armed conflict, through the Liberian Truth and Reconciliation Commission.

Authoritarian State Model: Brazilian National Truth Commission (CNV)

Brazil provides a recent example of how civil society movements promoted the inclusion of corporate complicity in the truth commission to expose the economic logic at the root of authoritarian state violence. The "Final Considerations" of Volume II describes the vision behind the coup and the dictatorship: to create a depoliticized, acquiescent, submissive, and productive working class under business and state authority control to generate higher

---

[68] Truth and Reconciliation Commission of South Africa, *Truth and Reconciliation Commission of South Africa Report*, Volume IV.
[69] Francisco De Roux, "Impunidad y conflicto armado," *El Tiempo*, August 2015.

capital accumulation. The truth commission acknowledges that the goal required a repressive labor system built through an alliance of business, police, and military that carried out torture, disappearance, illegal and arbitrary detention, and executions.[70]

The CNV locates economic actors' involvement in violence from the very origin of the authoritarian regime: the 1964 coup. Brazilian business elites mobilized proudly behind that coup, calling it a "Revolution."[71] The overthrow of democratically elected President João Goulart and the installation of the dictatorship began a capitalist and political transformation of the country. There was nothing secret about the central role of economic actors in the coup and the subsequent authoritarian regime it implanted. An article in *Fortune* magazine just six months after the coup, titled "When executives turned revolutionaries," outlined the involvement of an estimated 400 business groups in supporting the coup ideologically, financially (an estimated US$500 million), and militarily (providing counter-insurgency training and light arms).[72] A key academic text that drew on original business, business association, and government documents, further linked the business community to the repressive apparatus.[73] The business community not only did not deny its involvement; it considered its role heroic given its view that the spread of Communism threatened the country and the region, owing to Brazil's shared borders with all but two South American countries.

Despite widespread acknowledgment, the CNV mandate did not explicitly include corporate complicity. Mobilization from below – particularly by the trade union movement in the São Paulo state truth commission – succeeded in pressuring for the inclusion of corporate complicity in the national truth commission's final report. The decentralized nature of the truth commission process in Brazil – with grassroots commissions in states,

---

[70] Comissão Nacional da Verdade, 80–81.

[71] As evidence of this pride, two Brazilian industrialists boasted in interviews with Leigh A. Payne that the coup was hatched in their living room. Payne, *Brazilian Industrialists and Democratic Change*. See also Leigh A. Payne, "Cumplicidade empresarial na ditadura brasileira," *10a Revista Anistia: Cooperação econômica com a ditadura*, 2013.

[72] Philip Siekmann, "When Executives Turned Revolutionaries," *Fortune Magazine* (New York, September 1964). See also Felipe Amorim, "Revista Fortune revela já em 64 elo entre empresários de SP e embaixada dos EUA para dar golpe," *Operamundi* (São Paulo, January 2014), http://operamundi.uol.com.br/conteudo/reportagens/33603/revista+fortune+revela+ja +em+64+elo+entre+empresarios+de+sp+e+embaixada+dos+eua+para+dar+golpe.shtml?fb_ comment_id=460616454061037_2261867#f6ef5ef1194f58.

[73] René Armand Dreifuss, *1964: A conquista do estado, ação política, poder e golpe de classe* (Petrópolis, 1987). The book was based on Dreifuss's doctoral thesis research at the University of Glasgow conducted from 1976 to 1980. With more than 800 pages, Dreifuss's book provided ample evidence subsequently used in the truth commission investigations.

cities, communities, and universities springing up throughout the country – allowed civil society actors to pressure for participation in the national process. Such local agency was noted by the head of the São Paulo state's truth commission and former congressman, Adriano Diogo: "The Truth Commission cannot be seen as a movement isolated from society. It is a product of struggle. Neither the Brazilian state, political parties, nor governments, are the only and exclusive channels of civil society representation. The Truth Commission, the National one created by law, as well as the state and municipal ones ... are a product of that struggle and the resistance of the Brazilian people."[74]

The union movement's demand was bolstered by institutional innovators. The Brazilian Secretary of Justice called on the CNV to "investigate the corporations that financed the dictatorship" and acknowledge the private sector's responsibility for repression during the dictatorship;[75] the CNV created a task force to do so. CNV member and criminal lawyer Rosa Cardoso played a pivotal role demanding "institutional accountability" for business behavior during the coup and the dictatorship and contending that Brazil faced "not a military coup, but a civil-military coup that involved the entire business class."[76] As head of the São Paulo commission, Diogo proved instrumental in promoting local findings in the CNV's final report.[77]

The investigations carried out by national and local bodies generated documents, articles, videos, studies, books, and seminars.[78] Results of these projects made corporate complicity part of the CNV findings. The CNV, for example, links a business-supported group (IPES-OBAN) with the

---

[74] The commission was officially called the Rubens Paiva Truth Commission for the State of São Paulo (Comissão da Verdade do Estado de São Paulo, or CEV – "Rubens Paiva"). Quote by Adriano Diogo, Comissão da Verdade do Estado de São Paulo, Brasil, *Relatorio*, Volume 1, Part 1: Introduction (São Paulo, n.d.).

[75] Bohoslavsky and Torelly, "Financial Complicity: The Brazilian Dictatorship under the 'Macroscope,'" 259.

[76] Marsílea Gombata, "Comissão da Verdade quer responsabilizar empresas que colaboraram com a ditadura," *Carta Capital*, March 15, 2014.

[77] In Diogo's words quoted in Gombata (ibid.), "We defend the punishment of torturers and ... businesses ... [who] committed or incited crimes, they committed similar crimes or participated in the same crimes perpetrated by the military against the Brazilian people."

[78] For summaries of these investigations, see James-Allen et al., "Beyond the Truth and Reconciliation Commission: Transitional Justice Options in Liberia"; and ongoing investigations of Odebrecht Construction Company in Folha Transparencia, "Ministro determinou ajuda para empreiteira durante a ditadura," *Folha Transparencia*, 2014, www1 .folha.uol.com.br/poder/2013/03/1242058-ministro-determinou-ajuda-para-empreiteira-durante-a-ditadura.shtml. See also an edited volume summarizing the findings of the research: Joana Monteleone et al., *À espera da verdade: Empresários, juristas e elite transnacional, histórias de civis que fizeram a ditadura militar* (São Paulo: Alameda Editorial, 2016).

financing of the coup, the regime,[79] and its (DOI-CODI) repressive apparatus.[80] As stated in that final report, "The repressive structure of OBAN, oriented toward kidnapping, detention, torture, and execution of the opposition to the military regime, became such an efficient mechanism that it was subsequently used as a model diffused throughout the country in the DOI-CODI [torture] centers."[81]

The report acknowledges direct support for the violence through the creation of blacklists of workers considered "subversive elements," who faced detention, torture, and death or disappearance in the repressive apparatus. In addition, the report notes the role of business in supplying the instruments of repression of workers and others, i.e., vehicles, weapons, installations, and torturers themselves.[82] For example, allegedly privately-owned farms (e.g., Fazenda 31 de Março de 1964) and installations

---

[79] Journalist Denise Assis investigated business financial support for the coup and the propaganda network associated with it. She claims that 125 individuals and 95 entities were involved, including five economic groups (Listas Telefônicas Brasileiras, Light, Cruzeiro do Sul, Refinaria e Exploração de Petróleo União, and Icomi) providing more than 70 percent of the financial contributions. She contends that these funds were funneled to several advertising agencies – such as Promotion S.A., Denisson Propaganda, Gallas Propaganda, Norton Propaganda, and Multi Propaganda – that made at least fourteen propaganda films. See Gombata, "Comissão da Verdade quer responsabilizar empresas que colaboraram com a ditadura." For corruption activities, see Guilherme Amado, "Ditadura foi um oceano de corrupção," *Correio do povo*, March 16, 2014, www.correiodopovo.com.br/blogs/juremirmachado/?p=5770. This is an article based on the research carried out by historian Carlos Fico. Professor Pedro Henrique Pedreira Campos investigated the construction sector in terms of questionable profit-making practices during the dictatorship that helped sustain the regime itself. See Gombata, "Comissão da Verdade quer responsabilizar empresas que colaboraram com a ditadura." There are ongoing investigations of Odebrecht Construction Company and its role in financing the dictatorship, see Folha Transparencia, "Ministro determinou ajuda para empreiteira durante a ditadura."

[80] OBAN or Operação Bandeirantes, financed by business, allegedly helped create the repressive apparatus (Destacamento de Operações de Informações – DOI and the Centro de Operações de Defesa Interna – CODI) after 1969.

[81] Comissão Nacional da Verdade do Brasil, *Relatório da Comissão Nacional da Verdade*, Volume I, 2014, 755, www.cnv.gov.br.

[82] OBAN, created by a civil-military alliance, was located at 921 Rua Tutóia in São Paulo. It is the site of the well-known torture center DOI-CODI (Destacamento de Operações de Informação do Centro de Operações de Defesa Interna). Petrobras has also been accused of providing installations used as torture centers. In addition, General Motors allegedly provided DOI-CODI torturers with earplugs to more effectively carry out their work. See Gombata, "Comissão da Verdade quer responsabilizar empresas que colaboraram com a ditadura"; Correio do Brasil, "Empresários que apoiaram o golpe de 64 construíram grandes fortunas," *Correio do Brasil*, March 27, 2014, http://correiodobrasil.com.br/noticias/brasil/empresarios-que-apoiaram-o-golpe-de-64-construiram-grandes-fortunas/694263/.

(e.g., Boate Querosene) were used for clandestine detention, torture, and execution by the military.[83]

The CNV features Volkswagen as one of the emblematic companies involved in the repressive apparatus. Using archives, the CNV links the company with the DOPS police. Company reports found at the DOPS hinted at Volkswagen's use of informants. In a particular meeting recorded in the documents, Luiz Inácio Lula da Silva, the former trade unionist and president of the country, warned metalworkers about the surveillance at the factory under the company's director of security Coronel Adhemar Rudge.[84] The CNV provided testimony from Lúcio Bellentani, a metalworker at Volkswagen, as further evidence. While Bellentani was at work in the São Bernardo factory, he claimed he was approached by two individuals armed with machine guns. They handcuffed him and took him to the company's security office, where he was tortured, punched, and slapped. Twenty other people, mainly Volkswagen workers, were detained with him.

In rural areas, the CNV report emphasizes the concentration of land and the extractive sector in the hands of a few private individuals who perpetrated violence against rural workers, small landholders, and indigenous communities.[85] The report documents slave labor, land grabbing, and displacement.[86] It covers events in which landholders and companies are linked to the killing of workers and members of indigenous communities.

Without civil society – particularly union – demand, Adriano Diogo claims the information revealed in the São Paulo report would not have appeared in the CNV final report. In Diogo's opinion, CNV commissioners wished to keep the findings out of the final report. This could be explained because of localized, rather than national findings, the absence of a national mandate to include corporate complicity, or the orientation toward state, rather than non-state, actors. According to Diogo, "shaming," resulting from the intense mobilization from unions and the local São Paulo commission, succeeded in overcoming the CNV's initial reluctance.[87] A trade union leader concurs,

[83] Comissão Nacional da Verdade do Brasil, *Relatório da Comissão Nacional da Verdade*, Volume I, 806.
[84] Rudge had replaced the previous security chief at the factory, Franz Paul Stangl, when he was imprisoned in 1967 as a Nazi war criminal. Stangl had not even changed his name when he fled to Brazil and began working at Volkswagen. Comissão Nacional da Verdade, *Relatório da Comissão Nacional da Verdade*, Volume II, 67.
[85] Comissão Nacional da Verdade, *Relatório da Comissão Nacional da Verdade*, Volume II, 94.
[86] Ibid., 96.
[87] Interview with Adriano Diogo, São Paulo, Brazil, March 29, 2017.

emphasizing the significance of institutional innovators – Diogo and Cardoso – in bolstering civil society demand.[88]

We found no evidence of business veto players attempting to block the report.
This might be explained by the absence of a mandate; without it, economic
actors were not alerted to a possible accountability outcome affecting them. In
addition, their public history of support for the coup and the dictatorship,
including incontrovertible evidence of their involvement, would have undercut
efforts to deny the CNV findings. The blanket amnesty law, moreover, protected them from judicial action resulting from the commission findings. By the
time of the CNV, the business community lacked agreement over the merits of
the dictatorship, with key figures decrying business support for it, thereby
preventing strong veto power from emerging. Finally, business elites may have
underestimated the impact of civil society mobilization and institutional innovators in pressuring for corporate accountability in the truth commission.

The result of this process is the surprising CNV findings on corporate
complicity in past human rights violations. It names the highest number of
complicit economic actors compared to all other reports. It recommends
judicial investigations into possible criminal acts. It links business activity to
the very root of authoritarian state violence. While it might be seen as an
outlier, the CNV offers a model of how civil society can mobilize together
with institutional innovators to promote even a reluctant national truth commission to address corporate complicity.

Armed Conflict Model: Liberian Truth and Reconciliation Commission (LTRC)

The 2006 Liberian Truth and Reconciliation Commission (LTRC) aimed to
address the root causes of the armed conflict (1979–2003) that counted more
than 200,000 dead, one million displaced persons, and additional disappearances, torture, enslavement, sexual violence, false imprisonment, and economic crimes. In its mandate, the Commission defined economic crimes in
such a way as to link them to human rights violations: "business entities whose
economic activities contributed to gross human rights and/or humanitarian law
violations in Liberia or that otherwise perpetuated armed conflict in Liberia."[89]

The LTRC report finds the root of the human rights abuses in the illegal
trade that financed the violent conflict: "[President Charles] Taylor was setting
up deals for the exploitation of Liberia's natural resources . . . . Dealings, illicit
in nature and character, in timber, rubber, gold and diamonds, including

---

[88] Interview with Sebastião Neto, March 29, 2017.
[89] Truth and Reconciliation Commission of Liberia, *Final Report*, Volume I, 69.

diamonds from neighboring Sierra Leone, would prove crucial to sustaining Taylor's war efforts and prolonging the conflict."[90] In addition, the report states that, "[t]he rubber, timber, gold and shipping industries served as the sources and means for Taylor to obtain resources and weapons."[91] The report continues, "[t]his exploitation of natural resources to fund wars is well-documented. Often referred to as 'conflict' or 'blood' resources, these natural resources provided the revenue, logistical means, or camouflage to obtain weapons and fund wars. [...] Importantly, however, the origin of these resources was not confined to Liberia but international in scope."[92]

The report directly links the natural resource extraction and associated violence to "economic actors and economic activities [that] played a crucial role in contributing to, and benefiting from, armed conflict in Liberia. Successive governments, including the Taylor regime, established a massive patronage system with domestic and foreign-owned corporations in several critical economic sectors, such as timber, mining and telecommunications, and granted illegal benefits to the corporations in exchange for financial and military support."[93]

Economic crimes allegedly committed by the Liberian timber industry, one of Liberia's key economic sectors, undermined national and regional peace, security and rule of law in several ways. According to the report, logging revenue was unlawfully used by political elites and warring factions to fund armed conflict. The report alleges that logging companies shipped, or facilitated the shipment of, weapons and other military material to warring factions. It further notes the role of logging companies in facilitating, and contributing to, the movement of suspicious funds and illegal economic gains out of Liberia. The report also describes the companies' use of security forces that operated as, or were in fact, militia units that committed grave human rights abuses in Liberia and throughout the region. The report claims that the companies unintentionally contributed to conflict when logging operations were looted by warring factions, particularly when smaller logging companies and community members were violently removed from their land by larger logging operations supported by government militia and rebel factions.[94]

The LTRC further finds that the mining sector, particularly in diamonds, was not dissimilar from the lumber sector. "The [mining] sector also

---

[90] Ibid., 156.
[91] Ibid., 287.
[92] Ibid., 288.
[93] Ibid., 289.
[94] Ibid.

facilitated money laundering, terrorism, bribery of public officials and illegal arms trafficking. Security forces associated with mining companies also committed grave violations of human rights."[95]

The LTRC's investigations into key economic sectors and the related human rights abuses could be attributed to its innovative mandate. An important factor behind the mandate is international pressure. To end the violence and its destabilizing effect in the region, the Economic Community of West African States (ECOWAS) and the UN Mission in Liberia (UNMIL) promoted the LTRC. International Center for Transitional Justice researcher, Ruben Carranza, indirectly connects the LTRC's effective focus on the timber trade and associated human rights violations as "possible because of the collaboration among local civil society, government and international community representatives in the Forest Concessions Review Committee (FCRC), whose data the [L]TRC used. This suggests that when international technical expertise works with and respects local civil society and national government knowledge, corporate accountability in post-conflict contexts can be examined effectively."[96] The LTRC thus suggests that corporate complicity in truth commissions can be promoted through an effective alliance between local civil society groups, local institutional innovators, and international pressure.

Incorporating civil society participation in the truth-gathering process was an explicit part of the LTRC design. Nearly 20,000 testimonies were taken. Expert staff ran communication and sensitivity training to work with victims and their families traumatized by the war.[97] Civil society groups had formal roles within the structure, even in the diaspora. Hearings held in St. Paul, Minnesota sponsored by the Minnesota-based Advocates for Human Rights enabled Liberian refugees to participate in the LTRC process.[98]

These three forces – international pressure, civil society mobilization, and institutional innovation – provided critical support for the LTRC engagement of corporate complicity. During the process itself, little evidence of veto

---

[95] Ibid., 293.
[96] Carranza, "Transitional Justice, Corporate Responsibility and Learning from the Global South."
[97] See James Tonny Dhizaala, "Transitional Justice in Liberia: The Interface between Civil Society Organisations and the Liberian Truth and Reconciliation Commission," in *Advocating Transitional Justice in Africa: The Role of Civil Society*, ed. Jasmina Brankovich and Hugo van der Merwe (Cham, Switzerland: Springer, 2018), 54–55; William J. Long, "Liberia's Truth and Reconciliation Commission: An Interim Assessment," *International Journal of Peace Studies* 13, no. 2 (2008).
[98] See Laura A. Young and Rosalyn Park, "Engaging Diasporas in Truth Commissions: Lessons from the Liberia Truth and Reconciliation Commission Diaspora Project," *International Journal of Transitional Justice* 3, no. 3 (2009): 341–61.

players emerged. Nonetheless fierce opponents – powerful political and economic elites – re-emerged after the process to veto the implementation of the recommendations, particularly judicial action. They seem to have been successful. No courts in Liberia heard cases of economic actors' corporate complicity in human rights violations. Belgian and Dutch courts have, however, put these economic actors on trial.

The LTRC thus shows that the forces that coalesce behind corporate accountability in truth commissions can make impressive achievements, even acknowledging economic actors' role in the root causes of violence. The victories may prove fleeting, however. Sustaining civil society demand and institutional innovators' support against the reemergence of powerful veto players indicates that, at times, international pressure will be imperative.

EXPLAINING CORPORATE ACCOUNTABILITY IN TRUTH COMMISSIONS: ARCHIMEDES' LEVER

We employ the Archimedes' Lever analogy to explain when and why truth commissions have taken on corporate complicity. After exploring four factors critical to corporate accountability – international pressure, veto players, civil society mobilization, and institutional innovation – we examine how context shapes these processes.

International Pressure

As the Liberian case shows, international pressure can be fundamental to corporate accountability in truth commissions. The five internationally supported truth commissions with corporate accountability – El Salvador, Guatemala, Kenya, Liberia, and Timor-Leste partially reinforce the importance of the international pressure factor. These truth commissions are heavily represented among those with a mandate to investigate corporate complicity (three out of four).[99] Two are among the truth commissions with the highest number of economic actors identified as complicit in human rights violations (Guatemala and Liberia).

On the other hand, the international community generally appears indifferent to including corporate accountability in truth commissions. El Salvador provides an example. Although internationally supported, the truth commission had no mandate to investigate private sector support for death squad

---

[99] The three are Kenya, Liberia, and Timor-Leste. The only other such mandate is in Chad, but it did not end up holding those economic actors responsible.

violence. In the report, US Ambassador Alexander Hinton is quoted as saying, "I have never been able to understand the private sector's silence in the face of death squad activity."[100] We know, from US cable traffic and investigative journalism, that evidence of business financing of death squads exists.[101] While many of the economic actors assumed to have supported the death squads have links to the United States, even residing there, no discernible effort has been made to hold them responsible for gross violations of human rights in courts in El Salvador or in the United States. Victims therefore cannot rely on international pressure to advance corporate accountability. Even less evidence of pressure from abroad on corporate accountability exists in the other internationally-sponsored truth commissions.[102]

The absence of international pressure is also apparent in the other domestic truth commissions that did expose corporate complicity. In only a few cases has international pressure helped leverage corporate accountability in truth commissions. In most cases, victims have had to use their own force to counter the weight of veto power.

Veto Players

The Archimedes' Lever model assumes that economic actors' veto power weighs down corporate accountability. In the past truth commissions, little evidence supports this claim. Indeed, we argue that the absence of these veto players may explain how civil society demand and institutional innovators have managed to hold economic actors accountable in truth commissions.[103]

---

[100] US Ambassador interviewed at the Embassy in San Salvador 0349, July 18, 1983. See Comisión de la Verdad para El Salvador, *De la locura a la esperanza: La guerra de 12 años en El Salvador*, 27.

[101] See Abigail Reyes, Kathleen Kelly, and Laurel Anderson, "Death Squads and Miami Financiers," *National Security Archives Research*, February 5, 2003; Brendan Fischer, "US-Funded Death Squads in El Salvador Casts Shadow over GOP Ticket," *Alternet*, August 16, 2012, www.alternet.org/world/us-funded-death-squads-el-salvador-casts-shadow-over-gop-ticket; Raymond Bonner, *Weakness and Deceit: U.S. Policy and El Salvador* (New York, NY: Times Books, 1984).

[102] In Guatemala's report, for example, the naming of US-based Coca-Cola corporation as involved in human rights violations might have prompted some attention to corporate complicity more generally. It did not. Guatemalan workers and their families filed a suit in the Federal District Court in New York in 2010, alleging that the company engaged in a campaign of violence against union workers. The case is still pending.

[103] No discernible economic power differentials distinguish the four truth commissions that named the most companies – Brazil, Guatemala, Liberia, and South Africa – from the rest. Neither is it likely that state institutions or truth commissions in these four countries were more independent from business than in other countries. We also cannot assume that strong business veto power prevented truth commissions – the other half of our data base – from

This has begun to change. With greater visibility, and in new domestic political contexts, business veto power has emerged to block truth processes. This project thus confronts a moral hazard. The goal of making corporate complicity visible in truth commissions may provoke business veto players capable of shutting down such processes. Kenya, Liberia, Argentina, and Colombia provide examples of this hazard.

The internationally supported Kenyan truth commission included in its mandate investigation of human rights violations associated with corruption and land grabs. Leaked before its publication, veto players emerged to block those sections of the report. President Jomo Kenyatta, his family, and associates, implicated in the violent processes of self-enrichment through land acquisition, allegedly mobilized to block it. Protesting this use of veto power, three international commissioners stepped down from their roles.[104]

Veto players emerged in Liberia after the release of the truth commission report. They attempted to block the recommendations to investigate and prosecute those economic actors and others involved in crimes against humanity. As one observer recounts, "the forces that led the country down the path of conflict have not receded entirely. Many of the alleged perpetrators from the war continue determinedly to seek to recapture the state and create conditions that would perpetuate impunity and misrule."[105] These veto players have used legal claims – specifically constitutional challenges[106] – to block judicial action: "Legal scholars clearly state that when truth commissions name individuals for responsibility in contributing to or committing violations, 'the precise nature of the evidence against each named individual in respect of each attributed crime should be made explicit in the final report.'"[107] One scholar notes ironically that such legal mobilization was unnecessary given that "[a]ny attempt to pursue

naming names. Business veto power is surprisingly absent in most of the truth commissions' work.

[104] The three commissioners were the international representatives: Ambassador Berhanu Dinka, Justice Gertrude Chawatama, and Professor Ronald Slye. See Christopher Gitari Ndungú, "Lessons to Be Learned: An Analysis of the Final Report of Kenya's Truth, Justice and Reconciliation Commission," *International Center for Transitional Justice Briefing*, 2014, www .ictj.org/sites/default/files/ICTJ-Briefing-Kenya-TJRC-2014.pdf.

[105] Ezequiel Pajibo, "Civil Society and Transitional Justice in Liberia: A Practitioner's Reflection from the Field," *International Journal of Transitional Justice* 1, no. 2 (2007): 287–96.

[106] James-Allen et al., "Beyond the Truth and Reconciliation Commission: Transitional Justice Options in Liberia," 17.

[107] Mark Freeman, *Truth Commission and Procedural Fairness* (New York, NY: Cambridge University Press, 2006), 283 quoted in James-Allen et al., "Beyond the Truth and Reconciliation Commission: Transitional Justice Options in Liberia."

criminal accountability measures needs to bear in mind that Liberia's justice sector is still weak and susceptible to manipulation."[108]

In Argentina, a new truth commission on corporate complicity in the human rights violations during the Argentine dictatorship provides another example of veto power. Civil society and human rights groups mobilized behind the commission and institutional innovators helped promote the law. The timing was propitious, occurring during the presidency of Cristina Fernández de Kirchner, who had fought opponents in the business community throughout her administration.[109] Powerful Argentine companies within the Unión Argentina Industrial and their political allies, especially the party of then-presidential hopeful Mauricio Macri opposed it. Just weeks before President Macri took office, in November 2015, the legislation passed, allowing the creation of the commission that would be comprised of members of the two chambers of the National Parliament. Passing the legislation did not end the struggle. The political backdrop had changed with a new president with business links to the dictatorship.[110] Civil society groups mobilized to demand that the President and Congress implement the law. They also sought international pressure from the UN Special Rapporteurs and UN agencies to bolster their demand that the government fulfill its legal obligations.[111] Despite these efforts, the new truth commission is indefinitely stalled.

Business has organized to veto corporate accountability since the very beginning of Colombia's transitional justice process. The Consejo Nacional Gremial (National Guild Council), an association of the largest business associations in Colombia,[112] lobbied the government during the peace negotiations in Havana,

---

[108] James-Allen et al., "Beyond the Truth and Reconciliation Commission: Transitional Justice Options in Liberia," 19.

[109] Conflicts between the Fernández de Kirchner government and certain businesses, particularly the newspaper company Clarín, could be said to have initiated some efforts to expose companies' complicity in the past dictatorship. One particularly controversial example is the Papel Prensa case, in which Clarín was allegedly connected to the torture and forced takeover of the newsprint company, establishing a near monopoly over the print media during the dictatorship.

[110] El País Digital, "El grupo Macri y la dictadura: El comienzo de la expansión," *El País Digital*, March 24, 2018, www.elpaisdigital.com.ar/contenido/el-grupo-macri-y-la-dictadura-el-comienzo-de-la-expansin/15762; Telesurtv, "Los Macri y sus negocios durante la dictadura argentina," *Telesurtv*, 2015, www.telesurtv.net/news/Los-Macri-y-sus-negocios-durante-la-dictadura-argentina-20151112-0008.html.

[111] UN High Commission Office, "Argentina Dictatorship: UN Experts Back Creation of Commission on Role Business People Played," November 2015.

[112] This includes Andi (Asociación de Industriales de Colombia); Analdex (Asociación Nacional de Comercio Exterior); Asobancaria (Asociación gremial financiera colombiana); Asocaña (Asociación de Cultivadores de Caña de Azúcar); Fedegán (Federación Colombiana de Ganaderos); Cámara Colombiana de la Infraestructura, Fasecolda (Federación de

Cuba to block the inclusion of corporate accountability in the transitional justice mandate. Business also challenged its inclusion in the Special Jurisdiction for Peace (JEP) and won. Regarding the truth commission, business representatives have argued that it is not necessary when strong democratic institutions exist in the country. They further contend that the Commission could undermine other transitional justice institutions charged with investigating the armed conflict, such as the Historical Memory Center and the Special Jurisdiction of Peace.[113] The business veto over corporate accountability has gained power with the 2018 presidential election of President Iván Duque, publicly backed by the Consejo Nacional Gremial.[114]

In sum, civil society actors and institutional innovators historically promoted corporate accountability in truth commissions largely without business veto power blocking their efforts. Recent experiences suggest that powerful veto players are likely to emerge when civil society actors and institutional innovators achieve the goals of including corporate accountability in mandates, making commission findings visible, and advancing judicial recommendations. Thus, context can play an important role in corporate accountability.

Political Context

The early truth commissions benefited from a relatively neutral domestic and global context for corporate accountability. Neither international pressure nor domestic governments promoted corporate accountability, but neither did they oppose it. Certain openings for civil society mobilization also emerged at this time. The global human rights accountability norm brought widespread support for truth-telling efforts. The domestic shift away from authoritarian regimes and armed conflicts and toward democratic transition also opened up space for

Aseguradores Colombianos); ANDESCO (Asociación Nacional de Empresas de Servicios Públicos y Comunicaciones); and FEDEPALMA (Federación Nacional de Cultivadores de Palma de Aceite).

[113] These two institutions were preferable to economic actors no doubt because the Center had prepared a study recognizing business victims of the conflict and the JEP's mandate did not include corporate accountability.

[114] El Espectador, "Sector empresarial manifiesta su apoyo a Iván Duque," *El Espectador*, 2018, www.elespectador.com/elecciones-2018/noticias/politica/sector-empresarial-manifiesta-su-apoyo-ivan-duque-articulo-793181. The president of the Consejo Nacional Gremial manifestly opposed the results of our findings on corporate accountability and transitional justice. Jorge Humberto Botero, "Pax Christi," *Semana.com*, 2018, www.semana.com/opinion/articulo/jorge-botero-columna-pax-christi/559448. Our findings were presented at an open meeting in Bogota, see Nelson Camilo Sánchez et al., *Cuentas Claras: El papel de la Comisión de la Verdad en la develación de la responsabilidad de empresas en el conflicto armado colombiano* (Bogotá, 2018), www.dejusticia.org/publication/cuentas-claras-empresas/.

mobilization. In this neutral context, and with the absence of veto power by
business, civil society and institutional innovators required little force to hold
businesses accountable in truth commission final reports.

While the global context did not change dramatically, domestic contexts
varied among countries and over time. Most remained neutral. Even the
so-called pink tide (left-leaning) countries of Latin America neither opposed
nor advanced corporate accountability. One exception is the Cristina Fernández de Kirchner government that provided a much more favorable context,
owing to the President's battles with her corporate enemies. During her
administration, the new truth commission on corporate complicity was passed
through the legislature. In the other – neutral – domestic environments, civil
society and institutional forces attempted to exert more force than veto players.
As we have seen, sometimes veto players attempted to block truth processes
(Kenya, Liberia, Colombia). For the most part, veto players largely remained
passive in the face of corporate accountability in truth commissions.

The recent shift to the right in Latin America and in other parts of the world
foresees a much less neutral and less propitious environment for corporate
accountability. Where civil society actors and institutional innovators had a
chance against veto players in neutral contexts, the political shift portends a
much greater force holding down corporate accountability. In this unpropitious context, civil society and institutional innovators will have to redouble
their efforts to lift the weight of corporate accountability from under the force
of veto players.

Civil Society Mobilization and Institutional Innovators

Understanding how civil society mobilized in past truth commissions allows
us to consider future efforts. Testimony from victims was critical. Without
such testimony, and without a mandate to investigate corporate complicity,
claims against companies in the final report would not have been made by
staff. As Appendix D illustrates, truth commission reports with corporate
complicity involved victim testimony. There are only four exceptions.[115]
Specific institutional designs of truth commissions, such as the Liberian one
with ample popular participation, thus offer opportunities for civil society
groups to mobilize and advance the truth – through testimony – about
corporate complicity in past human rights violations.

---

[115] Truth commissions in Cote D'Ivoire and the three in South Korea did not include victim
testimony.

Yet civil society groups have not been deterred by a lack of a mandate or specific institutional designs to promote corporate accountability in truth commissions. At times, they create the opportunities to participate. The case of Brazil provides an example of union movement creativity in finding documents, locating witnesses, and persuading the national truth commission – through institutional innovators – to include corporate accountability in the final national truth commission report.

Other creative processes are not always planned by civil society actors or commission staff, but rather serendipitous. Corporate accountability in truth commissions sometimes emerges as a natural by-product of testimony by survivors of violence. The following section of Argentina's CONADEP truth commission report describes such a process:

> [CONADEP] met twice in the city of Villa Constitución and legally recognized the illegal detention center that operated in the Acindar company's building. The residents of the city spontaneously made testimony, leading to the identification of Aníbal Gordon. He was the head of the operations [when the massacre] took place in that city in January 1976. More than ten people were kidnapped and assassinated. One of the testimonies detailed events at the Acindar company at the end of 1975 [leading up to the massacre]. The 5,000 workers were ordered by the company to register with the Federal Police for a new National Identity Card, which would generate a new company identification card and new photographs. These photographs were later used by the security and military personnel to carry out the kidnapping and detention [of company employees].[116]

Without the efforts by commission staff, the testimony – the truth about corporate complicity in the violent past – would not have made it into the final report. Commission staff took the testimony of victims of corporate abuse and retained that testimony in the final report, thereby ensuring corporate accountability in truth commissions. Staff did not have to be ideologically committed to exposing the truth about corporate complicity; they simply had to be attuned to the information they were receiving about gross violations of human rights in which economic actors were involved. The preparation of the final report involves redaction since not all human rights violations can be included. That claims of corporate complicity do appear in these final reports, even when these violations are not part of the original truth commission mandates, suggests innovative acts – deliberate or not – on the part of institutional actors. Rather than strictly hewing to the

---

[116] Comisión Nacional sobre la Desaparición de Personas, *Nunca Más*, chap. 2.

commission mandate, truth commission researchers or other staff members sometimes advance victims' rights to truth about human rights abuses, even if committed by non-state actors. They did not edit out testimonies to the role of business in the violence. Without consciously or deliberately playing the role of innovators, commission staff exposed a truth about corporate complicity in past violations.

We sometimes wonder if we have played the role of innovators in our research method. In our first review of the Salvadoran truth commission report, for example, our keyword search did not reveal any names of economic actors involved in human rights abuses. Puzzled by this outcome, we cross-checked the members of the "Miami 8," mentioned in other documents as the businessmen who funded the death squads, to see if they were named in the report. They were, but the report identified them as "wealthy" Salvadorans, not one of our keywords. Our research thus revealed corporate accountability in the truth commission report through an innovative process. Guatemala is similar. Keyword searches did not reveal more than a handful of cases of corporate complicity. When we read through the lists of events in rural areas, we uncovered in the report the managers and owners of agricultural enterprises allegedly linked to gross violations of human rights.[117]

In sum, testimony is a key tool used by civil society and institutional innovators to advance corporate accountability in truth commissions. Without the testimony of victims and their families, truth commissions would not likely identify complicit companies. As institutional innovators, commission staff retained these testimonies and these truths in the final report. Testimony alone does not tell the full story of civil society mobilization for corporate accountability. Adding to civil society force to lift corporate accountability, two innovative tactics reveal the truths of corporate complicity in past human rights abuses: campaigns against certain companies or sets of companies for their corporate complicity, and direct action to "out" businesses for their complicity.[118]

---

[117] From the Guatemala report, it is difficult to determine the level of mobilization in rural communities to make testimony or demand corporate accountability.

[118] In the area of business and human rights, scholars have identified "bottom up" and nonjudicial forms of truth telling, such as naming and shaming, public protests, internet bashing, investor resolutions, and consumer boycotts. See Deva, "Multinationals, Human Rights and International Law: Time to Move beyond the 'State-Centric' Conception?," 23. See also the nonjudicial action discussed as a "bottom up" approach, such as National Human Rights Institutions (NHRIs), company mechanisms; multi-lateral financial institutions and loan conditioning; international treaty based grievance mechanisms, such as the International Labor Organization (ILO); regional human rights commissions; regional human rights courts; and collaborative initiatives. Drimmer and Laplante, "The Third Pillar." On campaigns against US companies, see Marcia L. Narine, "Living in a Material World – From Naming and Shaming

Campaigns

By campaigns, we mean organized efforts to inform the public about corporate complicity, targeting particular companies or sets of companies. On the annual 24 March anniversary of the Argentine coup, for example, protesters have added corporate complicity to the campaign for justice for past human rights abuses. Banners suspended over the main plaza announce the names of companies identified with state terror. "Democracy or corporations?" (see Image 4.1) is the question posed about a process of truth, justice, reparations, and guarantees of non-repetition that has left economic actors out of the accounting for past human rights violations. The rallies, organized by civil society groups, call for a recognition of business involvement in human rights abuses carried out by the security forces. As a result of the visibility of corporate complicity, references to the "military dictatorship" changed to the "civil-military dictatorship" to reflect the role of corporations and other non-state actors in the repression.[119] This mobilization was significant in the adoption of the new truth commission focusing on economic actors' violations during the dictatorship. It is also a way to make visible business involvement in the dictatorship without relying on the limited findings of the previous truth commission.

Campaigns in South Africa are closely connected to the country's TRC. Two campaigns in particular attempted to fulfill the goals of the TRC recommendations in holding businesses responsible for complicity in Apartheid-era violence. The social movement Jubilee South Africa, for example, targeted multinational corporations that repatriated profits outside the country, seeking, without success, both debt relief and reparations from those businesses. The ANC government under President Thabo Mbeki vociferously objected to efforts like these and the TRC's recommended "wealth tax." The government claimed these efforts would backfire, making it more difficult for the new South Africa to develop economically, and advance its social justice agenda, if it were perceived to be hostile toward business.

Frustrated at the unwillingness of the ANC government to hold business to account following the TRC findings, the Khulumani Support Group filed a

---

to Knowing and Showing: Will New Disclosure Regimes Finally Drive Corporate Accountability for Human Rights?" in *The Business and Human Rights Landscape: Moving Forward, Looking Back*, ed. Jena Martin and Karen E. Bravo (Cambridge: Cambridge University Press, 2015).

[119] Similar renaming of the past political regimes has occurred in Brazil, Chile, and Uruguay for the same reasons.

IMAGE 4.1 "Democracy or Corporations?"
Note: At the 2014 rally commemorating the anniversary of the Argentine coup, March 24, 1976, civil society groups rhetorically asked Argentines to choose between "democracy or corporations."
Photo by: Bernabé Rivarola. Reproduced by permission

lawsuit in the United States (see Chapter 2). The Mbeki government actively sought to undermine the lawsuit. Minister of Trade and Industry Alec Erwin claimed that the government would not enforce judgments made in US courts.[120] Minister of Justice Penuel Maduna attempted to have the case dismissed owing to its interference in South Africa's domestic process and state sovereignty. These combined actions were interpreted as efforts to reassure the business community of a positive investment climate.[121] It appeared that companies held veto power even in a socially-conscious ANC government owing to its fear of a corporate exodus from the country. Undeterred by these counter efforts on the part of the government, South African civil society groups continued to fight in US courts and in South Africa.

The timing of the 2010 Soccer World Cup offered an event and a stage for mobilization. Khulumani initiated a "Red Card" campaign stating, "Daimler

---

[120] Ginger Thompson, "South Africa to Pay $3,900 to Each Family of Apartheid Victims," *The New York Times*, April 16, 2013, www.nytimes.com/2003/04/16/world/south-africa-to-pay-3900-to-each-family-%0Dof-apartheid-victims.html.

[121] South African History Archive (SAHA), "TRC Category-4. Reparations," in *Traces of Truth: Documents Related to the Truth and Reconciliation Commission* (University of the Witwaterstrand, n.d.), http://truth.wwl.wits.ac.za/cat_descr.php?cat=4.

AG generously sponsored the German team in its quest to win the Soccer World Cup on South African soil, while ignoring calls to acknowledge and pay reparations for its 'sponsorship' of apartheid atrocities." In one poster produced in the campaign (see Image 4.2) the iconic Mercedes hood ornament was referred to as the "star of Apartheid."[122]

The nongovernmental organization Open Secrets[123] has also engaged in research and public exposure of the linkages between contemporary corruption and violent and illicit businesses with the Apartheid era. The organization's 2017 book, *Apartheid Guns and Money: A Tale of Profit*,[124] is an exposé linked to a public education campaign and call to action. As part of the education campaign, we observed a book launch in Cape Town's Khayelitsha Township organized by Open Secrets together with local community groups.[125] With Open Secrets, we have proposed a "blood banking" campaign that links Apartheid era and other authoritarian and conflict human rights crimes to the banks that sponsored those atrocities.

The most successful global campaign targets "blood diamonds," or conflict minerals more generally. Beginning in the late 1990s, governmental and nongovernmental organizations campaigned around the problem leading to the 2003 Kimberley Process in which governments certified legal import and export trade in diamonds. Popular awareness was no doubt heightened by the 2006 movie *Blood Diamond* starring Leonardo DiCaprio. Diamond and jewelry companies took notice and attempted to distance themselves from the blood diamond imagery. As a spokesperson for De Beers stated, "Diamonds are a luxury, not a necessity. No one wants to buy something that is intended to express love if it is tainted with blood."[126] Aware consumers are instructed through these campaigns to ask questions to avoid purchasing such a diamond, but not to accept easy answers. As one popular magazine suggests: "Don't settle

---

[122] Red Card Campaign, "Farewell Germany … But What about Daimler?," *Red Card Campaign*, 2010, https://redcardcampaign.wordpress.com/2010/07/08/farewell-germany-but-what-about-daimler/.

[123] See: Open Secrets, "Open Secrets," www.opensecrets.org.za.

[124] Hennie van Vuuren, *Apartheid Guns and Money: A Tale of Profit* (Open Secrets, 2017).

[125] The audience applauded the effort and expressed continued frustration with, and anger at, the ANC government's corruption. One young man, after expressing his respect for the work behind the book, raised the question of what can be done. As he stated, suing the government and its officials might bring in money, but the depth of the corruption implied that communities like Khayelitsha would never see a penny.

[126] Quote from presentation by Dr. Nicky Black, Head of Social Performance for De Beers, on October 24, 2014 at the Said Business School, University of Oxford. The presentation was given during the conference "Business and Human Rights – Aspects of International Law and Developments at the United Nations Human Rights Council," organized by the Oxford Institute for Ethics, Law, and Armed Conflict.

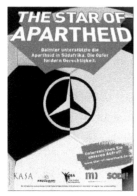

IMAGE 4.2 The World Cup and Apartheid-era Violence
Note: Civil society mobilization targeted multinational corporations sponsoring the 2010 Soccer World Cup in South Africa for their support for Apartheid-era violence.
Source: Khulumani Soccer World Cup Campaign, supported by KASA and medico international, 2010

for vague assurances about reputable suppliers or Kimberley Process certification – the KP does not ban diamonds that fund war crimes and human rights abuses by government forces. Nor does it address unfair labor practices or environmental degradation brought about by irresponsible diamond mining."[127] Despite the visibility of the campaign against blood diamonds that generated a film, consumer advice, country and company response, the problem of conflict minerals continues. As Global Witness states, "The illicit trade in diamonds has funded brutal wars and human rights abuses for decades. Despite significant progress, the problem has not gone away."[128]

These examples of civil society mobilization show that truth-telling about corporate complicity can occur outside formal commissions. These campaigns are visible, and capture media and public attention, in ways that truth commissions often do not. They aim to have a direct impact on public knowledge, and on governmental, international, and foreign policies of corporate accountability.

Outing

Efforts to publicly "out" business perpetrators for their past abuses also raise public awareness to corporate complicity. Argentina's well-known efforts at outing state perpetrators of past human rights violations, the so-called *escraches*

---

[127] Aryn Baker, "How to Buy an Ethical Diamond," *Time*, August 27, 2015, http://time.com/4013735/how-to-buy-an-ethical-diamond/.
[128] Global Witness, "Conflict Diamonds," n.d., www.globalwitness.org/en/campaigns/conflict-diamonds/.

organized by civil society groups (mainly H.I.J.O.S., or the sons and daughters of the disappeared), have been used in the last decade against corporate perpetrators. These are public acts aimed at holding human rights violators accountable when courts have failed to do so. The leaflets that circulate identifying the name of the perpetrator to be outed, the time, date, and place to meet (usually a public plaza), and the destination for the march (usually the perpetrator's home), also include the reason for the *escrache*: "If there is no justice, there will be outing!" (*Si no hay justicia, hay escrache*). The *escraches* are a popular form of accountability action to overcome impunity for past human rights violations.

We found one case in 2015 of an *escrache* in Buenos Aires to out Vicente Massot, the head of the newspaper *La Nueva Provincia*, and Carlos Pedro Tadeo Blaquier, the former head of the company Ledesma, for their "participation in crimes against humanity during the last civil-military dictatorship."[129] H.I.J.O.S. considers Massot responsible for the disappearance and death in 1976 of two workers and union delegates at the newspaper – Enrique Heinrich and Miguel Ángel Loyola – and for his role in aiding in the kidnapping, torture, and homicide of thirty-five additional people. The CONADEP report did not name either Massot or his newspaper. Ledesma is included in the report, as the excerpt at the beginning of this chapter shows. The *escrache* accused Blaquier and the sugar mill's manager of joint criminal activity with the armed forces in the kidnapping and repression of the company's workers and union leaders during "La Noche del Apagón" (Black-out Night) on the day of, and those following, the 1976 coup. The legal case (discussed in Chapter 5) is ongoing.[130]

A different sort of outing has occurred in Brazil.[131] Students, for example, mobilized to petition for the removal of a São Paulo street name associated with one of the businessmen connected to the coup and repression. The students created a short documentary film about their street action

---

[129] Andar, "La Red Nacional de H.I.J.O.S. convoca a un escrache a Massot y Blaquier," *Andar*, May 20, 2015, www.andaragencia.org/la-red-nacional-de-h-i-j-o-s-convoca-a-un-escrache-a-massot-y-blaquier/.

[130] See also Dandan and Franzki, "Entre analisis histórico y responsabilidad jurídica: El caso Ledesma."

[131] Brazil also has *escraches*, mainly led by a group called Levante Popular de Juventude, but we have not found evidence of its use for corporate complicity. Vladimir Safatle, "À sombra da ditadura," *Carta Capital*, December 30, 2011, www.cartacapital.com.br/politica/a-sombra-da-ditadura.

IMAGE 4.3 The *Escraches* in Buenos Aires
Note: The *Escraches* in Buenos Aires aimed at "outing" the connection between certain businesses and the repressive apparatus of the dictatorship.
Photo by: H.I.J.O.S. Capital and Mariano Portas. Reproduced by permission

called *Projeto Adeus Boilesen* (Project Good-bye Boilesen).[132] In the film they interview residents of the street in São Paulo, asking them about its name: "Do you have any idea who Henning Boilesen was?" One neighbor ventures a guess that he was German, given his name. Another confidently identifies him as a director of a business, pointing to a plaque under the street sign indicating those bare bones of his past. Most have no idea.

Boilesen could be said to be the face of corporate complicity in the 1964 coup and the dictatorship it implanted in Brazil. The truth commission report, drawing on already existing studies, identified him as financing the coup along with an estimated 125 other members of the business community. It also alleges that his company provided the repressive equipment used in the torture centers installed after the coup. Some claim he and other members of the business community participated in that torture. His open support for the coup and the dictatorship led to his assassination in 1971. Boilesen was gunned down in broad daylight near his home by the ALN (Ação Libertadora Nacional – National Liberation Action) urban guerrilla group.[133] A film about Boilesen – *Cidadão Boilesen* (Citizen Boilesen) – and his activities during the dictatorship leading to his murder a decade later circulated widely on YouTube.[134]

---

[132] Matheus Brant, *Projeto Adeus Boilesen* (Brazil, 2013), www.youtube.com/watch?v=SDM-PXdAS2w.

[133] See especially Comissão Nacional da Verdade do Brasil, *Relatório da Comissão Nacional da Verdade*, Volume I, 127, 317, 330–33.

[134] Chaim Litewski, *Cidadão Boilesen: Um dos empresários que financiou a tortura no Brasil*; Payne, "Cumplicidade empresarial na ditadura brasileira."

Shareholders' initiatives provide another sort of outing. At times these initiatives emerge from transnational advocacy based on local civil struggles, or STANs (shareholder transnational advocacy networks). One example occurred at a Volkswagen Company's annual shareholders' meeting in Hanover, Germany on May 13, 2014. The Association of Critical Shareholders raised the issue of the company's role in human rights violations in the Brazilian dictatorship. The document they prepared stated, "We demand that Volkswagen investigate and clarify immediately these cases [of collaboration in the dictatorship's repression], keeping in mind the recent fiftieth anniversary of the Brazilian military coup. Volkswagen must admit to and accept its historical responsibility."[135] The investigations underway in Brazil formed the basis for the outing of the company in Germany. The German media picked up on the local mobilization against the company, heightening pressure on the company to respond to the Brazilian demand for accountability. Shareholder activism reflects a form of civil mobilization within the company. It aims to influence the board of directors and management to address companies' involvement in human rights violations from within the company structure.[136] The protests and media coverage in Germany also bolster local demands for accountability in Brazil.

In South Africa, the "People's Tribunal on Economic Crime,"[137] illustrates innovative forms of "outing" and noninstitutionalized corporate accountability from below. Its "Final Report" recognizes that the aims of the TRC to bring justice for past abuses were not fully achieved by the National Prosecutor's Office. While one section of the report focused on the "pre-democracy" period, two other sections linked the economic crimes of that era to arms deals and state capture under the democratic government. Although not explicit, the report insinuates that the failure to fully investigate and prosecute economic crimes has perpetuated impunity that has endured to the present. In the pre-democracy period, the report focuses on those companies that ignored the binding UN embargo on South Africa. "Any sanction-busting operations

---

[135] Victor Sion, Felipe Amorim, and Patrícia Dichtchekenian, "Os acionistas críticos de Volkswagen, Siemens e Mercedes-Benz," in *À espera da verdade: Empresários, juristas e elite transnacional, histórias de civis que fizeram a ditadura militar*, ed. Joana Monteleone et al. (São Paulo: Alameda Editorial, 2016), 189.

[136] Ibid., 189–96.

[137] See The People's Tribunal on Economic Crime, *Final Report of the People's Tribunal on Economic Crime: First Hearings 3–7 February, 2018; Arms Trade: 20 September 2018*, 2018. For a discussion of South African people's courts, see Sandra Burman and Wilfried Schärf, "Creating People's Justice: Street Committees and People's Courts in a South African City," *Law & Society Review* 24, no. 3 (1990): 693.

aimed at propping up apartheid was, at the very least, equal to the crime of aiding and abetting the commission of the crime against humanity."[138] The document links funding from Kredietbank to "killings, torture, forced removals, wrongful imprisonment, and the like. Indeed, the regime's conduct would have been more difficult to sustain had it not been for the illegal trade in arms during this period."[139] In its recommendations, the report calls for judicial investigations and prosecution of the following companies that "aided and abetted the commission of the crimes of apartheid, a crime against humanity": KBL, Kredietbank, Thales, Norinco, and Ferrostaal.[140] The People's Tribunal calls for a special unit within the National Prosecuting Authority to carry out the investigations, to provide that information to the UN to establish an international criminal tribunal to investigate those crimes. Thus, the tribunal seemed to promote the TRC findings on corporate complicity and to advance justice for past crimes against humanity carried out by businesses.

The outing processes we have analyzed, like the campaigns, aim to make past corporate complicity visible. They are oriented toward popular justice – popular corporate accountability – as an outcome, an end in itself. In the process, they fill a void left by the invisibility of truth commissions' findings on corporate complicity.

CONCLUSION

Truth commissions constitute one of the singular most important nonjudicial official mechanisms for dealing with past human rights abuses in the world today. Operating for over three decades, since the creation of the 1983 Argentine CONADEP report to the 2018 truth commission in Colombia, twenty-three truth commissions in most regions of the world have investigated corporate complicity in violations of human rights during authoritarian periods and armed conflict. Very few of these investigations were mandated in the official truth commission design. That the commissions have included them speaks to the efforts by civil society forces and institutional innovators to raise awareness of corporate complicity within or outside formal truth

---

[138] See The People's Tribunal on Economic Crime, *Final Report of the People's Tribunal on Economic Crime: First Hearings 3–7 February, 2018; Arms Trade: 20 September 2018*, p. 4.
[139] Ibid., p. 5.
[140] Ibid., p. 7.

processes. We have shown that this success has also depended on neutral political contexts and passive veto players.

Nonetheless, these efforts have remained largely invisible. As such, they have played a limited role in transitional justice's corporate accountability efforts. These hidden truths mean that only rarely have they "narrowed the range of permissible lies"[141] about corporate complicity in violence. They have rarely raised the cost – even reputational – to companies for past human rights violations. The result is a limited contribution to advancing truth, justice, reparations, and guarantees of non-repetition for victims of corporate complicity.

These partial achievements notwithstanding, truth commissions have the potential to advance victims' rights. From our study, certain guidelines emerge that would likely enhance truth commissions' ability to achieve their goals of contributing to stronger human rights futures by addressing corporate complicity. We set those out here.

A first step is to define what corporate complicity means. As stated in the Introduction to this book, there is nothing incompatible about truth commissions or other transitional justice mechanisms holding corporations and other civil actors responsible for their complicity in human rights violations. The definition of these mechanisms is not restricted to state actors. Nonetheless, careful definition of complicity is crucial to avoid accusations of an ideological witch hunt led by anti-business forces. Defining the criteria by which business will be investigated demonstrates a serious inquiry into human rights abuses, rather than a hostility toward business. Four criteria correspond to jurisprudence in this area of law: joint criminal enterprise; slave labor; financing violence or repression; and violent illegal enterprises.[142] Clarification that direct and indirect crimes against humanity carried out by economic actors, and not simply doing business with, or profiting during, authoritarian and armed conflict periods, is imperative.

Second, truth commissions should outline why they are investigating corporations, and in particular link past human rights violence to a historical pattern of corporate abuse. Truth commissions should be involved where there is systematic and widespread corporate complicity that goes beyond a few "bad apples" within the business community. Presumably individual bad apples could be prosecuted by local judiciaries without a backlash from the

---

[141] Michael Ignatieff, *The Warrior's Honor: Ethnic War and the Modern Conscience* (New York, NY: Henry Holt and Company, 1997).
[142] Maassarani, "Four Counts of Corporate Complicity: Alternative Forms of Accomplice Liability under the Alien Tort Claims Act," 39–65.

business community. Truth commissions should investigate illegal economic enterprises and legitimate businesses that participated in gross violations of human rights under cover of impunity. Commissions should identify businesses and business activities that violated human rights. Such processes advance truth, accountability, and deterrence goals of truth commissions.

Third, particular institutional arrangements, even without a mandate, and particularly through victim and survivor testimony, enhance truth processes and contribute to restoring victims' dignity (reparative processes). Where victims' groups – such as unions, the families of the disappeared, indigenous and other communities – have participated, we have shown that commissions are more likely to make corporate violations and violators visible. Formalizing such investigations and testimony would thus promote victims' rights.

Fourth, the commission staff and those testifying to it require protection from potential corporate reprisals. In the last three years, the killing of Berta Cáceres and others who mobilized in Honduras against the large dam project, and the disappearance and killing of Santiago Maldonado in Argentina for his protest of Benetton's activities, show that businesses remain willing to use violent means to protect themselves from public campaigns and outing, protest, or condemnation. Although security has not yet been an issue for truth commissions investigating or revealing corporate complicity, with greater visibility to this aspect of truth commission work, it is likely to become a potential source of tension that could lead to threats of violence.

Fifth, international support would help guarantee the security and legitimacy of truth commissions engaging in this type of inquiry. While past commissions have often proved capable of carrying out these investigations without international support or even awareness, a serious effort to end economic actors' complicity – guarantees of non-repetition – would benefit from incorporating research into the design of truth commissions supported by international organizations such as the UN and the International Center for Transitional Justice.

Sixth, corporate complicity should be part of truth commission mandates where appropriate. Although civil society demand and institutional innovators have circumvented the lack of mandates in past truth commissions, the accountability and deterrence function of these processes would be enhanced by institutionalized and systematic, rather than ad hoc, investigations. Companies and business associations themselves have also hired researchers to investigate and divulge their past human rights violations as a commitment to avoid such activities in the future. National historical memory centers might conduct in-depth and emblematic case studies of events to deepen understanding of corporate complicity and its impact.

Seventh, the set of recommendations emerging from past truth commissions are often weak and poorly implemented. Greater attention to appropriate and enforceable recommendations would strengthen truth commission findings and address victims' rights. These recommendations must be appropriate to the country context and reflect the rights of victims. While prosecuting every company may not be possible, recommendations for investigations and sanctions through national human rights institutions or ombuds offices for firms willing to participate, and prosecution for others could advance accountability and deter future violations. This is the proposed strategy in Colombia to incorporate businesses complicit in the armed conflict into the accountability and peace process.

The guidelines set out here do not address business veto power explicitly. We suspect that businesses might use their veto power if truth commissions were to take on corporate complicity more openly. As we discuss throughout this book, institutional innovators have occasionally found ways around this veto power. International support may also provide greater leverage to commissioners, innovators, and governments attempting to break the cycle of impunity and to build new business cultures intolerant of human rights violations.

As transitional justice scholars have shown, truth commissions on their own are unlikely to improve democracy and human rights.[143] Thus, we would assume that closing the victims' gap will involve parallel and complementary truth commission and judicial processes. In the next chapter we explore the achievements of the judicial accountability efforts that are already underway.

[143] Olsen et al., *Transitional Justice in Balance: Comparing Processes, Weighing Efficacy*; Dancy et al., "Behind Bars and Bargains: New Findings on Transitional Justice in Emerging Democracies," 1–12.

5

Justice from Below

They [negotiators sent by the palm oil companies and the paramilitaries] would tell us "if you don't sell to us now, we will buy the land from your widow." If we did not sell we would lose access to the land. The best-case scenario was to sell to them and become a partner in the economic enterprise. They started tightening their grip. We started to lose access to our lands. The only way to hold on to something was to give up our land. They said that they would buy the land, but that was a lie. They paid whatever they wanted because it was all done under threat.
　　　　　—Victim of forced displacement in Colombia[1]

The demand for justice for human rights violations carried out by economic actors in dictatorships and armed conflicts often comes from below: from victims, their communities, and their advocates in the countries where the abuses occurred. It emerges in countries in the Global South transitioning from high levels of violence. When corporate complicity cases are taken to courts in those countries, the accountability outcomes are more likely than through "top down" international transitional justice models or "bottom-up" business and human rights strategies in Global North courts. This chapter examines the role of national courts in responding to victims' demands for corporate accountability, a process we call "justice from below."

The chapter also examines how the Archimedes' Lever analogy produces "justice from below." Civil society groups initiate the demand for justice for corporate wrongdoing. They rely on institutional innovators to translate those demands into judicial action: claim-making, indictment, convictions and adverse judgments. Judicial innovators develop tools, specifically the creative

---

[1] Testimony before the Prosecutor's Office of Miguel Ángel Hoyos Rivas, Member of the Communities of Curvaradó and Jiguamiandó, forcibly displaced by the AUC paramilitary groups and thirteen palm oil companies in the late 1990s in Colombia.

adaptation and blending of domestic legal instruments with international human rights law. With these tools, civil society demand and institutional innovators apply the force necessary to lift the weight of corporate account-ability. When the context (fulcrum) is closer to corporate accountability, they are likely to have sufficient force to lift it from under the weight of veto players, even in the absence of international pressure.

In lifting the weight of corporate accountability, "justice from below" advances international human rights. It does so in two ways. First, the very act of holding economic actors accountable for complicity in human rights viola-tions – legal practice – addresses victims' rights to truth, justice, reparations, and guarantees of non-repetition. Second, accountability efforts confirm – through legal interpretation – economic actors' binding and enforceable human rights obligations. Innovators use common legal practices available in most systems around the world (e.g., labor law, economic law, criminal law) coupled with international human rights norms often incorporated into national legislation. As corporate accountability tools available in different legal systems in various world regions, these processes can extend across Global South borders. "Justice from below," thus, acts as Archimedes' Lever: otherwise weak civil society actors and institutional innovators in the Global South employ effective tools in domestic courts to lift corporate accountability and thus global human rights through legal practice and legal interpretation.

In the first part of this chapter, we examine "justice from below" through our cross-national comparative analysis. We identify where, when, and what type of corporate accountability has been achieved. We also consider where progress toward corporate accountability from below through domestic courts has not been achieved. The next section attempts to explain those outcomes, drawing on a continuum of accountability outcomes and case studies to illustrate our argument. The conclusion to the chapter explores the trans-formative potential of domestic judicial action in shaping international human rights. It also sets forth guidelines for implementing "justice from below."

COMPARATIVE STUDY OF JUSTICE FROM BELOW

Our "from below" approach emerged from a systematic analysis of corporate accountability in judicial actions around the world. We find that the most successful outcomes for victims emerge from trials in domestic courts in the Global South, and not in international courts or foreign courts in the Global North. Not all of the initial efforts at judicial corporate accountability have ended in justice for victims, however. Instead, "from below" efforts have reached different stages on a continuum of accountability. This chapter explores some of the factors which influence where along that continuum various efforts lie.

Overview of Judicial Action Cases

Of the 104 judicial actions in post–World War II atrocities (committed after 1964), fifty-three (51 percent) were brought in domestic, rather than foreign or international courts. This split does not adequately reflect the role of the Global South compared to the Global North in corporate accountability. As we show in Chapter 2, international and foreign courts in the Global North produced few justice outcomes. Judicial action in Global South courts, on the other hand, rendered 75 percent of all guilty verdicts and adverse judgments for corporate accountability cases in the world (fifteen out of twenty).[2] These data confirm "justice from below": a majority of corporate complicity cases, and the majority of final judgments, occur in Global South domestic courts, and not in "bottom-up" processes in the Global North or in international courts.

The domestic judicial action data set shows that corporate accountability is part of transitional justice processes. As in accountability for state actors, corporate accountability for past human rights violations in conflict and authoritarian situations has occurred in international, foreign, and domestic courts. Yet corporate judicial accountability innovates on standard transitional justice processes. Civil actions, standard practice in business and human rights accountability cases, have been incorporated into the transitional justice toolkit. Indeed, in "bottom-up" corporate accountability processes in the Global North, criminal "prosecutions have not widely occurred ... and forms of civil relief remain the primary avenue through which human rights claims against business enterprises have been pursued."[3] Our data do not support that practice in corporate accountability and transitional justice cases. Although civil actions are used more frequently than in standard transitional justice cases, we do not find that they are the primary avenue for remedy.[4] Of the

---

[2]   Three are pending appeal.
[3]   Drimmer and Laplante, "The Third Pillar," para. 326.
[4]   By "civil trials," we mean any prosecution in which a civil court holds individuals, groups, companies, and/or the state accountable for human rights violations. We use the term "civil" as opposed to criminal or military courts. Thus, we include in our definition lawsuits in which plaintiffs bring legal complaints seeking remedy for damages through acts committed by individuals, groups, companies, and/or the state. By "remedy for damages," we mean monetary compensation, reparation, and nonfinancial remedies.

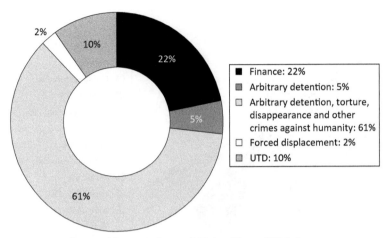

FIGURE 5.1 Distribution of Domestic Criminal Claims: Types of Violations
Source: Corporate Accountability and Transitional Justice database, 2016

fifty-three cases brought in domestic courts of the Global South, eight (15 percent) are civil, while forty-two (79 percent) are criminal.[5] Criminal trials are, thus, more frequent, but civil actions have provided innovative ways to advance corporate accountability and transitional justice.

Of the forty-two criminal actions, eleven (26 percent) accuse economic actors of indirect human rights violations, i.e., financing violence. The majority (thirty-one, or 74 percent) constitute claims of direct violations: aiding state security forces in arbitrarily detaining workers (two, or 5 percent), torture and disappearance of those who were arbitrarily detained (twenty-eight, or 67 percent), and a case in Colombia (one, or 2 percent) in which the company actively participated in the forced displacement of communities to appropriate their lands[6] (see Figure 5.1).

The business sectors accused in criminal and civil judicial processes are diverse. Companies operating in the agriculture sector are highly represented in the sample (twenty-two, or 39 percent), followed by natural resources (nine, or 16 percent). There are also cases involving companies operating in the construction, finance, manufacturing, media, metals, retail and transport

---

[5] Regarding the other three judicial actions, one is before a military court and the courts for the other two are unidentified.

[6] We could not find information about the specific type of violation in which the remaining two economic actors were involved.

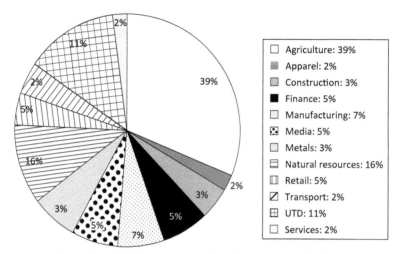

FIGURE 5.2 Distribution of Domestic Judicial Actions: Company-Level Variables
Source: Corporate Accountability and Transitional Justice database, 2016

sectors. We found no companies from the military or security sector. The data set shows that accusations of complicity have been made in nearly every sector of the economy (see Figure 5.2).

The majority of victims in cases brought to domestic courts have been workers, perceived members of political opposition groups, human rights defenders, and members of local communities. In some cases, the abuse was perceived to have had a widespread and general effect in the country. There is also one case where the victims were other members of the business community (see Figure 5.3).

The set of victims vary by country. The Argentine cases primarily involve workers and perceived members of political opposition groups. In Colombia, local community and the general public are the primary victims of business activity. This can be explained by the type of abuses that have been prosecuted in these countries. In Colombia, in twelve or 63 percent of the cases brought to the courts, the defendants are accused of financing paramilitary groups and the claims regarding victims tend to be very general. While in Argentina, financing only represents two cases (out of twenty-three, or 9 percent), and the other twenty (87 percent) refer to direct involvement in grave human rights violations committed against specific victims.[7]

---

[7]   In one case we could not find information about the type of violation.

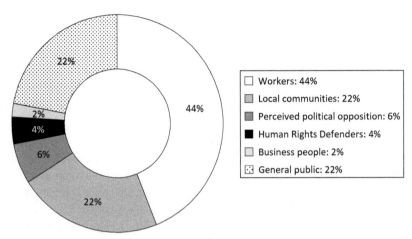

FIGURE 5.3 Distribution of Cases: Victimized Groups
Source: Corporate Accountability and Transitional Justice database, 2016

Latin American Protagonism and Archimedes' Lever

Nearly all of the domestic civil and criminal trials took place in Latin America (fifty-one out of fifty-three).[8] There are several possible explanations for the regional concentration of corporate accountability: type of companies, data and methods, context, and actors.

Regarding the type of companies, the Latin American cases involve mainly domestic economic actors accused of domestic actions, and thereby involve domestic jurisdiction. This contrasts with Asia and Africa, where the companies accused were transnational and thus faced judicial actions in foreign courts. Yet even the cases against the nineteen transnational companies accused of violating human rights in Latin America were heard mainly in national courts: in seven foreign courts;[9] four in both foreign and domestic

---

[8] Although we track, we do not delve into the two non–Latin American cases in the DRC. We have too little information on them. One was held in a military court, and the other court we have been unable to identify. As we discussed in different parts of this book, data collection on corporate complicity cases faces data availability challenges. Many corporate accountability initiatives have remained invisible to human rights organizations, academics and the general public. This weakness might be overcome with in-depth country case study research in other countries in Latin America and other regions of the world.

[9] The seven multinational cases heard in foreign courts include: Colombia – Airscan, BP Company, Cicolac-Nestlé, Dole Food Company, Occidental; Guatemala – Embotelladora Guatemalteca S.A./Coca Cola; and Argentina – Daimler Chrysler AG.

courts;[10] and eight in domestic courts.[11] These data suggest that when Latin American civil society actors and institutional innovators choose a judicial forum, they often opt for domestic courts over (or in addition to) foreign ones. This may reflect a stronger domestic legal culture in the region compared to other parts of the world. It most likely also reflects plaintiffs' lawyers' preference for litigating in their own domestic courts rather than in the courts of another country.

Access to data and the use of specialized methodologies may also reflect a research bias in favor of Latin American judicial actions. The Business and Human Rights Research Centre (BHRRC) online archive provided the main source of data for all corporate accountability cases in domestic, foreign, and international courts. The BHRRC itself has a bias in favor of Latin American cases since it has tracked those cases from its very inception and over a longer period of time. The BHRRC only later hired experts on other world regions who did not retroactively track older cases. In addition, because of active human rights organizations reporting on Argentina and Colombia, the BHRRC's local researchers had greater access to information from those two countries where we find the highest number of cases. We supplemented BHRRC data with online searches, but this has not revealed as many additional cases outside the region as we had hoped.

In addition, we had the opportunity to employ additional methodologies to find sources of information in the region. Given our own research and area expertise on Latin America, we had greater access to country experts who provided information on additional cases not included in the BHRRC. We also had access to judicial archives in Argentina and Colombia. Our collaboration with three human rights organizations (Centro de Estudios Legales y Sociales – CELS and Andhes in Argentina; Dejusticia in Colombia) allowed us to work with in-country researchers to mine specialized judicial archives to increase our set of cases in those two countries in the region. We know we do not have a complete set of cases in Latin America and most certainly outside the region, and that our data are skewed as a result of greater access to information in some countries and less in others. Nonetheless, this is the first data set of its kind. As such, it plays an important role in beginning to track and reveal patterns on a subset of corporate accountability and transitional justice processes.

In particular, this regional bias reveals that 89 percent of all domestic judicial actions occurred in three Latin American countries: Argentina (23),

---

[10]   The four cases of multinational corporations heard in domestic and foreign courts are: Colombia – Chiquita Brands and Drummond; Argentina – Ford; Ecuador – Chevron.

[11]   The eight heard only in domestic courts are: Brazil – Volkswagen, Fiat; Argentina – Acindar, Bank of America, Citibank, Mercedez Benz, Minera Aguilar S.A., Molinos Raíz de la Plata S.A.

Colombia (19), and Chile (5). This suggests that corporate accountability may be less of a regional phenomenon than the result of actions taken in specific countries of the region. There is judicial action in three other countries of the region – Brazil, Ecuador, and Peru – with only one case in Ecuador and Perú, and two in Brazil. These three countries represent a more typical process around the world, where only one or two corporate complicity cases advance in any court. The only non–Latin American domestic court case occurred in the DRC – in a military court. Despite corporate accountability's concentration in three countries in Latin America, we see regional characteristics reflected in the dynamic processes that led to those accountability outcomes.

We thus return to Archimedes' Lever. Latin American protagonism can be explained by the particular context in which these accountability processes emerged and the particular type of force applied by relatively weak actors who have overcome veto power. Context is critical. As we know from the mechanics of Archimedes' Lever, favorable contexts, in which the political climate moves closer to corporate accountability, requires less force on the part of civil society demand and institutional innovators to lift that weight. The global human rights accountability norm was at its most intense in Latin America following the transitions from authoritarian rule and armed conflict, thus moving the fulcrum to a more favorable position. In this propitious climate, some civil society groups began to extend the demand for justice for state and rebel actors to economic actors complicit in the violence. They did not only look to international institutions to address these demands. A model of domestic human rights trials emerged in the region, that, over the years, developed human rights expertise within the legal community. The global context thus opened up a political opportunity,[12] a propitious domestic context in which civil society groups and their advocates had greater opportunity than in other regions to mobilize and present their claims. The existence of human rights legal cultures in some countries of the region, built up through the promotion of, and experiences with, transitional justice, further explains how prosecutors and judges might be more amenable to advancing corporate accountability for past human rights violations.

Diffusion may also result from the so-called pink tide in Latin America. Left-leaning governments had achieved power throughout the region. Although these governments did not always or necessarily embrace human rights trials, they did not actively stop or prevent them. Moreover, civil society groups mobilizing against corporate wrongdoing – workers, unions,

---

[12] Doug McAdam, *Political Process and the Development of Black Insurgency, 1930–1970* (Chicago, IL: University of Chicago Press, 1982), 42.

communities – were the natural constituencies of these governments. In that way, the domestic context (fulcrum) moved toward corporate accountability, providing civil society groups and institutional innovators greater leverage over veto players pressing it down.

In other words, sets of mobilized civil society actors and institutional innovators had already emerged in the region; they sharpened their transitional justice advocacy and legal skills before applying them to corporate accountability. In the years after the transition, and through the pink-tide governments, existing elite control over political and economic structures proved less stable than during the authoritarian and armed conflict periods. Previously excluded and marginalized groups in society gained greater political access and leverage to advance their demands.[13] These groups could not count on global agents or binding and enforceable international human rights law to pressure for corporate accountability. They relied instead on a powerful set of tools – the creative blending of ordinary domestic law and international human rights norms incorporated into national legislation – to apply the necessary force for corporate accountability. This concentration of a propitious global and domestic context, civil society demand, and institutional innovators with effective tools may be a unique outcome of particular historic processes that have not yet emerged in other world regions or even throughout all of Latin America.

This is not to say that the corporate accountability models that emerged in Latin America are not transferable to other countries and regions of the world. Our Archimedes' Lever approach suggests that domestic processes have the potential of diffusing across borders, creating a cumulative effect in which businesses – like the heads of state before them – become less and less able to evade responsibility for their past human rights violations.

Context changes, however. The global emphasis on human rights accountability moved from active support (favorable context) to less engagement (neutrality) once the countries of the region had transitioned from conflict and authoritarian rule to democratic systems. The global context shifted in favor of building stable rule of law systems, but with an emphasis on commerce and trade over human rights.[14] Corporate accountability, moreover,

---

[13] McAdam, *Political Process and the Development of Black Insurgency, 1930–1970*, 42.

[14] Guillermo O'Donnell, "Polyarchies and the (Un)Rule of Law in Latin America: A Partial Conclusion," in *The (Un)Rule of Law and the Underprivileged in Latin America*, ed. Juan E. Méndez, Guillermo O'Donnell, and Paulo Sérgio Pinheiro (Notre Dame, IN: University of Notre Dame Press, 1999), 303–37; Tara L. Van Ho, "Corporate Complicity for Human Rights Violations: Using Transnational Civil and Criminal Litigation," in *Corporate Accountability in the Context of Transitional Justice*, ed. Sabine Michalowski (New York, NY: Routledge, 2013), 54.

never attracted attention from the international community, either in the early years of, or long after, the transition. This might have been different had more multinational corporations been under judicial investigation in domestic courts. A global backlash against corporate accountability in Latin America has not occurred; but neither is the global environment particularly propitious for these types of accountability processes. With the global context in a neutral position and without international pressure, civil society groups and institutional innovators must apply more force to lift the weight of corporate accountability. International pressure might emerge over time to help lift the weight of corporate accountability. The treaty process and the other legal initiatives in foreign courts discussed in Chapter 2 could generate greater international pressure for corporate accountability. For now, however, this is largely a domestic process.

Domestic context has begun to change in the region. The "ebbing of the pink tide" and the "right-wing backlash" began with the 2015 election of Mauricio Macri in Argentina and has continued to the 2018 election of Jair Bolsonaro in Brazil, with other countries in the region taking a turn to the right.[15] The movements that brought in the wave of right-wing governments have pressed to end human rights trials. Such a domestic context means that veto players are more likely to be emboldened. Unless international pressure is exerted, civil society groups, even with powerful tools in the hands of institutional innovators, may be hard-pressed to advance corporate accountability. Nonetheless one case – the conviction in Argentina of Ford Motor Company executives in 2018 – suggests that civil society mobilization and institutional innovation may still prove capable of overcoming unpropitious political climates.

Outcomes of Judicial Action Cases

Even in the most propitious context, the outcomes of judicial action for corporate accountability are not unambiguous. A dichotomous measure – legally culpable or innocent – produces unsatisfying results. The fifty-three domestic judicial actions rendered fifty-four outcomes. Twenty-five (46 percent) have reached judgment: fifteen (28 percent) ended in guilty verdicts or

---

[15] See The Financial Times, "The Ebbing of Latin America's 'Pink Tide,'" *The Financial Times*, December 2015; Omar G. Encarnación, "The Rise and Fall of the Latin American Left," *The Nation*, May 2018.

TABLE 5.1 *Levels of the Continuum: International,*
Foreign, and Domestic Courts

	(0) None	(1) Claims- Making	(2) Accusations*	(3) Tentative Final Judgment	(4) Confirmed Final Judgment
International	0	0	0	0	1
Foreign	28	8	10	0	4
Domestic	7[a]	30	2	3	12

Source: Corporate Accountability and Transitional Justice database, 2016
* *Includes settlements (9).*
[a] One domestic criminal action, in Chile, resulted in the conviction of one of the defendants, and the acquittal of the other. This case is counted in Stage 0 and in Stage 4.

adverse judgments for all business defendants (three of them are pending appeal);[16] ten, or 19 percent – ended in acquittal or dismissal (six original verdicts plus four dismissals pending appeal). With this dichotomous measure of outcomes, it appears that victims have a better chance of receiving a positive, rather than a negative, decision from domestic courts in their pursuit of justice.

The binary measure of outcomes does not account for the largest group of judicial actions, however: the twenty-eight cases that are still moving through the process toward judgment.[17] To capture that process, we devise an accountability continuum to better reflect "justice from below" outcomes. A fuller range of positions reflects processes leading to, or away from justice, advances and reversals. The accountability continuum includes five positions: no accountability; claim-making; accusation; tentative judgments (pending appeal); and final judgments.

Using these five levels of corporate accountability, we still find that "justice from below" has achieved more outcomes favorable to victims than "bottom-up" Global North courts or international tribunals, as illustrated in Table 5.1. Although international courts have achieved the highest-level accountability outcomes (final conviction), this involves only one (Rwanda "media") case. In foreign courts, outcomes are concentrated at no and low levels of accountability, sometimes achieving moderate levels, and seldom managing final convictions (four criminal cases) or adverse judgments (zero civil cases).

---

[16] These included: all business and nonbusiness defendants (seven), all companies (three), and all individuals working for a company (five).
[17] We were unable to determine the outcomes in one domestic judicial action.

In domestic courts, on the other hand, outcomes are distributed across the accountability continuum, as shown in Table 5.1.

Accountability Scale

The five positions on our accountability scale begin with zero, or no accountability. Some of these processes are not included in our analysis, since they remain at a preparatory stage. They nonetheless represent processes underway in which state agencies or international governmental organizations have begun to collect evidence. The Special Rapporteur on Economic, Social, Cultural and Environmental Rights (SRESCER) of the Inter-American Commission on Human Rights, for example, has initiated a process to recognize and advance such cases.[18] Similarly, we found situations where authorities have issued orders to investigate a case. In the case of Urapalma and other palm oil companies accused (and later convicted) of forced displacement in Colombia, the Inter-American Commission conducted an *in loco* visit and ordered the state to investigate the role of the companies in the violations of the human rights of Afro-Colombian communities displaced by the AUC paramilitary groups. The Commission ordered precautionary measures and the Inter-American Court ordered provisional measures, and only after these interventions did the criminal processes start to advance.[19] Although "no accountability" outcomes are achieved at this level, they nonetheless constitute progress toward accountability that we anticipate including in the future.

A second type of "no accountability" outcomes are included in our analysis. These involve cases that began to move along the accountability continuum but ended in acquittals or dismissals. In some instances, these cases only reach the low-level "claim-making" stage, before they are dismissed as lacking sufficient evidence to proceed. Thus, they revert to no official accountability. In other instances, they may advance all the way to a final adverse judgment or conviction. If they are reversed on final appeal, we contend that the judicial rejection of the case annuls all accountability effects. We have seven cases (13 percent) in this phase.

---

[18] We participated in a public consultation held in May 2018 called by the SRESCER "to receive information for the preparation of the thematic report on 'Business and Human Rights: Inter-American Standards.'" The SRESCER requested information on existing obstacles to the realization and enjoyment of human rights, including the context of transitional justice and corporate accountability. See www.oas.org/en/iachr/docs/pdf/2018/CuestionarioEmpresasDDHH-EN.pdf.

[19] Bernal-Bermúdez, "The Power of Business and the Power of People: Understanding Remedy and Corporate Accountability for Human Rights Violations. Colombia 1970–2014."

As cases move up the scale of accountability to level one, legal claims are made in the judicial system. At this stage, the official filing of a case prompts preliminary investigations in criminal or civil processes. This is a form of accountability because legal and public recognition is established through the claim. It thus provides a first phase by which victims can denounce wrong-doing, a kind of truth-telling effort. All of the cases in our data set made it into this phase initially, thus acknowledging "justice from below" at a very low level. Of our fifty-four outcomes, thirty (56 percent) never made it past this phase. The other half did, although one case that progressed was reversed on appeal.

The level two on the accountability continuum is achieved when a formal accusation is filed in criminal court and when the fact-finding phase of civil trials begins. At this stage, the defendants are notified of the accusations against them and evidence is presented in a court of law. In criminal cases, this stage is reached with an indictment. In civil actions, judicial notification to the accused of the claim filed against them would constitute the initiation of this stage. The degree of accountability remains low. While seventeen (31 percent) of the judicial action cases advanced through this phase, currently two (4 percent) have not moved beyond it.

At these lower stages, some might contend that no accountability is achieved, and these gains should not be counted as such. We disagree; when the odds against judicial action are so high, these advances recognize momentum toward justice. These are necessary stages to achieve higher levels of accountability, even if cases do not always advance to those levels. They therefore confirm the critical role of civil society actors and their advocates in establishing a foothold in the system, even if they later lose it or are otherwise unable to use it to climb higher in the "justice from below" hierarchy. Siri Glopen further argues, "even if the case is not decided in favor of the claimant, litigation might have a transformative impact. Authorities threatened with court action may settle out of court, and when courts provide a platform for social rights concerns, this might generate or intensify popular debate and create political momentum."[20]

As Glopen notes and as we discuss in Chapter 2, settlements may only reach low levels of accountability, but they nonetheless prove meaningful. They emerge from claim-making on behalf of victims. Moreover, formal charges are brought. The case is thus compelling enough for economic actors to negotiate a

---

[20] Siri Glopen, "Courts and Social Transformation: An Analytical Framework," in *Courts and Social Transformation in New Democracies*, ed. Roberto Gargarella, Pilar Domingo, and Theunis Roux (Burlington, VT: Ashgate, 2006), 42.

settlement rather than face possible conviction or adverse judgment. Although we do not have any evidence of settlements among the domestic judicial action cases, this level of accountability is relevant to the foreign (especially ATS) cases.

The third level of accountability is a conviction or civil judgment pending appeal. That is, the court renders a judgment against the defendant, but an appeals process is underway. Because we do not yet know the outcome of the appeal process, the conviction or the civil judgment is tentative. This court decision provides a high level of accountability by establishing the legal responsibility of the accused. Such a decision assigns legal judgment of wrongdoing. On the other hand, these convictions or civil judgments can be – and sometimes are – reversed. Our database reveals two convictions (4 percent) that were reversed on appeal that thus revert to "no accountability" status. We have three judgments in our database that are facing appeal, and thus could be reversed or upheld (two in Argentina and one in Colombia).

The highest level of accountability – four – is conviction or adverse judgment; we have twelve such outcomes. These processes have come to an end and these final judgments cannot be appealed. The parties either lost their opportunity to do so by failing to appeal within the applicable time period, or the last judgment was upheld at the highest level of appeal. While twelve such final judgments may seem relatively low in absolute terms, it is nearly a fourth of the total domestic cases. Within a context of tremendous procedural, financial and various "veto player" obstacles, this is a major accomplishment (see Figure 5.4).

Outcomes depend in part on the type of court. Although civil actions are less commonly used in "justice from below" cases, they achieve a higher level and rate of accountability. Three (38 percent) ended with final adverse judgments (Stage 4). The other five are divided between three pending judgments (Stage 1), one dismissal, and one acquittal (no accountability). The forty-two criminal actions have reached a similar range of outcomes, but are concentrated at lower levels of accountability. A fifth of those cases (nine or 21 percent) reached the highest level of accountability with final convictions, three ended in convictions but are pending an appeal, and over half (twenty-six, or 62 percent) are pending decisions and remain in the lower stages. Defendants in two criminal actions were acquitted, and two cases were dismissed (now under appeal), and thus achieved no accountability outcome (see Figure 5.5). Of the three remaining cases (one in military court and two with an undetermined court), all of them ended with no accountability.

Civil litigation is thus less frequently used in corporate complicity cases, but tends toward a higher level of accountability. Criminal cases have a variety of outcomes mainly at lower levels of accountability. This may reflect the higher

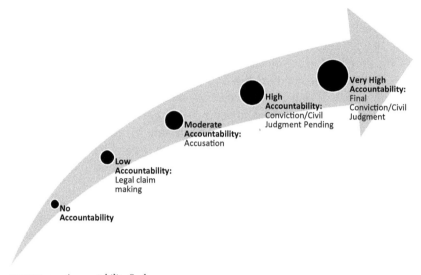

FIGURE 5.4 Accountability Scale
Source: The authors

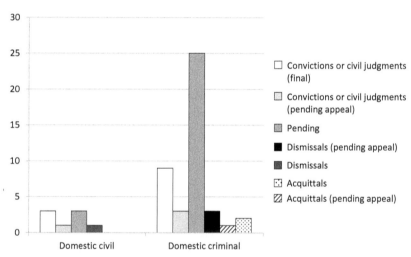

FIGURE 5.5 Outcomes of Judicial Actions: Type of Claim
Source: Corporate Accountability and Transitional Justice database, 2016

standards of proof and evidentiary requirements in such cases. These results suggest that judicial outcome is not merely a function of the type of case or court, but also the nature of the legal toolkit available to litigants. We explore these factors in more detail in the next section.

EXPLAINING JUSTICE FROM BELOW OUTCOMES

Our analysis of corporate accountability through domestic courts reveals a set of factors critical to moving along the continuum toward justice. Table 5.2 presents the outcomes of the cases in the domestic judicial action data set.

At the very first (claim-making) level of accountability, the importance of civil society demand is clear: in order to assert claims, civil society actors must be willing to do so. Civil society groups rarely act on their own, however, and instead require legal representation. Knowing how to move these cases forward through courts requires not only legal expertise, but also legal creativity, since these are not run-of-the-mill civil or criminal cases. Specialized courts that exist in other transitional justice situations have not yet appeared to address corporate complicity and, thus, no particular training for prosecutors or judges exist for these types of cases.

There is one exception. The Special Jurisdiction for Peace (JEP) in Colombia is the first specialized court in the world to put economic actors on trial for complicity in past human rights abuses. While the Constitutional Court ruled that the JEP cannot require businesspeople to come forward, it can try those economic actors who voluntarily do so. To date there are over three hundred businesspeople who have requested that special jurisdiction.[21]

Similarly, as the general discussion and the Andhes example from Chapter 2 show, the use of international human rights law is not easily adaptable to corporate complicity cases. Specific, settled, and enforceable human rights obligations on business do not yet exist, further requiring innovative strategies to advance corporate accountability. Thus, institutional innovators play a critical role in developing and litigating these cases. As mentioned earlier, Latin America has a uniquely strong and mobilized human rights and victims' community that benefits from well-trained, effective, motivated, and innovative legal advocates, and independent and open-minded judges.[22] The existence of these two factors in some countries of the region has allowed for the beginnings of accountability at the claim-making phase all the way up to the confirmed final judgment phase.[23]

---

[21] Submitting to the JEP will mean that, if they comply with the conditions and are found guilty, economic actors will receive a reduced sentence. If not, they face trial in ordinary courts with a much higher sentence.

[22] Javier A. Couso, Alexandra Huneeus, and Rachel Sieder, eds., *Cultures of Legality: Judicialization and Political Activism in Latin America* (New York, NY: Cambridge University Press, 2010).

[23] It might be argued that judicial accountability is a result of the public's positive perceptions of the effectiveness and independence of Latin American courts. However, institutional strength indicators cast doubt on the claims that Latin American courts are trusted more than those in

TABLE 5.2 *Distribution of Cases: Courts, Country, Business, and Outcomes*

Type of Court	Number of Judicial Actions	Country Where the Violation Took place	Name of Company or Business Person	Outcomes
Civil Courts	8	Argentina (4)	Bank of America and CitiBank, Banks (undetermined), Siderca, Techint S.A.	Pending (1), Dismissed (1), Convicted (1), Acquitted (1)
		Brazil (2)	Volkswagen, Fiat	Pending (2)
		Colombia (1)	Maderas del Darien, Multifruit	Adverse judgment
		Ecuador (1)	Chevron	Adverse judgment
Criminal Courts	42	Argentina (19)	Acindar (2), Adolfo Navajas Artaza, Editorial Atlántida, Ford, Fronterita, Héctor María Torres Queirel, La Nueva Provincia, La Veloz del Norte (2), Ledesma (3), Loma Negra, Mercedes Benz, Minera Aguilar S.A., Molinos Raíz de la Plata S.A., Papel Prensa S.A., Unknown (money laundering/stolen property case)	Acquitted/pending appeal (1), Convicted/pending appeal (2), Dismissed/pending appeal (3), Pending (13),
		Chile (5)[a]	CMPC Laja, Claudio Orregón Tudela, Juan Francisco Luzoro (3), Juan Guillermo Quintanilla, Mario Tagle Ramón, and Ricardo Tagle	Convicted (1), Acquitted (1), Pending (4)
		Colombia (19)[b]	Urapalma, Agropecuaria Palmas de Bajirá, Palmas de Curvaradó, Palmadó, Palmas, Inversiones Fregni Ochoa, Alfonso Ardila Hoyos,	Acquitted (1), Convicted (9), Convicted/pending appeal (1), Pending (7)

Type of Court	Number of Judicial Actions	Country Where the Violation Took place	Name of Company or Business Person	Outcomes
			Augura, C.I. Banafrut S.A., C.I. Unión de Bananeros de Urabá, Campo Elías de la Rosa, Manuel Morales, Chiquita Brands International, Drummond Ltd., Fondo Ganadero de Córdoba, Francisco Serna Palacios, Guillermo Gaviria Echeverry, Jaime Blanco Maya, Jairo Alberto Banquet Paez, Ocensa, Oscar Dario Ricardo Robledo, Oscar López, Pedro Nel Rincón, Uriel de la Ossa	
		Peru (1)	Hard Cotton and Desmontadora San Dionisio	Pending
Military	1	DRC (1)	Anvil Mining Ltd.	Acquitted

[a] One of the judicial actions has two outcomes, one defendant was convicted and the other acquitted. This is why there are 5 judicial actions, with 6 outcomes.
[b] Colombia has 19 domestic judicial actions, but we were not able to determine the outcome for one of the cases.
Source: Corporate Accountability and Transitional Justice database, 2016

The region may also have a unique set of legal tools available to institutional innovators. These innovative tools are the third set of factors for success. Analyzing justice outcomes reveals that existing models do not rely on obscure regulations, statutes, or laws unique to specific countries. Instead, institutional innovators have found very common forms of legal arguments to convince judges

other regions of the world. See for example the latest Rule of Law Index report of the World Justice Project https://worldjusticeproject.org/sites/default/files/documents/WJP-ROLI-2018-June-Online-Edition_o.pdf.

of the merits of the case. These legal arguments often blend domestic jurisprudence with international human rights law. Yet, not all regions of the world, or
countries within regions, have incorporated international human rights law into
their own jurisprudence. Latin American countries have largely done so, enabling institutional innovators to carry out this blending process that give the cases
legal standing in domestic courts. The incorporation of international human
rights standards into domestic legislation in Latin America has been referred to as
the "inter-Americanization" of national legal systems. Through a series of
"waves," Latin American constitutions have incorporated international human
rights standards into domestic law: "A first wave of constitutional reforms,
between 1988 and 1998, included clauses of the prevalence of human rights
(Constitution of Brazil of 1988), and grant constitutional status to human rights
treaties. They also include interpretation clauses in accordance with international human rights law (for example Colombia 1991, Peru 1993, Argentina
1994). These constitutional reforms were also accompanied by important decisions of the national courts. . . . A second wave of constitutional reforms extended
the incorporation of IHRL [International Human Rights Law] to soft law instruments (Venezuela 1999, Ecuador 2008, Bolivia 2009)."[24]

The domestic political context is relevant in that nearly all of the cases were
initially presented in courts during the pink-tide governments of the region.[25]
The propitious environment was open to justice claims on behalf of victims of
corporate abuse, with the assistance of institutional innovators representing
them in judicial actions and otherwise advancing prosecution. In the current
less propitious environment, the force that must be applied by civil society
actors and institutional innovators will have to be much greater to counter the
veto power enhanced by these political contexts.[26] We have found little

---

[24] Mariela Morales Antoniazzi, "Interamericanización como mecanismo del Ius Constitutionale
Commune en derechos humanos en América Latina," in *Ius constitutionale commune en
América Latina: Textos básicos para su comprensión*, ed. Armin von Bogdandy, Mariela
Morales Antoniazzi, and Eduardo Ferrer Mac-Gregor (Max Planck Institute; Instituto de
Estudios Constitucionales del Estado de Querátaro, 2017), 417–56, www.corteidh.or.cr/tablas/
136072.pdf. See also Daniel M. Brinks, *The DNA of Constitutional Justice in Latin America*
(Cambridge: Cambridge University Press, 2018).
[25] One exception is Colombia, where trials of corporate accountability began as early as 2005,
under a more conservative Álvaro Uribe administration.
[26] Take the case of Argentina, a transitional justice leader. According to the Public Prosecutor
Office, corporate complicity cases last, on average, almost six years after the public prosecutor
requests the initiation of a formal trial. We should note that this calculation excludes the first
stage of the litigation process in which prosecutors undertake preliminary investigation. Thus,
dramatic political shifts can take place during the course of the judicial action. See Fiscalía
General de la Nación de Argentina, "Informe estadístico sobre el estado de las causas por
delitos de lesa humanidad" (Buenos Aires, 2018), www.fiscales.gob.ar/wp-content/uploads/2018/
03/LESA-Informe-trayectoria.pdf.

evidence of international pressure, except in one case (Urapalma). We have also found little evidence of a fragmented set of veto players, except in the Fondo Ganadero de Córdoba case.

In the next sections, we explore these set of factors through case studies. They allow us to further test our operating assumptions regarding the mechanics of "justice from below" and illustrate how such justice is achieved. As such, they allow us to develop a set of models that can be replicated elsewhere to advance corporate accountability for past human rights abuses.

Level 0: No Accountability

We would expect that if the set of factors that explain justice outcomes are absent or insufficiently strong, no accountability would be achieved. In this section we have selected a set of cases without accountability outcomes to test our explanatory framework.

Financial Supporters (Argentina)

In 2009, Leandro Manuel Ibáñez and María Elena Perdighe, adult children of disappeared parents, brought a civil action alleging that foreign banks should be held accountable for lending money to the authoritarian regime, and the systematic mass repression that resulted from it.[27] The claimants alleged that the dictatorship's bankers consciously supported an authoritarian state's criminal apparatus which illegally kidnapped and disappeared their parents.[28]

They claimed reparations from the banks for complicity in crimes against humanity.The case involved powerful national and international human rights lawyers, with international pressure from New York University and the University of Essex, as well as local pressure from the well-known Argentine human rights organization Center for Legal and Social Studies (CELS, which filed *amicus curiae* briefs in support). The institutions alleged that banks should be held accountable for corporate complicity under international law and Argentine law and that the states should provide all the relevant information to establish the responsibility of banks for human rights violations. Despite the compelling and innovative legal strategy, the court rejected the claim on procedural grounds. The case applied international law and

---

[27] Juan Pablo Bohoslavsky, "Complicity of the Lenders," in *Outstanding Debts to Settle: The Economic Accomplices of the Dictatorship in Argentina*, ed. Horacio Verbitsky and Juan Pablo Bohoslavsky (Cambridge: Cambridge University Press, 2015).

[28] Horacio Verbitsky, "Los prestamistas de la muerte," *Página/12*, March 16, 2009, www.pagina12 .com.ar/diario/elpais/1-121607-2009-03-16.html.

domestic law, but it failed to overcome significant legal hurdles that impeded the development of innovative tools. The plaintiffs did not engage in pre-trial discovery to identify a particular responsible bank, but instead requested that the Central Bank provide detailed information on the regime's lenders, the amount and dates of the loans, in addition to other information critical to making an effective claim. These details, the claimants surmised, would reveal the impact of the transactions on the human rights violations during the dictatorship, allowing victims to claim damages from banks. While that is no doubt true, it left the judges in the situation of lacking a specific defendant against whom a claim could be made.

The civil judge who received the claim concluded that he had no jurisdiction over this type of claim and referred it to another judge who made a similar statement. From there, the case circulated through a legal labyrinth in which subsequent judges continued to make the same finding regarding their lack of jurisdiction.[29] Eventually, a judge rejected the petition, arguing that the claimants failed to provide sufficient information necessary to petition the Central Bank (e.g., the types of loans, possible lenders, etc.).[30] The case was dismissed. It is thus a case of "no accountability."

Because the claim was brought in a positive context for corporate accountability in Argentina, before President Macri took power, it might have succeeded had the institutional innovators developed better legal tools. Civil society mobilization was also lacking. Although the plaintiffs came from civil society, they did not mobilize strong civil society support. There was, for example, little media coverage of the case. Information and solidarity campaigns, such as those we analyze in successful cases (such as Veloz de Norte later in this chapter), never evolved. CELS played a limited role in the case, preparing an amicus brief, but not including the case in its campaigns or human rights reports.

The case suggests that certain "from below" elements are insufficient for accountability outcomes without the other factors. A favorable context existed, for example. The case was initiated under President Cristina Fernández's administration, which strongly favored judicial accountability for crimes against humanity in general. For example, it implemented important institutional reforms such as the truth commission to investigate corporate accountability (see Chapter 2). It also passed a reform of the civil code

---

[29] Nodal, "Investigarán la convivencia de la banca internacional con la dictadura militar," *Nodal Noticias de América Latina y El Caribe*, 2013, www.nodal.am/2013/09/investigaran-la-responsabilidad-de-la-banca-internacional-en-el-financiamiento-de-la-dictadura/.
[30] Ibid.

establishing that statutes of limitations do not apply to damages in the context of crimes against humanity. Powerful institutional innovators and even international pressure also emerged. The case was hamstrung, however, by underdeveloped legal tools. Insufficient discovery and evidence led the judges to reject the case, not on its merits but on procedural grounds. With stronger involvement of civil society, moreover, some of the limitations on discovery could have been overcome. Institutional innovators seem to have gambled – and lost – on a strategy and a local context, rather than building claims on a solid and convincing legal foundation.

Guillermo Gaviria Echeverri and the AUC (Colombia)

In 2010, as a result of the confessions of paramilitary leader Raúl Hasbún, the Prosecutor's office started a preliminary investigation of businessman Guillermo Gaviria Echeverri, who was accused of financing AUC paramilitary groups.[31] Gaviria was a well-known businessman in Antioquia and Urabá. His business activities were varied, including cattle ranches, banana plantations, gold mines, and the newspaper *El Mundo*.[32] He was among the founders of the companies Colanta, Uniban, and Carbocol. He also had strong political connections. He had served as senator, one of his sons was Mayor of Medellín and Governor of Antioquia (Aníbal Gaviria), and another was Governor of Antioquia (Guillermo Gaviria Correa, murdered by the FARC in 2003).

In November 2012 the prosecutor in charge of the case ordered the preliminary detention of Gaviria while he awaited trial.[33] He was represented in the criminal proceedings by the Foundation in Defense of the Innocent (Fundación Defensa de Inocentes). In 2013 the detention measure was revoked because the appeals court found that there was no merit to keeping Gaviria detained, though the criminal investigation continued.[34] In September

---

[31] Juan David Laverde Palma, "Las pruebas del caso Guillermo Gaviria Echeverri," *El Espectador*, April 25, 2012, www.elespectador.com/noticias/temadeldia/pruebas-del-caso-guillermo-gaviria-echeverri-articulo-341168; Verdadabierta.com, "Los testimonios que enredan a Guillermo Gaviria Echeverri," *Verdadabierta.com*, April 13, 2012, https://verdadabierta.com/los-testimonios-que-enredan-al-empresario-guillermo-gaviria-echeverri/.

[32] Ibid.

[33] Semana.com, "Decisión de peso: La orden de detención para Guillermo Gaviria," *Semana.com*, April 14, 2012, www.semana.com/nacion/articulo/decision-peso-orden-detencion-para-guillermo-gaviria/256397-3.

[34] Elpaís, "Revocan medida de aseguramiento a empresario Guillermo Gaviria," *El País*, 2013, www.elpais.com.co/judicial/revocan-medida-de-aseguramiento-a-empresario-guillermo-gaviria.html.

2013 Gaviria was acquitted because the court could not find evidence to substantiate the charge.[35] Gaviria died in 2015, and thus there is no likelihood that this case will move forward.

This case does not appear to have had the kind of civil society support and institutional innovation necessary to overcome the veto power of the Gaviria family and their legal support team. It demonstrates the great difficulty victims face in advancing cases through the judicial process when they lack sufficient force.

Techint[36] (Argentina)

In this case, María Gimena Ingegnieros sought financial compensation from the Argentine company Techint S.A. for its failure to protect the safety of her father, Enrique Roberto Ingegnieros. She claimed that the company should pay compensation for failing to protect her father's safety as an employee who disappeared from the firm during the civil-military dictatorship. According to testimonies given in the proceedings in the labor appeals court, state actors kidnapped Ingegnieros from his workplace on May 5, 1977. Ingegnieros reported to the company's administration office when he was informed that a relative was waiting for him there. He was never seen again.

The background to this incident is the company's emblematic role during the Argentine dictatorship of the 1970s. Techint was a leading steel corporation. Its director, Agostino Rocca, was considered one of the most influential businessmen at the time of the 1976 coup. He owned a number of companies, including the Argentine multinational steel company Siderca, also facing judgment for disappeared workers. During the dictatorship, the company experienced an unprecedented boom, providing it with substantial economic and political influence.

In the 1970s, the company faced a mobilized workforce. Tensions emerged before the coup and continued during the dictatorship. In particular, the company's workforce was represented by a faction of the Unión de Obreros Metalúrgicos (Metalworkers Union – UOM), regarded as one of the most activist trade union movements of the era. Because of the perceived radicalism

---

[35] El Espectador, "Absuelven a Guillermo Gaviria por vínculos con paramilitares," *El Espectador*, September 27, 2013, www.elespectador.com/noticias/judicial/absuelven-guillermo-gaviria-vinculos-paramilitares-articulo-449120.

[36] Payne and Pereira, "Accountability for Corporate Complicity in Human Rights Violations: Argentina's Transitional Justice Innovation."

of the UOM, during the dictatorship, dozens of Techint workers, including top union leaders, were illegally detained, tortured, and disappeared.[37]

After the dictatorship, former workers and victims' relatives mobilized for justice for these violations. They formed the Comisión de Familiares de Desaparecidos de Zárate-Campana (Committee of Families of the Zarate-Campana Disappeared). They participated actively in public protests and became directly and indirectly involved in judicial actions. They initiated, for example, criminal trials of state perpetrators as legal claimants and they provided evidence of human rights violations in various human rights trials of state and corporate abuses.

Human rights organizations accompanied civil society demand by publicly denouncing companies' involvement in disappearing workers. CELS, for example, included Techint in a report analyzing the participation in crimes against humanity of twenty-five companies across the country.

Institutional innovators translated civil society demands for justice into legal action. The claim against Techint creatively combined Argentina's standard labor law on worker safety with international human rights law regarding disappearance as a crime against humanity.[38] Had the legal argument hinged only on labor law, the case could be easily dismissed as falling outside the statute of limitations in worker safety cases. It took legal crafting to link the violation in domestic civil court and under domestic labor legislation to international law on crimes against humanity to overcome the statute of limitations defense.

The company denied its involvement in the disappearance. In addition, it rejected the claim on legal grounds. It argued that the two-year statute of limitations under the worker safety law had long since run out on this case that occurred more than thirty years before.

[37] Victorio Paulon, "Acindar and Techint: Extreme Militarization of Labor Relations," in *Outstanding Debts to Settle: The Economic Accomplices of the Dictatorship in Argentina*, ed. Horacio Verbitsky and Juan Pablo Bohoslavsky (Cambridge: Cambridge University Press, 2015), 174–85.

[38] A second case was brought to courts in April 2007 against the Siderca company following a similar strategy. Oscar Orlando Bordisso disappeared after he left his job at Siderca in 1977. He was never seen again. In 1995, his wife Ana María Cebrymsky claimed compensation from her husband's employer (Siderca) owing to its violation of Argentina's worker safety law that obliges employers to protect workers on entry and exit from the workplace. The company raised a statute of limitations defense. The first instance tribunal accepted the claim against the company. On appeal, the company again lost in the Provincial Supreme Court. The Court ordered compensation to Bordisso's widow; rejecting the defense's claim on statute of limitations grounds, since such statutes do not apply to crimes against humanity. There is no appeal available and, thus, the adverse judgment is final, the fourth stage of accountability is reached.

The decision in the first trial concurred with the company's position. The judge rejected the claim based on the statute of limitations. However, this decision was reversed on appeal in 2015. The court considered the company's failure to protect its workers to be a critical link in the causal chain of events leading to the disappearance of Ingegnieros. It further concluded that the statute of limitations did not apply because the case involved a crime against humanity. The appeals court thus ordered Techint to pay compensation to the victim's relative.[39]

Although the decision referenced international law, it did not rely on any particular international ruling or norms regarding corporations' human rights obligations. The judge referenced instead several sections of the preamble of the UN Draft Norms (see Chapter 2) to support his conclusion on the duty of the state to investigate and sanction corporate complicity. The same judge made quick reference to the Nuremberg Trials of businesses as precedent. Yet the decision applied domestic labor law rather than international norms in awarding financial compensation from the company to the victim's family. The ruling thus advanced the notion of victims' right to truth, justice, and reparations under a hybrid set of domestic and international legal tools.

Techint appealed the 2015 decision to the Argentine Supreme Court. Key institutional innovators continued to pressure for accountability. The Attorney General to the Supreme Court, for example, advised the High Court to confirm the conviction.[40] Nonetheless, the Supreme Court reversed the appellate court decision because of statutes of limitations in labor cases. In the end, Techint won.

This final decision reversed the progress toward corporate accountability. By the time of that judgment, a key factor limiting success had changed: the political context. The Mauricio Macri government, more hostile to and further away from corporate accountability, had replaced the once propitious government for corporate accountability under Cristina Fernández de Kirchner. While it could be argued that the political shift was too recent to explain the Supreme Court decision on Techint, a closer look reinforces our argument.

Early into Macri's administration, key supporting policies enabling advancements in truth, memory, and justice were reduced in scope, funding, or personnel, and others were dissolved.[41] Certain legislation that had passed

---

[39] Martín Piqué, "Condenaron a Techint a indemnizar a la hija de un obrero secuestrado en Siderca," *Infonews*, 2015.

[40] Diario Judicial, "Una indemnización que no prescribe," *Diario Judicial*, 2017, www .diariojudicial.com/nota/77561.

[41] Centro de Estudios Legales y Sociales (CELS), *Derechos humanos en la Argentina: Informe 2017* (Buenos Aires: Siglo XXI, 2018); Francesca Lessa, "Investigating Crimes against Humanity

prior to the change in government – such as the truth commission on economic actors passed in 2015 (see Chapter 4) – stalled. The government also dismantled the Argentine Central Bank's human rights unit which investigated economic complicity with the dictatorship.[42]

In addition, Macri's government has been characterized as a pro-business administration in various realms, not only with regard to corporate accountability.[43] One indication of a close relationship between the executive branch and private sector is the number of key public office posts in government and regulatory agencies held by high-profile members of the business community, the so-called "revolving door."[44]

According to a report issued by the Observatorio de las Élites Argentinas, the extension, magnitude and visibility of the revolving door phenomenon in Macri's times is unparalleled in recent Argentine history.[45] The report shows that 269 top officers in twenty governmental ministries are active in 890 domestic and transnational companies.[46] President Macri himself and seven of his closest advisors, ten ministers and thirty-two top officials continue to serve on the board of directors of private companies. Furthermore, a significant number of these government officials have links to economic groups

---

in South America: Present and Future Challenges," *Policy Brief*. Latin American Centre, University of Oxford.

[42] Centro de Estudios Legales y Sociales (CELS), *Derechos humanos en la Argentina: Informe 2017*.

[43] Control Risks, "Argentina's Mid-Term Elections: Will Macri's Pro Business Reforms Stand the Test?," *Forbes*, 2017, www.forbes.com/sites/riskmap/2017/03/23/argentinas-mid-term-elections-will-macris-pro-business-reforms-stand-the-test/#62bd4a5426ca; Graciela Mochkofsk, "What's Next for Mauricio Macri, Argentina's New President?," *The New Yorker*, December 2015, www.newyorker.com/news/news-desk/whats-next-mauricio-macri-argentinas-new-president; Nataniel Parish, "What Can Investors Expect from Argentina's Economy in 2018?," *Forbes*, June 2018, www.forbes.com/sites/nathanielparishflannery/2018/06/29/what-can-investors-expect-from-argentinas-economy-in-2018/#30417e4a1755; Kenneth Rapoza, "President Macri's Theme Song: Definitely Cry for Me, Argentina," *Forbes*, September 2018, www.forbes.com/sites/kenrapoza/2018/09/06/argentinas-president-macri-setting-the-table-for-future-peronista-government/#346d8cc93d02ta-government/#346d8cc93d02.

[44] This phenomenon, called revolving door in the business and human rights literature, is considered by human rights organizations as a means by which the economic elite undermine the realization of human rights and the environment by exerting undue influence over domestic decision-makers and public institutions. See ESCR-Net Corporate Accountability Working Group, "Corporate Capture: Definition and Characteristics," *ESCR-Net*, June 2019, https://drive.google.com/file/d/1IQ146Kb8WSj47NpbnlrOI-leZlZhVrKZ/view.

[45] Ana Castellani, "Cambiemos SA exposición a los conflictos de interés en el gobierno nacional: Los funcionarios con participación en empresas privadas a junio de 2018," *Informe de Investigación* No. 5 Parte 1, 8 (Buenos Aires: Universidad de San Martín, 2018), 8.

[46] The report refers to shareholding, legal representation, and board membership.

known for their direct and indirect support for the dictatorship, including Macri.[47]

A study of the Supreme Court that decided in favor of Techint further reveals the unpropitious environment for corporate accountability in the Macri era. Once a leader of transitional justice accountability efforts, the current Court has restricted the scope and sanctions in crime against humanity prosecutions since Macri took power. In 2017, the Court issued the so-called "2 x 1 decision," to reduce sentences of those convicted of crimes against humanity. After a national uproar, the legislation was eventually replaced and the Court reversed the "2 x 1" decision.

The Techint case exposes the anti-accountability views of certain Supreme Court justices. The vote was three to two. With such a narrow margin, the background of a key member is significant. Chief Justice Carlos Rosenkrantz was selected by Macri and approved by the Senate in 2016. He is considered to be the mastermind behind the roll-back on transitional justice accountability in Argentina.[48] In addition to holding a restrictive view on human rights protections and, specifically, crimes against humanity, he admits to a pro-business view. Before his appointment to the Court, he declared that he and/or his law firm legally represented almost 300 companies.[49] Even in the short-time as a Supreme Court judge, Rosenkrantz has failed to recuse himself from cases involving his firm's corporate clients.[50] In addition to legal connections,

[47] El País Digital, "El Grupo Macri y la dictadura: El comienzo de la expansión"; Telesurtv, "Los Macri y sus negocios durante la dictadura argentina," *Telesurtv*, 2015, www.telesurtv.net/news/Los-Macri-y-sus-negocios-durante-la-dictadura-argentina-20151112-0008.html.

[48] Rosenkrantz, and his colleague Justice Rossati, reached the Court amid an institutional scandal. President Macri made direct appointments through a presidential decree instead of following the public, participatory, and transparent procedure stipulated by the constitution and accompanying norms. Macri's move triggered strong public criticisms from a wide range of sectors of society. Eventually, Macri resubmitted their nominations through the constitutional procedure and the candidates were approved by the Congress. Andrés del Río Roldán, "Macri and the Judges," *Open Democracy*, January 21, 2016, www.opendemocracy.net/en/democraciaabierta/macri-and-judges/; José Miguel Vivanco, "Dispatches: Argentina's Supreme Court Appointments," *Human Rights Watch*, December 18, 2015, www.hrw.org/news/2015/12/18/dispatches-argentinas-supreme-court-appointments.

[49] Among these clients is Clarín, the powerful media company whose owners and CEOs have been accused of crimes against humanity in the Papel Prensa case. Ámbito Financiero, "Asume Rosenkrantz, un ex abogado de grandes empresas con extracto radical," *Ámbito Financiero*, September 11, 2018, www.ambito.com/asume-rosenkrantz-un-ex-abogado-grandes-empresas-extracto-radical-n4033383.

[50] Judge Rosenkrantz, in apparent violation of Argentine law, signed at least ten rulings in which some of his previous corporate clients were formal parties to the cases. Irina Hauser, "Rosenkrantz, de un lado y del otro," *Página/12*, May 12, 2019, www.pagina12.com.ar/193255-rosenkrantz-de-un-lado-y-del-otro.

Rosenkrantz enjoys social and political links with the Argentine business community. One relevant tie is to the Blaquier family, associated with the Ledesma company named in the crimes against humanity case discussed in Chapter 3.[51] The case against Blaquier is pending on appeal at the Supreme Court; Rosenkrantz has not declared a conflict of interest.

Three lessons can be extracted from the analysis of the Techint case. First, the success in the lower courts depended on very strong civil society mobilization accompanied by institutional innovators in a propitious corporate accountability political climate. Second, the tools employed by innovators – the creative blending of common labor law statutes and international human rights norms – could be used in a variety of contexts. They are not unique to Argentina. Worker safety legislation exists in most democratic countries. It allows for civil cases against companies to advance victims' rights, particularly where evidentiary constraints block access to criminal justice. By blending these labor laws with international human rights law, institutional innovators found ways around statutes of limitations. These are the kinds of tools in the hands of the weak that can achieve "justice from below." Third, however, the Techint case shows that civil society mobilization and institutional innovation can only go so far. With the unfavorable change in political context, the case was defeated. Techint thus illustrates the power of veto players in those contexts.

Level 1: Claim-Making

The litigation process starts when legal claims are brought to courts, and judicial officers initiate preliminary investigations. When the political context is propitious, we expect fewer barriers to legal claim-making and movement toward the next – formal accusation – stage on the continuum. Nonetheless, corporate accountability cases will not be initiated even in these political environments in the absence of civil society demand and institutional innovators with effective legal tools. Should the political environment shift, even in the presence of civil society demand and institutional innovators, we assume

---

[51] The Justice's wife serves on an NGO's board along with the former lawyer and nephew of Pedro Blaquier, the director and main shareholder of the company. Rosenkrantz has made public appearances in fundraising events together with the Blaquier family and officers of the Techint company. Also, as the president of San Andrés University, Rosenkrantz secured a substantive endowment to the University from the Blaquier family. Sofía Caram, "Blanquear a Blaquier," *Página/12*, July 7, 2019, www.pagina12.com.ar/204885-blanquear-a-blaquier.

that cases would get stuck at low levels of accountability. Claimants will have to amass considerable force, or the veto power of the defendants will have to decrease significantly, to move to higher levels of accountability in an unpropitious political context.

La Fronterita Case (Argentina)

In 2015, the public prosecutor's office initiated an investigation into the 1975–1983 activities of the managers and board members of La Fronterita sugar mill in Argentina. Prosecutor Pablo Camuña investigated their alleged participation in crimes against humanity during the 1975 "Operation Independence" and beyond. This was the period of state terror in Argentina beginning during an elected democratic government and continuing during the authoritarian junta that replaced it. According to Camuña's investigation, a clandestine detention center operated on-site at the mill for almost two years, company vehicles were used to kidnap workers, and the accused provided crucial information to the Army that identified the workers who were eventually kidnapped, tortured, killed or disappeared. A military command post with 260 troops had been set up in the region. Operation Independence had at least sixty-eight victims: forty-four La Fronterita employees and twenty-four residents of company housing. Fifty-one of those kidnapped were allegedly detained on-site before being sent to other clandestine centers. Many of the victims were union leaders who had actively protested against the company's labor policies.Based on the investigation, the prosecutor's office formally questioned the accused in a court hearing about the alleged human rights violations carried out between June and August 2017.[52] Following the hearing, the public prosecutor presented formal charges and requested their arrest. No decision has been made on the indictment. Thus, so far this case is blocked at the lowest level of accountability.

The case advanced to the first accountability stage largely owing to the public prosecutor's innovative set of legal strategies. Because some of the crimes committed occurred before the coup and formal assumption of power by the military junta in March 1976, they might not have fit a narrow interpretation of crimes against humanity. Limiting violations to the period of the military junta ignores historical accounts of large-scale civil-military involvement in systematic and widespread human rights violations before

---

[52] Ailín Bullentini, "Los empresarios cómplices del terror," *El País*, April 23, 2018, www.pagina12 .com.ar/110065-los-empresarios-complices-del-terror.

1976. The democratic government before the coup was also implicated in the set of crimes against humanity. Prosecutor Camuña's innovation involved challenging a narrow interpretation of crimes against humanity, drawing on legal reasoning developed during the human rights trials for state officials, and bolstered by the truth commission and other investigations into the full range of violations before and after the coup.

Second, the prosecutor relied on evidence and arguments presented in previous Operation Independence trials. Camuña was the prosecutor in a case in which ten state officials were found guilty in the violation of human rights of 271 victims in that incident. The facts of the case – the systematic violation of human rights – had been legally confirmed. In addition, discovery for the trial revealed crucial details in the La Fronterita case, such as the company's on-site detention center and the use of company vehicles in the crimes. These facts were supplemented with careful investigation of company files, further building the solid foundation for the accusations against the company.

Third, the prosecutor did not rely solely on the legal conventions associated with transitional justice litigation. In addition to standard domestic criminal law, he drew on elements of business criminal law, labor law, and international criminal and human rights law to identify the specific responsibility of the accused for wrongdoing, their duties to protect the victims as employers, and their degree of involvement in the crimes.

Fourth, innovation was not limited to the prosecutor's actions, but also involved the human rights organization Andhes. Andhes joined the prosecutor's case, representing one victim of disappearance, Fidel Jacobo Ortiz, who had been allegedly held and tortured in the company's on-site detention center. Ortiz was a union leader who had fought for labor rights during the 1970s. The information about Ortiz had emerged as part of a joint action-research project with the University of Oxford. The project involved collecting and coding data from judicial archives of corporate complicity during the period of state terror. From the set of cases, Andhes selected Ortiz as the individual victim with the strongest evidence for strategic litigation. Andhes' legal strategy reinforces Camuña's case, offering further evidence of one particular victim within the broader set of victims included in the case put forward by the public prosecutor's office. Andhes strengthened elements of international human rights law, broadening the legal claim around access to justice, the legal standard established by the Inter-American Court on Human Rights.

Together, the public prosecutor and Andhes acted as institutional innovators to bring justice for corporate complicity in Operation Independence.

They used sophisticated strategies to collect evidence, extend the notion of state terrorism to the company's role, and attribute legal responsibility to the defendants. The case advanced to a low level of accountability owing to these innovative processes. It has been stuck there, however, for the last three years.

In part, the failure to move to higher levels of accountability can be attributed to a shift in the political context from a more propitious to a less propitious context as reflected in the discussion on the Techint case. Neither strong civil society mobilization nor institutional innovation have emerged with sufficient force to outweigh the veto power of business in this context. Andhes and the prosecutor's office have essentially acted alone, without strong demand from other human rights, family, or victims' groups, workers' organizations, or community organizations. Institutional innovation has been blocked by the judge on the case who has failed to rule on the prosecutor's request for arrest. In addition, the judge has inexplicably agreed to consider the company's request for dismissal, even though the defendants have not produced a legal argument to support that action. No international pressure has been exerted. In this less propitious political context, the company has succeeded in blocking – but not yet reversing – advances toward justice.

Level 2: Formal Charges

Judicial cases move toward the second level of accountability when an official investigation generates formal charges against defendants. It is one step above claim-making by providing official backing of those claims. The same set of propitious political context, civil society mobilization, and institutional innovation factors explain the progress to this next level of accountability. Cases at this stage are unlikely to move forward to conviction or civil judgment in unfavorable political contexts, unless claimants manage to amass sufficient power and pressure to overcome the veto power of businesses, or the defendants' veto power is significantly diminished.

The Vildoza Money Laundering Case[53] (Argentina)

The Argentine 2000 money-laundering law (25.246) was creatively used in this case to bring to justice those perpetrators of human rights violations engaged

---

[53] Payne and Pereira, "Accountability for Corporate Complicity in Human Rights Violations: Argentina's Transitional Justice Innovation."

in illegal economic enterprises. Since the transition from authoritarian rule, there have been efforts to put on trial those who engaged in the theft of property of victims of the repression, a crime not covered by the amnesty laws. Money-laundering legislation added a new innovative legal mechanism for advancing justice for these crimes against humanity.

Naval officer Jorge Raúl Vildoza had allegedly created a company called American Data, S.A. as a front for stolen property from political prisoners detained at the infamous ESMA (Naval Mechanics School) clandestine torture center. The theft case against Vildoza had not included the money-laundering component until the state Financial Information Unit (UIF) signed on to the case. The UIF, headed by José Sbatella, called on the Federal Court of San Martín (City of Buenos Aires) to investigate the money-laundering dimension of Vildoza's property crime.[54] The UIF argued that, "[The case] involves establishing the trail of money illegally obtained as part of the implementation of a systematic plan of extermination and to determine the identity of the active duty officers engaged in the money-laundering of goods taken from the ESMA detainees."[55]

The Vildoza case is emblematic. It exposes the network of criminality associated with the repressive apparatus: from the clandestine and illegal detention of individuals, the relinquishing of their property under force to military officers, the use of those ill-gotten gains for personal profit by those officers through the resale of stolen properties, the creation of lucrative companies in appropriated buildings, sometimes using ESMA detainees as slave labor,[56] financial investments drawn from the profits of these illegal enterprises, and the cover-up by other officers and family members who benefited from the criminal acts. Those involved in criminal networks lack a legitimate "security" defense. Theft of property for personal gain does not fit the standard justification used by human rights violators that they were following orders or carrying out their patriotic duty to defend the country from subversion.

---

[54] 94diez.com, "Admiten a la UIF como querellante en la Causa Vildoza," *94diez.com*, March 5, 2014, www.94diez.com/noticias/leer/3842-admiten-a-la-uif-como-querellante-en-la-causa-vildoza.html.

[55] UIF legal case quoted in Alejandra Dandan, "Con el encuadre del lavado," *Página/12*, January 6, 2013, www.pagina12.com.ar/diario/elpais/1-211279-2013-01-06.html.

[56] Testimonies from ESMA detainees include one ex-Montonera (member of the urban guerrilla) who was extracted from her imprisonment to work by day as a receptionist at the public relations firm set up by her torturers. Another case involved the slave labor of a bricklayer detained at the ESMA who constructed the walls of a company created from stolen property.

6 Accountability from Below

On the surface, this case appears to involve few innovative human rights tools. It could be seen as a simple application of laws designed to prohibit money-laundering of stolen goods. Yet the UIF expressly linked the acts to crimes against humanity. Moreover, the human rights claims overcame a potential barrier posed by the retroactive application of the 2000 money-laundering law to acts committed in the 1970s. Legal precedent had already rejected the application of statutes of limitations for crimes against humanity, including those connected to the theft of property from detained-disappeared persons. A simple property theft case, moreover, did not have the same legal implications as the criminal network established through money-laundering. The innovation occurred with the establishment of a "causal nexus" between the original illegal appropriation of property and the continued profits from that theft that continued after the new money-laundering legislation was enacted. Rather than retroactive application of the law, the case addressed the ongoing crime of profiting from money-laundering of previously stolen property. The UIF argument reads: "Vildoza systematically appropriated goods from disappeared persons during the period of state terror between 1976 and 1983. To carry out and hide the appropriation of goods, he created the American Data S.A. firm, putting at the helm his son and his son-in-law. In this way, they tried to cover-up the illegal acquisition [of the company's assets] through Vildoza's criminal activity by transferring its management with the aim of generating profits from a company that would appear to have legal origin."[57] The national prosecutor's office accepted the UIF's judicial action. PROCELAC, a special prosecution unit dedicated to money laundering, together with the Crimes against Humanity Unit, intervened in the case seeking to freeze the accused's assets and to devise a legal strategy to return them to the victims. The prosecutor's office presented charges against the defendants and a formal process began.

Although the law used is not explicitly related to crimes against humanity, the case is. It connects the theft of property from forced disappeared people to money laundering by state perpetrators-cum-businessmen. This innovative strategy aimed to claim reparations for victims of human rights violations through the illegal profiting from property theft. It further uses contemporary legislation to identify the criminal networks operating within the repressive apparatus. It is a form of advancing victims' rights to truth, justice, reparations, and guarantees of nonrecurrence for past violations. Moreover, it recognizes

---

[57] Dandan, "Con el encuadre del lavado."

different forms of complicity by economic actors, in this case, military perpetrators who benefited from the repressive violence to form illegal enterprises. It
required institutional innovation to consider strategies to expose the criminal
networks established during the dictatorship, and to respond to victims'
demands for justice for the theft of their property.

The advances in this case are closely linked to the ESMA "megacausa"
(mass trial) for the atrocities committed at that clandestine torture and extermination center. The ESMA case is one of the most paradigmatic trials for
crimes against humanity in Argentina. Civil society has mobilized behind this
case since the 1980s. Its central importance in truth and justice relates to the
large number of victims, the top-ranking perpetrators of the human rights
crimes, and the range of abuses. It was pivotal in the struggle for truth and
justice following the civil-military dictatorship. The UIF and the national
prosecutor's office responded in an innovative way to this ongoing set of
investigations into the systematic repressive apparatus and its business dimension. It suggests how particular sets of laws governing economic transactions
can be used to investigate and prosecute crimes against humanity.

The Vildoza case has hit a significant hurdle, however.[58] Despite its initial
aggressive pursuit of justice, in 2016 the UIF withdrew its claim from the
Court. The unit dedicated to investigating corporate complicity had been
dismantled after the election of the Macri government. This reinforces the
notion that the election of President Macri has shifted the context from a
favorable to a less favorable environment for corporate accountability.
Although the national prosecutor's office continues to promote the innovative
money-laundering legal strategy, the case remains trapped at the second level
of accountability. No significant progress that we could find has been made to
advance to the third – tentative final judgment – stage. A less propitious
political context and the withdrawal of a key institutional innovator have
posed seemingly insurmountable obstacles.

The specifics of the profiting from ill-gotten gains by repressive regimes is
not unique to Argentina. The Philippines actively pursued these kinds of cases
in the aftermath of the Marcos' regime. Blood diamonds and other conflict
resources associated with crimes against humanity in Liberia and elsewhere
also suggest ways in which innovative judicial actors might seek some form of
truth, justice, and reparations for victims. What is significant and unique
about the Vildoza case is the blending of money-laundering legislation with

---

[58] It appears that Vildoza died in 2005 in Johannesburg, South Africa. If the case moves forward, it
will have to involve his heirs who are in charge of the company.

international human rights law found in domestic legislation to seek justice in domestic courts for economic crimes. But even this unique and innovative strategy can be stymied by a change in government that is less willing to support corporate accountability.

Volkswagen and Truth Trials (Brazil)

In September 2015, a civil lawsuit was filed in Brazil against Volkswagen alleging that the company collaborated with the 1964–1985 dictatorship, blacklisting and torturing former employees. The case was brought to the national prosecutor's office by the Workers' Forum for Remembrance, Truth, Justice, and Reparation, which is comprised of Brazil's ten workers' confederations, three large workers' unions, and human rights groups. The Forum represents twelve former employees who were allegedly arrested and tortured at Volkswagen's factory in São Bernardo do Campo. The case demands from the company a declaratory statement admitting to wrong-doing and collective reparations for the company's involvement in crimes against humanity.

The legal representatives of the unions and human rights groups as well as the public prosecutors taking the case developed an innovative strategy. They initiated the case fully aware that the general amnesty law enacted during the dictatorship retains its legal standing and would, thus, protect the company from prosecution and punishment for human rights violations. They envisioned the case as a preliminary prosecutorial investigation allowed under the amnesty law. Providing the prosecutors do not request a formal trial, the amnesty does not apply to the case. That allows prosecutors to produce evidence demonstrating the involvement of the company in human rights violations.[59]

In this regard, the case opens up the innovative legal mechanism of a truth trial. Truth trials were used by Argentine human rights organizations during the 1990s when the amnesty laws granted impunity to human rights

---

[59] A similar case was opened by a Brazilian public prosecutor against the Fiat corporation in June 2019 involving an investigation into the company's role in the repression of Fiat workers during the dictatorship. Gustavo Veiga, "Investigan a la Fiat en Brasil," *Página/12*, June 1, 2019, www.pagina12.com.ar/203628-investigan-a-la-fiat-en-brasil. The evidence suggests that the company cooperated with the state repressive apparatus to create a clandestine espionage network which operated within the company. Janaina Cesar, Pedro Grossi, Alessia Cerantola, and Leandor Demori, "145 Spies," *The Intercept*, February 25, 2019, https://theintercept.com/2019/02/25/fiat-brazil-spying-workers-collaborated-dictatorship/.

perpetrators of the last dictatorship in that country.[60] In general terms, under these trials, public criminal prosecutors and courts had the power to subpoena people suspected of crimes to appear and testify, yet they could not charge or convict them while the amnesty law had legal standing. The principle behind truth trials is that victims and relatives' right to truth requires courts to investigate the circumstances and hold accountable those responsible for human rights violations even though there is no possibility of punishment.[61]

The Volkswagen case has served as a mechanism for collecting evidence about the specific company operations as well as the broader truth regarding the business community's involvement in crimes against humanity during the Brazilian dictatorship. The public prosecutor's office took testimonies from former workers and victims and one of the accused, Colonel Adhemar Rudge, the head of the Security Division of the company.[62] It also held hearings in which the claimants and representatives of the company discussed the type of reparations the company should provide.[63] Although the company has offered individual monetary reparations to the victims and a memory plaque at the site, the union movement rejected the offer as inconsistent with its broader goals.

This case is perceived as an outgrowth of the work of both the National Truth Commission and the São Paulo Truth Commission (see Chapter 4).[64] Rosa Cardoso and Adriano Diogo, key institutional innovators who made possible the incorporation of corporate accountability into those commissions, are also the legal representatives of the claimants. The union leaders who brought the case led the union mobilization supporting the work of those commissions. In fact, the legal file included both evidence incorporated into the commission as well as new facts collected by the union members in the Forum. The prosecutorial investigations therefore supplement the evidence collected by the truth commissions. In this sense, the prosecutorial investigation serves the purposes of building truth about Volkswagen's involvement

---

[60] The truth trials were eventually established by the Inter-American Commission on Human Rights in a friendly settlement agreement between the Argentine state and human rights victims and relatives in 1999.

[61] Par Engstrom and Gabriel Pereira, "From Amnesty to Accountability: The Ebbs and Flows in the Search for Justice in Argentina," in *Amnesty in the Age of Human Rights Accountability: Comparative and International Perspectives*, ed. Francesca Lessa and Leigh A. Payne (Cambridge: Cambridge University Press, 2012).

[62] Mathilde Dorcadie, "When Volkswagen Handed Its Staff over to Brazil's Military Junta," *Equaltimes*, November 30, 2016, www.equaltimes.org/new-translation-quand-volkswagen# .WdPm12hSw2w.

[63] Interview with Sebastião Neto, São Paulo, March 29, 2017.

[64] Dorcadie, "When Volkswagen Handed Its Staff over to Brazil's Military Junta."

in human rights violations, but it also acts as an empowerment tool for the Forum. The prosecutor's office is working toward an agreement with the company that would include the establishment of a museum that would inform the public about the role of economic actors in the dictatorship. It also seeks funds from the company to support legal investigations into other companies' complicity. Although the parties have not yet reached an agreement, the truth trial has enabled them to engage in a conversation with the companies under the oversight of public prosecutors and to draw public attention to this example of corporate complicity.

The Brazilian case illustrates how innovative actors can effectively maneuver within an unpropitious political context featuring an amnesty law. The tremendous effort by institutional innovators and civil society mobilization, somewhat supported by pressure on the company by civil society actors in Germany,[65] has made it possible to advance this case to a low level of accountability. Nevertheless, the overarching political context presents an obstacle to moving toward adverse judgment. As long as the amnesty law remains in effect, that outcome is not possible. Undeterred, the union movement plans to continue to use the innovative truth trials to initiate other legal actions against more companies complicit in the dictatorship's human rights violations. Their goal is not adverse judgment, but a declaratory judgment from the company and collective reparations to address past human rights violations during the dictatorship.

Chiquita Brands (Colombia)

In 1959, the United Fruit Company, known today as Chiquita Brands, started operating in the region of Urabá in Colombia, through two subsidiaries (Banadex and Banacol). In 2007, the company admitted to the US Justice Department that it had paid a right-wing Colombian paramilitary group (Autodefensas Unidas de Colombia – AUC) $1.7 million from 1997 to 2004 to provide security. It also admitted to paying the FARC guerrilla group. The company pleaded guilty in 2007 to US criminal charges and settled the criminal complaint with the US Government paying a $25 million fine (with no reparation for victims). Since then, Colombian families of victims of paramilitary and guerrilla groups connected to Chiquita Brands have filed lawsuits in US Courts under ATS.[66] The courts dismissed the cases filed by

---

[65] Sion et al., "Os acionistas críticos de Volkswagen, Siemens e Mercedes-Benz."
[66] Business and Human Rights Resource Centre, "Chiquita Lawsuits (Re Colombia)."

Colombian victims for lack of jurisdiction. One additional case in US civil courts – filed by the families of US missionaries kidnapped and killed in the 1990s by the FARC guerrilla group connected to Chiquita – was scheduled for trial in February 2018. The company reached an out-of-court settlement with the victims on the day the trial was scheduled to begin.[67]

Colombian courts also initiated a criminal investigation of Chiquita Brands. In March 2012, a Medellín Prosecutor halted the investigation of former Chiquita executives in Colombia, referring to them as victims of extortion rather than perpetrators of human rights violations. The decision echoed the company's own defense. Yet, it contradicted findings by the Special Prosecution Unit for Justice and Peace. Three paramilitary leaders testified to the special prosecution that the company's involvement with the AUC was more extensive than the company admitted.[68] Because the Special Justice and Peace prosecutor's unit was designed only to adjudicate paramilitary violations, this unit requested that the national prosecutor's office follow up on these claims by initiating new investigations. It also called for measures to ensure that company assets would be available for possible reparations to victims.[69] In December 2016, the General Prosecutor declared financing paramilitary groups a crime against humanity, and informed the public that as part of a plan to prioritize cases related to patterns of macro-criminality, it would accelerate investigations of alleged financing of paramilitary groups by businesspeople operating in the Urabá banana region.[70] As a result of this decision, in August 2018, the Prosecutor General accused fourteen executives of the company (including Colombian nationals and US citizens) of financing paramilitary groups. Claims were made and formal accusations were lodged, thus, allowing the case to reach the second level of accountability along the continuum,[71] a step higher than that achieved in US foreign courts.

---

[67] Brendan Pierson, "Chiquita Settles with Families of U.S. Victims of Colombia's FARC," *Reuters*, 2018, www.reuters.com/article/us-usa-court-chiquita/chiquita-settles-with-families-of-u-s-victims-of-colombias-farc-idUSKBN1FP2VX.

[68] The three paramilitary leaders who confessed to Chiquita's role in the violence include: Raúl Hazbún (alias "Pedro Bonito"), Freddy Rendón Herrera (alias "el Alemán") and José Gregorio Mangonez Lugo (alias "Carlos Tijeras").

[69] El Tiempo, "Fiscalía cerró caso contra Chiquita por pagos a 'paras,'" *El Tiempo*, March 28, 2012 www.eltiempo.com/archivo/documento/CMS-11454061.

[70] El Tiempo, "Declaran delito de lesa humanidad financiación de bananeros a las AUC," *El Tiempo*, 2017, www.eltiempo.com/justicia/cortes/declaran-delito-de-lesa-humanidad-financiacion-de-bananeros-a-las-auc-41929.

[71] Semana.com, "Fiscalía revive el caso Chiquita Brands y llama a juicio a 14 empleados," *Semana.com*, 2018, www.semana.com/nacion/articulo/llaman-a-juicio-a-14-empresarios-de-chiquita-brands/581413.

Contrasting the two – foreign and domestic – cases illustrates the importance of key factors for "justice from below." The US case evolved during an
unpropitious context in the wake of the US Supreme Court's Kiobel ruling,
mentioned in Chapter 2. In that environment, moreover, the US company
had significant veto power compared to weak local civil society movements.
The company enjoyed strong veto power in the Colombia case that is evident
in its blocking preliminary investigations filed in 2007. Ten years later in 2017,
however, the Prosecutor General issued an order to prioritize the case.
Nevertheless, the veto power of the business remained constant over this
ten-year period, owing to its contribution to the local and national GDP.
Other factors changed: a more propitious political context; civil society mobilization grew; and institutional innovators emerged using innovative tools to
promote a criminal investigation.

The context had shifted with the election of President Juan Manuel Santos
in 2010. Once in office, he became a peace advocate, abandoning his earlier
support for the previous administration's emphasis on military defeat of the
armed rebels. His government made efforts to distance itself from any alliance
with paramilitaries. The Special Prosecutor of Justice and Peace Unit had also
advanced investigations, revealing the human rights violations of those paramilitary forces in alliance with other "third party civilians," such as politicians
and businesses. With a priority to investigate patterns of macro-criminality
related to grave human rights violations committed during the armed conflict,
the prosecutor's office provided a new context in which corporate accountability cases could move forward.[72] A Context Unit was formed in that office
charged with presenting the set of priority cases for legal investigation, including the role of banana growers and exporters allegedly financing paramilitary
groups. The Context Unit used evidence found in the dockets of former
paramilitary leaders that demobilized under the Justice and Peace process.
These institutional opportunities promoted innovation within the prosecutor's
office. At the same time, civil society mobilization pushing for prosecution of
economic actors involved in grave human rights violations increased after the
2016 Peace Agreement with the FARC.[73] There is little doubt that pressure
from civil society influenced the decision of the prosecutor to prioritize
cases where economic actors had been involved in financing illegal armed

---

[72] Fiscalía General de la Nación, "Fiscalía tendrá nueva Unidad Nacional de Análisis de
Contexto" (Bogotá, 2012), www.fiscalia.gov.co/colombia/noticias/fiscalia-tendra-nueva-unidad-
nacional-de-analisis-y-contexto/.
[73] Nelson Camilo Sánchez et al., *Cuentas Claras: El papel de la Comisión de la Verdad en la
develación de la responsabilidad de empresas en el conflicto armado colombiano.*

groups.[74] The context of accountability set forth by the Peace Agreement and the demobilization of the oldest guerrilla group in the world certainly altered the power structure at the local and national level, and put businesses on the defensive by opening spaces for victims to present their claims.

Nonetheless, the political context has shifted again. With the 2018 election of President Iván Duque, a less propitious political context for corporate accountability has emerged. His candidacy was supported by some of the strongest business associations in the country, including those who had opposed the Peace Process. Business veto players have a much stronger position within which to resist accountability. Institutional innovators may thus be stymied in their efforts to advance accountability. And it is unlikely that civil society organizations will receive much support from international forces to act as a counterweight to lift accountability beyond these low levels.

Level 3: Tentative Judgments Pending Appeal

The third level of accountability is one in which a guilty verdict or adverse civil judgment is rendered but an appeals process has begun, or is likely to begin. The initial judicial decision against the corporation is therefore tentative. Although a high degree of accountability is achieved through the judicial body establishing an economic actor's responsibility for past crimes against humanity, its decision could be reversed on appeal. While civil society mobilization and institutional innovation with or without international pressure worked together to achieve this level of high accountability, the political context in which it occurred could shift before the appeals process is completed. We anticipate that convictions or adverse judgments will occur in favorable contexts and they could be upheld in the same or similar political environments. The judgment is vulnerable to political shifts during appeals processes, however. In a more hostile environment, an appeals court could reverse the lower court's judgment. It may be that the veto strategy of business is to indefinitely delay a final decision – by using legal tactics discussed in Chapter 3 – to avoid a final judgment. We illustrate this category of cases by looking at Argentine criminal and civil trials of companies or company employees at La Veloz del Norte and Ford Motor Company. See Image 5.1 and Image 5.2.

---

[74] Interview with an official of the Prosecutor's Office, September 2017. He asked to remain anonymous.

La Veloz del Norte (Argentina)

A federal court in the Salta province of Argentina sentenced former bus company owner Marcos Levín to twelve years in prison in March 2016. The tribunal found evidence that Levín participated in the kidnapping and torture of employee and union leader Victor Cobos by providing crucial information to state agents that identified Cobos and resulted in his kidnapping and torture. Levín appealed his conviction. It was overturned in September 2017. The case has now been appealed to the Supreme Court.

In 1977, Cobos was a member of the Argentine Transport Association trade union. He was picked up and tortured in a police station together with other workers. Cobos was forced to sign a statement acknowledging that he had robbed from Levín's company and that his colleagues had done the same. Afterwards, Cobos was transferred to Villa Las Rosas detention center, and freed three months later.

On one hand, the case did not require elaborate innovative interpretations of criminal law to convict Levín. Public prosecutors and victims' lawyers presented strong evidence to the court that Levín had directly participated in criminal activities. The innovative action occurred when the court agreed to hear the case in the first place. Levín is the first businessman to be found guilty of committing human rights violations during the dictatorship in Argentina. The lawyers, prosecutors, and judges thus sought to extend criminal responsibility during the dictatorship to include actors who had never before been tried for human rights violations. The trial was unprecedented in its efforts to advance victims' rights embedded in international human rights law.

Although the tribunal convicted Levín as an individual, the decision referred to corporate crimes. Specifically, the ruling explicitly linked Levín to company interests. It claimed the company was motivated by worker mobilization and aimed to eliminate union leaders whose activity in defense of labor rights might cause economic losses to the company. Also, the ruling stated that the company as a corporate actor was involved in the developments leading to illegal detention and torture. The tribunal also stated that the company's assets were crucial for the commission of the crime. It provided to state forces the crucial information they needed to identify and locate workers, the vehicles necessary to illegally detain them, and to subsequently transport them across provincial borders.

The case was supported by strong civil society mobilization. Provincial and national human rights organization engaged in a visibility campaign that began in the very initial stages of judicial investigation and continued throughout the trial and appeal. The campaign included trial monitoring bolstered by CELS, that included trial developments in its highly influential annual human rights report. Human rights activist and prominent Argentine journalist Horacio Verbitsky covered the trial in articles published in the *Página/12* national newspaper. Other media outlets also covered the demand for justice in the Levín case, particularly when that demand began to be expressed at the national annual event on the anniversary of the coup. These civil society mobilizations received particular national attention as the verdict approached. Certain key individuals guaranteed heightened media attention. Cobos's sister, for example, is herself a human rights activist. The victim was represented by one of the most well-known human rights lawyers and activists in the country, David Leiva, who is also a member of the Asociación de Derechos Humanos Encuentro, Memoria, Verdad y Justicia de Orán. Thus, the Veloz del Norte case was more than a standard criminal case. It was one that extended the criminal acts of the dictatorship to economic actors who had not been legally linked to the repression previously. For that reason, and as the first such case in the country, it received widespread support from civil society and representation by institutional innovators.

The first and second trials corresponded to the favorable political climate during the Cristina Fernández de Kirchner government. The March 2016 conviction was not predicted by our model since it occurred after the political shift to the unsupportive Mauricio Macri government. We would have expected acquittal. However, it is plausible that this decision was rendered because Macri's term was just beginning and his policies had yet to be implemented. In those early days, it might have been possible for the massive civil society mobilization and creative institutional approach to overpower the business veto.

The obstacles to full accountability owing to the political shift may have subsequently begun to take hold. The appeals court overturned the conviction in September 2017. An appeal to the Supreme Court is underway. That appeal, almost two years after Macri's election, may mean that the accountability gains – as in the Techint case – will be reversed.

Ford Motor Company (Argentina)
In this unpropitious political climate in Argentina, the conviction in December 2018 of two Ford Motor Company executives for kidnapping and torture represents an exceptional case in many ways. First, this is the only case in which employees of a transnational company have been found guilty and

sentenced for crimes against humanity in a domestic court. The company's immense economic and global resources did not prove capable of vetoing the process. This is not because the company failed to try to escape justice. The sentencing in 2018 occurred after more than thirty years of efforts on behalf of victims to bring justice for past wrongdoing. Victims made testimony to the CONADEP truth commission (see Chapter 4). An initial judicial case was brought in 1984, put on hold while the general amnesty law was in effect, and then reinitiated after 2002 when those amnesty laws were challenged.[75] Victims also sought civil judgments against the company in the United States (US District Court in Los Angeles in 2004) and Argentina (Argentina's 35th Civil Court in 2006).[76] Over those years, the company repeatedly denied its involvement.[77] Nonetheless, forty years after the events, the First Federal Criminal Oral Tribunal of San Martín found aging executives (86 and 90 years old) guilty for their acts as company employees during the dictatorship, sentencing them to ten and twelve years in prison respectively.[78]

The accusations against Ford involved the 1976 kidnapping and torture of twenty-four workers at the General Pacheco plant outside Buenos Aires during the 1976–1983 dictatorship. The plaintiffs claimed that the defendants – former Ford executives Pedro Müller, the manufacturing director at the Argentine plant, and Héctor Francisco Sibilla, the security manager at the plant – had provided photographs, home addresses, and other personal information to facilitate their employees' abduction by the military. In addition, court documents show that the company had set up an on-site detention center inside the factory where the interrogations of the victims took place. "There they were handcuffed, beaten, and had their faces

---

[75] For a review of the legal process within and outside Argentina, see Alejandro Jasinski, "Reflexiones con ocasión del 'Juicio a Ford,'" *Notas: Periodismo Popular*, 2018, https://notasperiodismopopular.com.ar/2018/03/27/reflexiones-juicio-ford/.

[76] A lawyer on the legal team representing the victims, Tomás Ojea Quintana, claimed that the victory in Argentine courts could lead to success in US courts. He stated, "It is clear that Ford Motor Company had control of the Argentinian subsidiary during the '70s. Therefore, there is direct responsibility of Ford Motor Company" which "might give us the possibility to bring the case to the U.S. courts." Quoted in Cassandra Garrison and Nicolás Misculin, "Ex-Ford Argentina Executives Convicted in Torture Case; Victims May Sue in U.S.," *Reuters*, 2018, www.reuters.com/article/us-argentina-rights-ford-motor/ex-ford-argentina-executives-convicted-in-torture-case-victims-may-sue-in-u-s-idUSKBN1OA25H.

[77] Jasinski, "Reflexiones con ocasión del 'Juicio a Ford.'"

[78] The others accused in the original claim – the president of the company at the time of the alleged violations, Nicolás Courard, and the company's head of labor relations, Guillermo Galarraga – had died before the final judgment. Ibid.

covered so that they could not see who was interrogating them."[79] The victims' lawyer described the climate created inside the company: "The majority [of the victims] were kidnapped right off the assembly line. They were taken by rifle-toting military officers and paraded before the other workers so they could see what happened to their union representatives. This created an atmosphere of terror in the workplace that prevented any wage or working condition complaints."[80] After being picked up, the victims were subsequently fired by the company. The letters received by their families cynically justified the dismissals as their failure to appear for work, when some of those dismissed were at the time being subjected to torture in the plant's clandestine center. The testimony from two victims suggests that their union activism was the cause of their ill-treatment by the company. In response to the company's claims that they had called in the military to protect the company against guerrilla infiltration, worker-victims Pedro Troiani and Carlos Propato claimed they had "no involvement in political militancy and that they were held and tortured, alongside their colleagues because of their union activism."[81] The prosecution claimed that, "[t]he company acted in coordinated manner with the military."[82]

Propato expressed his views on the outcome of the trial: "My colleagues and I fought to arrive here. For me the success is having arrived at trial." Toriani hinted that this single verdict could achieve even more in terms of access to justice for others: "We want them to be held responsible and that our case serves as jurisprudence for other colleagues' whose cases are less advanced."[83]

What made the conviction possible in the unpropitious political context of the Macri government? Our model would not have predicted such an outcome. Yet, through the years of judicial action, key elements of "justice from below" proved crucial. The persistent struggle for justice by victims, their innovative advocates, and an innovative judge overcame the political context to render accountability. The victims and their families no doubt played a key

---

[79] Court papers cited in Garrison and Misculin, "Ex-Ford Argentina Executives Convicted in Torture Case; Victims May Sue in U.S."; Jasinski, "Reflexiones con ocasión del 'Juicio a Ford.'"

[80] Tomás Ojea Quintana quoted in Uki Goñi, "Argentina: Two Ex-Ford Executives Convicted in Torture Case," *The Guardian*, December 11, 2018, www.theguardian.com/world/2018/dec/11/pedro-muller-hedro-sibilla-ford-executives-argentina-torture-case.

[81] Nina Negron, "Ex-Ford Directors in Dock over Argentine Dictatorship Collaboration," *Abogado*, n.d., https://abogado.com.ph/ex-ford-directors-in-dock-over-argentine-dictatorship-collaboration/.

[82] Goñi, "Argentina: Two Ex-Ford Executives Convicted in Torture Case."

[83] Negron, "Ex-Ford Directors in Dock over Argentine Dictatorship Collaboration."

role in the process. Twelve of the thirteen living victims testified in the trial. The victims' demand for justice was accompanied by civil society forces within the labor movement, human rights groups, social movements, and academics. These civil society forces persevered over decades in the pursuit of justice. The legal representatives of the victims emphasized the unique collective efforts of a wide range of actors who have worked together for years to support the case. They particularly praised the distinctive activism of the company's former workers and relatives as a learning experience for those involved in accountability initiatives.[84]

In that process they benefited from institutional innovators. Legal innovators engaged in a multipronged strategy of finding courts – in the United States, in Argentina, criminal and civil – to hear the case. The lawyer for the victims, Tomás Ojea Quintana, has vast experience litigating human rights cases, such as the abduction of children during the authoritarian regimes on behalf of the Grandmothers of the Plaza de Mayo. His human rights career extends beyond national borders and includes the Inter-American Commission on Human Rights and the UN Office of the High Commissioner of Human Rights. Another attorney representing the victims is Elizabeth Gómez Alcorta, recognized by Front Line Defenders for taking on risky human rights cases, including many of the Argentine state terrorism causes, indigenous movements cases, and high-profile human rights cases. The National Human Rights Secretariat and the Buenos Aires Province Human Rights Secretariat were also named plaintiffs in the case. Evidence gathered by CELS and the Latin American Faculty of Social Sciences (FLACSO-Argentina) was used to bolster the testimony of victims in the case.[85] An innovative action-research strategy evolved in which scholars, legal advocates, NGOs, and victims worked together to pursue justice. The plaintiffs also benefited from the public prosecutor assigned to the case, Marcelo García Berro, regarded as one of the most experienced prosecutors for crimes against humanity in the country.[86] His remarks on the trial reflect a sensitivity to the victimization of workers during the dictatorship: "We were able to show during the trial that the company benefited economically during the period and how it used the repressive arm of the dictatorship to get rid of people that bothered them."[87]

---

[84] Tomás Ojea Quintana and Elizabeth Gomez Alcorta, "Alegato querella particular de los trabajadores," unpublished paper on file with the authors.

[85] See Centro de Estudios Legales y Sociales (CELS), "Ford," 2017, www.cels.org.ar/web/wp-content/uploads/2017/12/Ford.pdf.

[86] Ailín Bullentini, "El obrero fue transformado en enemigo," *Página/12*, 2014, www.pagina12 .com.ar/diario/elpais/1-250641-2014-07-13.html.

[87] Daniel Politi, "Argentina Convicts Ex-Ford Executives for Abuses during Dictatorship," *The New York Times*, November 12, 2018, www.nytimes.com/2018/12/11/world/americas/argentina-ford.html.

IMAGE 5.1 Ford Motor Company Protest
Note: Civil society groups use the well-known headscarves of the mothers and grandmothers of the Plaza de Mayo to denounce the alleged role of Ford Motor Company in the kidnapping, detention, and torture of workers.
Photo by: La Garganta Poderosa. Reproduced by permission

Yet, our conclusions about this victory remain tentative and cautious. An appeals process is underway with a powerful legal team representing the company.[88] On the other hand, the age of the defendants may mean that the appeal will not be decided in their lifetime.

Both La Veloz de Norte and Ford cases represent legal innovation in advancing litigation for corporate complicity in human rights abuses during the Argentine dictatorship. Because they are under appeal, they do not yet fall into the highest stage of accountability. They nonetheless illustrate the importance of civil society and victim demand for justice and institutional innovation to advance corporate accountability. They have shown that such factors can at least temporarily overcome even unpropitious political climates and the potential veto power of companies.

---

[88] The legal team defending the accused and their associates are regarded as being part of a select group of lawyers influencing judicial and political affairs in Argentina. Some of them have held influential government positions during authoritarian and democratic governments in Argentina. In the private sector, they have legally represented other powerful multinational companies operating in Argentina, high profile politicians, and businessmen. Alejandro Jasinski, "La conexión O'Farrell," *El cohete de la luna*, n.d., www.elcohetealaluna.com/la-conexion-ofarrell/.

IMAGE 5.2 Ford Motor Company Protest
Photo by: La Garganta Poderosa. Reproduced by permission

Level 4: Final Judgments

Final guilty verdicts or civil judgments not subject to appeal constitute the highest level of accountability. Again, to achieve this level requires civil society mobilization, institutional innovators, and a propitious political climate sufficient to overpower the veto power of business. In this section, we discuss three rare instances of final "justice from below": two in Colombia and one in Chile.

Urapalma (Colombia)[89]

The Urapalma case is a criminal conviction in Colombia of fifteen business people for their role in the violent forced displacement of Afro-Colombian communities by paramilitary forces in the late 1990s during the armed conflict. Several of the palm oil company's executives and former employees were convicted in October 2014, with some of the defendants sentenced to up to ten years in prison. They also faced significant fines: 2,650 minimum wages (approximately US$500,000) and were ordered to pay approximately

---

[89] Bernal-Bermúdez, "The Power of Business and the Power of People: Understanding Remedy and Corporate Accountability for Human Rights Violations. Colombia 1970–2014."

US$7,000 to compensate each victim. The court also ordered several state entities to guarantee and monitor the process of restitution of lands to the communities.

The innovation in this case is its expansion of the legal scope of the crime of forced displacement to convict company employees and recognize the rights of internally displaced people (IDPs) to return to lands occupied by private actors. The defendants appealed the ruling, arguing that only those holding the weapons and inflicting violence on the communities could be convicted for that crime. They lost on appeal when the Court confirmed the conviction in November 2016. The Court's initial decision found only low-level employees guilty. But that too changed. In June 2017, the same Tribunal revoked a lower court's ruling and convicted Antonio Nel Zuñiga-Caballero, a top officer at the company who was named by several of the people involved in the case as one of the leading actors behind the strategy of dispossession and displacement of these communities.

This is a clear case of the right tools in the hands of weak actors. The victims were marginalized Afro-Colombian communities. And yet they secured a precedent-setting judicial decision. They took advantage of a favorable local political context, where the demobilization of the AUC paramilitary group undermined existing political structures in the territories (made up of alliances between economic, political, and armed actors), and opened up the opportunity to victims to make their claims. In this propitious climate, the case advanced to the claim-making level of accountability.

The case relied on legal innovation to advance accountability. After the 1990s displacement, the communities received humanitarian assistance from the Catholic Church. When the Church group learned that the community's lands had been taken over by palm oil companies, it reached out to the Inter-Church Commission of Justice and Peace (CIJP), a human rights NGO with ample experience providing legal counsel to other displaced communities in the region of Urabá. This started a process of innovation that mobilized groups within civil society who gained support from global and foreign actors. By connecting international human rights law regarding race and land, a forceful transnational activist network emerged that included US members of the Black Congressional Caucus, international nongovernmental organizations such as the Washington Office on Latin America (WOLA), and governmental organizations (i.e., the Inter-American Commission and Inter-American Court on Human Rights). With this support, victims and their advocates overcame the veto power of the domestic business sector.

The claims and mobilization from the victims found a voice inside the prosecutor's office. After several petitions from the communities' advocates, the case was taken from the offices of local prosecutors in Chocó, to the office of Prosecutor Héctor Cruz, from the Human Rights Unit in Bogotá. Cruz had extensive experience using international human rights and international humanitarian law in well-known cases of massacres in Colombia. He took on the case and, as he told us, shielded it against all attempts from veto players to stop investigative efforts. He built a solid case after years of collecting evidence and connecting the crime to existing domestic and international law violations.[90]

On the surface, Urapalma could be viewed as a standard criminal case. And yet, without the international human rights dimension it is unlikely that it could have succeeded in developing the kinds of domestic and international support to persist and win against significant odds. It was institutional innovators who made the connection between international human rights, race, land, and violence that proved essential to the success of the case. The Urapalma case also demonstrates how international pressure could tip the justice scale on behalf of victims of corporate complicity.

Fondo Ganadero de Córdoba (Colombia)

This emblematic case of land appropriation and forced displacement in Colombia, like the Urapalma case, also occurred in the Urabá region. In 1995, the AUC paramilitary group forcibly displaced 130 families from 4,000 hectares of land in the region of Las Tulapas. Between 1998 and 2000, as a result of an alliance between executives of the Fondo Ganadero de Córdoba (Cattle Ranchers' Association of the Department of Córdoba) and Vicente Castaño, one of the leaders of the AUC paramilitary group, the Association started acquiring these lands. The peasants who owned the lands were pressured – through legal pressure and paramilitary coercion – to sell them. This case started to unravel with the confessions of Benito Osorio Villadiego, who belonged to the economic and political elite of Córdoba. He had held important public offices (Mayor of Cereté and ad hoc Governor of Antioquia), and also served as manager of the Fondo Ganadero de Córdoba. He was also close to former paramilitary leader, Salvatore Mancuso.[91] From confessions made during the Justice and Peace process, the prosecutor's office collected

---

[90] Interview with Héctor Cruz, Bogotá, Colombia, July 9, 2019. Mr. Cruz is a former prosecutor of the Human Right's Unit of the General Prosecutor's office and at the time of writing held a position as Auxiliary Magistrate of the Special Jurisdiction for Peace.

[91] Semana.com, "El hombre que entregó la información sobre el robo de tierras," *Semana.com*, November 2, 2014, www.semana.com/nacion/articulo/benito-osorio-informante-de-la-fiscalia-en-despojo-de-tierras-en-tulapas-uraba/376845-3.

enough evidence to detain in 2014 four executives of the Fondo Ganadero de Córdoba: Carlos Sotomayor Hodge (main shareholder), Benito Molina Laverde (majority shareholder), Orlando Fuentes Hessén, and Luis Gallo Restrepo (both former executive directors of the association). All were accused of forming alliances with paramilitary groups, forced displacement, and money laundering. Benito Molina Laverde pleaded guilty to the charges and in September 2015, a lower court in Medellín sentenced him to sixteen years and eight months in prison. He had been in charge of the Fondo at the time of the land transactions. The case was subsequently reviewed by an appeals court and by the Supreme Court of Colombia; both upheld the guilty verdict. The Supreme Court's final decision was issued on August 2, 2018.[92]

The high level of accountability in this case is the culmination of the successful mobilization of civil society actors with strong support from institutional innovators inside the Human Rights Unit of the General Prosecutor's office.[93] Like the Urapalma case, it also occurred during a propitious political environment. Nonetheless, unlike that case, it did not benefit from international pressure to apply the requisite force to overcome powerful veto players. Instead, those veto players lost power. This resulted from the exposure to close links between the Fondo and the paramilitary groups, which undermined the political influence of this once powerful veto player. Much less force on the side of civil society mobilization was necessary in the face of reduced veto power by business.

Paine (Chile)[94]

The Paine case in Chile is the only judicial case for corporate complicity in the Pinochet dictatorship resulting in a verdict. The case, presented in the opening of Chapter 1, featured six different economic actors accused of violent land displacement. Shortly after the September 11, 1973 coup and the installation of the Pinochet dictatorship, the military and landholders of this rural community, located twenty miles south of Santiago, kidnapped, tortured, assassinated, or disappeared an estimated seventy members of the community. They had been the beneficiaries of the agrarian reform program adopted by

---

[92] Alejandra Bonilla Mora, "Nueva condena a exintegrante del Fondo Ganadero de Córdoba por despojo paramilitar," *El Espectador*, 2018, https://colombia2020.elespectador.com/verdad-y-memoria/nueva-condena-exintegrante-del-fondo-ganadero-de-cordoba-por-despojo-paramilitar.

[93] Interview with Héctor Cruz, Bogotá, Colombia, July 9, 2019.

[94] Juan René Maureira Moreno, "Enfrentar con la vida a la muerte: Historias y memorias de la violencia y el terrorismo de estado en Paine (1960–2008)" (Universidad de Chile, 2009).

democratically-elected presidents Eduardo Frei Montalva (1964–1970) and Salvador Allende (1970–1973), who was ousted in the coup. The violence in Paine is sometimes linked to the wealthy Kast family and other large land-holders of the region who supported the coup and the subsequent dictator-ship. Under the cover of impunity, they allegedly violently retaliated against the rural community.[95]

Of the six defendants in the case, only one – Juan Francisco Luzoro Montenegro – has been sentenced so far. In 2016, Chilean High Court Judge (San Miguel Appeals Court), Minister Marianela Cifuentes Alarcón found Luzoro guilty of homicide and sentenced him to twenty years in prison and ordered him to pay compensation to the families of his victims. Some critics of the decision consider Luzoro an easy target. As an owner of a small transpor-tation company, he did not symbolize the ideological struggle to violently reverse agrarian reform policies. He might have been the safest defendant to convict, if the aim was to bring justice to victims without reopening the political polarization of the past. Of those we interviewed from Paine and in the Chilean human rights legal and NGO community, few believe that justice will be extended beyond this token guilty verdict to include the other – more emblematic – named defendants. However, we know from the Ura-palma and Fondo Ganadero cases in Colombia, that with the right set of factors even top business leaders have faced final conviction.

Even if the other cases do not progress, at least one unprecedented judg-ment was rendered. There is little doubt that the magistrate involved is an institutional innovator. In a confidential interview, we were told that only a couple of Appeals Court judges – including Cifuentes – are willing to take on human rights cases. The majority of the judges in this highest court of the country would like to end trials for past human rights violations. Pressure against trials of state perpetrators means even less motivation to hear cases of non-state business actors involved in those violations. In this judicial context, Cifuentes' conviction of Luzoro is particularly daring and innovative. Our informant was certain that other appeals court judges would not have reached the same decision and that future cases of justice for victims of corporate complicity will also depend on which particular judge is assigned to the case.

---

[95] Miguel Kast Rist, an economist trained at the University of Chicago, was Labor Minister and head of the Central Bank in the Pinochet regime. Other members of the Kast family are very connected politically, such as Deputy José Antonio Kast who ran for president in the 2017 elections. For further discussion of the Paine case, see Rebolledo Escobar, *A la sombra de los cuervos: Los cómplices civiles de la dictadura.*

The Paine case illustrates the need for mobilization to educate the public – including judges – regarding the violent and illegal human rights violations communities faced because of the business-military alliance before and following the coup. In the Paine case, that mobilization has been powerful, particularly since 2000. Survivors and relatives of the disappeared organized the Agrupación de Familiares de Detenidos Desaparecidos de Paine, with women playing a lead role. The human rights group has pursued a wide range of activities to achieve justice, memory, and truth. It extends its mobilization to those directly affected by the violence in Paine, but also to those who were indirectly affected. It has attracted significant support,[96] leading to the production of a documentary film and a highly publicized memorial site that has made Paine an emblematic case of illegal violence recognized throughout Chile. The Agrupación has also played a key role in the judicial action. It participated in Luzoro's court hearings and held public events throughout the trial.[97] The group has also made public the alleged involvement of other civilians in the crimes, such as the Kast family.[98]

Sensitizing judges to the experiences of victims and to the application of criminal law to non-state business actors in order to bring justice to victims does not necessarily involve novel legal practices. As judges recognize that their peers are taking on these cases, they may become more willing to do so themselves. The nongovernmental organization Londres 38 invited the Chilean legal community to a presentation and discussion of our findings on corporate accountability for past human rights violations in Latin America.[99] Although the judges who attended mainly comprised those sympathetic to human rights issues, the event may have reinforced their resolve to expand the understanding of perpetrators beyond state actors and the need to fill the victims' gap in corporate complicity. The NGO community thus attempted to advance victims' international human rights.

---

[96] Maureira Moreno, "Enfrentar con la vida a la muerte: Historias y memorias de la violencia y el terrorismo de estado en Paine (1960–2008)."

[97] Marga Lacabe, "Corte niega libertad a empresario implicado en desapariciones en Paine," *Desaparecidos.Org*, January 16, 2008, http://desaparecidos.org/notas/2008/01/chile-corte-niega-libertad-a-e.html.

[98] El Ciudadano, "Lorena Pizarro, Presidenta de la AFDD: 'Familia Kast está vinculada al terrorismo de estado,'" *El Ciudadano*, September 9, 2017, www.elciudadano.cl/justicia/lorena-pizarro-presidenta-de-la-afdd-familia-kast-esta-vinculada-al-terrorismo-de-estado/09/09/.

[99] Encuentro abierto: "Verdad y justicia sobre desaparición forzada: Responsabilidades del Estado y terceros actores," Instituto de Estudios Judiciales, Santiago, July 21, 2017.

These cases in Chile and Colombia illustrate that there is not a single model for corporate accountability from below. In some cases, success depends on the use of innovative tools by legal professionals working together with mobilized civil society groups. In other cases, international pressure adds the necessary force to deliver a judicial victory. Weak veto power also explains positive outcomes for victims. Even unpropitious climates can be overcome when the set of civil society and institutional innovation factors work effectively together to apply the requisite force.

CONCLUSION

Corporate accountability in domestic courts of the Global South illustrates the applicability of Archimedes' Lever in this context: the right set of tools in the hands of weak actors has the potential to lift corporate accountability. We have shown in this chapter that the lever has already begun to work. Outcomes of the corporate complicity trials of the Global South have held economic actors accountable, addressing the victims' gap and eroding economic actors' impunity for human rights violations during dictatorships and armed conflict. The global trend toward corporate human rights accountability is underway as evident in these successful cases.

These cases also play an interpretive function. Economic actors have been held accountable through a blend of domestic and international legal instruments, showing that legal tools do exist. Judicial action addresses states' duties to hold corporate actors accountable when they abuse human rights. It further establishes the conditions under which courts can prosecute individual economic actors or individuals working for companies involved in international human rights violations. Thus law-making from below has the potential to shape and strengthen international human rights law. "Justice from below" begins to raise the cost to businesses of being involved in such activity, potentially lowering the degree of corporate impunity and, correspondingly, lowering the threshold for establishing corporations' legal responsibility for human rights violations.

Global change is also potential through the diffusion and adaptation of successful models of "justice from below." We have shown that effective legal tools are transferable. Civil society demand and institutional innovators have emerged in some countries and have the potential to do so in others. Still, the small number of cases and outcomes have not yet established a discernible deterrence effect. The threshold question is relevant: how many executives would have to go to prison or pay hefty fines, in how many companies, in what types of companies, and in how many countries for such a deterrence effect to take hold? With few cases so far, economic actors may calculate that there is no need for them to change their human rights behavior. Too small a number of cases could backfire, in other words, and further entrench impunity and abusive human rights practices by business.

To avoid that outcome, the diffusion of the set of "justice from below" tools is imperative. Certain blocks or hurdles to the iterative process embodied in the notion of recursivity-as-law-making stymie the success of legal practitioners and their clients to effect global change.[100] There is little that can be done about the political context. Yet, even in propitious climates, our analysis of domestic cases reveals the necessity of mobilization and legal support, visibility, and acquisition of legal language and legal capacity.

For mobilization, civil society demand is key. Without it, these processes are unlikely to advance even to low levels of accountability. Much of the success we have seen in the domestic judicial action cases in Latin America have involved already existing groups in civil society, such as unions, workers, and communities mobilizing to demand corporate accountability. To advance judicial action, civil society groups require legal innovators. These include the litigants themselves, lawyers who take their cases to courts, public prosecutors who investigate cases, and judges who decide on and advance those cases. They might be found in the state, such as legislators and executive officers who design and create accountability policies, or in-practice innovators, such as public officials who, regardless of the inexistence of clear accountability policies and precedents, implement accountability practices. The two agents – civil society mobilization forces and institutional innovators – are thus indispensable in bringing about change at the local level.

Potential innovators can emerge through the visibility of effective models of accountability that diffuse within, and across, borders. Roundtables provide one way to make models visible. We conducted a series of roundtables with existing human rights organizations to reveal corporate accountability models in truth commissions, informal civil society mobilization, and judicial action. In each of the roundtables in which we participated, members of civil society groups were surprised at the absence of certain key companies in truth commission reports. In the case of Chile, for example, Londres 38 began to

---

[100] Liu and Halliday, "Recursivity in Legal Change: Lawyers and Reforms of China's Criminal Procedure Law," 911–50; Halliday and Carruthers, "The Recursivity of Law: Global Norm Making and National Lawmaking in the Globalization of Corporate Insolvency Regimes," 1135–202.

develop a new case – now formally filed – against the Pesquera Arauco company for its alleged participation in the transportation of people who were illegally detained in clandestine torture and extermination centers in the country during the dictatorship.[101] The roundtable further explored innovative tools to address corporate complicity. Drawing on the Holocaust and Rwanda cases, the roundtable considered the role media companies play in prolonging, promoting, and covering-up human rights violations.[102] The roundtable model thus suggests a strategy by which new mobilizations and innovative tactics can be pursued to address corporate complicity.

Exchanges with human rights lawyers, prosecutors, and judges can further develop advocacy tools on behalf of victims of corporate abuses. Because of the absence of clear, binding, and enforceable corporate human rights obligations in international law, these kinds of exchanges provide information about judicial strategies used and decisions made in other countries to advance human rights. Understanding that a set of practices exist can reassure legal professionals that these cases are not unfounded. The Appeal Court's decision on the Ingegnieros case, for example, referred to the Nuremberg Trials as a jurisprudential precedent establishing corporate obligations to provide financial reparations to their victims. Recognizing the violation as a globally condemned crime against humanity highlights its gravity and advances victims' international rights to truth, justice, reparations, and guarantees of nonrecurrence. As a crime against humanity, statutes of limitations constraints on domestic judicial action are avoided.

At the same time, adapting accessible local tools to these grave violations recognizes the crime in domestic legislation and increases the likelihood of justice. Adequately incorporating standard domestic law arguments resonates with judges. Evidence of wrongdoing based on local codes and statutes may lead even those judges skeptical of the human rights claim to rule on behalf of victims. Although some judges will be open-minded enough to accept innovative legal arguments, even they need solid legal argumentation and evidence to reach their decision.

[101] Memoria Viva, "Pesquera Arauco," *Memoria Viva*, n.d., www.memoriaviva.com/empresas/pesquera_arauco.htm.
[102] The Marta Lidia Ugarte Román case was discussed. The main newspapers at the time apparently knowingly covered up her torture, killing, and disappearance by DINA, Pinochet's security apparatus during the dictatorship. Her body washed up on the shores after she was thrown from a helicopter. The newspapers described the incident as a crime of passion, thereby deliberately hiding from the Chilean public the truth about the regime's repressive apparatus, https://web.archive.org/web/20120914202310/http://www.memoriaviva.com/Ejecutados/Ejecutados%20U/ugarte_roman_marta_lidia.htm.

Positive outcomes have resulted from substantiating the human rights violation through the use of the following sets of domestic legislation: (1) labor law: companies failed to protect the safety of workers through their participation in, providing information leading to, or directly engaging in, kidnapping, on-site detention, torture, disappearance, and killing; (2) slave labor law: individuals were forced to work for economic actors without pay while detained or under threat in rural communities; (3) tort law: victims claim remedy for damages caused by human rights violations at the hands of corporate actors; (4) economic regulatory law: money laundering or other legislation is used for violations that occurred as part of the human rights abuse, such as profiting from goods or property stolen at the time of illegal detention, disappearance, or assassination; (5) criminal law: economic actors provided material assistance to the direct perpetrators of a crime, or participated themselves in the commission of a crime. By relying on a combination of common legislation and codes, together with international human rights law, these legal strategies provide models transferrable and adaptable to a range of country contexts around the world. They thus advance accountability for the human rights violations by economic actors during dictatorships and armed conflicts, and expand global justice for human rights. Workshops or roundtables with human rights lawyers, prosecutors, and judges about these kinds of cases may produce more institutional innovators among them, or provide the support and confidence to those who already exist.

These tools are not only aimed at human rights advocates and judges. The blending of domestic and international law can also expand prosecutors' investigations that have corporate accountability implications. Rather than only pursuing the violations of paramilitary groups, in 2016 Colombia's national prosecutor's office determined that financing paramilitary forces constitutes a crime against humanity (not subject to statutes of limitations). This initiated new criminal investigations into the Bloque Bananero businesses complicit in paramilitary violence in the Northern part of the country."[103] We also discussed how in October 2017, the public prosecutor's office in Tucumán, Argentina opened a formal preliminary investigation of the owner and top executives of a sugar mill for human rights violations at an

---

[103] Redacción Judicial, "Fiscalía declara como crimen de lesa humanidad la financiación de grupos paramilitares," *El Espectador*, 2017, www.elespectador.com/noticias/judicial/fiscalia-declara-crimen-de-lesa-humanidad-financiacion-articulo-677924; Bernal-Bermúdez, "The Power of Business and the Power of People: Understanding Remedy and Corporate Accountability for Human Rights Violations. Colombia 1970–2014," 185.

on-site detention center operating during the 1970s–1980s dictatorship. As a crime against humanity, statutes of limitations would not apply.

There are certain hurdles that prevent the development of effective mobilization and support, visibility, and legal strategy. Local legislation itself acts as a barrier at times. The amnesty law in Brazil, for example, protected economic actors from criminal and civil judicial actions. To get around this obstacle, prosecutors adapted the Argentine truth trials model to carry out pre-trial investigation with the intention of obtaining a declaratory judgment and collective reparations. Civil society groups and their advocates worked together with the prosecutor's office to adapt and design appropriate local mechanisms to advance corporate accountability even within the existing legislative constraints.

Business veto power over judicial action is not always surmountable. An arsenal of legal tools can be used by economic actors and their advocates to delay, divert, and otherwise undermine judicial action. They have less detectable forms of veto power through connections to state officials, including judges, that weaken the chances of human rights claims against them. We provide evidence to show that economic elites do not always win their cases. Indeed, we have shown that their rate of success has been rather low, with only four final acquittals and two final dismissals. (Other acquittals (1) and dismissals (3) are currently under appeal.) These cases involve fairly powerless members of the business community, and not transnational corporations that have generally enjoyed impunity.

Some evidence supports the notion that convictions of even domestic businesses can weaken veto power. Members of the business community may choose to differentiate themselves from those held accountable. Within companies or communities, a decision may be taken to sacrifice an individual or firm to maintain the integrity of the larger entity. With reduced veto power, less force is required on the side of civil society actors and their advocates to promote corporate accountability. What can be done, therefore, is increasing the number of claims made and cases brought to fragment the business community and weaken its veto power.

The outcomes we have tracked also suggest that political context is a very important factor in "justice from below." Judicial corporate accountability actions began during a regional wave of human rights trials. With the current roll-back, owing to more conservative national governments, a less propitious context exists for corporate accountability. This does not mean that corporate accountability has failed to advance, but the force applied by civil society actors and their advocates has had to, and will have to, be redoubled in these contexts. There is little that can be done about the political context per se.

There are ways, however, to increase the force on the side of accountability. International pressure could tip the scale toward accountability. While such pressure has generally been negligible in domestic corporate accountability cases, where it has emerged, it appears to have made a difference. Adding international pressure could thus prove strategic in overcoming business veto power and unfavorable political contexts for corporate accountability.

As we discussed in Chapter 2, there are movements afoot to strengthen international human rights law related to corporate complicity, the proposed treaty in particular. With such a treaty, stronger pressure is likely to emerge from international institutions. We have also seen that the Inter-American System has increasingly addressed corporate complicity cases. Workshops with potential international actors who could apply pressure is a way to expose the victims' gap, and the capacity – with international support and pressure – to reduce corporate impunity and enhance victims' rights to truth, justice, reparations, and guarantees of nonrecurrence.

As the accountability efforts achieve success in some countries, and cross borders to achieve success in more countries, a body of practice that holds economic actors accountable for their complicity in the human rights violations in dictatorships and armed conflicts emerges. This may not settle law on the subject despite the evidence of state opinion and practice. Nonetheless, it can enhance the power of local actors around the world to overcome the weakness of international law and the powerful business veto that has perpetuated impunity. Such processes signify a turn in legal interpretation and put corporate accountability in practice "from below."

Conclusion

The Impact of Accountability from Below

"Give me but one firm spot on which to stand, and I will move the earth,"[1] Archimedes is quoted as saying in reference to the power of weak forces to move great weights by means of the right tool, a lever. The analogy is explored throughout this book to show how certain tools, even in the hands of weak actors of the Global South, have moved the great weight of corporate accountability for past human rights violations in authoritarian regimes and armed conflicts.

WEAK ACTORS

The weak actors are victims and survivors of corporate human rights abuses in authoritarian regimes and armed conflict. They are workers in factories or on farms. They may be union leaders or students. They are sometimes indigenous peoples or ethnic minorities living in poor and isolated communities. At times they are politically mobilized in political parties or organizations. Sometimes they include other, less powerful, economic actors.

These weak actors rely on institutional innovators to translate their demands into action, targeting key national institutions. Institutional innovators work within truth commissions or courts, law firms, human rights organizations, social movements, or unions. In their efforts, they confront powerful domestic and multinational businesses. They are relatively weak actors given the geographies and economies of power in the world.

The Ogoni people confronted Shell Oil in US courts for the atrocities it allegedly committed in connection with the Nigerian armed forces – including the killing of nine leaders. The company settled before a final judgment

---

[1] *The Oxford Dictionary of Quotations*, 2nd ed. (Oxford: Oxford University Press, 1953), 14.

was reached, providing reparations to the community. The International Criminal Tribunal of Rwanda took on the case of radio, television, and the print media for incitement of genocide against the Tutsi population. A very small organization of workers located in one of the poorest provinces in Argentina advocated for judicial accountability against one of the largest sugar mills in the country (Ledesma). Small (peasant) Chilean landholders in Paine brought to court economic actors connected to the domestic economic elite of that country. Poor and marginalized Afro-Colombian communities worked with the Church and local NGOs to confront powerful local economic elites who had escaped accountability efforts for years in their violent and illegal appropriation of lands.

How these relatively weak actors have been able to confront more powerful economic forces depends on a set of factors. We have observed that both civil society demand and institutional innovators emerge from previous "repertoires of collective action."[2] These may be mobilizations that do not directly engage the language of international human rights, for example, union movements, identity or ethnic movements, or student movements. They draw on resources (e.g., leadership, collective identity, organizational skills) to catalyze their demand into action.

In other cases, civil society actors and the institutional innovators who translate their demands into action originate in struggles for memory, truth, and justice before the end of the dictatorship or armed conflict. They honed their leadership, organization, mobilization, negotiation, and legal skills before they began to mobilize for corporate accountability for past human rights violations. As resource mobilization theory[3] explains, the harnessing of these skills empowers movements. Nonetheless, they remain relatively weak, given the global and local power of the economic actors they confront in their accountability efforts.

They are also relatively weak owing to their geographical location. An existing "bottom-up" approach to corporate accountability focuses on the potential of domestic courts in the Global North to affect international human rights change. Geographies and economies of power underly the logic of that approach. Because of the relative strength of those courts, judicial action is assumed to have an impact on consolidating international human rights law and establishing enforcement mechanisms to address business and human rights. Those courts could take on the most powerful businesses in the world:

---

[2]   Charles Tilly, *Regimes and Repertoires* (Chicago, IL: University of Chicago Press, 2006).
[3]   J. Craig Jenkins, "Resource Mobilization Theory and the Study of Social Movements," *Annual Review of Sociology* 9 (1983): 527–53.

transnational corporations. By doing so, they would fulfill the law-making criteria of state practice and state opinion, thereby crystallizing business's human rights obligations under international law. They would also have the power to promote the development of enforcement mechanisms at the international level to hold companies accountable when they violate those obligations.

Our "corporate accountability from below" approach, in contrast, relies on institutional innovators of the Global South. They respond to civil society demand to hold corporations accountable in domestic courts for complicity in international human rights violations. We contend that dynamic processes of accountability are underway in the Global South, achieving far higher levels of accountability than the international courts or foreign courts of the Global North. We further argue that these processes have the potential to shape international human rights through interpretive and legal practices.

GLOBAL WEIGHT

No one doubts the global power of business in general, or the particular power of multinational and large domestic corporations in economically weak countries. The capacity of these firms to thwart processes that make their human rights obligations binding and enforceable illustrates their power over corporate accountability and transitional justice.

This study has shown, however, that economic actors do not always possess sufficient power to shape outcomes. There was a moment after the Holocaust when consensus emerged that Nazi businesses had violated the customary laws governing human rights: the use of slave labor from concentration camps to work in factories; the production of poison gas used to kill Jews, Roma peoples, Communists, homosexuals, and others in extermination camps; banks that financed those camps. The realization of how integral business was to the Nazi regime and its atrocities moved the Allied forces to put the owners and managers of those companies on trial. Many were convicted and sentenced to prison. Some were executed.

At a specific political moment, the International Military Tribunal stood up to once powerful businesses to hold them accountable. Yet only a few years later, many of those imprisoned were granted clemency, released from prison, and their enterprises and means of production restored. They were viewed then, in a different Cold War context, as essential to the fight against Communism, the new global enemy. The historical moment of international accountability for corporate complicity seemed to have ended.

Efforts to recover the capacity of international institutions to check the power of business and to regulate its human rights behavior have not yet proved successful. A business lobby defeated the effort to consolidate existing laws regulating business human rights behavior in the UN Draft Norms. The members of the Human Rights Council that previously defeated the Norms were nearly all from the Global North. Current business lobbying focuses on maintaining the soft law and voluntary principles embodied in the UNGPs that replaced the Norms. The power of business continues to influence international human rights law away from binding obligations and enforcement mechanisms.

Since Nuremberg, and despite continued corporate complicity in human rights abuses around the world, only one international court (the UN Ad Hoc International Criminal Tribunal for Rwanda) has convicted economic actors for participating in past atrocities. And even then, no references were made to specific international instruments aimed at corporate accountability for human rights violations. No international law-making resulted from this effort.

The failure of international courts to adjudicate corporate violations motivated scholars to develop the "bottom up" approach. They contend that the best counterweight to powerful business lies with the courts in the powerful countries of the Global North. If those courts held powerful companies accountable using international human rights law, then they could be said to have implemented the state practice and the state opinion criteria to consolidate customary law on business human rights obligations. They would enhance victims' rights to truth, justice, reparations, and guarantees of nonrecurrence. They would also add the threat of prosecution that could bolster judicial initiatives around the world and reduce the level of impunity. Finally, they would legitimize and supplement the work of legal practitioners in their defense of victims' rights.

There is no doubt that foreign courts *could* make an enormous difference for victims and for advancing international human rights. Our data further show that foreign courts sometimes do advance corporate accountability and transitional justice. Belgian courts convicted two businessmen who financed repression in Liberia by doing business with the government of Charles Taylor (buying blood diamonds and selling weapons). Yet they were found guilty of illegal diamond possession, not for related war crimes or human rights violations. Empirical evidence does not support, therefore, the conclusion that courts in the Global North have become the counterweight to global business. In the area of corporate complicity, few cases have been brought, few have been adjudicated, and few have resulted in final judgments or convictions. Judicial systems in the Global North have begun to develop new legal instruments to hold economic actors accountable for human rights violations.

However, there is not yet evidence that these changes will contribute to corporate accountability in general, or to transitional contexts in particular.

The business and human rights literature has emphasized the power of multinational corporations in their use of complex management structures and legal strategies to avoid accountability. The evidence from our analysis suggests that economic actors have tended to avoid liability in the courts of the North by having cases dismissed or settling them. Monetary victories, through settlements, are the primary victories that victims achieve against multinational perpetrators in the Global North. Global businesses are powerful enough to avoid conviction or civil judgment, to keep the terms of settlement concealed, and to deny wrongdoing. Efforts to counter-balance that power has partially come from institutional innovators from the Global South promoting a draft international treaty to establish binding and enforceable human rights obligations on economic actors.

Another contribution that weak actors from the Global South have made to advance international human rights is in their courts and truth commissions. This is not to say that civil society demand for justice is being met. There is still a long way to go to achieve corporate accountability. Nonetheless, "accountability from below" models are being developed and have potential to lift international human rights.

THE RIGHT TOOLS

Relatively weak actors in weak countries of the Global South have used a set of effective tools to hold weighty businesses accountable. In Africa, Asia, and Latin America, truth commissions identified economic actors by name for their alleged involvement in human rights violations. Collecting and incorporating testimonies was part of the process of seeking truth about, and restorative justice for, victims of corporate complicity. Victims of those violations themselves and those supporting them in human rights organizations, trade unions, and local communities provided documentation to strengthen their claims of economic actors' violations during authoritarian regimes and armed conflicts.

For victims and their organizations and communities to be seen and heard, to have their experiences known and understood, to name and shame the perpetrators of those violations, requires institutional innovators in commissions. Institutional innovators have gone beyond the original scope of truth commissions to include corporate complicity in human rights violations. In sifting and winnowing through testimony, institutional innovators retained emblematic narratives of past violations by economic actors even if they fell outside the explicit commission mandate. These innovators are the commissioners, the researchers, and the redactors who see in these experiences of corporate complicity in human rights violations an injustice needing recognition.

Civil society mobilizations – campaigns and outing – are another tool used by weak actors. These include street mobilizations to draw attention to corporate complicity in human rights violations. They also require institutional innovators to plan public events and to design campaigns to correspond to global occasions like the World Cup or local ones like anniversaries of coups. These events target consumers to boycott blood diamonds or residents to replace street names to protest corporate sponsors of atrocity. These civil society mobilizations employ organizational tools to name and shame. They use them to raise the public and reputational costs to companies for committing abuses. They create peoples' courts that monitor and judge action by corporations and show the public that even "well-bred, highly educated, and sensible" people like Alfried Krupp, even companies like Ford, Chiquita Brands, or Shell Oil that provide jobs and goods, are capable of committing crimes against humanity.

The other tool weak actors use is judicial action. Institutional innovators have heard victims' stories and demands for justice and they respond to them. Up against powerful business forces and courts generally reluctant to confront them, they have to find novel forms of pursuing judicial action. One effective example of accountability from below is the blending of international human rights laws already incorporated into domestic law with ordinary domestic legal instruments like labor, tort, criminal, civil, and financial regulatory law. One key benefit of this approach is the lack of statutes of limitations in international human rights law for crimes against humanity. This allows victims to bring cases long after the harm occurred. Domestic law, with which domestic court judges are more familiar, attaches specific punishments for crimes committed. This blending of legal instruments enables courts to consider corporate liability under domestic law, rather than unclear, unfamiliar, and unsettled international law, but without statutes of limitations constraints.

These tools are transferable. They can travel across borders or within countries to promote judicial action. Institutional innovators can adapt these tools to litigation in a range of contexts. We have already begun to see the creation of transnational legal networks that are sharing accountability strategies and tools. Indeed, we have played a role in the diffusion of models across borders. These are the "right tools" used by weak actors to advance accountability from below and to confront the global weight of business.

LIFTING INTERNATIONAL HUMAN RIGHTS

These tools add force to civil society's demand for corporate accountability. Although a victims' gap still exists, accountability models have already begun to advance the right to truth, justice, reparations, and guarantees of nonrecurrence. There has been some accountability, some justice. The process has connected certain economic actors' behavior in the past to crimes against humanity. An interpretive shift has begun. In holding economic actors' accountable, the practice of advancing victims' rights is underway. "Corporate accountability from below" is thus beginning to have an impact. The victims' gap is narrowing.

Raising Human Rights for Victims

Based on our study, we can claim that "corporate accountability from below" has become part of the transitional justice process. It has advanced the rights to truth, justice, and reparations for victims of corporate complicity. Half of the final truth commission reports have named businesses for their alleged involvement in gross violations of human rights during authoritarian regimes and armed conflicts. This advances significantly victims' right to truth. Naming over 300 economic actors for allegedly financing and carrying out torture, arbitrary detentions, killings, and disappearances begins to document the seriousness of the violations in countries around the world. Some companies have paid reparations as a result of truth commission recommendations, judicial decisions, and out-of-court settlements. International, foreign, and especially domestic trials have held economic actors to account, winning justice for victims. With increasing knowledge of these forms of accountability, a deterrence function could begin to provide guarantees of non-repetition. We know that more needs to be done to address victims' rights. There is potential to meet that goal in the "accountability from below" model. We set out below some ideas for advancing that process.

Right to Truth

To address victims' right to truth, truth commissions need to be more systematic in their investigations into corporate complicity, make their findings more visible, and include authoritative recommendations to address corporate wrongdoing. Systematic investigations would involve including investigation into non-state business actors' role in the violence in the truth commission mandate. The preamble of the final report should carefully outline what the commission means by corporate complicity and the jurisprudence adapted to establish complicity (e.g., joint criminal enterprise, financing illegal violence, slave labor, and illegal violent enterprises). The preamble should also set forth the reasons for including corporate complicity, drawing on international human rights norms, the rights of victims, and the particular historical experience in the country as a whole, as well as in specific subnational settings. Together with affected individuals, groups, and communities, the commission should develop a strategy for investigation to reveal the truth. This would include victim testimony, the use of company and state archives, and the development of emblematic case studies to disclose patterns of corporate complicity.

The next step is the visibility of the findings. While the existing truth commission reports contain information on corporate complicity, most citizens are unaware of these findings. Short, well-made documentary films aimed at circulation on social media nationally and internationally could also be picked up in the print, televised, and radio media for further dissemination. These are most effective if they select a particularly emblematic event but cast it in a broader framework of complicity. Some of the models of campaigns and outings already initiated through civil society mobilization could be developed through the commission to gain visibility for its work and its findings. For certain kinds of complicity, international campaigns could be designed that link issue areas more widely across borders, similar to the blood diamond campaign.

In addition, setting out the international jurisprudence the commission utilizes in holding businesses accountable would establish clear guidelines for businesses. These could be promoted through closed workshops with businesses and their lawyers or open panel discussions with the public. These public education efforts would deepen understanding of business obligations in international law, violations of those obligations, and the tools that can be used to address them.

Right to Reparation

Based on the commission findings, appropriate, specific, and measurable recommendations need to be established in order to ensure accountability. Corporate reparations – individual and collective – must be a central part of the recommendations. Up to now, truth commissions have only occasionally recommended reparations for victims of corporate complicity. The South African Truth and Reconciliation Commission included the creation of a trust with voluntary contributions from business. No incentives accompanied the voluntary reparations recommendation. The most effective incentive may be reduced punishment in exchange for substantive individual and collective reparations for harm. While the symbolic appeal of putting abusers behind bars is powerful, victims face everyday concerns that will not be resolved by incarcerating corporate abusers. Moreover, the delay and other legal and extralegal tactics used by corporations' defense team may mean that the

victims will never realize retributive justice. Restorative justice through reparations might be possible if the program is established carefully to address the
needs of victims and identify incentives (reducing reputational costs or the
cost of imprisonment) for business to participate.

Collective reparations are designed to address victims' everyday needs, restore
their dignity and humanity. Individual reparations may be based on civil damages
and calculated by, or in accordance with, domestic civil proceedings to reach an
acceptable level of restitution. Collective reparations would target affected communities, focusing on restitution through housing, child care, health clinics,
jobs, skills training, and education programs. Such reparations should be costly.
By raising the financial cost of committing human rights violations, alternative
accountabilities – like their judicial counterparts – may reduce its recurrence.
The reparations program should be managed by professionals unrelated to the
company, with members of the community on the governing board. It should be
monitored to avoid the outcome we have observed whereby settlements are
reached but payments are not made to victims. Connecting reparations to
alternative accountabilities provides the threat of full-scale prosecution if the
terms are not met, further creating incentives to participate. National ombuds
offices would monitor the fulfillment of business' duties to repair harm.

Reparations without acknowledgment of wrongdoing fail to advance victims'
rights to truth. Settlements in civil courts tend to allow businesses to hide the
amount of the restitution paid and to disavow their role in human rights violations. Repairing harm and avoiding its recurrence involves recognition. Full
disclosure by perpetrators fulfills victims' right to truth; economic actors cannot
deny complicity if they provide a full accounting of their role in the harm.
Commission researchers would assist in this process with access to company
and official documents and records. It is based on this discovery that emblematic
cases would be developed and diffused widely to reveal the truth about corporate
complicity and the need to repair harm and guarantee nonrecurrence.

Right to Justice

The outcome of international "top down" and "bottom up" foreign trials in
the Global North has been disappointing, rendering only five total judgments
over more than half a century. A more dynamic process to advance victims'
right to justice for corporate violations has evolved in the Global South.
Despite the veto power of business, justice can be achieved with the right
set of legal tools utilized at propitious moments. We have shown that these
tools have also led to a range of models of "accountability from below" that
includes retributive (criminal trials), restorative (truth commissions), declara-
tive (truth trials), and reparative (civil trials for damages) forms of justice.

Our database includes examples of "accountability from below." They provide models for achieving justice and advancing victims' international human rights. These examples demonstrate a variety of judicial and nonjudicial mechanisms that can be utilized to advance justice: victim testimony; government and company archives; and blending of domestic civil law (i.e., labor, economic, and tort codes and statutes) and criminal law with international human rights law. Institutional innovators who have achieved justice for corporate complicity can provide the technical assistance needed for investigation and prosecution for similar crimes nationally or abroad.

Guarantees of Nonrecurrence

Less research has been conducted on the significance of truth commissions and trials to deter future violations and advance victims' rights to nonrecurrence. Deterrence theory claims that the credible and tangible high cost of certain behavior will reduce the likelihood of recurrence. Because this calculation is based on perception, our data could be interpreted as supporting deterrence claims that even a small number of high cost trials advances guarantees of nonrecurrence. None of the individual firms held criminally accountable in the International Military Tribunals and industrialist trials have been accused of violating human rights in subsequent authoritarian regimes or armed conflicts. This could suggest that those companies responded to the threat of prosecution. Alternatively, our data could challenge the view that high cost trials bring deterrence. After all, none of the Japanese firms that escaped judgment for allegations of slave labor and other crimes against humanity have committed subsequent atrocities.

On the other hand, low cost sanctions did not prevent multiple accusations against the companies that settled in US courts following the Holocaust, the companies named in truth commission reports, and companies identified in judicial actions for complicity in contemporary dictatorships and armed conflicts. None of the twenty accused of corporate complicity in human rights violations in more than one country and in more than one authoritarian or armed conflict situation has ever been held legally accountable. This would appear to reinforce deterrence theory regarding the negligible impact of low-level sanctions on guarantees of non-repetition.

Volkswagen was not held criminally responsible after the Holocaust by the International Military Tribunal but settled a US slave reparation case without any admission of wrongdoing. That company is once again facing judicial action, this time owing to its alleged complicity in the Brazilian repressive apparatus. These data suggest that judicial actions have not had a deterrent effect across time and context, within the business sector.

We might assume that one highly publicized guilty verdict would increase the perception among businesses of the risk of prosecution and incarceration for complicity in human rights violations. Yet more than one public and high cost outcome for economic actors' complicity in crimes against humanity in Nazi Germany – Tesch and Streicher's executions; Krupp's criminal sentence – failed to thwart subsequent complicity by companies around the world. The focus on convictions-as-deterrence may thus misrepresent business perceptions of cost. Businesses may not be deterred by the rare, even if dramatic, conviction. And the much more frequent outcomes of judicial actions without convictions (i.e., dismissals, settlements, clemency and pardon, or pending judgments) may signal to economic actors that they are likely to escape judgment if they use their substantial social, economic, and legal power effectively.

It is because of business power and perception, that "accountability from below" through truth commissions, civil society mobilization, and judicial action has not yet achieved the goals of filling the victims' gap. The best way to secure victims' right to the guarantee of nonrecurrence is to bolster "accountability from below" with international pressure on states and businesses to recognize the binding and enforceable human rights obligations on economic actors. Such an effort would change business perceptions of the likelihood of impunity for human rights violations.

Raising International Human Rights Law

An even bigger challenge for "accountability from below" than local-level corporate accountability processes is raising international human rights law. Specifically, an international legal framework would make explicit what scholars suggest already exists in a range of international instruments: the binding human rights obligations of business, states' duties to enforce those obligations, and the international community's commitment to back-up domestic enforcement with international accountability mechanisms. This would send a clear message to business of its human rights responsibilities. It would also reinforce for states their duties to respect, protect, and remedy human rights violations by business. It would bolster state's efforts to do so with international enforcement mechanisms, such as the International Criminal Court or foreign courts under the universal jurisdiction principle. This form of settled international law would support weak states that attempt to hold powerful businesses accountable. It would begin to close the impunity gap for corporate complicity.

We suggest three different ways in which weak states potentially have influence over international human rights law. First, states in the Global

South have proposed, and begun to develop, binding and enforceable human rights obligations on business. The movement behind a treaty on business and human rights exemplifies this initiative. Should these efforts succeed, they could fulfill a role of international law-making from below.

Transitional justice provides another means. We have shown with this study that transitional justice mechanisms have incorporated corporate accountability in practice. Truth commissions have named economic actors for alleged complicity in human rights violations. Legal processes for human rights violations by economic actors are underway at the domestic, foreign, and international level. What is missing is the explicit recognition of the use of these mechanisms to address the victims' gap. Few truth commissions include investigation for corporate complicity in human rights violations in their mandate. A more explicit recognition would bolster processes, such as that currently underway in Colombia. In addition, few truth commission recommendations include specific reparations or justice initiatives that address corporate complicity in past violations. Those who promote transitional justice could help close the victims' gap and strengthen international law by making clearer the responsibility of states through their transitional justice mechanisms to address economic actors' past violations of human rights.

Weak states also play a potential role in customary law-making. The accountability efforts in the truth commissions and courts of the Global South constitute two requisites for customary law-making: state practice and states' agreement on the interpretation of legal obligations. Those states that have begun to hold economic actors accountable for human rights violation thus constitute "custom pioneers,"[4] who through their interpretive acts and their practice break new legal ground in international human rights law. By blending domestic and international law in their corporate accountability practices, they show that they interpret economic actors' human rights obligations as binding and enforceable. They thus reinforce international human rights obligations on business and they act on their own understanding of state's duties to enforce those obligations by holding economic actors accountable for past human rights violations.

We acknowledge that only a few states have played the role of "custom pioneers," and, thus, as yet it cannot be argued that corporate accountability

---

[4] Michael P. Scharf, "Accelerated Formation of Customary International Law," *Faculty Publications – Case Western Reserve University (School of Law)*, 2014, http://scholarlycommons.law.case.edu/cgi/viewcontent.cgi?article=2166&context=faculty_publications; Scharf, *Customary International Law in Times of Fundamental Change: Recognizing Grotian Moments*, 306.

and transitional justice initiatives constitute "widespread" state practice or opinion. Nonetheless, we argue that the practice adopted in Latin America has the potential of developing Archimedes' Lever of corporate accountability and transitional justice. That is, an effective set of domestic tools transferable to actors in the Global South have begun to elevate the global normative and institutional framework of corporations' human rights obligations. Moreover, there is evidence to support the view that the tools in the hands of these relatively weak actors have partially achieved the objective of elevating international human rights in addressing victims' demand for truth, justice, reparations, and guarantees of non-repetition – through judicial and nonjudicial justice mechanisms from below. The region's potential to elevate customary and treaty law at the international level, and corresponding enforcement mechanisms, remains aspirational, but not completely unattainable.

A FIRM SPOT ON WHICH TO STAND

What allows weak actors to lift corporate accountability from under veto players' weight is not only force but, also the context, the position of the fulcrum, and the "firm spot on which to stand." We have observed that the context, or fulcrum, moves. It has not remained firmly in place over time. This alters the requirement of force on either side to lift (or suppress) the weight of accountability. The powerful role of business domestically and internationally has allowed economic actors to veto, or apply effective force, to weigh down corporate accountability even when the context is neutral, if they mobilize to do so. International pressure that was applied to overcome impunity for the previously untouchable regime leaders has not materialized for corporate actors complicit in those violations. No crystallized international human rights law renders such violations inviolable. No enforcement mechanisms credibly threaten prosecution. Without clear, settled, and enforceable laws, no pressure exists on states to advance processes of truth, remedy, and justice for victims of corporate complicity. International pressure could tip the scale on behalf of victims and toward accountability for human rights violations. Only rarely has it done so.

We have seen one time period in which institutional innovators in a favorable international context delivered justice: after the Holocaust and before the Cold War. A subsequent global context ended that propitious moment. Local contexts have, at times, proved more favorable, thus making "accountability from below" less dependent on international pressure to lift corporate accountability.

The concentration of corporate accountability in Latin America can be explained in part on local context: the prevalence of the human rights accountability norm and left-leaning pink-tide governments in the region. Even with the movement away from that context, we retain some expectations of continued corporate accountability efforts. For one, the innovative tools developed for justice and truth are now more firmly grasped by civil society groups and institutional innovators. They have the potential to deepen within borders and to cross borders to add to the force on the side of victims.

While veto players will likely enjoy enhanced power with center-right or right-wing governments, recent events may begin to weaken their power. Specifically, corruption scandals have shown that the "well-heeled" businesses and politicians – like war lords, drug czars, fly-by-night companies, and sketchy entrepreneurs – are not inexperienced in wrongdoing. The current timing on the world stage may be propitious for victims and their institutional innovator advocates to seek corporate accountability and transitional justice. Corruption scandals have raised attention to the link between human rights and economic crimes. Businesses are increasingly investigated for their involvement in such crimes. While states and rebel forces may have been able to convince sectors of civil society of the justification for political violence, these sectors do not countenance corruption. There is no such justification. This realization casts doubts on the ability of the business sector to self-regulate. Against the backdrop of legitimate companies involved in economic corruption, civil society mobilization against the violent practices of companies further maligns their image, reduces their veto power, and weakens the forces of impunity.

Recognition of the growing disparities between rich and poor around the globe, and the criminal and structural violence related to it, further erodes the reputation of economic actors. Ethical concerns place the onus on businesses to justify bonuses and obscenely high salaries for their directors when the real income of their employees, or the communities they allegedly serve, is falling. The occupy, *indignado*, one percent, *pingüino*, and other movements around the globe call for social, economic, and cultural justice. An important target for these calls is the global corporate community and its local economically and politically powerful representatives.

The accountability efforts emerging in the Global South – truth commissions, civil society mobilizations, civil and criminal judicial action, truth trials, the treaty initiative – do not directly link all of these current global problems and their local manifestations. There is a pattern of business abuse and impunity that existing laws and enforcement mechanisms have failed to address.

Looking back over the patterns of corporate human rights abuse during authoritarian rule and armed conflict, and the weakness of accountability efforts around the world, we have revealed the victims' gap. While victims of corporate complicity have the right to truth, justice, reparations, and guarantees of nonrecurrence, and transitional justice offers the mechanisms to address those rights, little has been done to advance them. The convergence of factors today – businesses' undue power and influence, abuse, impunity, lack of human rights enforcement – suggests that the time to address corporate complicity is now. Based on solid empirical evidence, this book has sought to provide the pathway to initiate those processes.

APPENDICES

APPENDIX A

Norms on Business and Human Rights

	Source	Year of Entry into Force	Obligations
Specialized Norms on Business and Human Rights			
Guidelines for Multinational Enterprises	Organization for Economic Co-operation and Development (OECD)	1976	Connects the norm that states and enterprises "should" respect human rights within "the framework of internationally recognized human rights, the international human rights obligations of the country;" Their supervisory mechanism (2000) established a general obligation on companies to respect the human rights of those affected by their activities
Tripartite Declaration of Multinational Enterprises and Social Policy adopted by the International Labor Organization	International Labor Organization (ILO)	1977	Includes a provision stating the general obligation of corporations to respect the UDHR and the corresponding covenants adopted by the United Nations General Assembly. Also, protection of labor rights such as arbitrary dismissals, protection of health and safety at work, among others

(continued)

(continued)

	Source	Year of Entry into Force	Obligations
Declaration on Fundamental Principles and Rights at Work	International Labor Organization (ILO)	1998	States are required to promote principles and rights in four categories: freedom of association and the effective recognition of the right to collective bargaining; the elimination of forced or compulsory labor; the abolition of child labor; and the elimination of discrimination in respect of employment and occupation
UN Global Compact	United Nations (UN)	2000	The Global Compact consists of ten principles outlining standards for corporate behavior in relation to human rights; Principle 1 establishes a general responsibility of business to protect human rights
Draft Norms on the Responsibilities of Transnational Corporations and Other Business Enterprises with Regard to Human Rights	UN Sub-Commission on the Promotion and Protection of Human Rights	2003	Under the General Obligations, the Draft Norms state that: "Within their respective spheres of activity and influence, transnational corporations and other business enterprises have the obligation to promote, secure the fulfillment of, respect, ensure respect of and protect human rights recognized in international as well as national law, including the rights and interests of indigenous peoples and other vulnerable groups;" Specifically about business complicity, under the Right to Security of Persons:

	Source	Year of Entry into Force	Obligations
			"Transnational corporations and other business enterprises shall not engage in nor benefit from war crimes, crimes against humanity, genocide, torture, forced disappearance, forced or compulsory labor, hostage-taking, extrajudicial, summary or arbitrary executions, other violations of humanitarian law and other international crimes against the human person as defined by international law, in particular human rights and humanitarian law;" It further states that businesses and their employees "shall refrain from any activity which supports, solicits, or encourages States or any other entities to abuse human rights"
UN Guiding Principles on Business and Human Rights	UN	2011	The UN Guiding Principles on Business and Human Rights are a set of guidelines for states and companies to prevent, address and remedy human rights abuses committed in business operations
Maastricht Principles on Extraterritorial Obligations of States in Economic, Social, and Cultural Rights	ETOs Consortium	2011	These principles are an expert opinion on the role that extraterritorial obligations (ETOs) have in the universal human rights protection system. The principles recognize transnational corporations as one of the actors that exert influence in the realization of economic,

(continued)

(continued)

	Source	Year of Entry into Force	Obligations
			social, and cultural rights around the world; Principle 12: Attribution of state responsibility for the conduct of non-state actors "State responsibility extends to: a) acts and omissions of non-State actors acting on the instructions or under the direction or control of the State; and b) acts and omissions of persons or entities which are not organs of the State, such as corporations and other business enterprises, where they are empowered by the State to exercise elements of governmental authority, provided those persons or entities are acting in that capacity in the particular instance"
International Peoples Treaty on the Control of Transnational Corporations		In process of being elaborated	This treaty is an effort from civil society and states in the Global South to create a binding instrument on transnational corporations and other business enterprises with respect to human rights; Since June 2014 the UN Human Rights Council created an open-ended intergovernmental working group with the mandate to elaborate a draft of this binding instrument; In February 2018 this group opened up consultations on the elements of the draft; In July 2019, a revised draft was circulated

	Source	Year of Entry into Force	Obligations
General International Law Treaties			
Universal Declaration of Human Rights (UDHR)	UN	1948	Transnational corporations and other business enterprises, as organs of society, are also responsible for promoting and securing the human rights set forth in the Universal Declaration of Human Rights (Article 30)
International Covenant on Economic, Social, and Cultural Rights	UN	1976	Article 5.1. reproduces the same text included in article 30 of the UDHR: "Nothing in the present Covenant may be interpreted as implying for any State, group or person any right to engage in any activity or to perform any act aimed at the destruction of any of the rights or freedoms recognized herein, or at their limitation to a greater extent than is provided for in the present Covenant"
International Covenant on Civil and Political Rights	UN	1976	Article 5.1. reproduces the same text included in article 30 of the UDHR: "Nothing in the present Covenant may be interpreted as implying for any State, group or person any right to engage in any activity or to perform any act aimed at the destruction of any of the rights or freedoms recognized herein, or at their limitation to a greater extent than is provided for in the present Covenant"
Convention against Corruption	UN	2004	State parties shall adopt measures to establish the liability of legal persons for participation in the offenses established in accordance with this Convention (Article 26)

(continued)

(continued)

	Source	Year of Entry into Force	Obligations
Treaties on Particular Rights or Groups			
Convention on the Elimination of all Forms of Racial Discrimination	UN	1969	Includes protections against discrimination by any person, group, enterprise, and organization
Convention on the Elimination of all Forms of Discrimination against Women	UN	1979	Includes protections against discrimination by any person, group, enterprise, and organization
Convention against Torture and Other Cruel, Inhuman or Degrading Treatment or Punishment	UN	1987	Requires states to ensure that the prohibited acts in the treaty are offenses under criminal law, including criminalization of "an attempt to commit torture and to an act by any person which constitutes complicity or participation in torture"
Slavery Convention	UN	1927	Requires states to take all necessary measures to prevent and suppress the slave trade; and to bring about, progressively and as soon as possible, the complete abolition of slavery in all its forms
Supplementary Convention on the Abolition of Slavery, the Slave Trade, and Institutions and Practices Similar to Slavery	UN	1957	Requires states to take all practicable and necessary legislative and other measures to bring about progressively and as soon as possible the complete abolition or abandonment of the following institutions and practices similar to slavery
Convention on the Rights of the Child	UN	1990	States should ensure that all actors of society respect the rights set forth in the convention

	Source	Year of Entry into Force	Obligations
Optional Protocol to the Convention on the Rights of the Child on the Sale of Children and Child Pornography	UN	2002	States should ensure that a series of offenses should be covered by criminal law whether they are committed by natural or legal persons, domestically or transnationally (Article 3)
Convention on the Prevention and Punishment of the Crime of Genocide	UN		Requires states to enact legislation to prosecute any actor involved in acts of genocide
International Convention on the Protection of the Rights of All Migrant Workers and Members of Their Families	UN	1990	Requires states to ensure that the rights of migrant workers are respected by all actors
Four Geneva Conventions and 2 Optional Protocols		1949	The contracting parties undertake to ensure the respect of the convention by all actors
Rome Statute of the ICC		1998	The Court has jurisdiction over individuals involved in the crime of genocide, crimes against humanity, war crimes and the crime of aggression; This includes businesspeople
UN Convention against Transnational Organized Crime	UN	2000	The convention looks to promote cooperation to prevent and combat transnational organized crime; The states are required to criminalize the participation in these types of groups; criminalize the laundering of proceeds of crime; and criminalize corruption; Article 10.1 establishes that: "Each State Party shall adopt such

(continued)

(continued)

	Source	Year of Entry into Force	Obligations
			measures as may be necessary, consistent with its legal principles, to establish the liability of legal persons for participation in serious crimes involving an organized criminal group"
Convention on Biological Diversity	UN	1992	This Convention relates to ways in which states should pursue sustainable development; It includes a set of limitations to the activities that could impact biological diversity
International Convention on Civil Liability for Oil Pollution Damage	International Maritime Organization	1996	Requires states to ensure proper compensation for persons who are affected by maritime casualties involving oil-carrying ships
Convention on Civil Liability for Damage Resulting from Activities Dangerous to the Environment	Council of Europe	1993	Requires states to ensure proper compensation for damages resulting from activities that are dangerous to the environment; In Article 1, an operator is defined as any person that controls a dangerous activity; And then it defines person as "[p]erson means any individual or partnership or any body governed by public or private law, whether corporate or not, including a State or any of its constituent subdivisions"
Declaration on the Right to Development	UN	1986	Requires states to take into consideration the self-determination and being consulted regarding policies of development

	Source	Year of Entry into Force	Obligations
Rio Declaration on the Environment and Development	UNESCO	1992	Principle 2 requires states to "ensure that activities within their jurisdiction or control do not cause damage to the environment of other States or of areas beyond the limits of national jurisdiction"
Plan of Implementation of the World Summit on Sustainable Development	UN	1992	The Plan refers to the role that states have to change unsustainable patterns of production; Particularly, regarding Africa, the Plan explicitly requires states to "[monitor] the performance and [improve] the accountability of public institutions and private companies" for the provision of public utilities
UN Millennium Declaration	UN	2000	Requires states to work together on sustainable development
Universal Declaration on the Human Genome and Human Rights	UNESCO	1997	The Declaration speaks to anyone who works with the human genome, including research facilities and firms
International Code of Marketing of Breast Milk Substitutes	World Health Assembly	1981	The Code requires states to take certain measures regarding the manufacturers of breast milk substitutes; These manufacturers are defined in Article 3 as: "a corporation or other entity in the public or private sector engaged in the business or function (whether directly or through an agent or through an entity controlled by or under contract with it) of manufacturing a product within the scope of this Code"

(continued)

(continued)

	Source	Year of Entry into Force	Obligations
Ethical Criteria for Medical Drug Promotion and the "Health for All in the Twenty-First Century"	World Health Organization	1997	Requires states to guarantee the right to health of the population, and in several parts of these documents the WHO urges states to keep firms involved in the health sector in check, and also take measures to prevent environmental degradation by all types of businesses, which eventually could affect the right to health
Convention against Discrimination in Education of the United Nations Education, Scientific, and Cultural Organization	UNESCO	1960	States are required to take legislative measures to avoid discrimination in educational institutions
Convention and Protocol Relating to the Status of Refugees	UN	1951	Requires states to take steps to protect the rights of refugees in the country of reception
Convention on Combating Bribery of Foreign Public Officials in International Business Transactions	OECD	2011	Contracting states commit to establish bribery by any person as a criminal offense
Regional Level Treaties			
American Convention on Human Rights	Organization of American States	1969	Everyone has a right to a remedy for protection against acts that violate fundamental rights committed even when the violation is committed by persons acting in their official capacity; It establishes that the protection of the right to freedom of thought and

	Source	Year of Entry into Force	Obligations
			expression prohibits private controls over the means of dissemination of information; The same regional treaty establishes that the right of reply and rights of the family also address protections against acts by non-state actors
Inter-American Convention to Prevent and Punish Torture	Organization of American States	1987	The convention stipulates that non-state actors may be liable if state officials are also involved
Inter-American Convention on the Prevention, Punishment, and Eradication of Violence against Women	Organization of American States	1995	The convention describes violence against women as a violation whether it occurs in the public or private sphere
European Convention for the Protection of Human Rights and Fundamental Freedoms	Council of Europe	1950	The convention sets out that "any state, group or persons" do not have the right to "engage in any activity or perform any act aimed at the destruction of any of the rights and freedoms set forth" in the Convention
European Social Charter	Council of Europe	1965	States parties to the Social Charter agree to pursue the attainment of the rights listed, which often implicate non-state actors, by all appropriate means
Convention on the Protection of the Environment through Criminal Law	Council of Europe	1998	States parties to the treaty are to establish criminal offense under domestic law when grave violations to the environment are committed

(*continued*)

(continued)

	Source	Year of Entry into Force	Obligations
			Whether states include criminal liability of companies or not, these offense have a bearing on the impact that businesses have on the environment
African Union Convention on Cyber Security and Personal Data Protection	African Union	2014	The Convention requires the state to take measures to regulate the behavior of data controllers, who are defined in Article 1 as: "any natural or legal person, public or private, any other organization or association which alone or jointly with others, decides to collect and process personal data and determines the purposes"
African Charter on Human and Peoples' Rights	African Union	1987	Protect particular rights from the actions of non-state actors such as in the case of the right to work, rights related to the family, and the right to equality; Also establishes that states parties should eliminate all forms of foreign economic exploitation particularly that practiced by international monopolies
Criminal Law Convention on Corruption	Council of Europe	2002	States are required to provide effective and dissuasive sanctions and measures that will also apply to corporations; Legal entities will also be liable and subject to effective criminal or non-criminal sanctions, including monetary sanctions (Article 18)

	Source	Year of Entry into Force	Obligations
Decisions by Regional Bodies			
	Inter-American Commission on Human Rights		The Commission has adopted several decisions where the violations of rights by states is related to business operations;[1] This has been a subject touched on by the Commission in individual cases, precausionary measures, country reports and thematic reports (e.g., In December 2015 the Commission published a report on extractive industries and human rights where it urged the home and host states to adopt measures to prevent, investigate, punish and repair the violation of human rights that result from these activities; and a report on the criminalization of human rights defenders) The Commission has also approved thematic hearings on the subject, focusing on the extractive industries and the rights of indigenous and Afro-descendants communities: "Denuncia de desplazamiento por proyectos de desarrollo" (2014); "Audiencia de situación de derechos humanos de los pueblos indígenas del Ecuador"; "Audiencia sobre el impacto de las actividades de empresas mineras canadienses sobre los derechos humanos en América Latina" (2015); "Audiencia

(*continued*)

(continued)

	Source	Year of Entry into Force	Obligations
			sobre empresas, derechos humanos y consulta previa en América" (2015); "Denuncias de ataques a personas defensoras de derechos humanos por empresas extractivas en Guatemala" (2017); Other hearings have included broader discussions of business involvement in human rights violations: "Justicia Especial para la Paz y responsabilidad de terceros en Colombia" (2017); "Industrias extractivas y el derecho a la identidad cultural de los pueblos indígenas en Ecuador" (2017); The two bodies of the Inter-American System have established that "certain acts or omissions by private actors can be directly treated as state acts [...] This occurs when such actors are "empowered to act in State capacity" (such as through a contract) and they act with the "acquiescence, collaboration, support or tolerance of state agents;"[2] State responsibility can also result when there is a failure to prevent, investigate, and punish rights violations (Article 25 of the American Convention of Human Rights)
Inter-American Court on Human Rights			The Inter-American Court has not referred extensively to states' responsibilities for business operations; It has granted provisional measures

	Source	Year of Entry into Force	Obligations
			to ensure the protection of rights that are threatened by business operations (mainly regarding the rights of indigenous groups); In some advisory opinions (e.g., on the rights of the child) and other decisions it has referred to third parties or non-state actors, but is yet to refer specifically to companies or businesses[3]
Decisions by UN Monitoring Bodies			
Recommendation 19	Committee monitoring the CEDAW	1992	States are responsible for private acts if they fail to act with due diligence to prevent violations of rights
General Comment 15	Committee on Economic, Social and Cultural Rights	2002	Requires states parties to prevent violations by private actors with respect to the right to water
"Statement on the Obligations of States Parties Regarding the Corporate Sector and Economic, Social and Cultural Rights E/ C.12/2011/1	UN Committee on Economic, Social and Cultural Rights	2011	Obligation of state parties to ensure that all economic, social and cultural rights laid down in the Covenant are fully respected and rights holders adequately protected in the context of corporate activities
General Comment 16	Committee on the Rights of the Child	2013	The committee adopted its General Comment 16 on state obligations regarding the impact of the business sector on children's rights
Regulations on the Jurisdiction of International and Regional Courts			
International Criminal Court			Corporations themselves could not be brought under the jurisdiction of international criminal courts, but individuals working for corporations could be prosecuted as natural persons

(continued)

(continued)

	Source	Year of Entry into Force	Obligations
International Criminal Tribunals for Yugoslavia and Rwanda			Corporations themselves could not be brought under the jurisdiction of international criminal courts, but individuals working for corporations could be prosecuted as natural persons
Special Tribunal for Lebanon			Has jurisdiction over corporate actors.
Protocol on Amendments to the Protocol on the Statute of the African Court of Justice and Human Rights	African Union	2014	Includes innovative provisions giving the Court jurisdiction over corporations in criminal matters; The Protocol grants the African Court jurisdiction over a broad range of crimes, including genocide, war crimes and crimes against humanity as well as mercenarism, corruption, money laundering, trafficking in persons, trafficking in drugs, trafficking in hazardous waste, and illicit exploitation of natural resources, among others

[1] Cecilia Anicama, "State Responsibilities to Regulate and Adjudicate Corporate Activities under the Inter-American Human Rights System," 2008.
[2] Alejandra Gonza, "Integrating Business and Human Rights in the Inter-American Human Rights System," *Business and Human Rights Journal* 1, no. 02 (2016): 358.
[3] Anicama, "State Responsibilities to Regulate and Adjudicate Corporate Activities under the Inter-American Human Rights System."

Corporate Accountability and Transitional Justice Database

	Transition to Democracy or Peace	Cases Mentioned in Truth Commissions Reports	Judicial Actions	Cases Mentioned by Paramilitary Leaders in the Justice and Peace Process
Latin America				
Argentina	1973, 1983	11	25	–
Brazil	1985	123	2	–
Chile	1989	16	5	–
Colombia	2007, 2016	–	30	459
Ecuador	1979	14	2	–
El Salvador	1984	9	–	–
Guatemala	1986	45	1	–
Haiti	1990, 1994	6	–	–
Honduras	1982	1	–	–
Paraguay	1989	3	–	–
Peru	1980, 1993	4	1	–
East Asia and North Africa; Asia				
Indonesia	1999	–	1	–
Iraq	1996, 2007	–	9	–
Myanmar	2007	–	5	–
Papua New Guinea	1996	–	1	–
South Korea	1988	3	–	–
Syria	1982	–	2	–
Timor-Leste	2007	1	2	–

(continued)

(continued)

	Transition to Democracy or Peace	Cases Mentioned in Truth Commissions Reports	Judicial Actions	Cases Mentioned by Paramilitary Leaders in the Justice and Peace Process
Africa				
Cote D'Ivoire	2000	1	–	–
Democratic Republic of Congo	1992, 2007	–	5	–
Ghana	1970, 1979, 1996, 1983	5	–	–
Kenya	2002	6	–	–
Liberia	1997, 1980, 2003	34	4	–
Nigeria	1970, 1979, 1999, 2004, 2007	9	6	–
Rwanda	1994	–	2	–
Sierra Leone	1996, 2000, 2002	7	–	–
South Africa	1988	30	1	–
Zambia	1991	1	–	–

World War II Cases: Holocaust and Japan

Holocaust Cases

	Dates of Trials	Number of Businesses on Trial	Number of Judicial Actions	Name of Company	Name of Defendant	Subsequent Outcomes
Nuremberg (International Military Tribunal)	1945–1946	2	3	Reichsbank (2 trials) Der Stürmer (1 trial)	Walter Funk, President of the German Reichsbank Julius Streicher Walter Funk and Schacht, Presidents of the German Reichsbank. Julius Streicher, founder and editor of the anti-semitic newspaper "Der Stürmer"	One of the trials ended in an acquittal for all counts. The other trial ended in an acquittal on Count 1 (Common Plan or Conspiracy) and conviction on Count 2 (Crimes against Peace); Count 3 (War Crimes); Count 4 (Crimes against Humanity). The defendant was sentenced to life imprisonment. The third trial ended in an acquittal on count 1 (common plan or conspiracy), and convicted on 4 (crimes against humanity). The defendant was sentenced to death.
Industrialist cases (US Military courts)	9 December 1946–13 April 1949	3	3	Flick Krupp: IG Farben	Friedrick Flick, Bernard Weiss, Otto Steinbrinck, Odilo Burkart, Konrad Kaletsch, Hermann Terberger	6 individuals were on trial for different counts of war crimes and crimes against humanity; as well as belonging to a criminal

organization. Two (Friedrick Flick and Bernard Weiss) were convicted for enslavement and deportation (7 and 2.5 years in prison respectively); one (Flick) was convicted for plunder of public and private property (7 years in prison); two (Flick and Steinbrinck) were convicted for financing the SS (7 and 5 years in prison) and 1 (Steinbrinck) was convicted for being a member of a criminal organization (5 years). Twelve leading officials were on trial. All were acquitted of charges of crimes against peace and common plan and conspiracy. 6 were convicted and 4 acquitted of plunder and spoliation. 11 were convicted and 1 acquitted

(continued)

Krupp, Mueller, von Buelow, Houdremont, Janssen, Eberhardt, Ihn, Loeser, Korschan, Lehmann, Kupke, Pfirsch Otto Ambros, Ernst Buergin, Heinrich Buetefisch, Walter Duerrfeld, Fritz Gajewski, Heinrich Cattineau, Paul Haefliger, Erich Von der Heyde, Heinrich Hoerlein, Max Ilgner, Friedrich Jaehne, August Von Knieriem, Carl Krauch, Hans Kuehne, Hans Kugler, Carl Lautenschlaeger, Wilhelm Mann, Fritz Ter Meer, Heinrich Oster, Hermann Schmitz, Christian Schneider, Georg Von Schnitzler, Karl Wurster

(continued)

Dates of Trials	Number of Businesses on Trial	Number of Judicial Actions	Name of Company	Name of Defendant	Subsequent Outcomes
					of crimes involving POWs and slave labor. Krupp was sentenced to 12 years in prison and forfeiture of all property; Mueller and von Buelow were sentenced to 12 years in prison; Houdremont and Janssen were sentenced to 10 years; Eberhardt and Ihn were sentenced to 9 years; Loeser was sentenced to 7 years; Korschan and Lehm were sentenced to 6 years; Kupke was sentenced to 2 years, 10 months and 19 days. Ten individuals were acquitted of all charges. None of them were found guilty of crimes against peace. 9 were found guilty of plunder and spoliation (Buergin, Haefliger,

Court	Years		Actions	Defendants	Description
					Igner, Jaehne, Kugler, ter Meer, Oster, Schmitz, and von Schnitzler) and 5 of using slave labor (Ambros, Buetefisch, Duerfeld, Krauch, and ter Meer). The sentences ranged from 1.5 to 7 years.
US Civil Courts	2000–2007	320	18 (6 consolidated actions)	A.S. Dr. A. Wander, A/S Nestlé Norge, ABB BV Rotterdam (the Netherlands), ABB Energo s.r.o. (Czechoslovakia), ABB S.p.A. (Italy), ABB Sp. Z.o.o. (Poland), AEG Aktiengesellschaft, AG Hermes (Switzerland), AG fur Dawa Produkte (Switzerland), AGFA Kamerawerke, AGFA-Gevaert AG, AXA Nordstern, Adam Opel AG, Ael Nordmark, Airal AG (Switzerland), Albers & Co., Alete Pharmazeutische Producte GmbH, Aligena AG (Switzerland), Allgauer Alpenmilch, Allianz AG	Voluntary dismissals: 10 of these judicial actions (3 of the consolidated actions) were voluntarily dismissed without prejudice by plaintiffs because this was a prerequisite to enter the compensation program organized by the German Foundation of "Remembrance, Responsibility and the Future," which used funds from the German government and different industries to compensate victims. Dismissals: 3 judicial actions ended in dismissals (2 arguing lack

(continued)

Dates of Trials	Number of Businesses on Trial	Number of Judicial Actions	Name of Company	Name of Defendant	Subsequent Outcomes
			Holding, Alsenische Portland-Cement Fabriken, Alubelge - L'Aluminium Belge S.A., Aluminium Rheinfelden GmbH (Germany), Aluminium Walzwerke Singen GmbH, Alusuisse Group AG, Anciens Etablissements Leon Sorg & Cia, Audi AG, Aurore (the Netherlands), BASF AG, Bakonyer Bauxit AG (Hungary), Banque National de Paris Paribas, Bauxita S.A.R. (Romania), Bayer AG, Bayerische Motoren Werke, Braunschweiger Portland-Cement, Breisgau Walzwerke GmbH (Germany), Breisgauer Portland Cementfabrik GmbH, Breitenburger Portland-Cement Fabrik, Brown Boveri & Cie, Bucher Industries, Buhler AG, Buhler Freres Burxelles		of jurisdiction and 1 for the lapse of time that had passed). Settlements: 3 judicial actions ended with settlements approved by the courts. One of them was one of the consolidated actions: the *Swiss Bank litigation* (*Victims Asset Litigation*). No data: There is no information about the outcomes of 2 judicial actions.

(Belgium), CIBA AG
(Switzerland), CIBA
Commercieel en Technisch
Bureau, CIBA Farver &
farmaceutike A/S, CIBA
S.A. Brussel (Belgium),
CIBA Society Anonyme
(France), CIBA chemisch-
pharmazeutische GmbH,
Cenovis GmbH, Cerberus
Pyrotronics, Inc., Chase
Manhattan Bank,
Chauffage Central Sulzer
S.A. (France), Chemische
Fabrik Goldschmieden,
Chemotextil, Chinoin AG
(Hungary), Ciba Berlin AG,
Ciba Industria Chimica S.p.
a. (Italy), Ciba S.A. St. Fons
(France), Ciba-Geigy,
Ciments d'Obourg S.A.
(Belgium), Clairant AG,
Clariant Masterbatch
GmbH, Colorex S.A.,
Colori Anilina Geigy S.A.,
Commerzbank AG,
Compagnie de
Construction Mecanique,
Continental AG, Daimler-
Benz AG (Daimler/Chrysler

(continued)

Dates of Trials	Number of Businesses on Trial	Number of Judicial Actions	Name of Company	Name of Defendant	Subsequent Outcomes
			AG), Danzas & Cie, Danzas A.E., Danzas Hellas A.E., Danzas Holding AG, Danzas OY, De Norske Melkefabriker, Degussa (Degussa-Huels AG, Evonik), Dehomag, Deutsche Bank AG, Deutsche Reichsbank, Deutz AG, Diamalt AG, Diehl GmbH, Diehl Stiftung & Company, Dr. A Wander AG, Dr. A. Wander & Co., Dr. A. Wander AG, Dr. A. Wander GmbH, Dr. A. Wander S.A., Dr. Wander GmbH, Draegerwerke, Dresdner Bank AG, Durand & Huguenin AG, Dynamit Nobel Aktiengesellschaft, Earste Nederlandse Cement Industrie, Erzinger Ziegelwerke, Ets. Geigy		

312

(continued)

Hunique, F. Hoffman-La
Roche & Cie., F. Hoffman-
La Roche & Co. AG., F.B.
Hatebur, Fabbrica
Lombarda Colori
D'Aniline, Fabrik
Medizinischer
Chirugischer, Fabryka
Uszlachetniania Folil
Aluminium, Farbwerke
Hoechst AG, Firma Albert
Herz, Fleischwarenfabrik
Wolf/Dorffler, Fonderie et
Aleliers Mecaniques, Ford
Werke AG, Frack-und
Kathreiner GmbH, Franck-
und Kathreiner, Franz
Eckert & Cie, Franz Klein
Mobeltransport-und Lageru,
Fratelli Buhler, Frisco-
Findus AG, Furst Bismarck-
Quelle, Fussel & Co. N.V.,
Gaba Holding f/k/a DOMA
AG, Galak Gecondenseerde
Melk Maatschaaplj,
Gaswerke AG, Gebruder
Buhler GmbH, Gebruder
Jung GmbH, Gebruder
Sulzer Ludwigshafen, Geigy
S.A., Geigy Verwaltung

313

(continued)

Dates of Trials	Number of Businesses on Trial	Number of Judicial Actions	Name of Company	Name of Defendant	Subsequent Outcomes
			GmbH, Geigy-Werke Schweizerhalle AG, General Motors Corporation, German Banks (including Deutsche Bank, Dresdner), Gessner & Co GmbH, Cessner AG, Gipswerk Wilhelm Ambrecht & Co. KG, Gleichrichter GmbH, Glucksklee-Milchgesellschaft, Goeringwerks, Gotthard Werke AG, Grada AG, HASAC, Harzer Grauhof-Brunnen, Hatebur Umformmaschinen AG, Hauserverwertungs AG CASA, Hebezeug-und Motoren Fabrikations AG, Heinkel AG, Henkel AG, Hesta AG, Hoechst Pharmaceuticals USA, Hoffman-La Roche Wien, Erzeugung und, Holderbank Financiere		

(continued)

Claris Ltd., Hollandsche
Fabriek van
Melkproducten, Hydro-
Nitro S.A., Ikaria GmbH,
Insecticides Geigy S.A.,
Interhamol, Irga GmbH,
Isolation AG, J.R. Geigy AG
(Germany), J.R. Giegy A.G.,
Joba/ISBA S.A., Junkers
Flugzeubeau un
Motorenwerke AG, Kraus &
Co., Krompacher
Kupferwerke, Kultura
Landwirtschaftsgesellschaft,
L. Schweisfurth Fleischerei,
L. Stromeyer & Co.,
L. Stromeyer & Co.,
Aluminium Industry, La
Quinoleine et ses Derives
S.A., Laboratories Ciba,
Laboratories Mexyl S.A.,
Laboratories Sandoz
S.A.R.L., Laborotories
ZYMA GALEN S.A., Laels-
Bucher GmbH,
Lavorazione Leghe Leggere
SA, Leica Holdings
Geosystems AG, Leica
Microsystems International

(continued)

Dates of Trials	Number of Businesses on Trial	Number of Judicial Actions	Name of Company	Name of Defendant	Subsequent Outcomes
			Holding, Leica Microsystems Wetzlar GmbH, Leiica Mikrosysteme GmbH, Lillian AG, Lonza Elektrizitattswerke und Chemisc, Lonza Group Ltd., Lonza-Werke GmbH, Lonzona AG fur Azetatprodukt, Maggi AG, Maggi GmbH Singen and Berlin, Maggi Spolka ZO.O, Magna International Inc., Maltex S.A., Mannesmann AG, Maschinenfabrik Augsburg Narnberg, Messerschmitt-Balkow-Blohm, Microtubes S.A., Misburger Portland-Cement Fabrik, N.V. Zyma Nederland, N.V. de Komeet, Natura Milch Exportges Bosch & Co., Nedlloyd Distribution Services, Nedlloyd Road		

(continued)

Cargo, Nestlé, Nestlé
Deutschland GmbH, Nestlé
Ostrerreich GmbH,
Neuselters Mineralquellen,
Otto Suhner GmbH, P.J.
Guisan S.A., Pabianicer AG
fur Chemische Industrie,
Paracelsus AG,
Pharmaanalytica Wander
S.A., Philipp Holzmann
AG, Polska Spolka
wytworow chemicznych,
Polskie Zaklady Elektryczne
Brown, Portland cement
fabrika Alemannia AG,
Portland cementwerk
Siegfried KG, Portland-
Cementwerk Schwanebeck
AG, Portlandcementfabrik
Holerdorf GmbH, Praz
Menou, Prodotti Roche,
Produits Geigy, Produits
Roche Societe Anonyme
Belge, R. Jung GmbH, RAG
Aktiengesellschaft, RSC
Hinique, RSC Konstanz,
RSC Weil/Rhein, Raiffeisen
Banking Group Austria,
Repromaterialien Vertriebs
GmbH, Rheinische Draht-

(continued)

Dates of Trials	Number of Businesses on Trial	Number of Judicial Actions	Name of Company	Name of Defendant	Subsequent Outcomes
			und Kabelwerke GmbH, Rheinmetall AG, Rhenser Mineralbrunnen Fritz Meyer, Rhodiaseta AG, Richard Hirschmann of America, Inc., Robert Aebi AG, Robert Bosch GMBH, Robert Schwarzenbach & Co., AG, Robert Victor Neher AG, Roche Grenzach, Roche Holding AG, Roche akcioya spolecnost pro chemicko, Roechling Enterprises, Romochim S.A.R., Rotti AG, Roux Combaluzier, S.A. Immobiliare Nizza-Monferrato, S.A. Schindler N.V., S.A. des Etablissements Wander, SA Bauxite de France, SAPIC SA, Salzburger Aluminium GmbH, Sandoz, Sandoz Producten N.V., Sandoz S. p.a., Sarotti AG, Saurer AG,		

(continued)

Schiesser AG, Schindler
Aufzugefabrik GmbH,
Schindler Management
Ltd., Schoellerische
Kammgarnspinnerei,
Schongrun AG,
Schweizerische Isola-
Werke, Schweizerische
Reederei AG,
Schweizerische
Schleppschiffahrtsgen,
Schweizerische
Teerindustrie AG, Sefar
Holding, Inc.,
Selectochemie AG,
Siemens AG, Sihl AG, Sihl
Benelux B.V.
the Netherlands, Sihl SNC,
Sika Finanz AG, Soceity
Francaise pour l'Industrie,
Societa Alluminio Veneto
Anonima, Societa
Bergamasca per l'Industria,
Societa Idroelettrica
Cismon per Azioni, Societa
Nestlé Milan, Societe
Anonyme Ciba, Societe des
Produits Nestlé S.A., Society
Anonyme CIBA, Spc/

319

(continued)

Dates of Trials	Number of Businesses on Trial	Number of Judicial Actions	Name of Company	Name of Defendant	Subsequent Outcomes
			Bergamaska per l'Industria Chimica, Stabelwitzer Kammgarnspinnerei AG, Stehli & Co GmbH, Steinoel Co. Factory, Steinoel Co. Ltd., Steyr-Daimler-Puch-AG, Stotz Apparatebau GmbH, Stotz Kontakt GmbH, Sulzer Centalheizungen GmbH (Germany), Sulzer Management Ltd., Susstoffsyndikat, Saurefabrik Schweizerhall, TPS-Technitube Rahrenwerke GmbH, TRICON Veredelungs GmbH, Teerfarben AG, Teerfarben AG Ciba, Telefunken AG, Tesch and Stabenow, Texta GmbH, Thomi & Fanck AG, Ugrovaca Minen AG, Unaxis Holding AG, UniCredit, VEBA AG, VVm (BAMC), Vantico AG, Vereinigte Aluminium-		

			Giessereien, Vereinigte Industrieunternehmungen AG, Verwohler Portland Cement Fabrik AG, Victoria Holding AG, Villiger Sohne AG, Villiger Sohne oHG, Volkswagen, Von Roll Holding Ltd., Von Roll Stahlgiesserei Biel AG, Vorarlberger Kammgarnspinnerei GmbH, WMF Group, Wander AG, Wiletal Kaffeemittel-Fabrik GmbH, Winterthur Technologie GmbH, Wollgarnspinnerei Schoeller Bregenz, Wuelfert GmbH, Wunsdorfer Portland-Cementwerke AG, Zyma GmbH, Zyma S.p.a.		
British Military Courts	1947	9	9	Ael Nordmark, Draegerwerke, Goeringwerks, Steinoel Co. Ltd., Unknown	Jakob Winkler, Walter Briezke, the rest unspecified.	Apart from one case where there was no data on outcomes, the other 8 cases ended with sentences: 1 of them, the Zyklon B case, ended with the sentencing of 2 defendants (Tesch and Weinbauer) to death and

(continued)

(continued)

	Dates of Trials	Number of Businesses on Trial	Number of Judicial Actions	Name of Company	Name of Defendant	Subsequent Outcomes
						the acquittal of 1 (Drosihn). Three of these cases involved defendants who were in charge of work camps.
German Civil Courts	1948–1949	1	2	HASAG		Both judicial actions ended with convictions.
Japanese Cases		13	10			
Japanese Criminal Courts	1998–1999	3	3	Mitsui Co, Nishimatsu Construction and Mitsubishi Materials Corp		One case ended with the conviction of Mitsui Co. for forcing Chinese citizens to work in its coalmines. The company was ordered to pay compensation, issued an apology and built a memorial. However, the Supreme Court of Japan reversed the ruling. Two cases ended with out-of-court settlements where companies (Nishimatsu Construction and Mitsubishi Materials

| | 2000–2016 | 10 | 7 | Mitsubishi Materials Corporation, Nippon Steel, Sumitomo Metal Corporation, Ishikawajima Harima Heavy Industries, Showa Denko K.K., Kawasaki Heavy Industries, Nissan Motor Company, Toyota Motor Company, Hitachi Ltd., NYK Line NA Inc./Nippon Yusen Kabushiki Kaisha. | Corp) compensated Chinese workers, issued an apology and built memorials. |
| US Criminal Courts | | | | | All cases ended with dismissals. They also involved cases brought by "Allied Prisoners of War" (POWs) for slave labor. |

Truth Commissions

	Name of the Commission	Year of Report	Hearings/ Testimonies of Victims	Number of Cases	Violations	Victims	Corporate Accountability Recommendations
Argentina	Comisión Nacional sobre la Desaparicion de Personas (CONADEP)	1983	Yes	11	Arbitrary detention, kidnapping, torture, disappearances, participation in repression	Workers and unionized workers	None
Brazil	Comissão Nacional da Verdade	2012	Yes	123	Financing and participating in repression, arbitrary detention, kidnapping, torture, extrajudicial killing, murder, disappearances, theft of property	Local communities, members of perceived political opposition, workers and unionized workers	In some cases the Commission recommended continued investigations to determine the circumstances and identify those responsible
Chile	Comision Nacional de Verdad y Reconciliacion – Rettig Commission	1990	Yes	14	Participation in repression, arbitrary detention, kidnapping, torture, disappearance	Members of perceived political opposition, workers and unionized workers	None
	Comisión Nacional sobre Prisión Política y Tortura – Valech Commission	2003	Yes	2	Arbitrary detention	Members of perceived political opposition	None

Cote D'Ivoire	Commission for Dialogue, Truth and Reconciliation	2011	No	1	Murder, environmental degradation	Local communities	None
Ecuador	Comisión de la Verdad para Prevenir la Impunidad	2007	Yes	14	Participation and financing repression, disappearance, murder, theft of property, murder	Human rights defenders, members of perceived political opposition, local communities, workers	Defensoría del Pueblo (Ombudsman) and Ministry of Justice to establish codes of conduct for companies consistent with international standards; prosecution of certain companies and investigation into others
El Salvador	Comisión de la Verdad para El Salvador	1992	Yes	9	Financing conflict, extrajudicial killing	General public	None
Ghana	National Reconciliation Commission	2004	Yes	5	Participation in conflict, arbitrary detention, murder, torture	Local communities, unionized workers, workers, members of perceived political opposition	Voluntary contributions to reparations fund; specific reparations with amounts to individuals harmed

(continued)

(continued)

	Name of the Commission	Year of Report	Hearings/ Testimonies of Victims	Number of Cases	Violations	Victims	Corporate Accountability Recommendations
Guatemala	Comisión para el Esclarecimiento Histórico	1997	Yes	45	Participation and financing conflict, arbitrary detention, extrajudicial killings, disappearances, torture, theft of property, kidnapping, murder	General public, local communities, human rights defenders, members of perceived political opposition, unionized workers, workers	None
Haiti	Commission Nationale de Vérité et de Justice	1995	Yes	6	Financing and participating in conflict, disappearances	General public, members of perceived political opposition, workers	None
Honduras	Comisión de la Verdad y la Reconciliación	2011	Yes	1	Arbitrary detention, extrajudicial killings	Human rights defenders, members of perceived political opposition	Break up oligarchic practices in media and improve media independence from government
Kenya	Truth, Justice and Reconciliation Commission	2009	Yes	6	Participation in conflict, theft of property	General public, local communities	Action on land inequality as source of conflict

Liberia	Truth and Reconciliation Commission	2006	Yes	34	Participation and financing conflict, arbitrary detention, murder, torture, slave and forced labor, child soldiers	General public, local communities, workers	Prosecution and investigation into corporations through an Extraordinary Criminal Tribunal; reparations for victims; compensation and restitution for gains
Nigeria	The Judicial Commission for the Investigation of Human Rights Violations (Oputa Panel)	1999	Yes	9	Participation and financing conflict, arbitrary detention, extrajudicial killings, kidnapping, murder, theft of property	Local communities, members of perceived political opposition, unionized workers	Workers reinstated; oil and gas company compliance with standards or face sanctions
Paraguay	Comisión Verdad y Justicia	2004	Yes	3	Participation in repression, arbitrary detention, extrajudicial killings, torture	Local communities, members of perceived political opposition, workers	Compliance enforced over TNCs to respect human rights; labor protections for indigenous peoples

(continued)

(continued)

	Name of the Commission	Year of Report	Hearings/ Testimonies of Victims	Number of Cases	Violations	Victims	Corporate Accountability Recommendations
Peru	Comisión de la Verdad y Reconciliación	2001	Yes	4	Participation in conflict, extrajudicial killings, kidnapping, arbitrary detention, murder	General public, local communities, unionized workers, members of perceived political opposition	Companies should recognize their complicity in the violence and accept their duties to compensate
Sierra Leone	Truth and Reconciliation Commission	2002	Yes	7	Financing conflict, murder	General public, local communities	Government must compensate victims of public and private violations; regulation on blood diamonds
South Africa	Commission of Truth and Reconciliation	1995	Yes	30	Participation and financing repression, extrajudicial killings, murder	General public, members of perceived political opposition, local communities, workers, unionized workers	Business should cancel odious debt, make social investments; contribute to reparations fund

Country	Commission	Year					
South Korea	National Committee for Investigation of the Truth about the Jeju April 3rd Event	2000	No	1	Arbitrary detention, torture	Members of perceived political opposition	None
	Presidential Commission on Suspicious Deaths	2000	No	1	Participation in conflict	Unionized workers	None
	Truth and Reconciliation Commission	2005	No	1	Participation in conflict, arbitrary detention, torture	Unionized workers	None
Timor-Leste	Commission for Reception, Truth, and Reconciliation (Comissão de Acolhimento, Verdade e Reconciliação)	2002	Yes	1	Financing conflict	General public, workers, members of perceived opposition	Contribute to reparations fund
Zambia	Munyama Human Rights Commission	1993	Yes	1	Participation in conflict	Workers	None

Cases by Type of Judicial Action and Court Hearing the Case

Type of Court	Nationality of the Court	Number of Judicial Actions	Country Where the Violation Took Place	Name of Company or Business Person	Outcomes
Civil Courts	US	33	Argentina (2)	Ford; Daimler Chrysler AG	Dismissed
			Colombia (8)	Chiquita Brands, Airscan Inc., BP Company, Dole Food Company, Drummond Ltd., Occidental	Pending (3), Dismissed (5)
			Ecuador (1)	Chevron (Texaco)	Dismissed
			Guatemala (1)	Embotelladora Guatemalteca S.A. (Coca-Cola)	Pending
			Indonesia (1)	Exxon Mobil Corp.	Pending
			Iraq (8)	Australian Wheat Board Limited; Banque National de Paris Paribas; Blackwater Lodge and Training Centre; CACI Premier Technology Incorporated; Titan Corporation; CACI International; Daoud & Partners; Kellogg Brown & Root	Dismissed (5), Pending (2), Settled
			Myanmar (2)	Unocal Oil Corporation	Settled
			Nigeria (6)	Chevron Nigeria Limited; Chevron Texaco Corporation; Chevron Texaco Overseas Petroleum Inc.; Royal Dutch Shell PLC; Shell Petroleum Development Company	Dismissed (3), Settled (3)

	No.	Location	Defendant(s)	Outcome
		Papua New Guinea (1)	Rio Tinto PLC	Dismissed
		South Africa (1)	53 companies, incl. Anglo American, Chevron, Coca-Cola, Colgate, Daimler, Dresdner Bank, Merrill Lunch, Commerzbank AG	All ended with acquittals; Only General Motors reached a settlement before the court's decision to acquit
		Timor-Leste (2)	Freeport McMoran Inc.	Dismissed
UK	1	Colombia	BP Company	Withdrawn
Canada	1	DRC	Anvil Mining Ltd.	Dismissed
France	2	Myanmar / Rwanda	TotalFinaElf (now Total) / BNP Paribas	Settled (1), Pending (1)
Criminal Courts				
US	1	Colombia	Chiquita Brands	Settlement
France	4	Syria, Myanmar and Liberia	Dalhoff, Larsen and Horneman; Lafarge; Qosmos and TotalFinaElf	Pending (2), Dismissed (2)
Switzerland	2	DRC, Colombia	Argor Heraeus, Nestlé	Dismissed
Germany	1	DRC	Danzer Group	Dismissed
Belgium	3	Liberia and Myanmar	Abbas Macky and Aziz Nassour; Leonid Minin and TotalFinaElf	Convicted (2), Dismissed (1)
Netherlands	2	Liberia	Guus Kouwenhoven and Frans Cornelis Adrianus van Anraat	Convicted

Source: Corporate Accountability and Transitional Justice database, 2016

Bibliography

94diez.com. "Admiten a la UIF como querellante en la Causa Vildoza." *94diez.com*, March 5, 2014. www.94diez.com/noticias/leer/3842-admiten-a-la-uif-como-querel lante-en-la-causa-vildoza.html.

Abbott, Kenneth W., and Duncan Snidal. "Hard and Soft Law in International Governance." *International Organization* 54, no. 3 (2000): 421–56.

Abrão, Paulo, and Marcelo D. Torelly. "O programa de reparações como eixo estruturante da justiça de transição no Brasil." In *Justiça de Transição – Manual para a América Latina*, edited by Félix Reátegui, 473–516. Brasilia/New York: Ministry of Justice/International Center of Transitional Justice, 2011.

"Resistance to Change: Brazil's Persistent Amnesty and Its Alternatives for Truth and Justice." In *Amnesty in the Age of Human Rights Accountability: Comparative and International Perspectives*, edited by Francesca Lessa and Leigh A. Payne. Cambridge: Cambridge University Press, 2012.

Albin-Lackey, Chris. "Corruption, Human Rights and Activism: Useful Connections and Their Limits." In *Justice and Economic Violence in Transition*, edited by Dustin N. Sharp, 139–63. New York, NY: Springer, 2013.

Albiston, Catherine. "The Rule of Law and the Litigation Process: The Paradox of Losing by Winning." *Law & Society Review* no. 33 (1999): 869–910.

Amado, Guilherme. "Ditadura foi um oceano de corrupção." *Correio do povo*, March 16, 2014, www.correiodopovo.com.br/blogs/juremirmachado/?p=5770.

Ámbito Financiero. "Asume Rosenkrantz, un ex abogado de grandes empresas con extracto radical." *Ámbito Financiero*, September 11, 2018, www.ambito.com/ asume-rosenkrantz-un-ex-abogado-grandes-empresas-extracto-radical-n4033383.

Amnesty International. "Defending Human Rights in the Americas: Necessary, Legitimate and Dangerous." Amnesty International: London, 2014.

"Letter from Joint NGO's to John Ruggie, Special Representative to the U.N. Secretary-General on Business and Human Rights, Joint NGO Position on the Interim Report from the Special Representative of the U.N. Secretary General on Business and Human Rights." In *International Human Rights: Law, Policy, and Process*, edited by David S. Weissbrodt, Joan Fitzpatrick, and Frank Newman. Cincinnati, OH: Anderson Pub. Co., 2001.

Amorim, Felipe. "Revista Fortune revela já em 64 elo entre empresários de SP e embaixada dos EUA para dar golpe." *Operamundi*, São Paulo, January 2014, http://operamundi.uol.com.br/conteudo/reportagens/33603/revista+fortune+revela+ ja+em+64+elo+entre+empresarios+de+sp+e+embaixada+dos+eua+para+dar+golpe .shtml?fb_comment_id=460616454061037_2261867#f6ef5ef1194f58.

Amorim, Felipe, and Rodolfo Machado. "Elite econômica que deu golpe no Brasil tinha braços internacionais, diz historiadora." *Operamundi*, March 2, 2014.

Andar. "La Red Nacional de H.I.J.O.S. convoca a un escrache a Massot y Blaquier." *Andar*, May 20, 2015, www.andaragencia.org/la-red-nacional-de-h-i-j-o-s-convoca-a-un-escrache-a-massot-y-blaquier/.

Anderson, Curt. "Settlement Reached in Chiquita Case Involving US Deaths." *Fox News*, February 2018.

Andrews, Edmund L. "Volkswagen to Create $12 Million Fund for Nazi-Era Laborers." *The New York Times*, September 11, 1998, www.nytimes.com/1998/09/11/world/ volkswagen-to-create-12-million-fund-for-nazi-era-laborers.html.

Anicama, Cecilia. "State Responsibilities to Regulate and Adjudicate Corporate Activities under the Inter-American Human Rights System," 2008.

Associated Press. "Japanese Firm Mitsubishi Used U.S. Prisoners of War as Slave Labor, Will Apologize 70 Years Later." *New York Daily News*, 2015, www.nydailynews .com/news/world/japanese-firm-u-s-prisoners-war-labor-article-1.2294061.

Atabongawung, Tamo. "Multi-Stakeholder Initiatives and the Evolution of the Business and Human Rights Discourse: Lessons from the Kimberley Process and Conflict Diamonds." In *The Business and Human Rights Landscape: Moving Forward, Looking Back*, edited by Jena Martin and Karen E. Bravo, 75–105. Cambridge: Cambridge University Press, 2016.

Austin, Ben S. "The Nuremberg Trials: Brief Overview of Defendants & Verdicts." Jewish Virtual Library, n.d., www.jewishvirtuallibrary.org/brief-overview-of-defend ants-and-verdicts-at-nuremberg-trials.

Avant, Deborah D. *The Market in Force: The Consequences of Privatizing Security*. Cambridge: Cambridge University Press, 2005.

Avery, Christopher. "Business and Human Rights in a Time of Change." In *Liability of Multinational Corporations under International Law*, edited by Menno T. Kamminga and Saman Zia-Zarifi, 17–73. Cambridge: Cambridge University Press, 2000.

"The Difference between CSR and Human Rights." *Corporate Citizenship Briefing*, August/September 2006, issue 89, www.business-humanrights.org/sites/default/ files/reports-and-materials/Avery-difference-between-CSR-and-human-rights-Aug-Sep-2006.pdf.

Babineau, Kathryn. "Business as Usual? Corporations and the Challenge of Human Rights Remedy in Peru." MPhil diss., University of Oxford, 2015.

Bah, Chernoh Alpha M. "Sierra Leone: Eight Lebanese Diamond Smugglers Jailed." *allAfrica*, December 13, 2004, https://allafrica.com/stories/200412140152.html.

Baker, Aryn. "How to Buy an Ethical Diamond." *Time*, August 27, 2015, http://time .com/4013735/how-to-buy-an-ethical-diamond/.

Ballentine, Karen, and Heiko Nitzschke. *Profiting from Peace: Managing the Resource Dimension of Civil War*. Project of the International Peace Academy. Boulder, CO: Lynne Rienner, 2005.

Balmer, John, Shaun Powell, and Stephen Greyser. "Explicating Ethical Corporate Marketing. Insights from the BP Deepwater Horizon Catastrophe: The Ethical Brand that Exploded and then Imploded." *Journal of Business Ethics* 102, no. 1 (2011): 1–14.

Barnett, Michael. *Eyewitness to a Genocide: The United Nations and Rwanda*. Ithaca, NY: Cornell University Press, 2002.

Bauer, Joanne, and Elizabeth Umlas. "Do Benefit Corporations Respect Human Rights?" *Stanford Social Innovation Review*, 2017.

Bazyler, Michael J. *Holocaust Justice: The Battle for Restitution in America's Courts*. New York, NY: New York University Press, 2003.

Holocaust, Genocide, and the Law: A Quest for Justice in a Post-Holocaust World. Oxford: Oxford University Press, 2016.

BBC News. "Chevron Wins Ecuador Rainforest 'Oil Dumping' Case." *BBC News*, 2018, www.bbc.com/news/world-latin-america-45455984.

Bellin, Eva. "The Robustness of Authoritarianism in the Middle East: Exceptionalism in Comparative Perspective." *Comparative Politics* 36, no. 2 (2004): 139–57.

Bernal-Bermúdez, Laura. "The Power of Business and the Power of People: Understanding Remedy and Corporate Accountability for Human Rights Violations. Colombia 1970–2014." PhD diss., University of Oxford, 2017.

Bernal-Bermúdez, Laura, and Tricia D. Olsen. "Business, Human Rights and Sustainable Development." In *The SAGE Handbook of International Corporate and Public Affairs*, edited by Phil Harris and Craig S. Fleisher. London: SAGE Publications, 2017.

Bernaz, Nadia. *Business and Human Rights History, Law and Policy – Bridging the Accountability Gap*. New York, NY: Routledge, 2017.

Bird, Kai. *The Chairman: John J. McCloy and the Making of the American Establishment*. New York, NY: Simon & Schuster, 1992.

Blackburn, Daniel. *Removing Barriers to Justice: How a Treaty on Business and Human Rights Could Improve Access to Remedy for Victims*. Amsterdam: Stichting Onderzoek Multinationale Ondernemingen (SOMO) and the Centre for Research on Multinational Corporations, August 2017, http://mhssn.igc.org/Removing-barriers-web.pdf.

Block, Fred. "The Ruling Class Does Not Rule: Notes on the Marxist Theory of the State." In *The Political Economy: Reading in the Politics and Economics of American Public Policy*, edited by Thomas Ferguson and Joel Rogers. Armonk, NY: M.E. Sharpe, 1984.

Bloomer, Phil, and Maysa Zorob. "Another Step on the Road? What Does the 'Zero Draft' Treaty Mean for the Business and Human Rights Movement?" In *Compilation of Commentaries on the "Zero Draft,"* 1–4. London: Business and Human Rights Resource Centre, 2018.

Bohoslavsky, Juan Pablo. "Complicity of the Lenders." In *Outstanding Debts to Settle: The Economic Accomplices of the Dictatorship in Argentina*, edited by Horacio Verbitsky and Juan Pablo Bohoslavsky. Cambridge: Cambridge University Press, 2015.

"El eslabón financiero en la justicia transicional uruguaya." *Revista uruguaya de ciencia política* 2, no. 21 (2012): 153–79.

Bohoslavsky, Juan Pablo, and Marcelo D. Torelly. "Financial Complicity: The Brazilian Dictatorship under the 'Macroscope.'" In *Justice and Economic Violence in Transition*, edited by Dustin N. Sharp. New York, NY: Springer, 2014.

Bohoslavsky, Juan Pablo, and Veerle Opgenhaffen. "The Past and Present of Corporate Complicity: Financing the Argentinean Dictatorship." *Harvard Human Rights Journal* 23 (2010): 157–203.

Bois-Pedain, Antje de. "Accountability through Conditional Amnesty: The Case of South Africa." In *Amnesty in the Age of Human Rights Accountability: Comparative and International Perspectives*, edited by Francesca Lessa and Leigh A. Payne, 238–62. Cambridge: Cambridge University Press, 2012.

Bonilla Mora, Alejandra. "Nueva condena a exintegrante del Fondo Ganadero de Córdoba por despojo paramilitar." *El Espectador*, 2018, https://colombia2020.ele spectador.com/verdad-y-memoria/nueva-condena-exintegrante-del-fondo-ganadero-de-cordoba-por-despojo-paramilitar.

Bonner, Raymond. *Weakness and Deceit: U.S. Policy and El Salvador*. New York, NY: Times Books, 1984.

Borkin, Joseph. *The Crime and Punishment of IG Farben*. New York, NY: Free Press, 1978.

Botero Caicedo, Mauricio. "Entre la ignorancia y la mala fe." *Las2Orillas*, 2018, www.las2orillas.co/entre-la-ignorancia-y-la-mala-fe/.

Botero, Jorge Humberto. "Pax Christi." *Semana.com*, 2018, www.semana.com/opinion/articulo/jorge-botero-columna-pax-christi/559448.

Bowsher, Josh. "Law & Critique: Transitional Justice as 'Omnus et Singulatim." *Law Critique* 29 (2018): 83–106.

Brant, Matheus. *Projeto Adeus Boilesen*. Brazil, 2013, www.youtube.com/watch?v= SDM-PXdAS2w.

Brinks, Daniel M. *The DNA of Constitutional Justice in Latin America*. Cambridge: Cambridge University Press, 2018.

Buhman, Karin. "Navigating from 'Train Wreck' to Being 'Welcomed.'" In *Human Rights Obligations of Business: Beyond the Corporate Responsibility to Respect*, edited by David Bilchitz and Surya Deva. Cambridge: Cambridge University Press, 2013.

Bullentini, Ailín. "El obrero fue transformado en enemigo." *Página/12*, 2014, www.pagina12.com.ar/diario/elpais/1-250641-2014-07-13.html.

   "Los empresarios cómplices del terror." *El País*, April 23, 2018, www.pagina12.com.ar/110065-los-empresarios-complices-del-terror.

Burman, Sandra, and Wilfried Schärf. "Creating People's Justice: Street Committees and People's Courts in a South African City." *Law & Society Review* 24, no. 3 (1990): 693.

Business and Human Rights Resource Centre. "BP Lawsuits (Re Casanare, Colombia)." *Business and Human Rights Resource Centre*, n.d.

   "Briefing: Is the UK Living up to Its Human Rights Commitments?" *Business and Human Rights Resource Centre*, n.d.

   "Chiquita Lawsuits (Re Colombia)." *Legal Accountability Report*, n.d., www.business-humanrights.org/en/chiquita-lawsuits-re-colombia.

   "Company Response Rates." *Business and Human Rights Resource Centre*, n.d., www.business-humanrights.org/en/company-response-rates.

   "Nestlé Lawsuit in Switzerland (Re Colombia)." *Business and Human Rights Resource Centre*, n.d., www.business-humanrights.org/en/nestl%C3%A9-lawsuit-re-colombia.

   "Reflections on the Zero Draft." *Business and Human Rights Resource Centre*, n.d.

"Total Lawsuit in Belgium (Re Myanmar)." *Business and Human Rights Resource Centre*, n.d., www.business-humanrights.org/en/total-lawsuit-in-belgium-re-myanmar.

Byers, Michael. "English Courts and Serious Human Rights Violations Abroad: A Preliminary Assessment." In *Liability of Multinational Corporations under International Law*, edited by Menno T. Kamminga and Saman Zia-Zarifi. The Hague: Kluwer Law International, 2000.

Cámara de Comercio de Bogotá, Unidad para la atención y reparación integral a las víctimas agencia colombiana para la reconciliación, Fundación Colombia con Memoria and Canal Capital. "Los sabores de la reconciliación," n.d., www.ccb.org.co/Transfor mar-Bogota/Paz/Acciones-por-la-Paz/Los-sabores-de-la-reconciliacion.

Canadian Centre for International Justice. "Anvil Mining (D.R. Congo/Canada)." Canadian Centre for International Justice, n.d., www.ccij.ca/cases/anvil-mining/.

Canal Capital. *Los sabores de la reconciliación: Beneficios y oportunidades para la paz.* Colombia, 2017, www.youtube.com/watch?v=jGeayQzKnUE&index=6&list= PLg3o8Sxb8FcFWSS6DIr_RrbFphNoGjGbx.

Cantón, Santiago A. "Leyes de amnistía." In *Víctimas sin mordaza: El impacto del sistema interamericano en la justicia transicional en latinoamérica: Los casos de Argentina, Guatemala, El Salvador y Perú*, edited by Due Process of Law Foundation and Comisión de Derechos Humanos del Distrito Federal, 219–44. Washington, DC: Due Process of Law Foundation; Comisión de Derechos Humanos del Distrito Federal; United States Institute of Peace, 2007, www.dplf.org/sites/default/files/1202485080.pdf.

Cantú Rivera, Humberto. "The Kiobel Precedent and Its Effects on Universal Jurisdiction and the Business & Human Rights Agenda: A Continuation to 'a Human Rights Forum in Peril?'" *Cuestiones Constitucionales: Revista Mexicana de Derecho Constituticional* 30 (2014): 209–22.

Caram, Sofía. "Blanquear a Blaquier." *Página/12*, July 7, 2019, www.pagina12.com.ar/204885-blanquear-a-blaquier.

Carillo, Nicolás. "Direct International Humanitarian Obligations of Non-State Entitites: Analysis of the Lex Lata and the Lex Ferenda." *Global Journal on Human Rights* 23, no. 2 (2015): 29–75.

Carranza, Ruben. "Plunder and Pain: Should Transitional Justice Engage with Corruption and Economic Crimes?" *International Journal of Transitional Justice* 2 (2008): 310–30.

"Transitional Justice, Corporate Responsibility and Learning from the Global South," April 28, 2015. http://jamesgstewart.com/transitional-justice-corporate-responsibility-and-learning-from-the-global-south/.

Carvalho Gomes da Silva, Rubens. "Values, Knowledge and Activism in the Brazilian Amazon: From the Boomerang to the Archimedean Lever." MSc diss., University of Oxford, 2010.

Cassel, Douglass, and Anita Ramasastry. "White Paper: Options for a Treaty on Business and Human Rights." *Journal of International and Comparative Law* 6, no. 1 (2016).

Castellani, Ana. "Cambiemos SA exposición a los conflictos de interés en el gobierno nacional: Los funcionarios con participación en empresas privadas a junio de 2018." *Informe de Investigación* No. 5 Parte 1, 8. Buenos Aires: Universidad de San Martín, 2018.

Center for Constitutional Rights. "Al Shimari v. CACI et al." n.d., https://ccrjustice.org/home/what-we-do/our-cases/al-shimari-v-caci-et-al.

"Wiwa et al. v. Royal Dutch Petroleum et al." n.d., https://ccrjustice.org/home/what-we-do/our-cases/wiwa-et-al-v-royal-dutch-petroleum-et-al.

Center for Economic and Social Rights. "Wiwa v. Shell Settlement Just One Small Step toward Ending Corporate Impunity," www.cesr.org/wiwa-v-shell-settlement-just-one-smallstep-toward-ending-corporateimpunity.

Center for International Law and Policy. "Briefing Report: Transitional Justice and Corporate Accountability." Boston, MA, 2016.

Centro de Estudios Legales y Sociales (CELS). *Derechos humanos en la Argentina: Informe 2017.* Buenos Aires: Siglo XXI, 2018.

"Ford." 2017, www.cels.org.ar/web/wp-content/uploads/2017/12/Ford.pdf.

Černič, Jernej Letnar. "Corporate Accountability for Human Rights: From a Top-down to a Bottom-up Approach." In *The Business and Human Rights Landscape: Moving Forward, Looking Back,* edited by Jena Martin and Karen E. Bravo. Cambridge: Cambridge University Press, 2016.

"An Elephant in a Room of Porcelain: Establishing Corporate Responsibility for Human Rights." *Global Journal on Human Rights* 24, no. 1 (2015): 5–32.

Cesar, Janaina, Pedro Grossi, Alessia Cerantola, and Leandor Demori. "145 Spies." *The Intercept,* February 25, 2019, https://theintercept.com/2019/02/25/fiat-brazil-spying-workers-collaborated-dictatorship/.

Chandler, Geoffrey. "The Evolution of the Business and Human Rights Debate." In *Business and Human Rights: Dilemmas and Solutions,* edited by Rory Sullivan. Sheffield: Greenleaf Publishing, 2003.

Chesterman, Simon. "Oil and Water: Regulating the Behavior of Multinational Corporations through Law." *New York University Journal of International Law and Politics* no. 36 (2004): 307.

CIDSE. "Value of a Future UN Treaty on Businesses and Human Rights Highlighted at EU Panel Debate." *CIDSE,* March 2017.

El Ciudadano. "Lorena Pizarro, Presidenta de la AFDD: 'Familia Kast está vinculada al terrorismo de estado.'" *El Ciudadano,* September 9, 2017, www.elciudadano.cl/justicia/lorena-pizarro-presidenta-de-la-afdd-familia-kast-esta-vinculada-al-terrorismo-de-estado/09/09/.

Clapham, Andrew. "The Question of Jurisdiction under International Criminal Law over Legal Persons: Lessons from the Rome Conference on an International Criminal Court." In *Liability of Multinational Corporations under International Law,* 139–95. The Hague: Kluwer Law International, 2000.

Clark, Phil. "Creeks of Justice: Debating Post-atrocity Accountability in Rwanda and Uganda." In *Amnesty in the Age of Human Rights Accountability: Comparative and International Perspectives,* edited by Francesca Lessa and Leigh A. Payne. Cambridge: Cambridge University Press, 2012.

Gacaca Courts, Post-Genocide Justice and Reconciliation in Rwanda: Justice without Lawyers. Cambridge: Cambridge University Press, 2010.

Cole, Wade M., and Francisco O. Ramírez. "Conditional Decoupling: Assessing the Impact of National Human Rights Institutions, 1981 to 2004." *American Sociological Review* 78, no. 4 (June 18, 2013): 702–25.

Colvin, Christopher J. "Overview of the Reparations Program in South Africa." In *The Handbook of Reparations*, edited by Pablo De Greiff. Oxford: Oxford University Press, 2006.

Comisión de la Verdad de Ecuador. *Informe de la Comisión de la Verdad de Ecuador*, Volumes I, II, 2010.

Comisión de la Verdad para El Salvador. *De la locura a la esperanza: La guerra de 12 años en El Salvador*, 1993.

Comisión de la Verdad y Reconciliación del Perú. *Informe final*, Volumes I, III, V, VII, 2003.

Comisión Nacional de Verdad y Reconciliación de Chile. *Informe de La Comisión Nacional de Verdad y Reconciliación*, 1991, www.derechoshumanos.net/lesahuma nidad/informes/informe-rettig.htm.

Comisión Nacional sobre la Desaparición de Personas en Argentina (CONADEP). *Nunca Más*, 1983.

Comisión para el Esclarecimiento Histórico. *Guatemala, memoria del silencio*, 1999.

Comisión Verdad y Justicia de Paraguay. *Informe final*, Volume I, 2008.

Comissão da Verdade do Estado de São Paulo, Brasil. *Relatorio*, Volume I, Part 1: Introduction. São Paulo, n.d.

Comissão Nacional da Verdade do Brasil. *Relatório da Comissão Nacional da Verdade*, Volumes I, II 2014, www.cnv.gov.br.

Commission d'Enquête du Ministère Chadien de la Justice sur les crimes du régime de Hissène Habré. *Report*. Chad, 1992.

Commission for Reception, Truth and Reconciliation in Timor-Leste. *Chega!*, 1999. www.cavr-timorleste.org/en/chegaReport.htm.

Commission Nationale de Vérité et de Justice. *République d'Haïti: Rapport de La Commission Nationale de Vérité et de Justice*, 1996.

Connolly, Kate. "German Railways Admits Complicity in Holocaust." *The Guardian*, January 23, 2008, www.theguardian.com/world/2008/jan/23/secondworldwar.germany.

Contraloría General de la República. "Análisis sobre los resultados y costos de la Ley de Justicia y Paz." Bogotá, 2017.

Control Risks. "Argentina's Mid-Term Elections: Will Macri's Pro Business Reforms Stand the Test?" *Forbes*, 2017, www.forbes.com/sites/riskmap/2017/03/23/argentinas-mid-term-elections-will-macris-pro-business-reforms-stand-the-test/#62bd4a5426ca.

Cooper, Neil. "State Collapse as Business: The Role of Conflict Trade and the Emerging Control Agenda." *Development and Change* 33, no. 5 (2002): 935–55.

Corporate Social Responsibility (CSR) Newswire. "Notre Dame Law Professor under Scrutiny for Accepting Chevron Funds to Attack Ecuadorian Villagers." *CSR News*, 2015, www.csrwire.com/press_releases/38291-Notre-Dame-Law-Professor-Under-Scrutiny-for-Accepting-Chevron-Funds-to-Attack-Ecuadorian-Villagers.

Correio do Brasil. "Empresários que apoiaram o golpe de 64 construíram grandes fortunas." *Correio do Brasil*, March 27, 2014, http://correiodobrasil.com.br/noti cias/brasil/empresarios-que-apoiaram-o-golpe-de-64-construiram-grandes-fortunas/694263/.

Corriher, Billy. "Big Business Taking over State Supreme Courts." *Center for American Progress*, 2012, www.americanprogress.org/issues/courts/reports/2012/08/13/11974/big-business-taking-over-state-supreme-courts/.

Cotton, James. "Understanding the State in South Korea: 'Bureaucratic-Authoritarian or State Autonomy Theory?'" *Comparative Political Studies* 24, no. 2 (1992): 512–31.

Couso, Javier A., Alexandra Huneeus, and Rachel Sieder, eds. *Cultures of Legality: Judicialization and Political Activism in Latin America.* New York, NY: Cambridge University Press, 2010.

Dallaire, Roméo. *Shake Hands with the Devil: The Failure of Humanity in Rwanda.* Random House Canada, 2003.

Dancy, Geoff, Bridget Marchesi, Tricia Olsen, Leigh A. Payne, Andrew Reiter, and Kathryn Sikkink. "Behind Bars and Bargains: New Findings on Transitional Justice in Emerging Democracies." *International Studies Quarterly* 63, no. 1 (2019): 1–12.

Dandan, Alejandra. "Con el encuadre del lavado." *Página/12*, January 6, 2013, www .pagina12.com.ar/diario/elpais/1-211279-2013-01-06.html.

Dandan, Alejandra, and Hannah Franzki. "Entre analisis histórico y responsabilidad jurídica: El caso Ledesma." In *Cuentas pendientes: Los cómplices económicos de la dictadura*, edited by Horacio Verbitsky and Juan Pablo Bohoslavsky. Buenos Aires: Siglo Veintiuno Editores, 2013.

Davis, Madeleine. *The Pinochet Case: Origins, Progress and Implications.* London: Institute of Latin American Studies, 2003.

"Universal Jurisdiction: National Courts and the Prosecution of Serious Crimes under International Law." *Human Rights Quarterly* 27, no. 2 (May 2005): 729–35.

Daviss, Bennett. "Profits from Principle: Five Forces Redefining Business." *The Futurist*, 1999.

de Gramont, Alexandre, Michael D. Igyarto, and Tatiana Sainati. "Divergent Paths: Settlement in US Litigation and International Arbitration." *Fordham International Law Journal* 40, no. 953–72 (2017).

De Roux, Francisco. "Impunidad y conflicto armado." *El Tiempo*, August 2015.

de Waal, Shaun. "Apartheid Killings and Awkward Questions." *Mail & Guardian*, March 23, 2018.

Deitelhoff, Nicole, and Klaus Wolf. "Business in Zones of Conflict: An Emergent Corporate Security Responsibility." In *The Business of Human Rights: An Evolving Agenda for Corporate Responsibility*, edited by Aurora Voliculescu and Helen Yanacopulos. London: Zed Books, 2011.

del Río Roldán, Andrés. "Macri and the Judges." *Open Democracy*, January 21, 2016, www.opendemocracy.net/en/democraciaabierta/macri-and-judges/.

Deutsche Welle (DW). "VW Worked Hand in Hand with Brazil's Military Dictatorship." *Deutsche Welle*, July 24, 2017, www.dw.com/en/vw-worked-hand-in-hand-with-brazils-military-dictatorship/a-39814070.

Deva, Surya. "Human Rights Lightly: A Critique of the Consensus Rhetoric and the Language Employed by the Guiding Principles." In *Human Rights Obligations of Business: Beyond the Corporate Responsibility to Respect*, edited by David Bilchitz and Surya Deva. Cambridge: Cambridge University Press, 2013.

"Multinationals, Human Rights and International Law: Time to Move beyond the 'State-Centric' Conception?" *Global Journal on Human Rights* 23, no. 2 (2015): 5–27.

Regulating Corporate Human Rights Violations: Humanizing Business. London: Routledge, 2012.

Dhizaala, James Tonny. "Transitional Justice in Liberia: The Interface between Civil Society Organisations and the Liberian Truth and Reconciliation Commission." In *Advocating Transitional Justice in Africa: The Role of Civil Society,* edited by Jasmina Brankovich and Hugo van der Merwe. Cham, Switzerland: Springer, 2018.

Diario Judicial. "Una indemnización que no prescribe." *Diario Judicial,* 2017, www.diariojudicial.com/nota/77561.

Donziger, Steven. "Blog: Amazon Watch Response to Decision to Uphold Flawed Chevron Retaliatory Lawsuit." 2016, http://stevendonziger.com/2016/08/08/amazon-watch-response-decision-uphold-flawed-chevron-retaliatory-lawsuit/.

Dorcadie, Mathilde. "When Volkswagen Handed Its Staff over to Brazil's Military Junta." *Equaltimes,* November 30, 2016, www.equaltimes.org/new-translation-quand-volkswagen#.WdPm12hSw2w.

Dougherty, Christopher. *Introduction to Econometrics,* 4th ed. Oxford: Oxford University Press, 2011.

Downs, George, David Rocke, and Peter Barsoom. "Is the Good News about Compliance Good News about Cooperation?" *International Organization* 50, no. 3 (1996): 379.

Dreifuss, René Armand. *1964: A conquista do estado, ação política, poder e golpe de classe.* Petrópolis, 1987.

Drimmer, Jonathan, and Lisa J. Laplante. "The Third Pillar." In *The Business and Human Rights Landscape: Moving Forward, Looking Back,* edited by Jena Martin and Karen E. Bravo. Cambridge: Cambridge University Press, 2015.

Drumbl, Mark A. *Atrocity, Punishment, and International Law.* Cambridge: Cambridge University Press, 2007.

The Economist. "BNP Paribas Faces Accusations over the Rwandan Genocide." *The Economist,* 2017, www.economist.com/finance-and-economics/2017/07/08/bnpparibas-faces-accusations-over-the-rwandan-genocide.

Encarnación, Omar G. "The Rise and Fall of the Latin American Left." *The Nation,* May 2018.

Engstrom, Par. "The Inter-American Human Rights System: Notable Achievements and Enduring Challenges." In *Contemporary Challenges for Understanding and Securing Human Rights in Practice,* edited by Corinne Lennox. London: School of Advanced Study, 2015.

Engstrom, Par, and Gabriel Pereira. "From Amnesty to Accountability: The Ebbs and Flows in the Search for Justice in Argentina." In *Amnesty in the Age of Human Rights Accountability: Comparative and International Perspectives,* edited by Francesca Lessa and Leigh A. Payne. Cambridge: Cambridge University Press, 2012.

Epstein, Lee, William M. Landes, and Richard A. Posner. "How Business Fares in the Supreme Court." *Minnesota Law Review* 97 (2013): 1431.

ESCR-Net. "About the Proposed Treaty." *ESCR-Net,* n.d., www.escr-net.org/corporateaccountability/hrbusinesstreaty/about-proposed-treaty.

ESCR-Net Corporate Accountability Working Group. "Corporate Capture: Definition and Characteristics." *ESCR-Net,* June 2019, https://drive.google.com/file/d/1IQ146Kb8WSj47NpbnlrOI-leZlZhVrKZ/view.

El Espectador. "Absuelven a Guillermo Gaviria por vínculos con paramilitares." *El Espectador*, September 2013.

"Sector empresarial manifiesta su apoyo a Iván Duque." *El Espectador*, 2018, www .elespectador.com/elecciones-2018/noticias/politica/sector-empresarial-manifiesta-su-apoyo-ivan-duque-articulo-793181.

Farah, Youseph. "Toward a Multi-directional Approach to Corporate Accountability." In *Corporate Accountability in the Context of Transitional Justice*, edited by Sabine Michalowski, 27–51. New York, NY: Routledge, 2013.

Faunes Amigo, Martín, Eugenia Hortvitz, and Oscar Montealegre. "Paine: Testimonio de Alejandro Bustos 'el Colorín' sobreviviente de los fusilamientos realizados por civiles y militares." *Facebook*, 2015, www.facebook.com/notes/martin-faunes-amigo/paine-testimonio-de-alejandro-bustos-el-colorín-sobreviviente-de-los-fusilamient/ 10153474782834416/.

Federman, Sarah. "Genocide Studies and Corporate Social Responsibility: The Contemporary Case of the French National Railways (SNCF)." *Genocide Studies and Prevention: An International Journal* 2, no. 2 (2017): 16.

Felstiner, William L.F., Richard L. Abel, and Austin Sarat. "The Emergence and Transformation of Disputes: Naming, Blaming, Claiming." *Law & Society Review* 15, no. 3/4 (1980): 631–54.

The Financial Times. "The Ebbing of Latin America's 'Pink Tide.'" *The Financial Times*, December 2015.

Finder, Joseph. "Ultimate Insider, Ultimate Outsider." *The New York Times*, April 12, 1992, www.nytimes.com/1992/04/12/books/ultimate-insider-ultimate-outsider.html? pagewanted=all.

Finnemore, Martha, and Kathryn Sikkink. "International Norm Dynamics and Political Change." *International Organization* 52, no. 4 (1998): 887.

Fiscalía General de la Nación. "Fiscalía tendrá nueva Unidad Nacional de Análisis de Contexto." Bogotá, 2012, www.fiscalia.gov.co/colombia/noticias/fiscalia-tendra-nueva-unidad-nacional-de-analisis-y-contexto/.

Fiscalía General de la Nación de Argentina. "Informe estadístico sobre el estado de las causas por delitos de lesa humanidad." Buenos Aires, 2018, www.fiscales.gob.ar/ wp-content/uploads/2018/03/LESA-Informe-trayectoria.pdf.

Fischer, Brendan. "US-Funded Death Squads in El Salvador Casts Shadow over GOP Ticket." *Alternet*, August 16, 2012, www.alternet.org/world/us-funded-death-squads-el-salvador-casts-shadow-over-gop-ticket.

Fisher, Daniel. "Appeals Court Upholds Sanctions against Donziger over $9.5 Billion Chevron Judgment." *Forbes*, August 2016, www.forbes.com/sites/danielfisher/ 2016/08/08/appeals-court-upholds-sanctions-against-donziger-over-chevron-litiga tion-in-ecuador/.

Folha Transparencia. "Ministro determinou ajuda para empreiteira durante a ditadura." *Folha Transparencia*, 2014, www1.folha.uol.com.br/poder/2013/03/1242058-ministro-determinou-ajuda-para-empreiteira-durante-a-ditadura.shtml.

Folkman, Ted. "The Access to Justice Gap in Transnational Litigation." *Letters Blogatory*, 2011, https://lettersblogatory.com/2011/08/02/the-access-to-justice-gap-in-transnational-litigation/.

Footer, Mary E. "Human Rights Due Diligence and the Responsible Supply of Minerals from Conflict-Affected Areas: Towards a Normative Framework?" *Global Journal on Human Rights* 24, no. 1 (2015): 51–100.

Ford, Jolyon. *Regulating Business for Peace: The United Nations, the Private Sector, and Post-Conflict Recovery.* Cambridge: Cambridge University Press, 2015.

Fortune. "Fortune Global 500." *Fortune*, 2018, https://fortune.com/global500/search/.

Freeman, Mark. *Necessary Evils: Amnesties and the Search for Justice.* Cambridge: Cambridge University Press, 2009.

Truth Commission and Procedural Fairness. New York, NY: Cambridge University Press, 2006.

Freshfields Bruckhaus Deringer. "Landmark Supreme Court Opinion Shuts Door to ATS Suits against Foreign Corporations." *Freshfields Bruckhaus Deringer*, April 2018.

"UK Considers Reforms on Holding Companies Liable for Economic Crime." *Freshfields Bruckhaus Deringer*, 2017.

Frey, Barbara A. "The Legal and Ethical Responsibilities of Transnational Corporations in the Protection of International Human Rights." *Minnesota Journal of Global Trade* 6, no. 153 (1997): 188.

Friedman, Milton. *Capitalism and Freedom.* Chicago, IL: University of Chicago Press, 1963.

"The Social Responsibility of Business Is to Increase Its Profits." *The New York Times Magazine*, September 13, 1970, www.colorado.edu/studentgroups/libertarians/issues/friedman-soc-resp-business.html.

Frontline Defenders. "Break-in at Home of Human Rights Defender Mr Danilo Rueda and Theft of Items Containing Sensitive Information." 2011, www.frontlinedefenders.org/en/case/case-history-danilo-rueda.

"Shots Fired at Vehicle of Human Rights Defender Father Alberto Franco." 2013, www.frontlinedefenders.org/en/case/case-history-father-alberto-franco.

"Threats and Harassment against Members of the Comision Intereclesial de Justicia y Paz." 2013, www.justiciaypazcolombia.com/threats-and-harassment-against-members-of-the-comision-intereclesial-de-justicia-y-paz/.

Frumkin, Si. "Why Won't These SOBs Give Me My Money? A Survivor's Testimony." In *Holocaust Restitution: Perspectives on the Litigation and Its Legacy*, edited by Michael J. Bazyler and Roger P. Alford. New York, NY: New York University Press, 2006.

Frydman, Benoît, and Ludovic Hennebel. "Translating Unocal: The Liability of Transnational Corporations for Human Rights Violations." In *Business and Human Rights*, edited by Manoj Kumar Sinha. Thousand Oaks, CA: SAGE Law, 2013.

Garrison, Cassandra, and Nicolás Misculin. "Ex-Ford Argentina Executives Convicted in Torture Case; Victims May Sue in U.S." *Reuters*, 2018, www.reuters.com/article/us-argentina-rights-ford-motor/ex-ford-argentina-executives-convicted-in-torture-case-victims-may-sue-in-u-s-idUSKBN1OA25H.

George, Erika R. "The Enterprise of Empire: Evolving Understandings of Corporate Identity and Responsibility." In *The Business and Human Rights Landscape: Moving Forward, Looking Back*, edited by Jena Martin and Karen E. Bravo, 19–50. Cambridge: Cambridge University Press, 2015.

Global Witness. "Conflict Diamonds." n.d., www.globalwitness.org/en/campaigns/con flict-diamonds/.

Glopen, Siri. "Courts and Social Transformation: An Analytical Framework." In *Courts and Social Transformation in New Democracies*, edited by Roberto Gargarella, Pilar Domingo, and Theunis Roux, 35–60. Burlington, VT: Ashgate, 2006.

Gombata, Marsílea. "Comissão da verdade quer responsabilizar empresas que colaboraram com a ditadura." *Carta Capital*, March 15, 2014.

Goñi, Uki. "Argentina: Two Ex-Ford Executives Convicted in Torture Case." *The Guardian*, 2018, www.theguardian.com/world/2018/dec/11/pedro-muller-hedro-sibilla-ford-executives-argentina-torture-case.

Gonza, Alejandra. "Integrating Business and Human Rights in the Inter-American Human Rights System." *Business and Human Rights Journal* 1, no. 02 (2016): 357–65.

Gonzalez-Ocantos, Ezequiel. "Communicative Entrepreneurs: The Case of the Inter-American Court of Human Rights' Dialogue with National Judges." *International Studies Quarterly*, 2018.

Shifting Legal Visions: Judicial Change and Human Rights Trials in Latin America. Cambridge: Cambridge University Press, 2016.

Gready, Paul, and Simon Robins. "From Transitional to Transformative Justice: A New Agenda for Practice." *International Journal of Transitional Justice* 8 (2014): 339–61.

Grear, Anna, and Burns H. Weston. "The Betrayal of Human Rights and the Urgency of Universal Corporate Accountability: Reflections on a Post-Kiobel Lawscape." *Human Rights Law Review* 15, no. 1 (2015): 21–44.

Green, Shannon. "On the Rocks: Tunisia's Transitional Justice Process." *Center for Strategic & International Studies: Commentary*, 2015, www.csis.org/analysis/rocks-tunisias-transitional-justice-process.

Greenwood, Christopher. "Presbyterian Church of Sudan v. Talisman Energy Inc, Republic of the Sudan Civil Action, 374 F. Supp. 2d 331 (S.D.N.Y, 2005), No.01 CV 9882 (AGS)," n.d.

Grossman, Joel B. "Social Backgrounds and Judicial Decision-Making." *Harvard Law Review* 79, no. 8 (1966): 1551–64.

The Guardian. "Germany Approves Plans to Fine Social Media Firms up to €50m." *The Guardian*, June 2017.

"Lafarge Charged with Complicity in Syria Crimes against Humanity." *The Guardian*, June 28, 2018, www.theguardian.com/world/2018/jun/28/lafarge-charged-with complicity-in-syria-crimes-against-humanity.

Haas, Peter M. "Epistemic Communities and International Policy Coordination." *International Organization* 46, no. 1 (1992): 1–35.

Haberstroh, John. "In Re World War II Era Japanese Forced Labor Litigation and Obstacles to International Human Rights Claims in U.S. Courts." *Asian American Law Journal* 10, no. 2 (2003): 253–94.

Halliday, Terence C., and Bruce G. Carruthers. "The Recursivity of Law: Global Norm Making and National Lawmaking in the Globalization of Corporate Insolvency Regimes." *American Journal of Sociology* 112, no. 4 (2007): 1135–202.

Hathaway, Oona. "Do Human Rights Treaties Make a Difference?" *The Yale Law Journal* 111, no. 8 (2002): 1935–2042.

Haufler, Virginia. "Disclosure as Governance: The Extractive Industries Transparency Initiative and Resource Management in the Developing World." *Global Environmental Politics* 10, no. 3 (2010): 53–73.

Hauser, Irina. "Rosenkrantz, de un lado y del otro." *Página/12*, May 12, 2019, www.pagina12.com.ar/193255-rosenkrantz-de-un-lado-y-del-otro.

Hayes, Peter. *Industry and Ideology: IG Farben in the Nazi Era*, 2nd ed. Cambridge: Cambridge University Press, 2001.

Helm, Toby. "Germany to Compensate Nazi Slave-Labourers." *The Telegraph*, May 31, 2001, www.telegraph.co.uk/news/worldnews/europe/germany/1332474/Germany-to-compensate-Nazi-slave-labourers.html.

Herz, Richard L. "The Liberalizing Effects of Tort: How Corporate Liability under the Alien Tort Statute Advances Engagement." *Harvard Human Rights Journal* 21 (2008): 207–39.

Hilbink, Lisa. *Judges beyond Politics in Democracy and Dictatorship: Lessons from Chile*. Cambridge: Cambridge University Press, 2007.

Hinton, Alexander Laban. *Man or Monster? The Trial of a Khmer Rouge Torturer*. Durham, NC: Duke University Press, 2016.

Holly, Gabrielle. "Access to Remedy under the UNGPs: Vedanta and the Expansion of Parent Company Liability." *EJIL:Talk!*, October 2017.

Holt, Charlie, Shira Stanton, Daniel Simons, and Greenpeace. "The Zero Draft Legally Binding Instrument on Business and Human Rights: Small Steps along the Irresistible Path to Corporate Accountability." In *Compilation of Commentaries on the "Zero Draft,"* 9–11. London: Business and Human Rights Resource Centre, 2018.

Horrigan, Bryan. *Corporate Social Responsibility in the 21st Century: Debates, Models and Practices across Government, Law and Business*. Cheltenham: Edward Elgar, 2010.

Huckerby, Jayne, and Aya Fujimura-Fanselow. "The Truth about Rendition and Torture: An Inquiry in North Carolina." *Just Security*, December 14, 2017, www.justsecurity.org/49343/truth-rendition-torture-nongovernmental-inquiry-north-carolina/.

Human Rights Council. "Resolution A/HRC/34/L.7." New York, 2017.

Human Rights Violations Investigation Commission (Oputa Panel). *Human Rights Violations Investigation Commission*, Volume III, 2005, 43.

Huneeus, Alexandra V. "Judging from Guilty Conscience: The Chilean Judiciary's Human Rights Turn." *Law and Social Inquiry* 35, no. 1 (2010): 99–135.

Hutto, Christopher, and Anjela Jenkins. *Report on Corporate Complicity Litigation in the Americas: Leading Doctrines, Relevant Cases, and Analysis of Trends*. Austin, 2010.

Ignatieff, Michael. *The Warrior's Honor: Ethnic War and the Modern Conscience*. New York, NY: Henry Holt and Company, 1997.

Im, Hyung Baeng. "The Rise of Bureaucratic Authoritarianism in South Korea." *World Politics* 39, no. 2 (1987): 231–57.

Inter-American Commission on Human Rights. "Criminalization of Human Rights Defenders." Washington, DC, 2015, www.oas.org/en/iachr/reports/pdfs/criminalization2016.pdf.

International Center for Transitional Justice. "Tunisia." *International Center for Transitional Justice Reports*, 2018, www.ictj.org/our-work/regions-and-countries/tunisia. "What Is Transitional Justice?" 2009, www.ictj.org/about/transitional-justice.

International Chamber of Commerce and International Organization of Employers. "Joint Views of the IOE and ICC on the Draft Norms on the Responsibilities of Transnational Corporations and Other Business Enterprises with Regard to Human Rights. U.N. ESCOR, 55." In *International Human Rights: Law, Policy, and Process*, edited by David S. Weissbrodt, Joan Fitzpatrick, and Frank Newman. Cincinnati, OH: Anderson Pub. Co., 2001.

International Coalition of Sites of Conscience. "Memorial Paine," n.d., www.sitesof conscience.org/en/membership/memorial-paine-corporacia-paine-un-lugar-para-la-memoria-chile/.

International Commission of Jurists. "Corporate Complicity & Legal Accountability." Geneva, 2008, www.icj.org/wp-content/uploads/2012/06/Vol.1-Corporate-legal-accountability-thematic-report-2008.pdf.

"Proposals for Elements of a Legally Binding Instrument on Transnational Corporations and Other Business Enterprises." Geneva, 2016, www.icj.org/wp-content/ uploads/2016/10/Universal-OEWG-session-2-ICJ-submission-Advocacy-Analysis-brief-2016-ENG.pdf.

International Court of Justice. LaGrand (Germany v. United States of America) – Judgment (2001).

International Crimes Database. "The Prosecutor v. Alfred Musema."

"The Public Prosecutor v. Guus Kouwenhoven." *International Crimes Database*, n.d., www.internationalcrimesdatabase.org/Case/2238.

International Criminal Court. "Statement of ICC Prosecutor, Fatou Bensouda, on the Conclusion of the Peace Negotiations between the Government of Colombia and the Revolutionary Armed Forces of Colombia – People's Army." September 1, 2016, www.icc-cpi.int/Pages/item.aspx?name=160901-otp-stat-colombia.

International Criminal Tribunal for Rwanda. "The Prosecutor v. Elizaphan and Gerard Ntakirutimana Cases No. ICTR-96-10 & ICTR-96-17-T." Trial Chamber I, 2003.

International Federation for Human Rights (FIDH). "Corporate Accountability for Human Rights Abuses: A Guide for Victims and NGOs on Recourse Mechanisms." *Globalisation and Human Rights Report*, May 11, 2016, www.fidh.org/IMG/ pdf/corporate_accountability_guide_version_web.pdf.

Ite, Uwem. "Multinationals and Corporate Social Responsibility in Developing Countries: A Case Study of Nigeria." *Corporate Social Responsibility and Environmental Management* 1, no. 11 (2004).

La Izquierda Diario. "Amplio repudio a la carta de blanquier a Myriam Bregman." *La Izquierda Diario*, August 29, 2016, www.laizquierdadiario.com/Amplio-repudio-a-la-carta-de-Blaquier-a-Myriam-Bregman.

Jabarin, Shawan, and Maha Abdallah, Al-Haq. "The 'Zero Draft' Treaty: Is It Sufficient to Address Corporate Abuses in Conflict-Affected Areas?" In *Compilation of Commentaries on the "Zero Draft,"* 4–6. London: Business and Human Rights Resource Centre, 2018.

Jagers, Nicola. "Transnational Corporations and Human Rights." In *To Baehr in Our Minds*, edited by Mielle K. Bultermann, Aart Hendriks, and Jacqueline Smith. Utrecht: Netherlands Institute of Human Rights, 1998.

James-Allen, Paul, Aaron Weah, and Lizzie Goodfriend. "Beyond the Truth and Reconciliation Commission: Transitional Justice Options in Liberia." *International Center for Transitional Justice*, 2010, www.ictj.org/publication/beyond-truth-and-reconciliation-commission-transitional-justice-options-liberia.

Jasinski, Alejandro. "La conexión O'Farrell." *El cohete de la luna*, n.d., www.elcohe tealaluna.com/la-conexion-ofarrell/.

"Reflexiones con ocasión del 'Juicio a Ford.'" *Notas: Periodismo Popular*, 2018, https://notasperiodismopopular.com.ar/2018/03/27/reflexiones-juicio-ford/.

Jenkins, J. Craig. "Resource Mobilization Theory and the Study of Social Movements." *Annual Review of Sociology* 9 (1983): 527–53.

Jewish Virtual Library. "Nuremberg Trial Defendants: Walter Funk." *Jewish Virtual Library*, n.d., www.jewishvirtuallibrary.org/nuremberg-trial-defendants-walter-funk.

"An Overview of the Human Rights Accountability of Multinational Enterprises." In *Liability of Multinational Corporations under International Law*, edited by Menno T. Kamminga and Saman Zia-Zarifi, 75–93. The Hague: Kluwer Law International, 2000.

Joseph, Sarah. *Corporations and Transnational Human Rights Litigation: Human Rights Law in Perspective*. Oxford: Hart, 2004.

Jungk, Margaret. "Why Businesses Say Human Rights Is Their Most Urgent Sustainability Priority." *Business and Social Responsibility*, October 13, 2016.

Kagan, Sophia. "The 'Media Case' before the Rwanda Tribunal: The Nahimana et al. Appeal Judgement." *The Hague Justice Portal*, April 24, 2008.

Kaleck, Wolfgang, and Miriam Saage-Maaß. "Corporate Accountability for Human Rights Violations Amounting to International Crimes: The Status Quo and Its Challenges." *Journal of International Criminal Justice* 8 (July 2010): 699–724.

Kamminga, Menno T., and Saman Zia-Zarifi. "Liability of Multinational Corporations under International Law: An Introduction." In *Liability of Multinational Corporations under International Law*, 1–15. The Hague: Kluwer Law International, 2000.

Kaplan, Margo. "Carats and Sticks: Pursuing War and Peace through the Diamond Trade." *International Law and Politics* no. 35 (2003): 559–617.

Keck, Margaret E., and Kathryn Sikkink. *Activists beyond Borders: Advocacy Networks in International Politics*. Ithaca, NY: Cornell University Press, 1998.

Keefe, Patrick Radden. "Reversal of Fortune." *The New Yorker*, 2012, www.newyorker.com/magazine/2012/01/09/reversal-of-fortune-patrick-radden-keefe.

Keller, Edmond J. "The State in Contemporary Africa." In *Comparative Political Dynamics: Global Research Perspectives*, edited by Dankwart A. Rustow and Kenneth Paul Erickson. New York, NY: Harper Collins, 1991.

Kelly, Michael J. "Atrocities by Corporate Actors: A Historical Perspective." *Case Western Reserve Journal of International Law* 50 (2018): 49–89.

Prosecuting Corporations for Genocide. New York, NY: Oxford University Press, 2016.

"Prosecuting Corporations for Genocide under International Law." *Harvard Law Policy Review* no. 6 (2012): 339–67.

Kempster, Norman. "Agreement Reached on Nazi Slave Reparations." *Los Angeles Times*, December 15, 1999, http://articles.latimes.com/1999/dec/15/news/mn-44055.

Kersten, Mark. "The Great Escape? The Role of the International Criminal Court in the Colombian Peace Process." *Justice in Conflict*, October 13, 2016.

Kim, Hun Joon. "Seeking Truth after Fifty Years: The National Committee for Investigation of the Truth about the Jeju 4.3 Events." *International Journal of Transitional Justice* 3 (2009): 406–23.

Kopp, Pierre. "Improving Sanctions through Legal Means." In *Profiting from Peace: Managing the Resource Dimensions of Civil War*, edited by Karen Ballentine and Heiko Nitzschke. Boulder, CO: Lynne Reinner Publishers, 2005.

Kopylova, Ekaterina. "Akhbar Beirut S.A.L. Guilty of Contempt, STL Found: One Small Verdict for a Tribunal, a Giant Leap for International Justice?" *Opinio Juris*, 2016, http://opiniojuris.org/2016/08/04/akhbar-beirut-s-a-l-guilty-of-contempt-stl-found-one-small-verdict-for-a-tribunal-a-giant-leap-for-international-justice/.

Lacabe, Marga. "Corte niega libertad a empresario implicado en desapariciones en Paine." *Desaparecidos.Org*, January 16, 2008, http://desaparecidos.org/notas/2008/01/chile-corte-niega-libertad-a-e.html.

Lagorio-Chafkin, Christine. "This Billion-Dollar Founder Says Hiring Refugees Is Not a Political Act." *Inc.*, 2018, www.inc.com/magazine/201806/christine-lagorio/chobani-yogurt-hamdi-ulukaya-hiring-refugees.html.

Laufer, William. "Social Accountability and Corporate Greenwashing." *Journal of Business Ethics* 43, no. 3 (2003): 253.

Laverde Palma, Juan David. "Las pruebas del caso Guillermo Gaviria Echeverri." *El Espectador*, April 2012.

"Legally Binding Instrument to Regulate, in International Human Rights Law, the Activities of Transnational Corporations and Other Business Enterprises – Zero Draft." 2018, www.business-humanrights.org/sites/default/files/documents/DraftLBI.pdf.

Leigh Day & Co. "Leigh Day Submission to the Joint Committee on Human Rights Inquiry on Business and Human Rights." 2016, www.leighday.co.uk/LeighDay/media/LeighDay/documents/Corporate accountability/2016_08_31-LEIGH-DAY-SUBMISSION-TO-THE-JCHR1.pdf.

Lessa, Francesca. "Investigating Crimes against Humanity in South America: Present and Future Challenges." *Policy Brief*. Latin American Centre, University of Oxford, 2019.

Lessa, Francesca, Tricia D. Olsen, Leigh A. Payne, Gabriel Pereira, and Andrew G. Reiter. "Overcoming Impunity: Pathways to Accountability in Latin America." *The International Journal of Transitional Justice* 8 (2014): 75–98.

Lessa, Francesca, Leigh A. Payne, and Gabriel Pereira. "Overcoming Barriers to Justice in the Age of Human Rights Accountability." *Human Rights Quarterly* 27 (2015): 728–54.

Levit, Janet Koven. "Bottom-Up International Lawmaking: Reflections on the New Haven School of International Law." *Yale Journal of International Law* 3, no. 32 (2007).

  "Bottom-Up Lawmaking: The Private Origins of Transnational Law." *Indiana Journal of Global Legal Studies* 15, no. 1 (2008): 49–73.

Lim, Alwyn, and Kiyoteru Tsutsui. "Globalization and Commitment in Corporate Social Responsibility: Cross-National Analyses of Institutional and Political-Economy Effects." *American Sociological Review* 77, no. 1 (February 1, 2012): 69–98.

Lindblom, Charles Edward. *Politics and Markets: The World's Political-Economic Systems.* New York, NY: Basic Books, 1977.

Liptak, Adam, and Alicia Parlapiano. "Conservatives in Charge, the Supreme Court Moved Right." *The New York Times,* June 28, 2018, www.nytimes.com/interactive/2018/06/28/us/politics/supreme-court-2017-term-moved-right.html.

Litewski, Chaim. *Cidadão Boilesen: Um dos empresários que financiou a tortura no Brasil.* Brasil, 2013, www.youtube.com/watch?v=yGxIA9oxXeY.

Liu, Sida, and Terence C. Halliday. "Recursivity in Legal Change: Lawyers and Reforms of China's Criminal Procedure Law." *Law and Social Inquiry* 34, no. 4 (2009): 911–50.

Lohner, Andreas, and Nicolai Behr. "Corporate Liability in Germany." *Global Compliance News Backer McKenzie,* n.d.

Long, William J. "Liberia's Truth and Reconciliation Commission: An Interim Assessment." *International Journal of Peace Studies* 13, no. 2 (2008).

Lutz, Ellen L., and Caitlin Reiger, eds. *Prosecuting Heads of State.* Cambridge: Cambridge University Press, 2009.

Maassarani, Tarek F. "Four Counts of Corporate Complicity: Alternative Forms of Accomplice Liability under the Alien Tort Claims Act." *New York University Journal of International Law and Politics* (2005): 39–65.

Madani, Dorsati. "A Review of the Role of Impact of Export Processing Zones." *Policy Research Working Papers.* Washington, DC: World Bank, Development Research Group, Trade, 1999.

Manchester, William. *The Arms of Krupp, 1587–1968.* Boston, MA: Back Bay Books, 2003.

Mantilla, Giovanni. "Emerging International Human Rights Norms for Transnational Corporations." *Global Governance* 15, no. 2 (2009): 279–98.

Marlise, Simon. "Rwandan Pastor and His Son Are Convicted of Genocide." *The New York Times,* 2003, www.nytimes.com/2003/02/20/world/rwandan-pastor-and-his-son-are-convicted-of-genocide.html.

Martin, Jena, and Karen E. Bravo. "Introduction: More of the Same? Or Introduction of a New Paradigm?" In *The Business and Human Rights Landscape: Moving Forward, Looking Back,* edited by Jena Martin and Karen E. Bravo. Cambridge: Cambridge University Press, 2016.

Mason, Peter. *Blood and Iron.* Victoria, Australia: Penguin Books, 1984.

Maureira Moreno, Juan René. "Enfrentar con la vida a la muerte: Historias y memorias de la violencia y el terrorismo de estado en Paine (1960–2008)." Universidad de Chile, 2009.

McAdam, Doug. *Political Process and the Development of Black Insurgency, 1930–1970.* Chicago, IL: University of Chicago Press, 1982.

McCarthy, Bill. "New Economics of Sociological Criminology." *Annual Review of Sociology* 28 (2002): 417–42.

Media Part. "Crimes against Humanity: The Ongoing Case against Qosmos at the Paris High Court." *Media Part,* October 28, 2018, https://blogs.mediapart.fr/jamesinparis/blog/281018/crimes-against-humanity-ongoing-case-against-qosmos-paris-high-court.

Meeran, Richard. "Liability of Multinational Corporations: A Critical Stage in the UK." In *Liability of Multinational Corporations under International Law,* edited by Menno T. Kamminga and Saman Zia-Zarifi, 251–64. The Hague: Kluwer Law International, 2000.

Memoria Viva. "Pesquera Arauco." *Memoria Viva*, n.d., www.memoriaviva.com/
empresas/pesquera_arauco.htm.
Mendienta Miranda, Maximiliano. "Hydrocarbon Extraction in Guaraní Ñandeva
Territory: What about the Rights of Indigenous Peoples?" In *Human Rights in
Minefields: Extractive Economies, Environmental Conflicts and Social Justice
in the Global South*, edited by César Rodríguez Garavito. Bogotá: Dejusticia,
2015.
Merry, Sally Engle. "Transnational Human Rights and Local Activism: Mapping the
Middle." *American Anthropologist* 108, no. 1 (2006): 38–51.
Mesquita, Bruce Bueno, and Lawrence E. Cohen. "Self-Interest, Equity, and Crime
Control: A Game-Theoretic Analysis of Criminal Decision Making." *Criminology*
33, no. 4 (1995): 483–518.
Michalowski, Sabine, ed. *Corporate Accountability in the Context of Transitional
Justice*. Abingdon: Routledge, 2013.
Michel, Verónica. *Prosecutorial Accountability and Victims' Rights in Latin America*.
Cambridge: Cambridge University Press, 2018.
Miliband, Ralph. *The State in Capitalist Society*. London: Quartet Books, 1973.
Mills, C. Wright. *The Power Elite*. New York, NY: Oxford University Press, 1959.
Mochkofsk, Graciela. "What's Next for Mauricio Macri, Argentina's New President?"
The New Yorker, December 2015, www.newyorker.com/news/news-desk/whats-
next-mauricio-macri-argentinas-new-president.
Monteleone, Joana, Haroldo Ceravolo Sereza, Vitor Sion, Felipe Amorim, and
Rodolfo Machado. *À espera da verdade: Empresários, juristas e elite transnacional,
histórias de civis que fizeram a ditadura militar*. São Paulo: Alameda Editorial,
2016.
Morales Antoniazzi, Mariela. "Interamericanización como mecanismo del Ius Con-
stitutionale Commune en derechos humanos en América Latina." In *Ius Constitutionale Commune en América Latina: Textos básicos para su comprensión*,
edited by Armin von Bogdandy, Mariela Morales Antoniazzi, and Eduardo Ferrer
Mac-Gregor, 417–56. Max Planck Institute; Instituto de Estudios Constitucionales
del Estado de Querátaro, 2017.
Moran, Michael. "Misunderstanding of the Regulatory State?" *British Journal of
Political Science* no. 32 (2002): 391–413.
Moreno Ocampo, Luis. "Foreword." In *Prosecuting Corporations for Genocide*, edited
by Michael J. Kelly. Oxford: Oxford University Press, 2016.
Moyn, Samuel. *Not Enough: Human Rights in an Unequal World*. Cambridge, MA:
Harvard University Press, 2018.
Muchilinski, Peter T. "Attempts to Extend the Accountability of Transnational Corpor-
ations: The Role of UNCTAD." In *Liability of Multinational Corporations under
International Law*, edited by Menno T. Kamminga and Saman Zia-Zarifi. The
Hague: Kluwer Law International, 2000.
Nagarkatti, Karan, and Gary McWilliams. "International Tribunal Rules in Favor of
Chevron in Ecuador Case." *Reuters*, September 2018.
Nagin, Daniel S. "Criminal Deterrence Research at the Outset of the Twenty-First
Century." *Crime and Justice* 23 (1998): 1–42.
Narine, Marcia L. "Living in a Material World – From Naming and Shaming to
Knowing and Showing: Will New Disclosure Regimes Finally Drive Corporate

Accountability for Human Rights?" In *The Business and Human Rights Landscape: Moving Forward, Looking Back*, edited by Jena Martin and Karen E. Bravo. Cambridge: Cambridge University Press, 2015.

National Committee for Investigation of the Truth about the Jeju April 3 Incident in South Korea. *The Jeju 4.3 Incident Investigation Report*, n.d., www.jeju43peace.or.kr/report_eng.pdf.

National Reconciliation Commission of Ghana. *National Reconciliation Commission Final Report*, 2004.

"Nazi-Era Claims against German Companies." *The American Journal of International Law* 94, no. 4 (2000): 682.

Ndungú, Christopher Gitari. "Lessons to Be Learned: An Analysis of the Final Report of Kenya's Truth, Justice and Reconciliation Commission." *International Center for Transitional Justice Briefing*, 2014, www.ictj.org/sites/default/files/ICTJ-Briefing-Kenya-TJRC-2014.pdf.

Negron, Nina. "Ex-Ford Directors in Dock over Argentine Dictatorship Collaboration." *Abogado*, n.d., https://abogado.com.ph/ex-ford-directors-in-dock-over-argentine-dictatorship-collaboration/.

Nestlé. "Annual Review 2017." 2018, www.nestle.com/asset-library/documents/library/documents/annual_reports/2017-annual-review-en.pdf.

Nocera, Joe. "Behind the Chevron Case." *The New York Times*, 2014, www.nytimes.com/2014/09/23/opinion/joe-nocera-behind-the-chevron-case.html.

"Chevron's Longtime Nemesis Hits the End of the Road." *Bloomberg Opinion*, 2018, www.bloomberg.com/view/articles/2018-07-12/chevron-nemesis-steven-donziger-pays-a-price-for-ecuador-lawsuit.

Nodal. "Investigarán la connivencia de la banca internacional con la dictadura militar." *Nodal Noticias de América Latina y El Caribe*, 2013, www.nodal.am/2013/09/investigaran-la-responsabilidad-de-la-banca-internacional-en-el-financiamiento-de-la-dictadura/.

Nolan, Justine. "The Corporate Responsibility to Respect Human Rights: Soft Law or Not Law?" In *Human Rights Obligations of Business: Beyond the Corporate Responsibility to Respect*, edited by David Bilchitz and Surya Deva. Cambridge: Cambridge University Press, 2013.

O'Donnell, Guillermo. "Polyarchies and the (Un)Rule of Law in Latin America: A Partial Conclusion." In *The (Un)Rule of Law and the Underprivileged in Latin America*, edited by Juan E. Méndez, Guillermo O'Donnell, and Paulo Sérgio Pinheiro, 303–37. Notre Dame, IN: University of Notre Dame Press, 1999.

Offe, Claus, and Helmut Weisenthal. "Two Logics of Collective Action: Theoretical Notes on Social Class and Organizational Form." *Political Power and Social Theory* no. 1 (1980): 67–115.

Office of the Prosecutor. *Situation in Colombia – Interim Report*, 2012, www.icc-cpi.int/NR/rdonlyres/3D3055BD-16E2-4C83-BA85-35BCFD2A7922/285102/OTPCOLOMBIAPublicInterimReportNovember2012.pdf.

Olsen, Tricia D., and Leigh A. Payne. "Corporations and Human Rights Database," 2014.

Olsen, Tricia D., Leigh A. Payne, and Andrew G. Reiter. *Transitional Justice in Balance: Comparing Processes, Weighing Efficacy*. Washington, DC: USIP Press, 2010.

Open Secrets. "Open Secrets." n.d., www.opensecrets.org.za.

Orentlicher, Diane. "Report of Diane Orentlicher, Independent Expert to Update the Set of Principles to Combat Impunity – Updated Set of Principles for the Protection and Promotion of Human Rights through Action to Combat Impunity E/CN.4/2005/102/Add.1." New York, NY: United Nations, 2005, https://documents-dds-ny.un.org/doc/UNDOC/GEN/G05/109/00/PDF/G0510900.pdf?OpenElement.

Overy, Richard. "The Nuremberg Trials: International Law in the Making." In *From Nuremberg to The Hague: The Future of International Criminal Justice*, edited by Philippe Sands, 1–29. Cambridge: Cambridge University Press, 2003.

The Oxford Dictionary of Quotations, 2nd ed. Oxford: Oxford University Press, 1953.

Oxford Pro Bono Público. "Obstacles to Justice and Redress for Victims of Corporate Human Rights Abuse." Oxford, 2008.

Paine Municipality. "Estudio de abogados de Nelson Caucoto visita el memorial Paine." *Paine Municipality*, 2017, www.paine.cl/estudio-de-abogados-de-nelson-caucoto-visita-el-memorial-paine/.

El País. "Revocan medida de aseguramiento a empresario Guillermo Gaviria." *El País*, 2013, www.elpais.com.co/judicial/revocan-medida-de-aseguramiento-a-empresario-guillermogaviria.html.

El País Digital. "El grupo Macri y la dictadura: El comienzo de la expansión." *El País Digital*, March 2018, www.elpaisdigital.com.ar/contenido/el-grupo-macri-y-la-dictadura-el-comienzo-de-la-expansin/15762.

Pajibo, Ezequiel. "Civil Society and Transitional Justice in Liberia: A Practitioner's Reflection from the Field." *International Journal of Transitional Justice* 1, no. 2 (2007): 287–96.

Paper, Lewis J. *Brandeis: An Intimate Biography of One of America's Truly Great Supreme Court Justices*. Secaucus, NJ: Citadel, 1983.

Parish, Nataniel, "What Can Investors Expect from Argentina's Economy in 2018?" *Forbes*, June 2018, www.forbes.com/sites/nathanielparishflannery/2018/06/29/what-can-investors-expect-from-argentinas-economy-in-2018/#30417e4a1755.

Paul, Genevieve, and Judith Schonsteiner. "Transitional Justice and the UN Guiding Principles on Business and Human Rights." In *Corporate Accountability in the Context of Transitional Justice*, edited by Sabine Michalowski. London: Routledge Press, 2013.

Paulon, Victorio. "Acindar and Techint: Extreme Militarization of Labor Relations." In *Outstanding Debts to Settle: The Economic Accomplices of the Dictatorship in Argentina*, edited by Horacio Verbitsky and Juan Pablo Bohoslavsky, 174–85. Cambridge: Cambridge University Press, 2015.

Payne, Leigh A. *Brazilian Industrialists and Democratic Change*. Baltimore, MD: Johns Hopkins University Press, 1994.

"Cumplicidade empresarial na ditadura brasileira." *10a Revista Anistia: Cooperação econômica com a ditadura*, 2013.

Payne, Leigh A., and Gabriel Pereira. "Accountability for Corporate Complicity in Human Rights Violations: Argentina's Transitional Justice Innovation." In *Outstanding Debts to Settle: The Economic Accomplices of the Dictatorship in Argentina*, edited by Horacio Verbitsky and Juan Pablo Bohoslavsky. Cambridge: Cambridge University Press, 2015.

Payne, Leigh A., Gabriel Pereira, and Laura Bernal-Bermúdez. "The Business of Transitional Justice." In *The Oxford Handbook of Transitional Justice*, edited by

Jens Meierhenrich, Alexander Laban Hinton, and Lawrence Douglas. Oxford University Press, forthcoming.

Pensky, Max, and Mark Freeman. "The Amnesty Controversy in International Law." In *Amnesty in the Age of Human Rights Accountability: Comparative and International Perspectives*, edited by Francesca Lessa and Leigh A. Payne. Cambridge: Cambridge University Press, 2012.

The People's Tribunal on Economic Crime in South Africa. *Final Report of the People's Tribunal on Economic Crime: First Hearings 3–7 February, 2018; Arms Trade: 20 September 2018.*

Perosino, Maria Celeste, Bruno Nápoli, and Walter Bosisio. *Economía, política y sistema financiero: La última dictadura cívico-militar en la CNV.* Buenos Aires: Comisión Nacional de Valores, 2013.

Peskin, Victor. *International Justice in Rwanda and the Balkans: Virtual Trials and the Struggle for State Cooperation.* Cambridge: Cambridge University Press, 2008.

Phillips, Harlan B. *Felix Frankfurter Reminisces: An Intimate Portrait as Recorded in Talks with Dr. Harlan B. Phillips.* New York, NY: Reynal, 1960.

Pierson, Brendan. "Chiquita Settles with Families of U.S. Victims of Colombia's FARC." *Reuters*, 2018, www.reuters.com/article/us-usa-court-chiquita/chiquita-settles-with-families-of-u-s-victims-of-colombias-farc-idUSKBN1FP2VX.

Pion-Berlin, David. "To Prosecute or to Pardon? Human Rights Decisions in the Latin American Southern Cone." *Human Rights Quarterly* 16, no. 1 (1994): 105.

Piqué, Martín. "Condenaron a Techint a indemnizar a la hija de un obrero secuestrado en Siderca." *Infonews*, 2015.

Politi, Daniel. "Argentina Convicts Ex-Ford Executives for Abuses during Dictatorship." *The New York Times*, November 2018, www.nytimes.com/2018/12/11/world/americas/argentina-ford.html.

Porter, Michael E., and Mark R. Kramer. "Strategy and Society: The Link between Competitive Advantage and Corporate Social Responsibility." *Harvard Business Review* 84, no. 12 (2006): 78.

Poulantzas, Nicos Ar, and Timothy O'Hagan. *Political Power and Social Classes.* London: Verso, 1978.

Powell, Colin L. "Designation of the AUC as a Foreign Terrorist Organization." Department of State Archive, 2001, https://2001-2009.state.gov/secretary/former/powell/remarks/2001/4852.htm.

Power, Samantha. *A Problem from Hell: America and the Age of Genocide.* New York, NY: Basic Books, 2003.

Punto Final. "Camioneros en la represión." *Punto Final*, 2016, www.puntofinal.cl/850/camioneros850.php.

Quimbo, Nathan Gilbert. "The Philippines: Predatory Regime, Growing Authoritarian Features." *Pacific Review* 22, no. 3 (2009): 335–53.

Quinn, Joana. "Tradition?! Traditional Cultural Institutions on Customary Practices in Uganda." *Africa Spectrum* 49, no. 3 (2014): 29–54.

Radio Santafe. "Sodexo, reconocida por la ACR gracias a sus esfuerzos en empleabilidad." *Radio Santafe*, December 14, 2016, www.radiosantafe.com/2016/12/14/sodexo-reconocida-por-la-acr-gracias-a-sus-esfuerzos-en-empleabilidad/.

Ramasastry, Anita. "Corporate Complicity: From Nuremberg to Rangoon, an Examination of Forced Labor Cases and Their Impact on the Liability of Corporations." *Berkeley Journal of International Law* 20, no. 1 (2002): 91–159.

"Corporate Social Responsibility versus Business and Human Rights: Bridging the Gap between Responsibility and Accountability." *Journal of Human Rights* 14, no. 2 (2015): 237–59.

Rappeport, Alan, and Emily Fitter. "Congress Approves First Big Dodd-Frank Rollback." *The New York Times*, May 22, 2018, www.nytimes.com/2018/05/22/business/congress-passes-dodd-frank-rollback-for-smaller-banks.html.

Rapoza, Kenneth. "President Macri's Theme Song: Definitely Cry for Me, Argentina." *Forbes*, September 2018, www.forbes.com/sites/kenrapoza/2018/09/06/argentinas-president-macri-setting-the-table-for-future-peronista-government/#346d8cc93d02ta-government/#346d8cc93d02.

Rasche, Andreas. "Corporate Criminal Liability in Germany – An Idea Whose Time Has Come." *The Business of Society*, November 2017.

Rebolledo Escobar, Javier. *A la sombra de los cuervos: Los cómplices civiles de la dictadura*. Santiago de Chile: Ceibo Ediciones, 2015.

Red Card Campaign. "Farewell Germany … but What about Daimler?" *Red Card Campaign*, 2010, https://redcardcampaign.wordpress.com/2010/07/08/farewell-germany-but-what-about-daimler/.

Redacción Judicial. "Fiscalía declara como crimen de lesa humanidad la financiación de grupos paramilitares." *El Espectador*, 2017, www.elespectador.com/noticias/judicial/fiscalia-declara-crimen-de-lesa-humanidad-financiacion-articulo-677924.

Reno, William. "African Weak States and Commercial Alliances." *African Affairs* 96, no. 383 (1997): 165–86.

Revista Dinero. "Las Zomac ya tienen 407 nuevas empresas." *Revista Dinero*, 2018, www.dinero.com/pais/articulo/407-empresas-se-han-creado-en-las-zomac/258141.

Reyes, Abigail, Kathleen Kelly, and Laurel Anderson. "Death Squads and Miami Financiers." *National Security Archives Research*, February 5, 2003.

Rikhof, Joseph. "Analysis: The Special Tribunal for Lebanon: A Unique Institution." *Institut Philippe Kirsch*, 2018, www.kirschinstitute.ca/analysis-special-tribunal-lebanon-unique-institution/.

Risse, Thomas, and Stephen Ropp. "Introduction and Overview." In *The Persistent Power of Human Rights*, edited by Thomas Risse, Stephen Ropp, and Kathryn Sikkink. Cambridge: Cambridge University Press, 2013.

Roht-Arriaza, Naomi. *The Pinochet Effect: Transnational Justice in the Age of Human Rights*. Pennsylvania Studies in Human Rights. Philadelphia, PA: University of Pennsylvania Press, 2005.

Rojas Corral, Hugo Andrés. "Indifference to Past Human Rights Violations in Chile: The Impact on Transitional Justice Success, 1990–2017." PhD diss., University of Oxford, 2018.

Ruggie, John Gerard. "Business and Human Rights: Further Steps toward the Operationalization of the 'Protect, Respect and Remedy' Framework." 2010, www2.ohchr.org/english/issues/trans_corporations/docs/A-HRC-14-27.pdf.

"Comments on the 'Zero Draft' Treaty on Business and Human Rights." In *Compilation of Commentaries on the "Zero Draft,"* 6–9. London: Business and Human Rights Resource Centre, 2018.

"Interim Report of the Special Representative of the Secretary-General on the Issue of Human Rights and Transnational Corporations and Other Business Enterprises U.N. Doc.E/CN.4/2006/97." In *International Human Rights: Law, Policy, and Process*, edited by David S. Weissbrodt, Joan Fitzpatrick, and Frank Newman. Cincinnati, OH: Anderson Pub. Co., 2001.

Just Business: Multinational Corporations and Human Rights. New York, NY: W.W. Norton & Company, 2013.

"Kiobel and Corporate Social Responsibility – An Issues Brief." 2012.

Ryf, Kara. "Burger-Fischer v. Degussa Ag: U.S. Courts Allow Siemens and Degussa to Profit from Holocaust Slave Labor." *Case Western Reserve Journal of International Law* 33, no. 1 (2001): 155–78.

Ryngaert, Cedric. "Transnational Private Regulation and Human Rights: The Limitations of Stateless Law and the Re-entry of the State." *Global Journal on Human Rights* 2, no. 23 (2015): 77–108.

Safatle, Vladimir. "À sombra da ditadura." *Carta Capital*, December 30, 2011, www.cartacapital.com.br/politica/a-sombra-da-ditadura.

Sagafi-nejad, Tagi, and John H. Dunning. *The UN and Transnational Corporations: From Code of Conduct to Global Compact*. United Nations Intellectual History Project (Series). Bloomington, IN: Indiana University Press, 2008.

Sahagun, Louis. "Suit on WWII Slave Labor in Japan Voided." *Los Angeles Times*, 2000, http://articles.latimes.com/2000/sep/22/news/mn-25128.

Saki, Otto. "How Companies Are Using Lawsuits to Silence Environmental Activists – and How Philanthropy Can Help." Ford Foundation: Equals Change Blog, 2017, www.fordfoundation.org/ideas/equals-change-blog/posts/how-companies-are-using-law-suits-to-silence-environmental-activists-and-how-philanthropy-can-help/.

Sánchez, Nelson Camilo, Leigh A. Payne, Gabriel Pereira, Laura Bernal-Bermúdez, Daniel Marín López, and Miguel Barboza López. *Cuentas Claras: El papel de la Comisión de la Verdad en la develación de la responsabilidad de empresas en el conflicto armado colombiano*. Bogotá, 2018, www.dejusticia.org/publication/cuentas-claras-empresas/.

Sandoval, Clara, Leonardo Filippini, and Roberto Vidal. "Linking Transitional Justice and Corporate Accountability." In *Corporate Accountability in the Context of Transitional Justice*, edited by Sabine Michalowski. London: Routledge Press, 2013.

Sands, Philippe, ed. *From Nuremberg to The Hague: The Future of International Criminal Justice*. Cambridge: Cambridge University Press, 2003.

Schabas, William. "War Economies, Economic Actors, and International Criminal Law." In *Profiting from Peace: Managing the Resource Dimensions of Civil War*, edited by Karen Ballentine and Heiko Nitzschke. Boulder, CO: Lynne Rienner Publishers, Inc., 2005.

Scharf, Michael P. "Accelerated Formation of Customary International Law." *Faculty Publications – Case Western Reserve University (School of Law)*, 2014, http://scholarlycommons.law.case.edu/cgi/viewcontent.cgi?article=2166&context=faculty_publications.

Balkan Justice: The Story behind the First International War Crimes Trial since Nuremberg. Durham, NC: Carolina Academic Press, 1997.

Customary International Law in Times of Fundamental Change: Recognizing Grotian Moments. Cambridge: Cambridge University Press, 2013.

Schorri, Martín. "Industrial Economic Power as Promoter and Beneficiary of Argentina's Refounding Project (1976–1983)." In *Outstanding Debts to Settle: The Economic Accomplices of the Dictatorship in Argentina*, edited by Horacio Verbitsky and Juan Pablo Bohoslavsky. Cambridge: Cambridge University Press, 2015.

Segran, Grace. "Mary Robinson: Human Rights Are Good for Business." *Insead: Knowledge*, 2008, https://knowledge.insead.edu/ethics/mary-robinson-human-rights-are-good-for-business-2093.

Semana.com. "Decisión de peso: La orden de detención para Guillermo Gaviria." *Semana.com*, April 2012.

"El hombre que entregó la información sobre el robo de tierras." *Semana.com*, November 2, 2014, www.semana.com/nacion/articulo/benito-osorio-informante-de-la-fiscalia-en-despojo-de-tierras-en-tulapas-uraba/376845-3.

"Fiscalía revive el caso Chiquita Brands y llama a juicio a 14 empleados." *Semana.com*. 2018, www.semana.com/nacion/articulo/llaman-a-juicio-a-14-empresarios-de-chiquita-brands/581413.

Sharp, Dustin N. "Interrogating the Peripheries: The Preoccupations of Fourth Generation Transitional Justice." *Harvard Human Rights Journal* 26 (2013): 149.

Justice and Economic Violence in Transition. San Diego, CA: Springer, 2014.

Siekmann, Philip. "When Executives Turned Revolutionaries." *Fortune Magazine*. New York, September 1964.

Sierra Leone Truth and Reconciliation Commission. *Witness to Truth: Report of the Sierra Leone Truth and Reconciliation Commission*, Volumes I, II, IIIA, IIIB, 2004.

El Siglo. "Condenan a civil por violaciones de DDHH en 1973." *El Siglo*, 2017, www.elsiglo.cl/2017/11/17/condenan-a-civil-por-violaciones-de-ddhh-en-1973/.

Sikkink, Kathryn. "From Pariah State to Global Protagonist: Argentina and the Struggle for International Human Rights." *Latin American Politics and Society* 50, no. 1 (2008): 1–29.

The Justice Cascade : How Human Rights Prosecutions Are Changing World Politics. Norton Series in World Politics. New York, NY: W.W. Norton, 2013.

Sion, Victor, Felipe Amorim, and Patrícia Dichtchekenian. "Os acionistas críticos de Volkswagen, Siemens e Mercedes-Benz." In *À espera da verdade: Empresários, juristas e elite transnacional, histórias de civis que fizeram a ditadura militar*, edited by Joana Monteleone, Haroldo Ceravolo Sereza, Vitor Sion, Felipe Amorim, and Rodolfo Machado. São Paulo: Alameda Editorial, 2016.

Sirleaf, Matiangai. "The African Justice Cascade and the Malabo Protocol." *International Journal of Transitional Justice* 11, no. 1 (2017).

Skinner, Gwynne. "Nuremberg's Legacy Continues: The Nuremberg Trials' Influence on Human Rights Litigation in US Courts under the Alien Tort Statute." *Albany Law Review* 71, no. 1 (2008).

Skocpol, Theda, and Margaret Somers. "The Uses of Comparative History in Macrosocial Inquiry." *Comparative Studies in Society and History* 22, no. 2 (1980): 174–97.

South African History Archive (SAHA). "TRC Category-4. Reparations." In *Traces of Truth: Documents Related to the Truth and Reconciliation Commission*. University of the Witwatersrand, n.d., http://truth.wwl.wits.ac.za/cat_descr.php?cat=4.

Stanley, William. *The Protection Racket State: Elite Politics, Military Extortion and Civil War in El Salvador.* Philadelphia, PA: Temple University Press, 1996.

Steinhardt, Ralph G. "Kiobel and the Weakening of Precedent: A Long Walk for a Short Drink." *The American Journal of International Law* 107, no. 4 (2013): 841–45.

Struck, Jean-Philip. "Historian Reveals Ties between Brazilian Volkswagen Affiliate and the Military Dictatorship." *Folha de São Paulo*, April 8, 2017, www1.folha.uol .com.br/internacional/en/brazil/2017/08/1907170-historian-reveals-ties-between-bra zilian-volkswagen-affiliate-and-the-military-dictatorship.shtml.

Subotić, Jelena. *Hijacked Justice: Dealing with the Past in the Balkans.* Ithaca, NY: Cornell University Press, 2009.

"The Transformation of International Transitional Justice Advocacy." *International Journal of Transitional Justice* 6, no. 1 (2012): 106–25.

Sunstein, Cass Robert. "Social Norms and Social Roles." *Columbia Law Review* 96 (1996): 903–68.

Supreme Court of the United States. Jesner et al. v. Arab Bank, PLC, 138 S. Ct. 1386 2018.

Tapias-Torrado, Nancy and the Inter-American Commission on Human Rights. "Criminalization of Human Rights Defenders." Washington, DC, 2015.

Teitel, Ruti G. "Transitional Justice and Judicial Activism – A Right to Accountability?" *Cornell International Law Journal* 48 (2015): 385–422.

"Transitional Justice Genealogy." *Harvard Human Rights Journal* 69 (2003).

Transitional Justice. New York, NY: Oxford University Press, 2000.

Telam. "Myriam Bregman calificó de 'intimidatorio' un escrito de abogados de Carlos Pedro Blanquier." *Telam*, 2016, http://memoria.telam.com.ar/noticia/bregman-llamo–intimidatorio–a-un-escrito-de-blaquier_n6625.

Telesurtv. "Los Macri y sus negocios durante la dictadura argentina." *Telesurtv*, 2015, www.telesurtv.net/news/Los-Macri-y-sus-negocios-durante-la-dictadura-argentina-20151112-0008.html.

Thompson, Ginger. "South Africa to Pay \$3,900 to Each Family of Apartheid Victims." *The New York Times*, April 16, 2013, www.nytimes.com/2003/04/16/world/south-africa-to-pay-3900-to-each-family-%0Dof-apartheid-victims.html.

Thompson, Robert, Anita Ramasastry, and Mark Taylor. "Translating Unocal: The Expanding Web of Liability for Business Entities Implicated in International Crimes." *The George Washington International Law Review* 40, no. 4 (2009): 841–902.

El Tiempo. "Declaran delito de lesa humanidad financiación de bananeros a las AUC." *El Tiempo*, 2017, www.eltiempo.com/justicia/cortes/declaran-delito-de-lesa-humanidad-financiacion-de-bananeros-a-las-auc-41929.

"Fiscalía cerró caso contra Chiquita por pagos a 'paras.'" *El Tiempo*, March 28, 2012, www.eltiempo.com/archivo/documento/CMS-11454061.

"Por invertir en antiguas zonas de conflicto se pagarán menos impuestos." *El Tiempo*, 2017, www.eltiempo.com/politica/proceso-de-paz/plan-de-inversion-para-las-zonas-mas-afectadas-por-el-conflicto-zomac-139498.

Tilly, Charles. *Regimes and Repertoires.* Chicago, IL: University of Chicago Press, 2006.

Tófalo, Inés. "Overt and Hidden Accomplices: Transnational Corporations' Range of Complicity in Human Rights Violations." In *Transnational Corporations and*

Human Rights, edited by Olivier De Schutter, 335–58. Portland, OR: Hart Publishing, 2006.

Tolbert, David. "Hope Amidst Angst: The Tunisian Truth and Dignity Commission." 2018, www.linkedin.com/pulse/hope-amidst-angst-tunisian-truth-dignity-commission-david-tolbert.

Trial International. "Alfred Musema." *Trial International*, 2016, https://trialinterna tional.org/latest-post/alfred-musema/.

Trust Africa. "The Kiisi Trust to Benefit the Ogoni People." *Trust Africa*, n.d., www .trustafrica.org/en/programme/philanthropy-advisory-services/kiisi-trust-fund.

Truth, Justice and Reconciliation Commission of Kenya. *Report of the Truth, Justice and Reconciliation Commission*, Volumes III, IV, 2013.

Truth and Reconciliation Commission of Liberia. *Final Report*, Volume I, 2008, http:// trcofliberia.org/reports/final-report.

Final Report, Volume II, 2009, http://trcofliberia.org/resources/reports/final/volume-two_layout-1.pdf.

Mandate, 2006, http://trcofliberia.org/about/trc-mandate.

Official Website, n.d., http://trcofliberia.org.

Truth and Reconciliation Commission of South Africa. *Truth and Reconciliation Commission of South Africa Report*, Volumes IV, V, 1998.

Truth and Reconciliation Commission of South Africa Report, Volume VI, section 2, chapter 5, 1998.

Tsebelis, George. *Veto Players: How Political Institutions Work*. Princeton, NJ: Russell Sage Foundation, 2002.

United Nations. "Guidance Note of the Secretary-General: United Nations Approach to Transitional Justice." New York, NY: United Nations, 2010, www.un.org/ruleof law/files/TJ_Guidance_Note_March_2010FINAL.pdf.

United Nations General Assembly. "Basic Principles and Guidelines on the Right to a Remedy and Reparation for Victims of Gross Violations of International Human Rights Law and Serious Violations of International Humanitarian Law A/RES/60/ 147." New York, NY: United Nations, 2005, https://documents-dds-ny.un.org/doc/ UNDOC/GEN/N05/496/42/PDF/N0549642.pdf?OpenElement.

United Nations High Commission Office. "Argentina Dictatorship: UN Experts Back Creation of Commission on Role Business People Played." November 2015.

United Nations Human Rights Council. Human Rights and Transnational Corporations and Other Business Enterprises Res. 26/22, U.N. Doc. A/HRC/RES/26/22, 2014, https://documents-dds-ny.un.org/doc/UNDOC/LTD/G14/062/40/PDF/G1406240 .pdf?OpenElement.

"Elaboration of an International Legally Binding Instrument on Transnational Corporations and Other Business Enterprises with Respect to Human Rights A/HRC/26/L.22/Rev.1." New York, NY: United Nations, 2014, https://docu ments-dds-ny.un.org/doc/UNDOC/LTD/G14/064/48/PDF/G1406448.pdf?Open Element.

United Nations Human Rights Office of the High Commissioner. "Guiding Principles on Business and Human Rights: Implementing the United Nations 'Protect, Respect and Remedy' Framework." New York and Geneva: United Nations, 2011, www.ohchr.org/ Documents/Publications/GuidingPrinciplesBusinessHR_EN.pdf.

United Nations Secretary General. "United Nations Approach to Transitional Justice." 2010, www.un.org/ruleoflaw/files/TJ_Guidance_Note_March_2010FINAL.pdf.

"Other Multilateral Instruments and Guidelines for Corporate Behavior." n.d., http://hrlibrary.umn.edu/business/omig.html.

"Universal Declaration of Human Rights." New York, NY: United Nations, 1948, www.un.org/en/universal-declaration-human-rights/.

United Nations Sub-Commission on the Promotion and Protection of Human Rights. "Commentary on the Norms on the Responsibilities of Transnational Corporations and Other Business Enterprises with Regard to Human Rights, U.N. Doc. E/CN.4/Sub.2/2003/38/Rev.2." New York, 2003.

"Norms on the Responsibilities of Transnational Corporations and Other Business Enterprises with Regard to Human Rights." United Nations, 2003.

United States Congress. "28 U.S. Code Part IV Chapter 85 § 1350," n.d., www.law.cornell.edu/uscode/text/28/1350.

United States Holocaust Memorial Museum. "Incitement to Genocide in International Law." *Holocaust Encyclopedia*, n.d.

United States Institute of Peace. Truth Commission: Kenya, n.d.

Truth Commission: Liberia, 2006, www.usip.org/publications/2006/02/truth-commission-liberia.

UN News. "UN Tribunal Convicts 3 Rwandan Media Executives for Their Role in 1994 Genocide." *UN News*, December 2003.

U.S. District Court for the Central District of California. "Doe I v. Unocal, 963 F. Supp. 880 (CD.Cal.1997)." 1997.

van den Herik, Larissa, and Jernej Letnar Černič. "Regulating Corporations under International Law: From Human Rights to International Criminal Law and Back Again." *Journal of International Criminal Justice* 8, no. 3 (2010): 725–43.

van der Wilt, Harmen. "Corporate Criminal Responsibility for International Crimes: Exploring the Possibilities." *Chinese Journal of International Law* 12, no. 1 (2013): 43–77.

Van Ho, Tara L. "Corporate Complicity for Human Rights Violations: Using Transnational Civil and Criminal Litigation." In *Corporate Accountability in the Context of Transitional Justice*, edited by Sabine Michalowski, 52–72. New York, NY: Routledge, 2013.

van Vuuren, Hennie. *Apartheid Guns and Money: A Tale of Profit.* Open Secrets, 2017.

Veiga, Gustavo. "Investigan a la Fiat en Brasil." *Página/12*, June 1, 2019, www.pagina12.com.ar/203628-investigan-a-la-fiat-en-brasil.

Verbitsky, Horacio. "Los prestamistas de la muerte." *Página/12*, March 16, 2009, www.pagina12.com.ar/diario/elpais/1-121607-2009-03-16.html.

Verbitsky, Horacio, and Juan Pablo Bohoslavsky, eds. *Cuentas pendientes: Los cómplices económicos de la dictadura.* Buenos Aires: Siglo Veintiuno Editores, 2013.

Outstanding Debts to Settle: The Economic Accomplices of the Dictatorship in Argentina. Cambridge: Cambridge University Press, 2015.

Verdadabierta.com. "Los cuestionamientos a bananeros detrás del No." *Verdadabierta.com*, 2016, https://verdadabierta.com/los-cuestionamientos-a-los-bananeros-detras-del-no/.

"Los testimonios que enredan a Guillermo Gaviria Echeverri." *Verdadabierta.com*, April 2012.

Vivanco, José Miguel. "Dispatches: Argentina's Supreme Court Appointments." *Human Rights Watch*, December 18, 2015, www.hrw.org/news/2015/12/18/dis patches-argentinas-supreme-court-appointments.

Vogel, David. "Why Businessmen Distrust Their State: The Political Consciousness of American Corporation Executives." *British Journal of Political Science* 1, no. 8 (1978): 19–43.

Wallace, Denise. *Human Rights and Business: A Policy-Oriented Perspective*. Studies in Intercultural Human Rights. Leiden, the Netherlands: BRILL, 2015.

War.Wire. "Japanese High Court Overturns Order to Pay Chinese Forced Labourers." *War.Wire*, 2004, www.nytimes.com/1999/09/15/world/ex-pow-s-sue-5-big-japanese-companies-over-forced-labor.html.

Wawryk, Alex. "Regulating Transnational Corporations through Corporate Codes of Conduct." In *Transnational Corporations and Human Rights*, edited by Jedrzej George Frynas and Scott Pegg. Palgrave Macmillan, 2003.

Weissbrodt, David S. *The Beginning of a Sessional Working Group on Transnational Corporations within the UN Sub-Commission on Prevention of Discrimination and Protection of Minorities*. London: Kluwer Law International, 2000.

Weissbrodt, David S., and Muria Kruger. "Human Rights Responsibilities of Businesses as Non-State Actors." In *Non-State Actors and Human Rights*, edited by Phillip Alston, 315–49. Oxford: Oxford University Press, 2005.

Whytock, Christopher A., and Cassandra Burke Robertson. "Forum Non Conveniens and the Enforcement of Foreign Judgments." *Columbia Law Review* 111, no. 7 (2011).

Wilkens, John, and Peter Rowe. "Lester Tenney, Army Tank Commander Who Survived Bataan Death March during World War II, Dies at 96." *Los Angeles Times*, 2017, www.latimes.com/local/obituaries/la-me-lester-tenney-20170227-story .html.

Wolf, Klaus Dieter, Nicole Deitelhoff, and Stefan Engert. "Corporate Security Responsibility." *Cooperation and Conflict* 42 (2007): 294–320.

Wuerth, Ingrid. "Wiwa v. Shell: The $15.5 Million Settlement." *American Society of International Law*, September 9, 2009, www.asil.org/insights/volume/13/issue/14/ wiwa-v-shell-155-million-settlement.

Young, Laura A., and Rosalyn Park. "Engaging Diasporas in Truth Commissions: Lessons from the Liberia Truth and Reconciliation Commission Diaspora Project." *International Journal of Transitional Justice* 3, no. 3 (2009): 341–61.

Zerk, Jennifer A. *Corporate Liability for Gross Human Rights Abuses: Towards a Fairer and More Effective System of Domestic Law Remedies*. Geneva: UN High Commissioner of Human Rights, 2014.

Index

Acindar. *See* Argentina

Africa
  economic actors and armed conflict, 10
  truth commissions and corporate complicity
    extrajudicial killings and disappearances, 183
    property and environmental violence, 183
    truth commissions and types of victims of corporate complicity, 177

African Charter on Human and Peoples' Rights, 298

African Court on Human and Peoples' Rights
  Malabo Protocol, 106

African Union Convention on Cyber Security and Personal Data Protection, 298

Airscan Inc. *See* Colombia

Akhbar Beirut S.A.L. *See* Special Tribunal for Lebanon

Al-Assad, Bashar. *See* Syria

Alessandri, Jorge. *See* Chile

Ali, Ben. *See* Tunisia

Alien Tort Statute (ATS), 63, 96
  Apartheid trial, 150
  and corporate accountability, 81–85
  definition of, 80
  Jesner ruling (2018), 82–85, 91, 145
  Kelly, Michael, 82
  Kiobel ruling (2013), 82–85, 91, 145, 252
  Sotomayor, Sonia (Justice), 84

Allende, Salvador. *See* Chile

American Convention on Human Rights, 296

American Declaration of the Rights and Duties of Man, 27

Amnesty International, 26, 101, 141

amnesty laws, 17, 28–30, 33, 45, 54, 245, 248, 256

Andhes, *See* Argentina

Anglo American, *See* South Africa

Anvil Mining Ltd. *See* Canada

Archimedes' Lever.
  corporate accountability, 49
  corporate accountability from below, 19
  corporate accountability from below and the role of domestic courts, 221–23
  corporate veto power, 160
  weak actors, 274–86

Aredez, Olga. *See* Argentina

Argentina
  Acindar, 125, 201, 230
  Andhes (Northeastern Argentine Association of Lawyers of Human Rights and Social Studies), 110, 112, 220, 229, 243
  Bank of America, 131, 230
  Bregman-Blaquier incident, 113–14
    Aredez, Olga, 113
    Blaquier, Carlos Pedro Tadeo, 207
    Bonasso, Miguel, 113
    Bregman, Myriam, 113
    Figueroa, Laura, 114
  CELS (Centro de Estudios Legales y Sociales), 233–34, 237, 255, 258
  Citibank, 131
  CONADEP (truth commission), 165–66, 201, 207, 210, 256, 326
  CONADEP (truth commission) and types of victims of corporate complicity, 177
  CONADEP (truth commission) testimonies and corporate complicity, 201
  corporate accountability, 15
  Daimler Chrysler AG, 118, 205, 334
  escraches and "outing," 206–7

365

For EU product safety concerns, contact us at Calle de José Abascal, 56–1°,
28003 Madrid, Spain or eugpsr@cambridge.org.

www.ingramcontent.com/pod-product-compliance
Ingram Content Group UK Ltd.
Pitfield, Milton Keynes, MK11 3LW, UK
UKHW020402140625
459647UK00020B/2609